Cooking of the
American Southwest

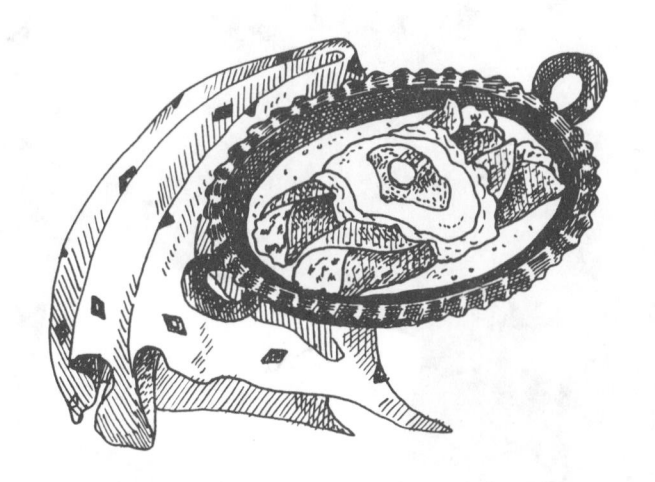

THE FEAST OF
SANTA FE

Huntley Dent

Illustrations by Susan Gaber

A FIRESIDE BOOK
Published by Simon & Schuster
NEW YORK   LONDON   TORONTO   SYDNEY   TOKYO   SINGAPORE

FIRESIDE

Rockefeller Center
1230 Avenue of the Americas
New York, New York 10020

First Fireside Edition 1993

FIRESIDE and colophon are registered trademarks
of Simon & Schuster Inc.

Designed by Eve Kirch
Manufactured in the United States of America

9 10
9 10   (PBK)

Library of Congress Cataloging-in-Publication data
Dent, Huntley.
The feast of Santa Fe.
Includes index.
1. Cookery, American—Southwestern style.   2. Cookery
—New Mexico—Santa Fe.   3. Santa Fe (N.M.)—Social life
and customs.   I. Title.
TX715.D43   1984   641.5979   84-20217
ISBN: 0-671-47686-6
ISBN: 0-671-87302-4 (PBK)

The author gratefully acknowledges permission to reprint the map on page 12 from
Historical Atlas of New Mexico, by Warren A. Beck and Ynez D. Haase. Copyright ©
1969 by the University of Oklahoma Press.

ACKNOWLEDGMENTS

In the course of writing this book, which was largely a solitary endeavor, I began to feel a deepening comradeship with the writers who preceded me in their affection for New Mexico and its cuisine, among them Ronald Johnson, Jim Douglas, Erna Fergusson, and the wonderfully evocative Fabiola Cabeza de Baca Gilbert. All of them are very much required reading for anyone who wants to learn about Santa Fe cookery. For a broad perspective on the New Mexican people, I thank Paul Horgan, the most devoted of modern writers on Santa Fe.

I owe thanks to Henry Hubert, who first suggested that I write a cookbook for Simon and Schuster, and to Susan Victor, who first edited and organized the great unformed mass of manuscript. Carole Lalli subsequently edited the manuscript for publication, showing exemplary intelligence and tact—every recipe owes something to her talents. My friends Eric and Diane Gould have always been kind in their support of my writing, but Diane in particular deserves the bouquet, for she thought of a Santa Fe cookbook in the first place. It says something about her sagacity that I began writing it the next day.

HUNTLEY DENT
Denver, Colorado
April 1984

*My love of cooking
comes from my mother, Eola Lorance Dent,
to whom this book is lovingly dedicated,
but I know she would want to
share it with our whole family—
Gene, Dee, Johnny, and Bill.*

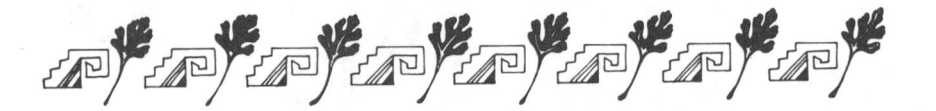

CONTENTS

TRADITIONS

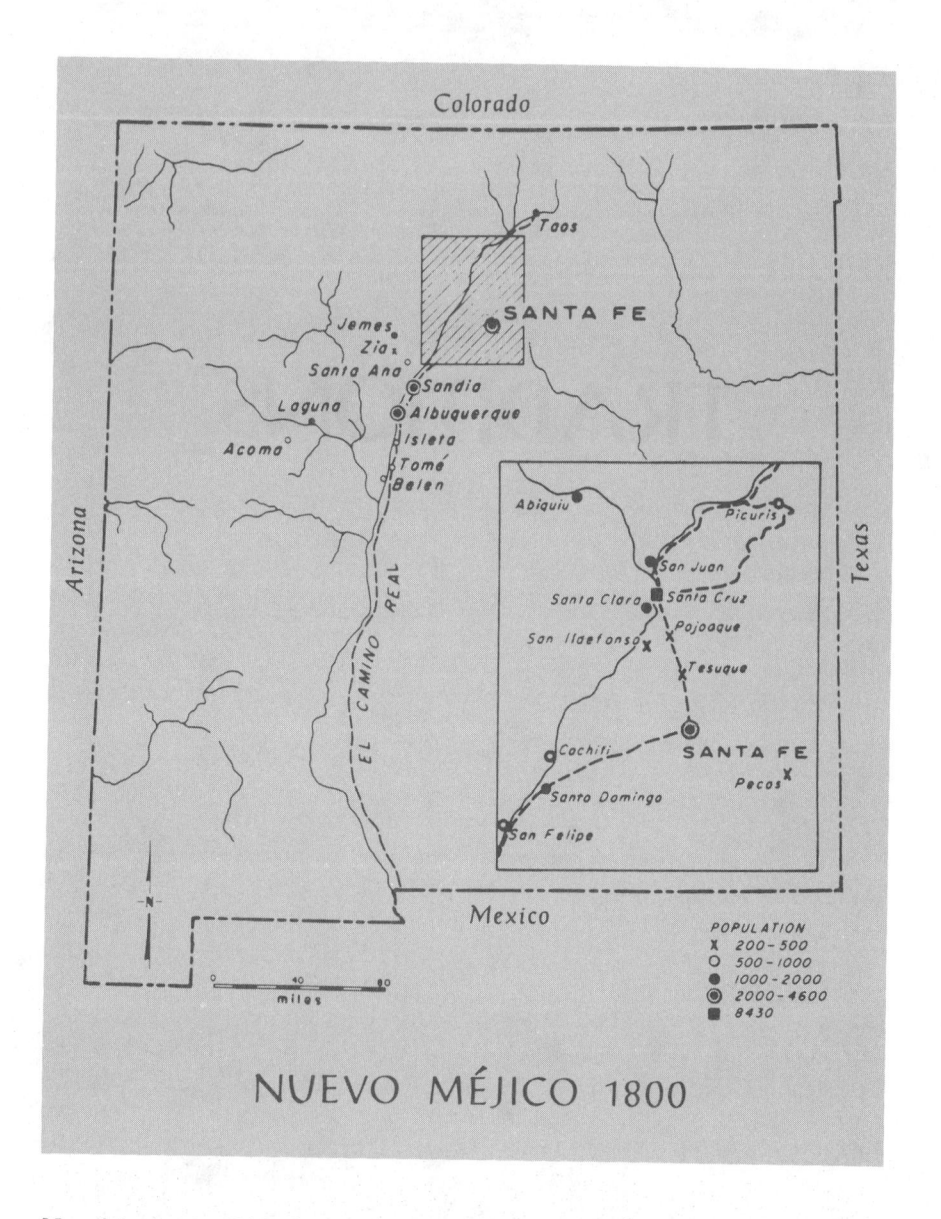

Colorado

Taos

SANTA FE

Jemes
Zia
Santa Ana
Laguna   Sandia
          Albuquerque
Acoma   Isleta
          Tomé
          Belen

Abiquiu   Picuris

          San Juan
Santa Clara   Santa Cruz
San Ildefonso   Pojoaque
                 Tesuque

      Cachiti   SANTA FE
                     Pecos
      Santo Domingo
   San Felipe

Arizona

Texas

EL CAMINO REAL

Mexico

POPULATION
X   200-500
O   500-1000
●   1000-2000
◉   2000-4600
■   8430

-N-

0   40   80
     miles

NUEVO MÉJICO 1800

New Mexico in 1800, during the period of Spanish rule. Santa Fe, now the
capital, had a population of less than 5,000 and was accessible from Mexico
only by the royal road. The smaller place names surrounding it represent
Indian pueblos.

Source: *Historical Atlas of New Mexico,* by Warren A. Beck and Ynez D. Haase
(University of Oklahoma Press).

A ROYAL CITY

Santa Fe, New Mexico, is a city of mixed cultures, and this cookbook contains recipes from each—Pueblo Indian, Spanish, Mexican, pioneer Anglo-American, as well as the cuisine of modern Santa Fe, which evolved from all of them. Here you will find directions for making the specialties that travelers expect when they come to New Mexico, for it would be foolish to leave out *enchiladas* and *chiles rellenos*, or to pass by so colorful a thing as the blue corn tortilla. Santa Fe food is as soul-satisfying as it is mostly because of its simplest native dishes.

But unlike New Orleans, that other American city whose mixed cultures gave rise to more than one notable style of cooking, Santa Fe is not a culinary byword. For a long time its fascinating potential for good cooking was not known to the rest of the country. That was due in part to the town's tiny size, its location, which is high, remote and severe, and its Spanish heritage, which was slow to assimilate. The southern part of New Mexico was almost thoroughly Anglicized at a time when the villages of the north continued to speak Spanish. Indeed, although it is tempting to romanticize the melding of cultures, the food of the Indians and the Hispanic cooks stands out in high relief in the Santa Fe area because of their stubbornness toward change. The whole early history of Santa Fe when it was part of Nuevo Mejico is a chronicle of the Spanish subduing the Indians by force and the Indians murdering or driving forth their Spanish masters, only to have them return, reconquer the territory and execute the Indian rebels. The pattern of hostility abated in time as New Mexico was annexed by Mexico and, in the 1840s, by the United States. Out of antagonism and conflict a new culture was emerging, but to an American from the outside it remained as strange as its Indian and Spanish antecedents. Even now, the linking of Santa Fe to the rest of the nation by railroad is less than a century old, and statehood came within living memory.

But despite some harsh obstacles, thousands of cooks were funneled into early Santa Fe. Some came up from the south following the Chihuahua Trail that unwound its immense, tortuous length to Mexico City and eventually the sea. Along this route came all the foodstuffs that the indigenous economy could not supply. The land around Santa Fe consists of high desert plain, with the city itself sited in the spectacular Rio Grande valley that incises the whole plateau. But once you have taken away the view, the land is not generous. For centuries the Indians lived here on corn, squash and beans. They hunted rabbits, deer, and even such meager prey as wild mice. They foraged for wild plums and for nuts in the cracks of pine cones, and still their existence was marginal.

The Spaniards benefited by making virtual slaves out of the Pueblos, and they had many years to subdue the landscape, turning it into truck gardens, cattle ranches of the most barren kind, orchards and, once you go south far enough to reach the mission at El Paso del Norte, vineyards. All this could be accomplished only after incessant laboring, and the fruits eventually reached Santa Fe. In comparison to the thousands of tractless miles around it, the city had life, color, trade and politics, not to mention slavery, war and a painful religious rectitude that Spanish conquest invariably brought in its wake. After its founding in 1609 as a *villa real,* or royal city—its entire name in Spanish translates to "The Royal City of the Holy Faith of St. Francis of Assisi"—Santa Fe was the colonial seat of government for the entire vastness of the Southwest.

The Spaniards and the Indians had almost 200 years to live and eat together before an American citizen ever set eyes upon Santa Fe. They worked out a most uneven truce, as we can see from their diets. The Indians subsisted on corn gruel and chili, the poorer Spanish blended into that fare some pinto beans, tortillas and little else, while the great families along the river, fervently eager to preserve intact their Castilian ways and, even more precious, their Castilian blood, lived with the aloof elevation of aristocrats. Along the trail from Mexico they imported the silver, lace, chocolate and tobacco without which their lives would have been unthinkably drab. Looking to their local market, the plaza in front of the governor's palace which still exists and still operates as a market, the gentlefolk saw squalor and few amenities. The staples for sale were corn, chili, onions and beans, augmented when farmers came to hawk their cheese, eggs and orchard fruit in season.

Naturally the lives of the river families (or *ricos*) could not remain untouched by the Indians, who at the very least were their servants. Cornbread began to appear as often as raised white bread, chili and beans were eaten, and the two opposed camps unavoidably developed a cuisine of melded cultures. Now the basic Santa Fe style was laid down, although it is almost silly to call it that, for this food born of barren necessity mixed with memories of the European table in truth prevailed all over New Spain, not just here. But the old style is still easily distinguishable here, and when visitors come to Santa Fe, they immediately head for the Mexican restaurants, eating the indigenous chili as though the whole era of pioneer domestication did not take place.

The pioneer era, officially called the "Territorial" period, coincided with the capture of Santa Fe by the United States after the Mexican War of 1846. It brought in ranchers, pioneer settlers, and all the trade that flowed down the Santa Fe Trail from Missouri. What these new people ate is more or less the stuff of cowboy legend; there is no particular reason to think of settler food—son-of-a-gun stew or dropped biscuits—as markedly peculiar to Santa Fe, except that the slow merging of culinary currents now had something more to work on. It was like overlaying Mexico City with Kansas City.

Still the basic characteristic of the food continued to be its scarcity. In real life, Willa Cather's famous fictional prelate in *Death Comes for the Archbishop* was Bishop Jean Baptiste Lamy of Santa Fe, a man as devoted to frugal eating as he was to the faith, if we are to judge by one incident when he sent a missionary father on horseback to Colorado with nothing to sustain him beyond a sack of roasted cornmeal. In Lamy's day, roughly the latter half of the nineteenth century, remote pastors under his jurisdiction often lived on nothing more or better than tortillas and beans.

So it seems somewhat grim and ironical to note the arrival in our time of artists and writers and their followers to Santa Fe—the single event that has romanticized the city, at the same time that it saved it from destruction. This historic refuge of poverty turned into a cultural facade, the fabled Old Santa Fe. The good and bad of what was done by shoals of New Englanders and British who embraced the city a generation ago is not the point here. They brought art, sophisticated manners, a hunger for Southwestern color and—here is where this book takes off—a taste for New Mexican food.

Suddenly money was available to make Santa Fe a shrine for local culture. The tendency for wealth to gravitate here has not slacked, and every day new millionaires come to Santa Fe, populating its restaurants, searching every nook for potential romance and flavor. The rest of us are of course in the swim, too, but hardly anyone has considered that every sort of trader, conqueror, tourist and native is a contributor to the process of building a cuisine.

Now that you know the basic antecedents you are going to work from, such as the Indian corn, the Spanish *chile* (coincidentally also learned from Mexican Indians, in fact), the pioneer beef and the modern Santa Fean's love for all the rest that has preceded him, you will see what a rich opportunity Santa Fe food represents. What's left to tell is a bit more about the physical conditions of cooking here.

THE SANTA FE KITCHEN

Unless you are fortunate enough to live and cook in a desert setting, your kitchen is fundamentally different from that of a Santa Fe cook. Hers is lined, oftener than not, with Mexican tiles of simple design, daubed with cactus green or Sonoran brown in a quick, repetitive pattern. If the house is old enough, the kitchen walls are molded of adobe, that most malleable and plastic of building materials, capable of following any curve a human hand can shape it to. In that way it resembles bread dough, another fundamental and plastic human material, except that the ruddy tone of the adobe makes it appear like dough that was pulled directly out of the landscape, pushed from nature's hands directly into walls of no more artifice than desert hills or arroyos.

To put it in one phrase, the ever-present landscape flows in and through a Santa Fe kitchen. It comes in as a stream of brilliant sunlight; as the smell of piñon nuts whose mother trees can be seen across every acre of land; as the inescapable layer of desert dust which no one tries overly hard to keep out, and, of course, as the food itself. The corn you might see in the summer garden, like the chilies that overflow entire valleys, is the basic stuff of the kitchen as well as the basic stuff of the land.

The equipment of the Santa Fe kitchen may be very meager. In remote hill villages, where wheat tortillas (paler, bigger, and thinner than the corn kind, but still aromatic) and chili are really an everyday diet, the cook may use a flat hand griddle, a *comal*, for roasting her daily bread. More likely she merely resorts to the griddle plate on the top of her range. In place of a blender or processor she uses her hand, massaging the husks off the dried Chimayó chilies which go into red chili sauce. Particularly if she is Indian, there is no question of measuring cups and spoons, for the ingrained habit of making tortillas and *frijoles* every day makes her unaware that flour and water have to be measured at all.

The stone mortars used in Mexico might also be in the house. In them a garlic is crushed, then roasted green chili flesh added, the whole to be mashed into the *chile verde* paste that gives the meals their savor, for customarily the bread is not salted and the *frijoles* are flavored only with chunks of salt pork. This all seems to us like a throwback, not just to another time but to another world. That sensation gave me much pleasure throughout the stages of writing and testing recipes; I had the lingering impression that very ancient and foreign ways were being brought to light.

One not-so-minor note is that most traditional cooking was never done indoors at all, but in clay ovens brought here by the Spanish and cannibalized by the Indians as their own beehive ovens. From these came bread, pumpkins, feast-day stews and the ubiquitous beans, which were set over heat nearby instead of directly inside the oven. Game was roasted on spits, imparting the incomparable smoky flavor a modern barbecue strains to imitate.

Corn, chili, sunlight, dust and adobe do not exactly constitute a complexity of materials, but they hang together. And they belong here by nature. Whatever you can buy elsewhere in a chain supermarket, you can buy in downtown Santa Fe. As the ratio of vacationing millionaires begins to edge up on the ratio of natives, it is ever more likely that corned-beef brisket, Atlantic bluefish, and Dungeness crab will begin to appear on the shelves. But no diversity of tastes, however the clever cook manages it, can quite be of a piece the way corn and chilies are. They are that way naturally and almost effortlessly. Whether you are Hispanic or Indian or Anglo, the land belonged to the corn and *chile* before it belonged to you. This book was written in an attempt to bring their unity into your kitchen, wherever you live.

THE QUESTION
OF AUTHENTICITY

A Santa Fe dish is only as authentic as its cook and its heritage. Because the city is fortunate in having a long heritage and many stubborn-minded cooks, you can find food here which is as untouched, or nearly so, as a *cassoulet* cooked within the walls of Carcassonne. Even that medieval fortress town would have to bow before the antiquity of the Rio Grande pueblos, whose cooks passed on versions of their tortillas and jerked meat to the Spanish while conserving the ageless originals to be cooked without change to this day.

The merging of Indian and Spanish styles, taking three centuries to mature, created the cooking that forms the center of this book, the old way that is most intimate, flavorful and unsmoothed. Then, in the century that passed after America annexed the Southwest according to its Manifest Destiny, more change took place in the kitchen than under the Spaniards in treble the time. Everything we call Tex-Mex, cowboy cooking, pioneer and settler cooking; all that the New Mexicans lump under "Anglo" food; all that was imported by the railroad and its food service, the Harvey company—all of it swept in to alter or drive out the Hispanic style as new tastes dictated. The changeless changed.

There is a good chance that the Southwestern style might not have survived at all. Reticence about the un-American qualities of New Mexican food was abroad, for one thing, but just as compelling was the newfound desire to glamorize a diet that by any measure was stark and even monotonous throughout its history. The avocado, for example, could no more survive in the northern reaches of New Mexico than a papaya, but it rushed in with the advent of supermarkets and the late-'40s fad for sun-drenched California living. To complicate matters, Southwestern cooking had acquired a romantic image among the New Englanders who were moving in to adopt and preserve Old Santa Fe. When they were followed by the art crowd and later by millions of tourists, a new style of restaurant cooking sprang up to accommodate them. Much of it was honorably dedicated to the native foods, but almost all of it was standardized, too: a combination plate of blue-corn *enchiladas* with *posole* and beans on the side began to stand in for a whole cuisine.

So much of this food is good, both old and new, that I did not want to leave any out, even the obvious imports and bastardizations. In my own mind, I divided the recipes into categories and assigned each its relative importance. The categories were

—Spanish cooking that was little modified in the New World
—Mexican cooking, modified or not, as it came to New Mexico
—Anglo cooking, primarily the food of the wagon trains and the American settlers
—ranch-house and Tex-Mex hybrids of Mexican food
—Santa Fe restaurant cooking in the modern tourist era
—modern home cooking using Southwestern inspirations.

Even native New Mexicans may be surprised that their food is so complicated, for in their minds a dinner of *guacamole*, chili con carne, green corn *tamales* and chocolate mousse, a dinner that you could buy on any night in a typical Santa Fe restaurant, is merely one thing; they don't think of it as a melding of Aztec, Spanish, Mexican, ranch house and tourist styles. As time passes, these styles no doubt will blend even more; already you can buy cookbooks from New Mexico with Santa Fe quiche and baklava in them.

This cookbook was not written just to preserve the old Hispanic cuisine of northern New Mexico—that was done well and faithfully thirty years ago by Fabiola Cabeza de Baca Gilbert in her delightful book *The Good Life*, written in the last days before irreversible changes set in. Without it, none of us outside that closed tradition would know of its ancestral ways and its pleasures in the midst of scarcity. But one reading convinced me that no one would want such splendid asceticism today, except in brief snatches. Yet who would want only ranch-house biscuits, *vaquero* stew, or Canyon Road quiche, for that matter?

In the end, I decided not to untangle the complications of Southwestern food too much, for the nature of the life is in the tangling. Such things as did not appeal to me, like tamale pie and chili con carne, were given minor mention, while the simple glories, like all manner of *enchiladas*, were allowed to spread out as far as they wanted. These decisions were subjective, and somewhat capricious. I soft-pedaled restaurant cuisine, having the notion that anyone who really loved to cook would want to explore beyond the borders of commercial cookery; and where I had no legitimate knowledge, the obvious area of my ignorance being the conservative pueblos of the Rio Grande valley, I did not intrude too far with invented recipes.

I had the good fortune to be able to consult a wealth of materials— fiesta programs, out-of-print cookbooks, Southwestern novels and memoirs —which filled in a picture of cooking that most Americans do not realize is in their midst. To the eye, Santa Fe continues to look like a foreign city. Its carved portals and winding streets, its adobe walls and dry *acequias*, even the mountain stream lined with cottonwoods that runs through the town, are duplicated nowhere else in the country. By gathering in the food that nourished its builders and citizens, I hope that this loveliest of Spanish gifts will retain another living dimension. Much of the cooking here will remain as remote as a vacated penitential chapel in the *néomejicano* desert, but much, too, can be made to live anywhere.

TWELVE FEASTS IN SIMPLICITY

The luxuriousness of modern Santa Fe is a veneer, recently applied, and everyday food in particular has lapsed far from the austerity of the old city. The ancient hard diet of the Indians gave way to a Spanish diet just barely softened, and only 200 years later came the amenities which could be brought overland by Yankee traders. The changes were so slow in coming that as we look back we see mostly the hardness and little of the softening. The land had few gifts to offer even into this century. Daily nourishment centered on chili, corn and beans, and when a feast day came around, the food was chili, corn and beans again, but with minor variations. We who can secure a dozen vineyard-fattened snails with the flick of a can opener find it hard to conceive such frugality—to realize that adding molasses and raisins to dough meant bread splendid enough for a festive day.

The hardness of the old New Mexico villages is not forced upon us— we feast in simplicity for no other reason than pleasure. What the early village cooks worked upon—the meat and chili, the flour tortilla, the aniseed cookies—they eventually perfected, and now we can attune our mental palates to the subtle importance of a red chili pod added to a stew, and the weight of difference made because it is not a green chili. At first it barely seems credible that a stew could be satisfying if it consisted *only* of meat, onion and red chili, so cookbook writers rush in to clothe the naked and begin to amplify. As the recipes are expanded, more ingredients are added. The modern authors pour in tomato puree, another kind of chili or two, some herbs, dried and fresh—in other words, they "civilize" the cooking. As well they might, since the whole context of a simple New Mexican meal is difficult to grasp when its proper time and place are lost.

In her cookbook *The Good Life*, which is also an annal of the old cherished ways among New Mexican villagers, Fabiola Gilbert writes of an autumn day spent in the hills around Santa Fe harvesting piñon nuts. An entire family comes to pick them—one should say "pick up," for they lie everywhere scattered under the piñon pines—and their time is spent bent over, gleaning the pounds and pounds of seeds. At the end, the labor accomplished, the mother of the family unpacks a picnic. It consists of a goat's cheese made fresh at home and molded by her hands; large rounds of deep-fried bread called *buñuelos* (these first two are eaten with molasses, also home-pressed); a roasted leg of kid; and the first red chili sauce of autumn, seasoned with wild oregano gathered on the same hillsides where the family is eating. As you read the episode, the scene, the people, and the food seem stopped in time, not wishing to move or change.

I want to be there with them and eat that food. I can taste it and know how delicious it must have been on a fading afternoon described as the last fall day before the snow. Just to see such a piñon-rich land-scape spreading itself around Santa Fe today makes you hungry for that experience. Since I cannot have it, the only surrogate that matters is the food, which at least can be prepared in the right spirit. The human feel-ing that ties events together, food and family, work and a day, is never wholly lost in a cookbook.

Like the other writers, I am, in the end, going to throw in the tomato puree at times and the several kinds of chilies, too. Vegetable shortening will be quietly substituted for lard. Mention of roast kid will be made, but only in the spirit of hopefulness, since most of us will never eat it. If you have ever seen Santa Fe, you will want to recapture it as a human scene, and not knowing on what day and with what people you had your experiences, I will give just the bare instructions for simple feasting; I hope that you can adapt them in a personal spirit.

Needless to say, all of this food is good eaten alone, accompanied by imagination, or with one person who understands food and, better yet, what you are after. Tell that person about piñon picking, and the goat cheese and *buñuelos* you are eating will be "authentic," even if the scene is a suburban kitchen shining all around with Cuisinarts. Tell him too about Father Latour, the archbishop in Willa Cather's novel *Death Comes for the Archbishop* and a Frenchman used to good food as his birthright. He came to New Mexico and tried to make a Christmas feast for himself at a time when remote Santa Fe did not even have a "blessed lettuce." A cook will know exactly what it meant when Father Latour rode 1,500 miles to and from Old Mexico with a bottle of *real* olive oil in his saddlebags—the situation called for drastic measures—or how he wished mournfully for leeks as he dined on plain onion soup as his main treat that Christmas night (but was grateful to have any soup, let it be said).

The food of Santa Fe is not offered merely so that you can imitate austerity. Even without the adobe-colored hills, the rounded junipers and the New Mexican sun, there is still in this cooking a quality of unsmoothed touch, or as Cather called it, "that irregular and intimate quality of things made entirely by the human hand." As home cooks, we can still give our food that intimacy.

Here, then, are twelve such feasts in simplicity:

DAY ONE. Roast a green chili over an open flame, peel it and mash the flesh with garlic into a simple relish (*chile verde*). Knead flour and water for tortillas, roll them out after the dough has rested, and then bake some bread for yourself on the griddle. Eat the first triumphant tortilla with butter and a little of your relish. Eat all the others that way, too, or sprinkle on some grated soft white cheese.

DAY TWO. Boil a kettle of dried red or pink beans with onion and oregano for savor. Eat them with fresh tortillas and the green chili of the first day.

DAY THREE. Soak red chili pods in hot water to extract their pulp, from which you make red chili sauce (*chile colorado*). Mix the sauce into some, but not all, of your leftover beans, and repeat the meal of the previous day. If you lived in a pueblo or on a poor village farm, you would be repeating some version of this meal hundreds and thousands of times. Eventually there would be no more need for a rolling pin for the tortillas or measuring spoons for anything else.

DAY FOUR. Have ready a large piece of pork shoulder. Cut the greater part of it into thin strips for curing in *chile colorado*. Simmer the remainder in its chili sauce to eat today, accompanied by bread, beans and the green chili *salsa*.

DAY FIVE. If there are still beans in the pot, revive them by frying in oil with some onion added for flavor. Mash them with a spoon to make refried beans, then stir in shreds of white cheese. Eat with part of the stew meat you cured in red chili and, of course, tortillas.

DAY SIX. Take some more strips of meat that have cured in red chili and sauté them in oil, then add water to make a stew. Prepare a dish of rice and onions to go with the stew; embellish it with a handful of *garbanzos*—and you have "dry soup."

DAY SEVEN. Roll out your first corn tortillas today and bake them exactly as you did the flour ones on the first day. Fold a few tortillas around shreds of white cheese and some chopped onion and then heat in the oven with red chili sauce to cover—these are the simplest and yet the best of *enchiladas*.

DAY EIGHT. Take yet some more strips of cured pork and stew them for half a day with water and swelled hominy, which makes *posole*. Tortillas and green chili relish go along.

DAY NINE. Stew a chunk of pork shoulder, tear it into long shreds, and mix with enough red chili sauce to moisten. Work some hominy meal and lard with water or pork broth into a doughy paste. Spread a layer of paste on corn husks, fill with the shredded pork, and roll the husk packages into *tamales*. These are steamed for an hour and then eaten with more red chili sauce.

DAY TEN. Make a yeast dough for bread and divide it into four parts. Roll the first part into flat triangles thin enough to puff up like a pillow when they are deep-fried; these are *sopaipillas*. The second part is sweetened with molasses and raisins and shaped into rolls; these baked sweet rolls are called *molletes*. The third part of the dough is rolled into balls between your palms and fried as fritters, or *buñuelos*. Eat the "sofa pillows" with butter and honey, the others with a white goat cheese. Save the fourth part of the dough.

DAY ELEVEN. The fourth part of the yeast dough is reserved for turnovers, half-moons in shape stuffed with pork mincemeat, raisins and spices. Regular-size turnovers are called *empanadas*; choicer, smaller ones are *empanaditas*.

DAY TWELVE. The culmination is to make all of your preceding dishes on one day, which means a vast meal of *tamales* and sweet rolls, mincemeat turnovers and stewed pork in red chili sauce, flour tortillas with refried beans, and separate bowls of *posole*, green chili *salsa*, "dry soup" and goat cheese. With extra energy you might produce *enchiladas*, but they certainly are not so important as desserts—either double-crust pies filled with dried apples, or a soft egg custard lightened with whipped egg whites, or anise-speckled cookies baked along with your bread. A good feast must have all three, according to the old cooks.

You might have guessed by now that the twelfth day was the feast of Christmas. Everything in it duplicated the daily food, but there was more, and more variety. Everything was handmade and therefore essentially irregular and intimate. Hardly anything deviated from the corn, beans and chili which formed the platforms of everyday food, along with wheat flour, onions and pork. Native New Mexicans also did have wild greens to gather, or they cultivated a kitchen garden to produce the "blessed lettuce." Potatoes were grown in the fields, and from the earliest days of the Spanish conquerors there flourished orchards of apples, pears and plums, not to mention wine-grape vineyards. Still, the basic repetitive rhythm of everyday cooking comes across as you imaginatively follow the twelve days. Moreover, one can actually cook this way and be satisfied with the results.

No one seems to have put piñon nuts in their dishes, however, which seems strange. In Fabiola Gilbert's book, the piñons are eaten by themselves by the main characters, a family and some neighbors, who form a larger communal family as they gather around a fireplace through long winter evenings to gossip and crack piñons. The father and mother in her book are always present, at first with their son, who later marries and moves away. A goatherd who has been adopted into the family sparks the gossip and plays the guitar, eyed by an old woman, a former slave in Spanish colonial days, who now wanders the hills to gather wild herbs, functioning as herbal healer for all the surrounding families. She soon will die, and being illiterate, cannot pass on her formulas. For the moment, though, the timeless unit is complete. There will be coffee at midnight, then a sleep before the coming day, which will center on some chore involved with food. Green chilies to roast, red chilies to dry, dried chili to make into sauce, sauce to cure the meat, meat to cook into stew—one gets the feeling that there are no artificial interludes of the kind we call menus, meal planning or even recipes—only the intertwined experiences of the people and their hard-won daily fare.

If you want to follow up this imaginative schedule by cooking any of the simple foods described, here is a list of recipe locations:

Roasted Green Chili with Garlic, p. 94
Flour Tortillas, p. 119
Boiled Pinto Beans, p. 294
Red Chili-Powder Sauce, p. 73
Shredded Pork, p. 99
Pork Cured in Red Chili, p. 264
Refried Beans, p. 296

"Dry Soup," p. 305
Corn Tortillas, p. 114
Red Chili *Enchiladas*, p. 216
Posole, p. 266
Tamales with Pork Filling, p. 240
Sopaipillas, p. 127
Buñuelos, p. 331
Empanadas, p. 345
Soft Egg Custard (*Natillas*), p. 353
Aniseed Cookies (*Bizcochitos*), p. 346

A SANTA FE LARDER

Although a larder has come to mean a stockpile of ingredients, it is also literally a place—what would have been the "dispensary" in a New Mexican colonial village or hacienda. A walk into this dispensary would tell any cook a great deal about the meals to come, and particularly about the advantages and limitations facing the kitchen. If you look at the roster of dried foods sold in current Santa Fe groceries, you still can get the feeling imparted by the old storerooms. A typical list runs like this:

Dried red chilies
Dried chili powder
Dried green chilies
Whole *pequín* pods
Nixtamal (dried hominy)
Blue cornmeal
Blue corn flour
White cornmeal
Panocha flour
Cumin

Coriander
Saffron
Wild tea
Mexican chocolate
Posole
Chicos (dried corn)
Pinto beans
Corn husks
Piñon nuts

Since this is a modern list, primarily concentrating on native goods not found in supermarkets, it does not have quite the right historical emphasis. A Santa Fe woman of past centuries would have thought most highly of, and guarded most preciously, such imported luxuries as her chocolate, sugar, cinnamon and tobacco. They would have held place with her linens and silver, also brought across the ocean or up the tremendous length of the Chihuahua Trail.

On the other hand, some of her humblest ingredients were ones not easily come by today, such as the flanked strips of dried venison, usually cured with red chili, the vats of fresh lard manufactured in slaughtering season, and local dried melon and summer squash, preparations acquired from the Indians. Nonetheless, even such a sketch of ingredients is more than enough to conjure up chili stews, *tamales*, *posole*, refried beans and a dozen other marks of Santa Fe cooking.

What follows is a fleshed-out description of the larder as you, a modern cook, will need to know about it. If you already understand the methods and techniques of Mexican cooking, this chapter will be practically enough to indicate the ways the cooking of northern New Mexico (and the American Southwest in general) differs from the cooking of Mexico proper. If you are new to all manner of Mexican food, except for the sort presented on restaurant menus around the country, this section is a good place to get your bearings. We are fortunate that it takes only a small effort of orientation to begin to produce home-cooked Mexican food that leaves the restaurants far behind, something you could not truthfully say about Japanese, Chinese or French cooking.

The only thing lacking, should you be conscientious enough to read all these larder ingredients through, is a feeling for the place itself. Once experienced, a sympathy for Santa Fe lingers of its own accord, and there is no pretending that it can be infused through the pages of a book. Particularly intangible in these days of new Southwestern prosperity is the hardness and austerity that gives local cooking the same unyielding edges as the landscape. The first Europeans were hard-pressed indeed not to find their situation barbaric, and where we see comforting earth tones, their hearts must have pined for a wider color palette. There is no denying that what they created out of their situation, and one does not mean only food, breathes an unspoken somberness which is not at all the same quality as the impromptu gayness of similar Mexican food. But what was there made a good life, and the goodness is easily felt to this day.

Herbs and Spices

In New Mexico, herbs were used more for medicine than for cooking, but the old women who kept the herbal lore certainly knew where on the mesa they could gather wild *orégano*, *azafrán* and *yerba buena*. These and a few other cooking herbs were meant to approximate the ones remembered from Spain and Mexico. In some cases, as with the wild saffron, the substitute was very approximate indeed. Other indigenous herbs, such as *chimajá*, were not really like anything else—you see it variously described as wild celery, thyme or parsley. And if the landscape seemed barren of desirable plants to the casual observer, the herb hunter could find many varieties of certain ingredients, particularly if they went under the name of sage or sagebrush. (However, the wild black sage, which is closely akin to culinary bottled sage, was not much used in Santa Fe cooking, at least according to preserved recipes.)

Spices were also suited to the tastes of Spain and Mexico. Because they all had to be imported, the spices were highly valued and preciously guarded. Although you might not notice much call for cinnamon, clove and nutmeg, you can be sure that these were lavishly used on feast days or for flavoring such a dish as the stuffed roast chicken which was to be the centerpiece of a wedding supper. The commonest spice, then as now, was cumin, just as the common dried herb was oregano.

The following herbs and spices are in frequent use and therefore appear in this cookbook:

Aniseed (*anís*) is used whole to give a licorice taste to sweet pastries, particularly the holiday cookie called *bizcochitos*. To impart the same flavor fennel seed is perfectly all right also, but star anise (used in Chinese and Mexican cooking) would have to be ground first before adding it to dough.

Coriander seed is at times called for as a sweet baking spice, but by far the greater use comes from the green coriander leaf (*cilantro*). It is the main fresh herb in the Santa Fe kitchen, employed both as a flavoring and as a garnish to finished dishes. *Cilantro* was never as continually available in New Mexico, however, as in the warmer climates of California or Mexico proper, and many local restaurants apparently do without it altogether to this day. The taste and smell are peculiar enough to put you off when you first encounter green coriander, but soon the memory is as haunting as fresh basil is to a native Italian. Regular parsley, which has never haunted anybody, is not a substitute. If you do not want to snip a few *cilantro* leaves onto your *enchiladas* or grind them into your *guacamole*, then do without.

Green coriander stores the least well of any standard herb. It is best to wash the bunch free of sand, shake out the excess moisture, and then unwrap the twine which holds the stems together (and promotes rotting). Pick off the browned, wilted leaves that inevitably come along and place the cleaned herb in a plastic bag. Once refrigerated, *cilantro* keeps well for a few days, and sometimes a week. Some authorities advise wrapping the bunch in wet paper towels or standing the cut stems in water to prevent wilting, but I have never gone to the trouble.

In parts of the country where *cilantro* is not a supermarket item, it should be available in Oriental groceries as "Chinese parsley." If you have to make a trip to locate some, I still do not advise buying it in quantity. It is true that the surplus leaves can be chopped up and added to your bottled *salsas* or blended with water and frozen in the form of coriander ice cubes, but there is always a drastic loss in taste. Frozen coriander also tends to turn brown, which is not too desirable.

The best way to chop *cilantro* is by hand, using either scissors or a knife. Attempting to chop the delicate leaves by machine will only plaster them against the sides of the container or else turn them to pulp. Chop at the last moment if you can, for chopped *cilantro* will wilt and lose its freshness in a matter of minutes, even when refrigerated.

Cinnamon is used in stick or powdered form. Its taste adds a gala touch to desserts and festive menus, not to mention the daily cups of chocolate. However, the elaborate spicing of Mexican cooking, where cinnamon, clove and ground coriander seed are tossed in with abandon, is foreign to the more austere ways of Santa Fe.

Cumin (*comino*) was picked from the seedpods of a wild plant to be used both whole and ground. It adds a prominent flavor to almost any chili-based sauce but particularly to the red. Once again, the austere tastes of Santa Fe make this an optional flavoring, but many cooks employ it as freely as we would salt or pepper.

Bay leaf (*laurel*) comes from a different tree in the new world than the old, with a somewhat stronger flavor. It can be used to taste in sauces and soups; the recipes in this book mainly call for it in conjunction with beans and lentils, two foods that are enhanced by the bay leaf flavor, even to the point of overuse.

Orégano in New Mexico usage means wild marjoram. It appears freely in any sauce or soup recipe that needs an herb taste, and seems especially right with dried red chilies and tomatoes. Because the leaf is spiky and catches between the teeth, Santa Fe cooks preferred ground to whole oregano. Use whichever you happen to like; my choice at home is whole-leaf Greek oregano, which is quite strong. To keep its flavor intact, I store it in small bags in the refrigerator. For that matter, it is also good to refrigerate any perishable spice, such as cumin, ground coriander (these two are especially short-lived before they turn to tasteless dust), black pepper and ground cinnamon.

Black pepper, preferably freshly ground, is also called for in practically every seasoned dish. Although we also call chilies by the name of pepper, the two ingredients are not related, so you will need black pepper in your sauces even after you have added green or red chilies.

These are the main flavorings relied upon on a daily basis. They are supplemented on occasion by saffron (*azafrán*), one of the most valuable of Spanish herbs, but not found in the New World; safflower, a yellow coloring agent used in place of saffron by cooks who could not afford the real thing; ground clove and ginger, both used as sweet spices, particularly in mincemeat; and wild mint (*yerba buena*), which can replace green coriander as a flavoring or fresh garnish. If it suits your taste, you can put sage into sauces in place of oregano. Another wild substitute favored by Santa Fe cooks is *chimajá*, but its dried leaves or ground roots are not widely available. The root was the main flavoring for Chimayó whiskey, one of the stuffs of New Mexican drinking legends.

Cooking Oils

The dismaying truth is that Santa Fe food is properly cooked in lard. It was unthinkable in a subsistence economy to discard this abundant byproduct of pig-slaughtering season. In addition, lard keeps well with minimal refrigeration. In the days before cholesterol, Hispanic cooks had no fear, either, of tossing bits of pork cracklings (*chicharrones*) into a pan of refried beans as they merrily sizzled away in lard. Heated to the smoking point, lard was used for softening the daily tortilla or for browning flour to thicken chili sauces. In hardened form it became the shortening for pastries, or it could be whipped to a state similar to our canned vegetable shortening for making cookie dough and bread.

Having said this much, I am not requiring lard in any recipes in this book. The factory-made lard sold in the supermarket in snow-white blocks is not the gutsy lard of home or village renderers. There is little to be gained by frying with it unless you already happen to like it. Vegetable oil, olive oil, butter and vegetable shortening will come into play as they are needed. Still, it's abstractly comforting to know that you can, theoretically, live without them so long as you have a tub of lard.

I primarily recommend lard for pastry making. The "Spanish pies" that so frequently appeared on festive occasions in Santa Fe, by which were meant double-crust tarts like the French *tourte*, and the half-moon fried pies (*empanadas*), which also were the marks of a fiesta mood, all require good, tender pastry. Their traditionally thin layers of filling make them "more crust than pie," at least as observed by Anglo cooks used to their own cobblers and chess pies. Lard imparts a particular flakiness to good pastry that Southern cooks still pride themselves upon. They will be the last ones, I suppose, to heed the bad news about pork fat, or to fret over its social unacceptability. So the pastry recipes in this book merely indicate how to work lard into your pastry, leaving you to choose. Properly rendered lard is not salty or strong in meat flavors, so leftover bacon fat or even high-quality salt pork is not a substitute for it.

The everyday oil for frying tortillas is now probably Crisco. It may not be the product you use yourself, but make sure your choice is economical—the exposure of the frying fat to tortillas and foods made with chili renders it unfit to recycle. You will need a fresh supply every time you fry.

Shallow-frying: I respect the modern squeamishness over deep-frying, although none of our ancestors worried. My experience shows me that even food that was traditionally deep-fried, such as fritters or *buñuelos*, can be shallow-fried in no more than ½ inch of oil. The round-bottomed shape of a wok conserves the amount of oil needed better than a flat-bottomed frypan. An electric wok is best of all since it offers the added attraction of allowing you to control the temperature of the cooking fat, unlike a wok set down over the range. It is also much less likely to tip over on you, a genuine threat with most conventional woks except for those that are heavy or well secured to the range top, which few are.

However, the flat-bottomed shape of a small skillet is preferable for softening tortillas.

Of course, some people will not want to use a wok for cooking Santa Fe food, no matter how convenient it is. Likewise, they may seek out authentic clay vessels for stewing beans, and a Mexican *comal* for roasting chilies. I always picture such cooks standing before their four-burner stoves with microwave and warming oven, the processor humming in the distance, but thinking in their imaginations that they are in fact barefoot and wearing sombreros.

Fruits and Vegetables

In modern Santa Fe, as anywhere else, you can walk into a local supermarket and buy mangoes or artichokes if that is what you crave, but for the purposes of this book, you will need only the fruits and vegetables that cling close to the native New Mexico spirit. Mexican cooking is famous for its rainbow medley of garden produce, and much of it is attractive to cooks in Santa Fe. Their own austere climate could not raise avocados, pineapples, or oranges, but the culinary influences from Mexico proper have brought them into play here, along with *nopales* (cactus), *jícama*, pomegranate (its seeds appear in the traditional Christmas Eve salads), and other semitropical delights.

This abundance is a far cry from the Indian staples of corn, beans and squash, the oldest garden crops which the short native growing season supported, later amplified under Spanish rule by the remaining familiar garden produce—zucchini, bell peppers, tomatoes, potatoes, melons and a particular Pueblo favorite, the watermelon. The usual Indian way of cooking their summer vegetables (not the melons) was to mix them all together in one casserole for baking in the *horno*, or beehive oven. The earthenware pots stood in the gentle oven heat for several hours, eventually emerging as a uniformly soft—we would say mushy—melange. No seasoning, not even salt, was called for, and the kinds of vegetables used were determined by the season. The lavish abundance of green chilies, zucchini, tomato, and green corn in high summer gave way to pumpkins, acorn squash, red chilies and dried corn (*chicos*) in autumn.

When winter was on the horizon, all the Pueblo and Spanish gardeners devoted full days to drying produce for the many months when the earth was barren of crops. Not only were chilies, corn and beans dried, but also such unlikely foods as green summer squash and melons. The process was simplicity itself, since all that had to be done was to cut the fruit or vegetable into strips, impale them on forked green twigs and leave them outside to dry in the arid New Mexico climate. Modern practice is to dry them on clotheslines, holding the strips with clothespins.

Settlers to this barren country quickly made orchards in it, but the really suitable land for fruits and nuts lay south of Santa Fe. We are told that by 1850 the produce peddlers lounging under the portals of the plaza had grapes and peaches to offer in season, along with apples, apricots and plums. These must have come as a grateful respite from the sameness of local onions and beans. Fruits that stored well over winter were most prized, giving rise to pastry fillings based on dried apples and raisins, or else dried apricots and almonds. Families also foraged the land for wild plums, berries and piñons as their respective seasons came around, all to be tucked into the winter larder with everything else. The weeks of provisioning were a crucial part of the year's labor up until recent memory. The great reward for all this work came at fiesta time, which coincided with fall harvesting, and later of course with Christmas. Then the unassuming, shriveled produce was transformed into mincemeat tarts, dried-apple turnovers (*empanaditas*), and all manner of vegetables stewed with meat (which had also been dried over winter). In our days of abundance, it is possible to feel almost envious of a child who woke up to the smells of apples and raisins stewing since dawn, and knew it must be Christmas.

In the recipe section I have adhered as much as possible to the indigenous ingredients of the Santa Fe area, but the extensive cottage industry of canning, drying and putting by has been omitted for lack of space. Since most of the produce called for is not out of the ordinary, I am restricting my comments in this section to the ingredients which may be unfamiliar to many cooks or which require special handling.

Lettuce and wild greens: Although Southwestern restaurants invariably use iceberg lettuce for garnishing, the more authentic variety is romaine. It has a definite flavor and smell as well as much less water content than iceberg, but it quickly wilts after being placed on top of a hot *taco* or *enchilada*. The best way to handle it is to take as many of the outer leaves as you need for your garnish, stack them one on top of the other, and slice into ¼- to ½-inch strips. Having the center rib facing up helps your knife to dig in, as does holding the blade at an angle rather than straight across the leaf. In any case, you do not have to be precise about cutting fine shreds—broader strips seem to add character to the garnish.

Precut romaine can be put into a plastic bag and stored in the refrigerator for an hour or two until needed. The small, pale inner leaves of this lettuce make excellent scoops for *guacamole*.

Before the arrival of modern agriculture, the old way to make a salad in Santa Fe was to use wild greens. One finds recipes that call quite often for watercress and *quelites*, or lamb's-quarters. Specialty markets in many cities now carry similar unusual greens, so feel free to employ them in your own improvised New Mexico salads. Fresh herbs, particularly those in the mint and oregano families, are also authentically used in this region. If you do resort to iceberg lettuce after all, either as a salad green or garnish, there is no great harm done—it is a matter of trading taste for crunch.

Onions: Onions are pervasively used in New Mexican cooking as a basic flavoring, most prominently in sauces and garnishes. Many native cooks do not make much distinction between types of onion, so you find many recipes where ordinary white or yellow onions are used everywhere. For myself, I am not able to enjoy quantities of yellow onion as a raw ingredient in uncooked table *salsas* and *guacamole*, and I like it only in very small amounts sprinkled over finished dishes as a garnish. Therefore, the amounts of onion have been considerably reduced in certain of my recipes, and as a rule chopped green onion (scallion) is called for as the garnishing I prefer. Where it made a distinct difference to my palate, mild red onion has been substituted for yellow onion in uncooked *salsas* and *guacamole*. However, what seems an improvement to me may not be to you, so feel free to increase the amounts of onion as you become more skilled in New Mexican cooking, and use the varieties you prefer. Even "gourmet" onions like the imported sweet Maui onion are worth experimenting with, although they are a far cry from the humble staples of Santa Fe root cellars.

Tomatoes and tomatillos: If you can find the proverbial "firm, ripe, bright-colored red tomato," then by all means use it wherever tomatoes are called for in this book. Whether to peel them or not is a matter of personal preference. I have never peeled a tomato for any New Mexico sauce, garnish or salad, but I have heard that it is absolutely standard practice among many other (more genteel) cooks. When fresh tomatoes are out of season or too sorry-looking to bother with, any recipe can be prepared with canned ones (except for the few where fresh tomatoes alone are specified).

Green tomatoes or *tomatillos* are a separate fruit, not botanically kin to the ordinary tomato, so an unripe garden tomato (commonly called a green tomato) will not be a satisfactory substitute. Mexican cookbooks frequently require *tomatillos* as the basis for green sauces, usually but not always combined with green chilies. I have not discovered very many such recipes in New Mexico, however, and to my taste at least the green, sour flavor and tobaccolike smell of the *tomatillo* are not pleasant. If you are curious about green tomatoes and want to use them, I have indicated a very few variations in the recipe sections that call for them. However, real lovers of *tomatillos* can incorporate them into any green chili recipe simply by parboiling some for five minutes in salted water, peeling off the papery brown husks and pureeing the flesh in a blender or food processor. The puree is added to the sauce along with the green chilies and needs at least 15 minutes of cooking to get rid of its raw taste. One pound of fresh *tomatillos* yields about 1½ cups of puree.

Fresh *tomatillos* range in size from cherry tomatoes to medium-small—never as big as red ones. Only firm ones should be bought; avoid those that feel mushy or have dampness on the husks. Unlike red tomatoes, you cannot test fresh uncooked *tomatillos* either by taste, smell or texture, for they always seem totally unripe. The canned ones, on the other hand, are invariably precooked to mush. They need no further preparation except to drain them, puree the fruit and add to the sauce as it cooks. The canned sort can also be directly incorporated into *guacamole* if you like their sour taste there.

Avocado: A tropical fruit not native to the Santa Fe area (any more than pineapple is), but now thoroughly assimilated into the local cuisine. See p. 151 for more details about handling avocados.

Chilies: A major cash crop in New Mexico, these are the backbone of all Santa Fe cooking. Since a thorough knowledge of how to use both green and red chilies is indispensable to sauce making before anything else, see pp. 59–72 in the chapter on sauces for an extensive discussion of local varieties and practices.

Corn: This is one of the heroic triad of New Mexican foodstuffs, along with chilies and beans. For a detailed discussion of its many uses, see pp. 111–13.

Dried beans, chick-peas and lentils: A casual diner in a New Mexico café would suppose that the pinto bean is king—and he would be right—but Santa Fe cooking includes quite a variety of other dried beans and legumes. See p. 293 for details.

Jícama: A tropical vegetable, not native to northern New Mexico, nonetheless has a few interesting uses in Santa Fe cooking, mostly as a salad ingredient. See p. 175 for details.

Meat and Poultry

All the meat eaten by the Pueblos was wild game, and every generation that came to Santa Fe later hunted in its turn. The domesticated dogs and turkeys that lived in Indian villages were not raised for food, so it took the Spanish to introduce salt pork, mutton, ranch-raised beef and cured meats of every domestic kind. Sun-dried strips of meat, or jerky, could be eaten raw or stewed in place of fresh meat. The everyday meat of the hill villagers was mutton, but being Spanish, they liked to have their spring lamb or kid slaughtered very young. By the era of the Santa Fe Trail there was such an abundance of accumulated meat recipes, however scarce or seasonal some meats might have been, that the only problem for the cookbook writer is what to select.

What was free in the wild to Indians is now prohibitively expensive for us, so I have eliminated venison and wild turkey recipes—we won't even speak of prairie dog, bison and beaver—but it is worth remembering that the hunt is not at all dead in New Mexico, and cooks still exchange recipes for venison stews and sausages. The Pueblo hunt for deer was a ceremonial affair that came around once in winter and once in spring, but rabbits were snared quite often; therefore, one could use today's domesticated young rabbits found in supermarkets to represent game meat, along with turkey. Stews with complicated chili-and-spice sauces, the famous *moles* of Mexico, have been pushed aside in favor of simpler Santa Fe stews. A few I think of as cowboy stews, or *vaquero* stews if the cowboy spoke Spanish, but others involve first stewing the chunks of meat and then frying them with spicy flavorings, an ancient Aztec cooking method which has an exact counterpart, strangely enough, in the oldest curries of India.

The Pueblos, in common with most Indians, spit-roasted or stewed their meat with very little added, usually not even salt, so there is not much question of turning their diet into acceptable modern recipes. In the spirit of their way of cooking, however, a way passed on directly to the Spanish and later to the Anglo pioneers, the meats in this cookbook are mostly barbecues and stews. Since there exist countless marinades and table sauces for both, and a good variety of chicken, turkey, pork, kid goat, lamb and beef to work with, you do not have to worry about monotony. Just the combinations of meat, chili and tortillas could occupy an inventive cook for a lifetime. If you are accustomed to unadorned ground beef, which the run-of-the-mill Mexican restaurant uses as the only meat stuffing for tortillas, I particularly want to point you toward the spiced minced meat called *picadillo*. Its mix of raisins, chilies and spices is far more interesting than plain ground beef, and its faintly sweet flavor goes back as far as medieval Spanish cookery.

Salted and cured meats are now on the list of suspicious characters for modern eaters, so there is no reason in my mind for perpetuating recipes, however authentic, which rely heavily on fatback, pork rind, ham, sausages and the rest. However, a few sausage recipes must be put in for their taste alone. Otherwise, it does not bother me that a traditional Santa Fe cook deprived of her salting vats and curing rooms would be lost. This is not a historical cookbook; it is simply one that keeps tradition as its guide.

Most of us avoid indoor grilling because of the mess it makes in modern ovens. I have tried to minimize that and to provide good recipes using charcoal. Cooks are also bothered by the uncertainty of timing meat dishes, particularly if it is a matter of pleasing adamant diners who will not tolerate rare or well-done beef, whichever is the case. With a few exceptions, the recipes in this cookbook do not depend for success on exact timing. Where barbecue is concerned, a cooking method notorious for producing either raw or charred meat, it is almost ridiculous either to provide spurious exact timings or to leave the cook to a hit-or-miss guessing game. The solution is to char the meat over the coals and then transfer it to the controlled heat of an oven. With the widespread use of kettle barbecues in which coals can be smothered and conserved simply by closing the vents, it is no longer wasteful to fire up the barbecue for ten minutes. The charcoal works perfectly well a second and even a third time.

I have been fairly scrupulous about pairing sauces and meats after a traditional manner, which means that braised meat like *carne adovada* calls for pork, as it should. I see no real barrier, though, to braising the dark meat of, say, a turkey in just the same manner. Wherever possible, the recipes encourage you to substitute lamb for beef, turkey for chicken, and so on. But American cooks tend to shy away from lamb, and there are any number of people who avoid it altogether except for the Irish stew dished out in college cafeterias or an occasional rib chop at a fancy dinner party. For those who have missed so much, therefore, I have leaned on the lamb a bit, knowing full well that real *vaqueros* of course threw into the pot the beef they lived with and tended.

Chorizo: This has become a generic term for almost any sort of spiced Mexican pork sausage, although the Spanish have their own version. Wherever you find it, whether in a supermarket or a Mexican butcher's, the meat is encased in a sausage skin that must be removed. Simply slit it from end to end, peel the casing away from the meat and chop the sausage into a coarse mince with a knife. A processor is likely to grind it up, which is not what you want. Exactly what you are getting when you buy *chorizo* depends entirely upon your source. Besides garlic, cumin and red chili, the pork itself can taste rather like Polish sausage. The *chorizos* sold in Mexican groceries in the Southwest are often surprisingly mild despite their chili-orange color. To make your own *chorizo*, see recipes on p. 103 and p. 205.

Jerky: Until the recent revival of beef jerky as food for backpackers, preservation by sun-drying had been long banished by the advent of refrigeration. The Indians set out strips of meat for jerking on forked twigs along with the corn, squash and melons that needed to be stored over winter. The technique was passed to the Spaniards, and it is still employed in the mountain villages and pueblos where venison strips are hung out in the autumn sun, though now they are attached to the back-yard clothesline instead of a cottonwood sapling.

Mexico proper abounds in dried-meat dishes. Steaks from the fore-quarters of the beef carcass are cut along the grain into accordion pleats, then unfolded and dried as *cecina,* and this, once it is cooked and shredded, becomes a Sonoran specialty called *machaca.* I give a recipe for eggs with beef jerky on p. 203 which is close to the Mexican *machaca,* but in deference to the price of supermarket jerky (about a dollar an ounce, even here in the West), the proportion of meat to eggs has been reduced, in contrast to these dishes as made by Mexican cooks, who often sauté over a pound each of meat, onions and tomatoes before scrambling just two eggs in the same skillet.

Jerky can also be cut into cubes and added for flavoring to green or red chili stews, but I do not find this is much different from the *chorizo* on p. 103, which is much cheaper. Since supermarket jerky also has such dubious improvements as liquid smoke and corn syrup added, no specific recipes for it are given in the main-dish category. Although the Pueblos plump their jerked meat and flavor it at the same time by stewing in red chili sauce, there is a preparation called New Mexico jerky, or *carne seca,* to denote its Hispanic origins, in which the meat strips are rubbed before drying with generous amounts of salt, vinegar and powdered red chilies. This would have been eaten through the winter when fresh meat was scarce, needing only to be grilled or stewed in water.

Fish

An indigenous fish recipe is hard to find in New Mexico. A high mountain town like Santa Fe depends upon long transportation lines to bring it any food from the sea. The native game fish from the Rio Grande and other high-country waters is usually trout (although the modern rainbow trout is an import), which is at its most delicious fresh-caught and simply grilled. The requirements for Catholic fast days were largely met here without fish, although dried shrimp that had traveled the route from Acapulco do appear in traditional egg fritters, or *torrejas.* A supply of dried and salted fish from the same source could be reconstituted into a mash with cream and eggs along the lines of the traditional Spanish preparations for salt cod (*bacalao*), but in fact there is no real evidence that this was done. One does not encounter many fish dishes in Santa Fe even today, so the recipes in this book are restricted to the trout and little else.

All our ancestors were so passionate about oysters that barrels of them trekked the immense distance from the sea to Santa Fe even before the railroad came in the 1880s. These were eaten at gala moments with champagne, also trudged in. We realize now, as they knew then, that oysters on ice can survive up to four weeks in their shells, but I do not regard oysters on the half shell as an indigenous dish. You could use a plate of oysters to preface a meal, of course, and probably it would be quite right to spike it with a dash of chili *salsa* to make it a Santa Fe oyster.

Cheese

For centuries the daily cheese in Santa Fe was sheep or goat cheese, manufactured in the surrounding villages from fresh milk and rennet. A moist curd cheese called *resquesón*, something like our modern cottage cheese, was used for light-textured fillings in *enchiladas* or the quichelike tarts called *quesadillas*. In modern Santa Fe the markets mostly sell Monterey Jack as the all-purpose cheese; it is suitably mild and soft, but it has none of the rank, woolly taste that lovers of goat cheese so enjoy. Rather than bothering about true *queso blanco* from Mexico or the currently popular California goat cheese, I have indicated that you use Monterey Jack in almost all the recipes calling for cheese in this book. However, if you like the taste of goat cheese, feel free to substitute it instead. That includes using it in sweet dishes, for the New Mexicans doted on the combination of goat cheese and honey (you can even eat the two as dessert by themselves, along with warm, crusty bread).

In Tex-Mex cooking, and wherever the Anglo influence is dominant, the most popular cheese is some form of orange Cheddar-type cheese, primarily Colby and Longhorn. These are salty and sharp compared to Monterey Jack. Devotees of New Mexican cooking might look on such products as also too blatantly orange to be right in an authentic dish. Whether or not you resort to Cheddar cheese ultimately depends upon your own taste, but considering its ever-present use in commercial cooking, I like to buy Monterey Jack instead. Although it is really authentic in California rather than New Mexico, Monterey Jack approximates the taste and texture you are looking for. Santa Fe cooks sometimes made use of *queso añejo*, a hard grating cheese that resembles Parmesan or Romano, but that too is no longer much kept up. If you want to mix a little fresh-grated Parmesan into the melting cheese that will go on top of some *enchiladas*, or if you want to sprinkle a spoonful into a bowl of *frijoles* or *posole*, feel free to try it.

Once Monterey Jack has been shredded, it begins to soften at room temperature and then to clump together. For easiest handling, shred the cheese at the last moment and keep it cool. I shred cheese by hand on the largest holes of a four-sided grater because my processor tends to gum up on Monterey Jack. Newer models come with blades that do the job nicely, I understand. If your shredded cheese has to stand for any time, keep it lightly covered with waxed paper to prevent drying out.

Melted cheese should be soft and glossy. If you are melting some in a pan, as for *chile con queso*, first heat the other ingredients to boiling, then add the shredded cheese off the heat. Stir until almost melted, then return to *gentle* heat to finish the process. Never bring cheese to a boil, for high heat will toughen it and cause it to break down. For dishes topped with cheese and oven-baked, use a moderate oven (300°–350°F.) and cook for only a few minutes. High temperatures will make cheese stringy and will brown it, which you do not want in Santa Fe cooking. If you are oven-broiling the cheese topping, place it 6 inches or more from the broiling element and watch the dish closely.

Nuts

Piñons (pine nuts): Pine nuts, which ripen in the crevices of pine cones throughout the desert Southwest, are the native article in Santa Fe cooking. By an irony of fashion and commerce, this essentially free ingredient, hand-gathered in the wild since the days of the earliest Indians, now costs as much as hazelnuts and more than pecans. To buy pine nuts at all in some places you must go to Italian groceries, where they sell under the name of *pignoli*, or to the better-stocked Hispanic and Greek groceries. Canned *pignoli* are frequently salted, so you must rinse them under cold water before making desserts with them. The unsalted pine nuts that you occasionally run across in supermarkets seem to have comparatively little pine oil in them, and the oil is what gives the taste to piñons, making them preferable to slivered, blanched almonds, their nearest equivalent in texture. Good, strong-flavored piñons are worth searching for, since they are the right ingredient for certain Santa Fe dishes, and I have not substituted where they are really needed.

Pecans: Southern New Mexico grows a considerable crop of pecans, excuse enough for including recipes for two delightful Southern sweets, the pecan pie and the praline. The pioneer heritage of Santa Fe, what is called without animosity the Anglo influence, brought pecan pie to the frontier. By the time of the railroad's arrival in the 1880s, any of the countless American pies that a dining-car chef chose to make had become standard fare. I think the choicest ones are the old Southern chess pies, overweeningly sweet and thus able to be kept for long storage without refrigeration. Traditional pecan pie is really a chess pie with nuts in it.

Almonds: As far as Spanish sauces and puddings go, the almond is the common nut. A few recipes using it have been included, but several are frankly hybrids and imports, reminiscences of Old Spain and Mexico. And, because the crunch and bitterness of walnuts form such a good complement to ripe avocado, I have put them together a few times, although once again the spirit is more native to another place—California—and not New Mexico.

A MODERN
APPROACH

PLANNING YOUR LABOR

Like other American cities, but unlike Mexico, Santa Fe does not have a class of kitchen helpers, either hired or attached to the family, who are free to spend hours making tortillas or even stewing pinto beans. In the mother culture of Mexico there are street vendors of fresh tortillas, not to mention *tacos* and *tamales*. And there are still relatives—*tía* this-or-that—who realize that their place in the world is to run the home kitchen, every day preparing for the large to huge afternoon meal, the *comida*, which some call the center of Mexican life.

None of that is Santa Fe. In homes, as in restaurants, you are likely to encounter the one-plate Mexican dinner, which by purist standards is all wrong. Its *tacos* and *burritos* should rightly be eaten as snacks, not as dinner food. The *salsa* and refried beans likely as not come from a can. The tortillas almost certainly came from plastic bags in the supermarket refrigerator section. And the meal is eaten on the go. Make of them what you will, these are facts of present-day Santa Fe eating.

My object is not to enable you to eat like a visitor to a Santa Fe restaurant, so I will not tell you how to go about producing a combination plate. But neither are you going to need Tía Sofía backing you up on the tortilla press. The trick is to plan your kitchen labor so that a degree of handmade authenticity is achieved without physical exhaustion. I think making your own sauces, for example, is far more important than stamping out your own tortillas. For the first there is no commercial equivalent that passes for homemade; for the second there is. I leave it to you whether or not you want to peel your own green chilies. I absolutely believe you should buy wheat tortillas, ready-made, along with canned chicken and beef broth and good canned tomatoes. My conscience often provokes me to pass by canned pintos, kidney beans and garbanzos, but even they show up in my dishes on those occasions when I do not have five hours free to prepare them from their dried state. I say five hours, instead of the requisite two or, more improbable yet, one and a half that cookbooks usually mention. Dried beans are quite capable of taking a *long* time to cook, and their proteins are completely unpalatable when still the least bit raw. (Even pureeing half-cooked beans in a processor does not seem to help. It is not just the hard texture of the beans that makes them unusable, but their basic raw flavor.)

Pressure cookers and Crockpots are proven laborsavers in the cooking of beans or of meat to be braised and shredded. Recipes will indicate their use when it is advisable. The only mechanical aids that are indispensable, however, are the food processor and the electric blender. Mexican cooking is so labor-intensive that you will be following enough steps without having to bother about hand mixing when the processor will do the work so much faster. My directions always call for using a processor if it is obviously the easiest method, but I have limited use of its attachments to one—the regular metal blade. In my own kitchen the only other blade ever to come into play is an adjustable slicer, which I use for making onion rings.

Canned and bottled ingredients also come under the heading of labor management in your kitchen. The section "Mexican Convenience Foods" (pp. 52–56) is a critical appraisal, by no means complete, of the packaged products you will encounter in your supermarket's Mexican food section.

The crucial thing to say about labor is that Santa Fe cooking looks far more daunting on the recipe page than it actually feels under your hands. Experience will gradually free you from fixed recipes altogether, except for the more finicky sorts of pastries. Even the sauces, unlike those in French cuisine, depend as much on whim as on rigid formulations. This is essentially the cooking of mixed cultures, as you read time and again. It hangs together only because individual cooks have followed the given rules—those imposed by the subsistence landscape—only to outwit them by their personal ingenuity. When you can see *guacamole* or *chile con queso* in your own mind as a series of steps and a body of flavors, you too will be liberated from the domination of a cookbook. You will be well on the way to being a good cook in general and not just a good Santa Fe cook.

Nevertheless, Mexican cooking holds a reputation for requiring hours of kitchen labor, and this is easy to transpose to New Mexican cooking, which is its stepchild. The advent of the electric blender and the food processor has made it possible to prepare almost all the food in this book about as quickly as you might prepare good standard American fare. You need only consult the recipe for *tamales* on p. 240 to see that I am not coaxing you with false promises. The most laborious tasks, such as shredding pork for the *tamal* filling, are whizzed along with a few seconds in the processor. The machine also purees the red chili sauce and the *tamal* dough itself. (The old recipe for *tamales* began with the instruction, "Whip some lard by hand until it is the consistency of whipped cream.") Unless you are a stickler for authentic touches, the customary soaking and rolling of corn husks will be bypassed with aluminum foil, which has no ethnicity about it—only ease for the cook.

Similar convenience has been unashamedly provided, usually without comment, everywhere that it was possible to save time. More time translates into more dishes for you to explore, after all, and it is the writer's aim to have this book actually used. I mean to do more than pass along the folkways of a culture that relied for centuries on unpaid labor. But there are still some remarks to make for the cook who has never approached Mexican cooking of any sort and who is baffled by the new techniques of assembling and saucing so many dishes based on chilies.

Sauces to make ahead: The finest New Mexican cooks are masters of the improvised sauce, and once you get a feeling for the basic components —chilies, tomatoes, onion and garlic—you will find that new sauces spring to your fingertips. Unlike a more set cuisine in France or China, this cooking is not tied down by rule books. A red *enchilada* sauce is a guide only, and no two try to be the same. Since a restaurant cook is mainly interested in speed and quantity, however, the visitor to Santa Fe may begin to think that there is only basic red chili and basic green chili, with a large empty space between them. It is not so, as you will see for yourself, but the restaurant cooks are right in one respect: you can be a faster and less harried cook if you keep one good red chili sauce on hand, such as the variety on p. 73 concocted from powdered chili. This is the backbone of everyday cooking. A green chili sauce is not so necessary to store, however, since it is needed less often.

The only other sauce to store is some kind of sour table sauce, like the green one on p. 91 with or without tomatoes added. It becomes an all-purpose relish when you are too busy to make one fresh, and it is also good to have for spooning over any bland food like pinto beans.

Knowing what must be fresh: A recipe writer is forced to repeat the phrases "serve fresh" and "serve immediately" even though he shares with his reader the realities of cooking—not everything can be hot, fresh and instantly delivered all at once. Uncooked *salsas* will keep for a time, with the important exception of *guacamole*, and all the cooked sauces are good for weeks. Stewed meats can wait, but not tortilla dishes—they really do have to be rushed out almost as soon as a sauce touches them. All forms of beans can sit over low heat for an hour or more, but fresh preparations using corn and squash, like the *calabacitas* on p. 318, lose their sweetness if they stand around. So when all is said and done, it is really just the tortilla preparations that must be rushed, and you will quickly learn to plan around them. One great advantage of New Mexico food is that none of it was developed with refrigeration in mind, so you will have to worry about a minimum of curdling, spoiling and turning rancid. This is food that likes to stand in an adobe room and feel the breezes pass through.

Avoiding complications: If you are in doubt about how many dishes to include in your meal, err on the side of simplicity. New Mexico food is not just a repetition of red chili, beans, and tortillas, as you will quickly learn, but it is all too easy to repeat these ingredients in one meal. Don't overlap chili flavors too often from one dish to the next and do try to set off bland, creamy dishes against stark red chili sauces. Look for contrast wherever you find it, and there will be no danger of falling into the monotony of standard combination plates as served in neighborhood *taco* parlors.

PROCESSOR TECHNIQUES

Avid and casual cooks alike now own a food processor, but how many, I wonder, have fully adapted to it? If you were already conscientious about learning proper knife technique, it takes a few months before you feel comfortable with the machine and know for certain when its work is as good as a chef's knife. Often it isn't, and lax cooks who try to chop everything by machine are liable to relegate it to the shelf once it has liquefied an onion or turned mashed potatoes into glue when the cook's back was turned. True adaptation to a processor demands that you learn new habits —getting used to the incessant scraping down of the bowl with a spatula, changing your time frame to seconds instead of minutes (cake batters, for instance, are zipped up in five seconds), and resigning yourself to washing the bowl and blade ten times in one afternoon.

Once you make the effort to adapt, however, the processor turns out to be invaluable for sophisticated cuisines, and perhaps even more for the simple but labor-intensive cooking of Mexico and New Mexico. The maiden aunt who patted out tortilla dough, mixed up piecrusts, mashed out chili purees and chopped onions is now electrified. Here are some of the basic techniques employed in this cookbook, all of them requiring no more than a standard processor equipped with a standard metal blade.

To chop garlic: Turn on the machine and drop the peeled whole cloves in through the feed tube.

To chop herbs: The same technique as for garlic, but not very effective if the leaves are delicate or moist. Parsley works, green coriander doesn't, unless it goes in with other ingredients.

To chop onions: Peel and cut whole white or yellow onions into quarters. Then place them in the processor bowl a few at a time and pulse quickly in separated, repeated bursts. Look through the sides of the bowl to see how the chopping is going, stop after four good bursts, and lift off the cover. Scrape down the sides of the bowl with a spatula and give the onion one or two more pulses. Trying to chop an onion at continuous speed will invariably turn it to mush. If your pulsing has chopped most of the onion but left one or two intractable large chunks, remove them for the next batch rather than risking turning everything to pulp by further processing. Scallions do not generally process well unless you first cut them into short lengths, since the action of the blade on large bits of green onion stem plasters them unchopped on the side of the bowl.

To chop green chilies: Large chilies like Anaheims or bell peppers are first cored and deveined, then cut into chunks and processed with short, repeated bursts. They take longer to chop than an onion, thanks to their tougher skins, and often there are unchopped bits remaining, even when you scrape down the sides once or twice. Small chilies like *jalapeños* and *serranos* are dropped into the whirring blade through the feed tube, but be careful to avert your face from the upward rush of chili vapor— it can immediately induce a coughing fit and running eyes.

To chop foods in sequence: If you have to chop garlic, chilies and onions together, first drop in the smaller things (garlic and small chilies) through the feed tube while the processor is on, then stop the machine, place in the chunks of onion or large chilies, and continue to chop them

with the repeated pulse technique. It is invaluable to know this technique since so many recipes have such sequences in them.

To mix batters: The chief concern here is to process the batter thoroughly without working the flour so much that its gluten toughens. As every curious cook infatuated with a new processor has learned, a few extra seconds in the machine can produce strange, extreme results. The general technique with cake batters is to process them just a few seconds, or until the dry ingredients are no longer separate, then to scrape up the batter from the bottom of the bowl with a spatula and process for a very few seconds more. Butter creamed with sugar, as well as melted chocolate, particularly needs to be scraped up, since it readily sinks beneath the blades.

To make pastry: Although many books tell you confidently that you can mix pastry in your processor, the danger is that the blades will generate too much heat, causing your shortening to turn oily, and then the dough will roll up into a homogenized ball of flour and fat—no good at all for pastry. The best compromise technique that I have found is to use the machine for cutting in the shortening (even then the butter needs to be well chilled or actually frozen) and afterward add only a minimum of water to moisten the dough. Work with pulses and do not let the pastry get beyond the stage where it looks like meal or flakes. Now the half-finished dough is poured into a bowl and worked lightly by hand, pressing and turning it quickly with the knuckles of your fist, until it coheres into one mass. This technique is more or less the same as the French method of scraping the pastry along the pastry board in order to work in the shortening.

To puree soups and sauces: Processors are not always better at lique- fying soups or sauces than an electric blender would be, because the blade cannot always catch on to solids that are suspended in too much liquid. It is usually effective to liquefy small batches at a time or to strain off some of the cooking liquid and puree only solid matter first. If you try to add a solid to the machine while it is working on a liquid (if, for example, you drop a whole garlic clove or *jalapeño* into a chili sauce), the blade will probably just whir it around without chopping it up at all, much less puree it. Have your solid ingredients in the bowl at the start— especially if more than a cup of liquid is called for later.

To puree vegetables: A processor does a much better job of making a textured puree than a blender can: Carefully used, it produces vegetable purees and uncooked chili *salsas* that do not resemble baby food. Watch the progress of pureeing closely, however, stopping the machine at two- second intervals to scrape down the sides of the bowl and check on the texture. It also makes quite a difference to the final taste of a puree if it is rough, smooth, or in between. You can verify this for yourself by changing the texture of your *guacamole* from time to time.

To mix bread dough: The machine is the most effective on simple, unraised doughs, for conventional bread dough is usually prepared in fairly large quantity and may stall the motor. Luckily, there are several such unraised breads in this cookbook. Details for making their doughs in the processor are provided in the appropriate recipes. The doughs for biscuits and *sopaipillas*, which need to remain quite soft, are best made by hand.

To shred meat: Pork, beef, chicken and turkey are shredded in chunks after they are cooked by using the dull plastic blade. More detailed directions are given on p. 100. This is the sole instance in which you need a different blade from the standard metal one.

POTS, PANS AND UTENSILS

A good kitchen can be put together by a habit of scavenging. If your instincts lead you, quite correctly I think, to eschew fancy gourmet cookware in favor of a constant hunt for honest, heavy, usable implements, then this section probably has nothing to tell you. There will always be mistakes, needless to say: pasta machines and electric ice-cream makers, Chinese steamers and imported charlotte molds, bought in a fit of hunger, and now thrust into corners like toys in the attic. This book is not going to add to the pile.

We rely here on quite ordinary pots and pans, just as the list of ingredients relies on food you can buy in supermarkets. My own favorite cookware is Le Creuset, heavy iron coated with enamel. It is no longer cheap, as it was when Elizabeth David first began to recommend it in her cookbooks, but at least you can find it anywhere. I also welcome Teflon and Silverstone lining in skillets, albeit they are plastered onto lightweight aluminum for the most part. Tin-clad copper is a joy to work with, but we do not all live on a trust fund. Pictures of kitchens hung round with copper pans, copper bowls and copper molds amuse me, for, having actually spent an afternoon polishing the intricate grooves of a cherished old copper mold in the shape of a lion, I cannot imagine making a habit of it.

I actively warn you against thin stainless-steel pans, the sort painted with a thin bottom of copper, too skimpy to do any good as far as transmitting heat goes; they are so light that they slide around the burner while you are stirring, and frequently they topple off the stove altogether if you accidentally bump into their handles. Plain aluminum of some weight transmits heat well without serious hot spots, but the oxidation of its interiors on contact with acidic foods rules it out for me; I am not willing to put up with the metallic taste, and I have seen such pans turn Béarnaise sauce an inedible purple.

Investing in a tortilla press is not a bad idea, though it is certainly a prime candidate for toy-in-the-attic status later. An electric wok makes a good deal of sense, as I explain under "Cooking Oils" (p. 31), and it has the advantage of being useful for every imaginable cuisine. Mexican *comales*, chocolate frothers and Oaxacan ceramic pots are not needed unless you are encouraged to your best efforts by local color.

Almost all the food described in this book benefits from gentle heat, whether it is prepared by barbecuing, braising or baking. The adobe ovens of the Indians and Spaniards, fueled by wood and charcoal, cooked slowly enough for all the tastes of the food to marry. The outdoor baking ovens called *hornos* would be a delight to own, but only in your imagination. (New Mexican cookbooks which give detailed instructions for building your very own backyard *horno* make me laugh once again.) Of all the foods one strives to duplicate in a city kitchen, the indigenous breads are the least reachable. I shall do without a *horno*, I'm afraid, but I know that means I will not have the intricate flower breads of the Pueblo Indians, the dark bread of Taos, the whole pumpkins baked after the bread is finished, or the real Spanish tarts, either.

MEXICAN CONVENIENCE FOODS

There is no denying that traditional New Mexican food requires a good deal of repetitive labor. Besides not making their own tortillas by hand, many cooks are now tempted to resort as well to canned sauces, canned chilies and varieties of "instant" mixes. The extensive selection of such conveniences can be baffling to the uninitiated, and the various brands are very inconsistent in quality. Where it is possible, recipes will be given for improving upon the better bottled and canned products. But first, in order to orient you to the long shelf of Mexican goods, here is a brief consumer guide:

Canned and Bottled Sauces

These come in both red and green, including red ones that are called green because the chilies used in them are fresh green ones in red tomato bases. The cans are usually marked mild, medium or hot, but that is going by an Anglo scale. It is a rare commercial *salsa* that is more than a bit tingly. Although you would expect the brands with Spanish names to be better than the mass-market Americanized imitators, they often have the thinnest texture and the most powdered ingredients so that they can be sold cheaply.

Powdered ingredients there are aplenty in commercial sauces: witness a sample of canned *enchilada* sauce admitting to garlic powder, onion powder, beef powder and *jalapeño* powder. Its only unprocessed ingredient is water. If you want products that are free of these additives, you can still find them, though at higher prices, in many natural-food markets and sometimes in well-stocked supermarkets that are not afraid of off brands. The primary difference between several traditional lines from Texas or California and the Americanized ones like Del Monte is that the ethnic brands generally underplay the tomatoes and sugar. Sauces marked *salsa* are usually uncooked table sauces meant to be spooned over any dish at will. *Salsas* of this kind are not intended for cooking, although the generic word for any sauce in Spanish is *salsa*.

Red enchilada sauce: After finding certain Spanish-label brands bitter and thin, the Americanized ones too sweet and tomatoey, I plumped for Old El Paso red *enchilada* sauce marked "hot." Directions for turning it into rather a respectable instant red chili sauce are on p. 80.

Green enchilada sauce: By usage and custom, this is hotter than the red, but is not hot at all when it comes from a can; in fact, several of them taste of nothing stronger than vinegar. Most lines are to be avoided, since a vinegar taste is rarely what you want. Old El Paso, although quite meek, is at least green. Use it for the instant green chili sauce on p. 83.

Taco sauce: Many of these are green and come in bottles. Practically all are quite sour—more like pureed pickles than a chili sauce—so their only use is for sprinkling as a garnish over *tacos*. Do not be deceived into thinking they will make a green sauce for *enchiladas*.

Salsa jalapeña: Basically the same product as *taco* sauce, but much hotter. Remember, if you use it to hot up a dish, that the vinegar in it will also make it quite sour.

Green chili salsa: These vary considerably, but they are typically another variety of uncooked table sauce, to be used as a condiment. Some are green, some are red, some are sour, and some are very sweet. None are used for cooking.

Salsa picante: Literally speaking, any hot sauce is a *salsa picante*, but the bottled ones are uncooked liquid relishes containing green chilies, onion, tomatoes and garlic in varying proportions. Some of them make respectable substitutes for uncooked sauce (*salsa cruda*), to accompany grilled meats, though not nearly so good as your own.

Chili sauce: The chili sauces sold in ketchup bottles are a variety of ketchup, more or less. They have a good consistency for adding to a New Orleans-style *rémoulade*, but they are not used in this cookbook.

Tabasco and other red-hot sauces: Some are good products, but they add the taste of vinegar to whatever they touch. It is better to hot up a dish with mashed canned *jalapeños* (the kind packed only in water) or powdered cayenne.

Canned Green Chilies

Under this heading come many products, some of them quite necessary if you want to make Santa Fe food often but are not prepared, as almost no cook is, to roast and peel fresh green chilies every time. If you are not certain about the product you are buying, look on the label for some indication that the chilies inside are mild, medium or hot. Unlike many other "hot" canned goods, the *jalapeños*, including *chiles chipotles*, are the ultimate in fieriness. Handle them with caution. Ortega, perhaps the major line of Mexican canned chilies distributed in the West, marks its mild products with a blue label, its hot ones with an orange label.

Whole green chilies: This name applies to flame-roasted, peeled Anaheims, and happily for us they are practically as good for *chiles rellenos* or green chili sauces as ones you laboriously roast yourself. Small cans contain only a few and tend to be relatively expensive, so buy the largest you can find and freeze the remainder, or puree any leftovers into sauce. If you need to store canned chilies in the refrigerator, be sure to remove them from the can. A bad taste can otherwise develop in no more than a day. The phrase "whole green chilies" generally means mild ones; whole *jalapeños* are labeled as such. The phrase also usually indicates that the chilies are packed in salted water instead of vinegar, but check any unfamiliar brand to make sure of it.

Chopped green chilies: These are quite finely chopped, and their flavor is comparable to home-prepared, but seeds are intermixed freely with pulp, which can be a drawback. If you have a need for only a small amount of chopped chili, a fresh one from the grocery will make do, even without peeling. Like the whole ones, "chopped green chilies" generally means mild.

Whole jalapeños: Two sorts exist. The pickled ones are not always labeled *en escabeche*, as they should be, but the ingredients list will note the presence of vinegar. These are used for garnish and to eat whole by themselves, providing you can tolerate them. For the cooking of green sauces, look for the other sort, whole *jalapeños* in salted water; citric acid is also commonly added as a preservative. The pickled *chiles chipotles* which certain recipes in this book call for are a delightfully smoky version of pickled *jalapeño*.

Pickled peppers: These are wax peppers pickled and sold in super-markets alongside the other pickles; they are not suitable for general cooking purposes but can be used as garnishes.

Canned beans and refritos: The motto which applies here is that if you must, you must. Cooked beans of every kind become afflicted with mushiness when canned, but if they are added to a dish two minutes before it is taken from the heat, they usually are acceptable. Even canned chick-peas, or *garbanzos,* which are the toughest survivors, should be rinsed to remove the canned taste, though it is fairly indelible. Canned *refritos* taste good to most of us because Mexican restaurants are our reference, and every Mexican restaurant uses them. They are not called for in this cookbook, nor are the dreadful bean dips of all description.

Canned tomatillos: With their texture turned almost to liquid and their fresh flavor overwhelmed by the taste of the can itself, they make a sorry substitute for fresh *tomatillos.* It is hardly necessary to buy them in any case, as fresh *tomatillos* are readily available, and their use often optional. If you go ahead and open a can anyway, you should know that the *tomatillos* inside need no blanching before going into your sauce.

Sopaipilla mix: Many restaurants use this mixture of flour, baking powder and lard, to which only water has to be added. For home pur-poses, if you do not want to make the extremely easy dough yourself, packaged biscuit mixes like Bisquick amount to the same thing as instant *sopaipilla* mix; both of them incline to be oversalted. The proportions for the biscuit mix are approximately one cup mix to three tablespoons water.

Tomatoes with jalapeños: For dishes that call for tomatoes and hot green chilies together, there is a ready-made canned product sold as "tomatoes with *jalapeños.*" It contains good-quality whole peeled tomatoes packed in very hot tomato juice—the actual pieces of green chili are not much in evidence. Besides using it for the quick red chili sauce on p. 79, you can substitute this excellent product anywhere that canned tomatoes are used, but be sure to adjust for the added hotness as you proceed with the recipe instructions.

Corn-tortilla products: If you elect not to make your own tortillas by hand, perfectly acceptable ones can be found in the refrigerator section of the supermarket. Outside the areas where Mexican cooking is popular you may have to resort to frozen tortillas—there should be little loss in quality—or to the decidedly inferior canned variety. If all you can find is canned tortillas, use them in recipes where their tired taste will be well disguised by a chili sauce, and plan to make a batch of fresh tortillas as soon as you can. Frankly, since commercial corn tortillas are adequate for almost any dish, I would perfect my tortilla skills on flour tortillas first; their commercial equivalents never seem to have the fragrance of the homemade kind.

Store-bought varieties of *taco* and *tostada* shells work quite well, too, but they improve greatly if reheated in a 300° oven for a few minutes before filling them. Store-bought tortilla chips, or *tostados*, are good enough for dipping, but they are too flimsy to cook with. If you can find a brand that is thick and sturdy enough to be baked into *nachos*, stick with it. Any cook who lives in the West should also search his area markets for ready-made blue-corn tortillas. These may be hard to find, but an obliging Mexican grocery might be willing to order them for you. If a source is not known, try the address for Josie's tortillas given on p. 112. Unless you happen to live in Santa Fe, the local supply of blue-corn tortillas is likely to be quite erratic at the best of times, so don't plan on blue-corn *enchiladas* until you have bagged the tortillas to begin with.

SAUCES, RELISHES AND FILLINGS

Chilies—The Soul of the Sauce

COOKED SAUCES
Basic Red Chili Sauce (Chile colorado)
Red Chili Sauce from Whole Chilies
Adaptable Red Chili Sauce with Tomatoes
Instant Red Enchilada *Sauce*
Basic Green Chili Sauce (Chile verde)
Instant Green Enchilada *Sauce*
Ranch-Style Pan Sauce (Salsa ranchera)
Avocado-and-Zucchini Sauce

UNCOOKED SAUCES
Basic Table Salsa (Salsa fresca)
Quick Tomato Salsa • *Sour Green Chili* Salsa
Scorpion Chili Paste • Guacamole *Sauce*

RELISHES
Green Chilies for the Table (Chile verde)
Roasted Green Chili Relish
Sweet-and-Sour Relish for Barbecue • *Chili Vinegar*

FILLINGS
Hand-Shredded Beef • *Shredded Pork*
Shredded Turkey Breast
Spiced Ground Beef with Raisins and Almonds (Picadillo)
Sausage to Taste Like Chorizo • *Sage Cheese*
Fillings Based on Goat Cheese or Cream Cheese
Other Cold Fillings • *Other Hot Fillings*

CHILIES—THE SOUL
OF THE SAUCE

Corn is the earth in Santa Fe cooking, and chilies are the fire. From the
Hispanic viewpoint, the correct word is *chile*, pluralized to *chiles*. In
Anglo usage, which historically came later but is nonetheless unyielding,
it is *chili* and the plural is *chilies*. When Columbus first spotted them
growing wild on Santo Domingo, he continued in the same delusion which
had led him to name the aboriginal natives "Indians," and he called chilies
"peppers." After all, he supposed that he had reached the Indies, whose
fabled wealth rested in no small part upon black pepper and other spices.
Chilies in fact are *capsicums*, to be botanical about it, and they interbreed
with no encouragement, giving rise to hundreds of variants.

The nomenclature of chilies is made complicated by several unrelated
facts. First of all, the habit of spontaneous interbreeding blurs the line
between one chili and another. Second, the same chilies are called by
different names throughout Mexico, California and the Southwest. Finally,
and most confusingly, the names applied to specific kinds of chilies are
often misnomers which would not be used at all were the world of chilies
an orderly one. If terminology were more important to us than taste, we
would all be lost among the chilies.

Cooking with chilies, however, is a more casual matter than the be-
wildered city-bound reader might suppose as he glances over the long lists
of *poblanos, pasillas, tepíns, anchos* and *jalapeños* that preface Mexican
cookbooks. All chilies grow fresh on the vine in a green state and proceed
to ripen through various stages of yellow, orange, flame red, dark red and
brown-red. For commercial purposes, the green chilies are sold to be eaten
immediately or else pickled, while the red-ripened fruit is dried to be sold
either whole or as a powder.

For the sake of simplicity, we can say that you will use green chilies

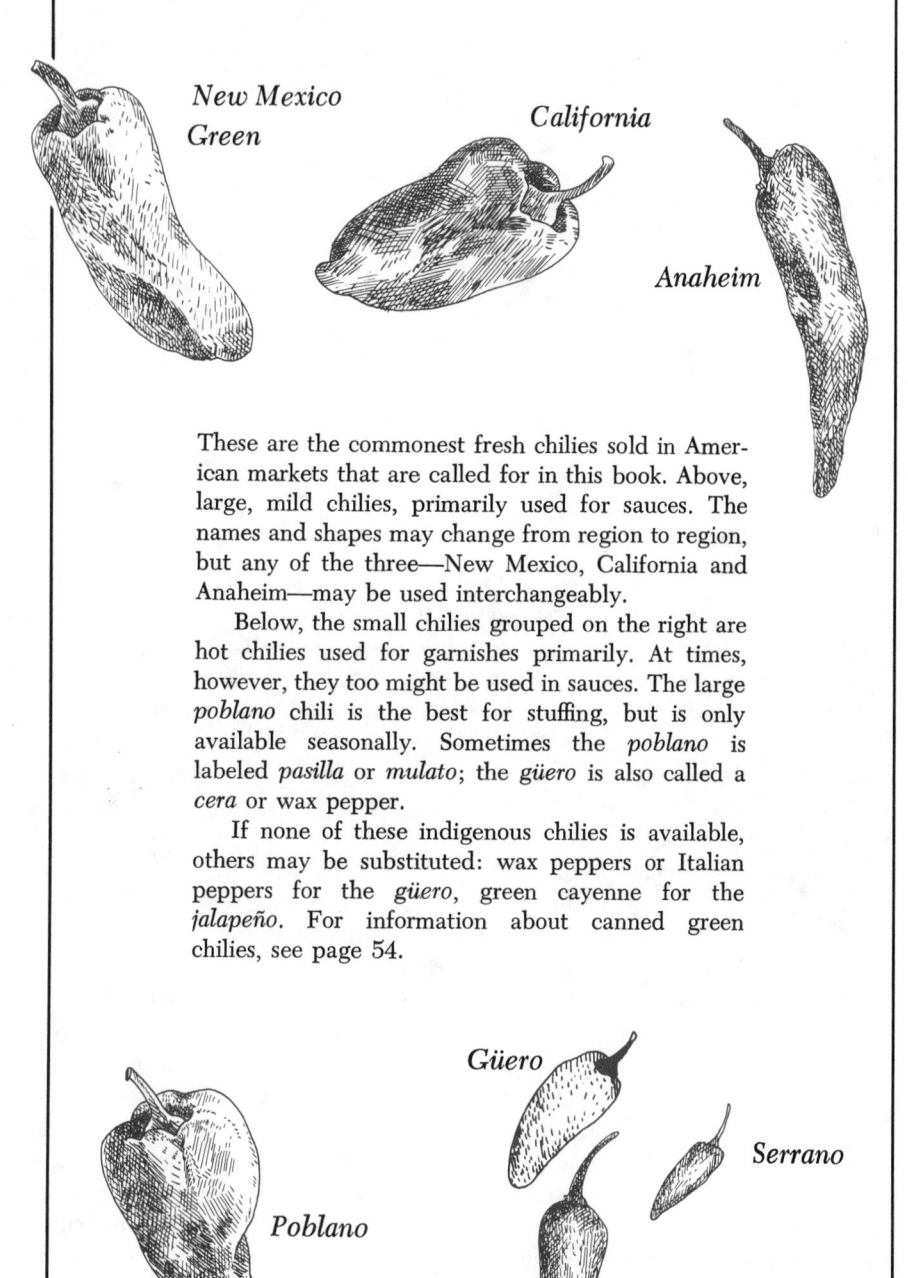

New Mexico Green

California

Anaheim

These are the commonest fresh chilies sold in American markets that are called for in this book. Above, large, mild chilies, primarily used for sauces. The names and shapes may change from region to region, but any of the three—New Mexico, California and Anaheim—may be used interchangeably.

Below, the small chilies grouped on the right are hot chilies used for garnishes primarily. At times, however, they too might be used in sauces. The large *poblano* chili is the best for stuffing, but is only available seasonally. Sometimes the *poblano* is labeled *pasilla* or *mulato*; the *güero* is also called a *cera* or wax pepper.

If none of these indigenous chilies is available, others may be substituted: wax peppers or Italian peppers for the *güero*, green cayenne for the *jalapeño*. For information about canned green chilies, see page 54.

Güero

Serrano

Poblano

Jalapeño

*Chile de Ristra or
dried California*

Ancho

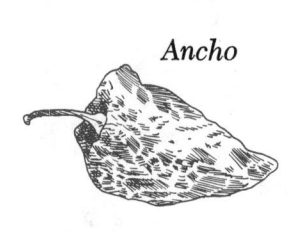

The same classes of chilies as the fresh green but in dried form. At top left is the chile de ristra, or dried California chili (often loosely called *pasilla*). At top right is the *ancho* (the dried *poblano*), which is used much less in New Mexico than in California or Mexico proper.

At lower left is a group of small, very hot chilies; note that the *chipotle* imparts a strong, smoky taste to any dish it is used in.

Below right are the small hot chilies known as cayenne or *japónes*, but any dried chili in this shape can be substituted.

In powdered form, the mild chilies are sold as *chile primero, molido, pasilla* or simply New Mexico (or California) red chilies. For powdered hot chilies, choose a good-quality cayenne or flaked *chile caribe*.

Chile Chipotle

Tepín

*Cayenne
or Japónes*

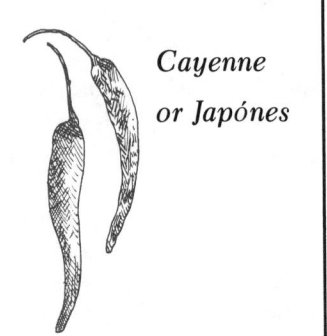

Pequín

primarily after they have been roasted and peeled, and you will use red chilies in the form of a ground powder. Understood that way, from a culinary rather than a botanical point of view, chilies become altogether easier.

Green Chilies

The one green chili all of us are familiar with is the supermarket bell pepper. Curiously, it is also hardly ever called for in New Mexican cooking (some purists would say never). When a mild green chili is needed for any purpose except to be stuffed, cookbooks tell us to use the Anaheim, a pointed light green chili which is more or less interchangeable with the New Mexican *chile de ristra* and the California green chili. Whatever name it goes by, this particular type looks like a witch's hat that has been stamped on. If the cook is making stuffed chilies (*chiles rellenos*), the preferred variety is the darker, thick-fleshed *poblano*, whose shape is stubby, gnarled and strawberry-like. In our times of popular gourmetism, the Anaheim chili is easy to find year round in the supermarket, but the *poblano* remains seasonal in spring and fall.

Before they can be used, green chilies must be roasted and peeled. Upon that point there is really not much compromise, I'm afraid. If you skip the roasting process and leave the chili unpeeled, you miss the characteristic flavor and texture of Southwestern green chili. An unpeeled *chile relleno* is little better than any stuffed pepper you might run across in a cafeteria. However, the roasting and peeling operation, novel as it is when you first try it, soon becomes tedious. The prospect of charring a dozen Anaheim chilies over a gas burner, which is just the first of several steps pursuant to producing a dish of *chiles rellenos* for six people, can be especially dismal.

Sometimes you can sidestep the problem by substituting bell peppers for Anaheims, however nonpurist that may be. Except to a chili aficionado, the taste is altogether comparable, or at least acceptable. More important, the task of charring them is much less finicky than working with small pointed chilies with nooks from which it is difficult to pluck bits of skin. You will still be several steps ahead of those cooks—their numbers are legion—who prefer to buy cans of "whole peeled green chilies" and be done with it. But that is an alternative, too, as we shall see later on.

Besides the Anaheim and the bell pepper, most chain supermarkets now sell small green chilies of varying degrees of hotness. The larger one, which averages about 1½ inches in length—big enough so that it must be deveined and picked clean of seeds—is the *jalapeño*. Strictly speaking, it is a garnishing chili, most often eaten in pickled form (*jalapeños en escabeche*) rather than added to sauces. Its smaller relation, a little darker in color, is the *serrano*. It often is sold in sizes smaller than an inch, and it has the advantage of being so tiny that you do not have to rid it of veins and seeds. Connoisseurs can taste the difference between *jalapeños* and *serranos*, but to most of us both are so hot that hardly any other sensation, much less another taste, is detectable after you bite into one.

An important caution about handling hot green chilies: For complex reasons having to do with the way they ripen, chilies vary widely in hotness. Today's *serrano* may be almost mild and tomorrow's intolerably fiery. The volatile oils that produce the heat reside principally in the inner white veins of the chili—it apparently is not correct to think that the seeds are hot, although that is a most common belief—but any time you expose your fingers to any part of the inner flesh of a hot chili you are in danger of spreading the chili oil to your mouth, nose or eyes. Burns can be very painful, and at the least irritating. Because the oil is so volatile, you must be cautious when handling chilies. Here are some tips gained from practice:

- Chop or cut green chilies on a nonporous surface like china, glass or metal rather than on your regular cutting boards. Wood readily soaks up the burning oil and passes it along to the next food chopped on it, with sad results if that happens to be, say, strawberries.
- Do not cut chilies under running water, either hot or cold. The oil is carried up by the water vapor and can cause immediate coughing fits just from breathing over the sink.
- Avert your face if you are processing chilies or sautéing them in hot oil. Both operations release plenty of the burning vapors.
- To rid your fingers of chili oil, follow the same method Julia Child prescribes for garlic and onion. First wet your hands with cold water, then briskly rub them together with a teaspoon or so of salt, as if you were using soap. Now actually wash them with soap and warm water. This method has worked for me without fail. I also happen to believe that you can chop chilies and peel onions safely by clenching a wooden match between your teeth. The reason is that the grimace this evokes narrows the corners of your eyes where the tear duct is exposed to onion or chili vapors. You can do equally well by simply grimacing as if you were holding a match between your clenched teeth, but it is easy to forget this pretense—you relax and all is lost. The match provides the involuntary grimace necessary.

Storing green chilies: Fresh chilies tend to refrigerate badly, because they are susceptible to damp rotting, but you do have to keep them moist and cool; otherwise, the skin quickly starts to shrivel and the taste loses its snap. Wrapping chilies in dry paper towels and then refrigerating them in a plastic bag is a good solution; the towels act as a kind of insulation against the dampness. I prefer to buy only two or three at a time, or a quantity no greater than I need for the week ahead. Also, when you are faced with surplus perishables like green chilies or, worse yet, coriander leaf (*cilantro*), you can also salvage them by pureeing them into an existing jar of green chili *salsa* or *salsa picante*. Simply place the chilies and a little *salsa* in a blender jar, whir for a few seconds, and return the newly flavored sauce to the refrigerator. This additional authenticity is a help, particularly for commercial *salsas*, to which even the most conscientious of us turn on occasion.

Canned chilies: On the question of whether or not to use canned green chilies I am no purist. As much as they might lose in texture, canned chilies, chopped or whole, mild or hot, can be found in the kitchen of every Santa Fe cook. They are indispensable to restaurant cooking, needless to say, for the little person who is willing to peel a hundred green chilies in a day's work is as rare as the one who stands by and patiently pats out tortillas by hand. I describe the use of canned chilies in the recipes as they come up. Suffice it to say here that no sauce which depends for its essence on either green chili or green tomatoes (*tomatillos*) will come out quite right when it is produced *exclusively* from canned ingredients.

Roasting and peeling green chilies: These operations are essential in all Hispanic cooking from California southward. Essentially, what you do is blister a whole chili intact over—or under—a flame and then peel off the blistered and blackened skin. It is a novel technique to anyone who has never attempted it before because, first of all, the hissing chili does not explode, although it does limply deflate as soon as the grilled flesh is cooled. The amount of charring that is necessary is also surprising, for the pepper can be turned into a blackened little monstrosity before all the skin has been reached by the fire. But it is certain that the skin, which is tedious enough to pick off after the operation is finished, will refuse to come off at all from any portions that are *not* charred.

Here is the technique in some detail:

1. Direct-gas method—recommended for a few peppers. Turn the gas burner of a range on medium or high and place the whole Anaheim, *poblano*, or bell pepper directly on the burner plate (the same that holds up the saucepans). If your range is electric, or if you fear that the chilies will fall through the trivet, place a cake rack over the eye and proceed. Never let the skin of the chili come in direct contact with the electric element.

2. As the skin in contact with the flames starts to char, rotate the chili using ordinary kitchen tongs. Try not to puncture the skin as you turn it. Turn the chilies occasionally for as long as it takes to blacken and blister every outside part. This means that at some points in the operation you will have to hold the chilies patiently in your tongs—they like to roll around the burner and cleverly keep out of the flame just the part you want to blister next. Since the entire operation takes a little time, at least five

ROASTING
FRESH GREEN CHILIES

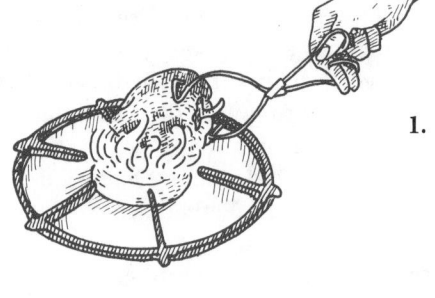

1. Roast whole chili over open flame until thoroughly charred, turning with tongs to catch any hidden peel.

2. Gently pull away charred skin under cold running water.

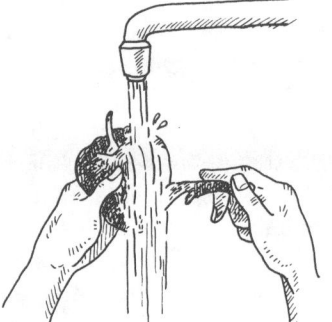

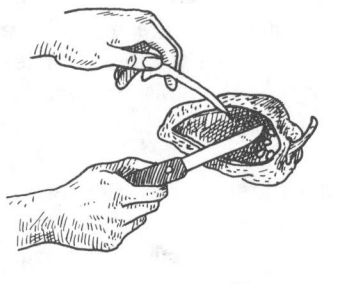

3. Using fingers and a paring knife, remove inner ribs and seeds. Try to leave chili whole with stem intact if meant for *chiles rellenos*. (For other uses, remove stem end of chili and do not bother with a side incision.)

minutes per chili, you can be roasting one on every burner simultaneously without worrying about how each little blister is coming along. No matter how blackened a section turns, the flesh underneath seems to come through intact and flavorsome.

3. Remove the charred chili from the range and cool it. You can do this by 1. plunging the fruit under a cold-water tap, 2. tossing it into a plastic or paper bag and sealing closed, or 3. placing it under several layers of moist kitchen towel. The latter two methods are supposed to help steam the skin and separate it from the flesh, which makes it easier to peel. This is a matter of conjecture, however, and I prefer simply to dunk the charred peppers under cold water and go on with the peeling.

4. Holding the chili under a thin stream of cold running water, just as you would a hard-boiled egg, begin to peel. Any method which doesn't drive you to distraction is called for here. The charred skin tends to flake off in maddeningly small bits, leaving behind plenty of stubborn particles. In general, you should peel from the stem end, working toward the point. The object is not to tear open the chili, particularly if you are planning to stuff it later on. Tearing, of course, is of no great moment if making a green chili *salsa* is your only aim. Really deft cooks can peel a whole chili leaving the stem end entirely intact. They then make one long cut, stem to point, from which veins and seeds are removed. Finally, they carefully place the stuffing inside the chili, close the gap, and thus are able to present perfectly re-formed *chiles rellenos* to their guests. The proof of their skill is the telltale stem, which is left peeking above the sauce.

The less skillful peel chilies any way they can. They then reach in to pull out and discard the inner veins and seeds. Deveining doesn't have to be perfect. One method is simply to cut off the stem end, scrape off the char, and pull out the veins and seeds with fingers and a paring knife. You will almost certainly revert to this rough-and-ready way by the time you arrive at your sixth chili of the afternoon unless you are blessed with extraordinary patience. In truth, even the sloppiest green chili can be stuffed and cooked without regard for its imperfect peeling. But leaving the stem on as long as possible does help to hold the chili together. Do not worry if a few charred spots remain despite your best efforts; they add to the charm of the home-peeled product.

5. If you are not using the chilies immediately, wrap them well with plastic wrap or store them with enough water to cover in the refrigerator.

Caution: Do not attempt to char the small hot *jalapeños* and *serranos*—no recipe in this book calls for that.

You can try blistering chilies under a broiler if you have quite a number to roast. This method still requires constant attention, and the broiler must be hot enough and the chilies close enough to the flame to actually char the skin. Oven baking will not do, by the way, since the temperature cannot be raised high enough, and prolonged baking at a lower temperature ruins the inner flesh. Finally, avoid recipes that advise you to deep-fry the chilies as an alternative to roasting. The dangers of splattering, the mess of peeling greasy chilies, and the altered taste brought on by frying are more than enough reasons to reject this method.

Dried Red Chilies

Dried red chilies are more important in Santa Fe cooking than fresh green ones, primarily because they are less seasonal. In the days before supermarkets, green chilies appeared only from mid- to late summer, and raising them required a garden or a desert farm that could be irrigated. Once it ripened to its red stage, however, the chili could be strung in long bunches called *ristras*, and in that form stored for many months. A *chile de ristra* was used in several ways: by crumpling it into large pieces (a technique mostly reserved for rustic stews), grinding it into a powder, or soaking the chili pod until its softened pulp could be readily turned into a paste.

The dried chili commonly met with in Santa Fe is variously called a New Mexico red, *pasilla*, or *chile de ristra*. By whatever name, it is basically the ripened and dried version of the green chilies one buys as an Anaheim, New Mexico or California chili. In other words, it looks long and pointed and bears thin flesh compared to a *poblano* (which in its dried state is sold as an *ancho*). All New Mexico dried chilies vary unpredictably from very mild to hot. Long storage reduces the hotness, as does long cooking, because the oils that carry the hotness evaporate or lose their volatility. A dried chili which has been scrupulously picked clean of its veins and seeds will also lose much of its fieriness.

The hottest among the numerous other dried chilies are the tiny ones. Some are round and the size of peas; others are tapered and thin, miniature versions of large red chilies. As far as Spanish labeling goes, the words *"tepín"* and *"pequín"* appear most frequently on the rounded sort, while the skinniest long ones are called Japanese chilies (*japónes*), or are simply packaged as "hot red chile."

As soon as you become involved with the complexity of identifying various chilies, you have entered the province of Mexican cooking proper. To the New Mexican cook, as often as not, the availability of a mild red chili and a hot red chili is enough. Many cooks probably get by with one, the generic product sold as "New Mexico chile powder." If the chilies that went into it are good ones from the prime area of Española and not sweepings from the sorting-room floor, so to speak, such a powder is eminently useful. (The flaked form packaged with all the seeds is called *chile caribe*. It is as hot as cayenne but often lacks flavor.)

It is nice to collect chilies to use them as you please. Among the large, milder ones, the general names to be found are *pasilla*, *mulato* and *ancho*.

The Mexican *ancho*, which is more brown than red and as wrinkled as an old avocado, brings to any dish a sweet, earthy taste that New Mexico chilies lack. Grinding a bit of it into your own chili powder would be a desirable touch. I find much less to choose from when it comes to the hot little chilies. Indeed, since *capsicums* are now a universal plant, you could diversely stock your kitchen with commercial cayenne pepper, imported hot and sweet Hungarian paprikas and New Mexico chili powder, with no one the wiser. Hungary boasts a chili culture as passionate and complex as Mexico's, as one glance through a mail-order catalog of paprikas will prove to you. It always needs saying, however, that you should avoid the commercial American product found on spice racks as "chili powder." It is meant strictly as a seasoning for chili con carne Texas style, and therefore contains garlic salt, cumin, oregano and the sweepings from the sorting-room floor which you were trying at all costs to avoid.

Making your own powdered chilies: Once you actually decide on grinding your own chili powder, the method is a simple one. Roast the whole dried chilies for only a few moments in an ungreased heavy skillet, shaking the pan from time to time to avoid any scorching. This can be done on the range or in a 350° oven. The point is simply to stiffen the outside of the chili so that it can be easily cracked apart; the incidental mild roasted flavor is a nice sidelight. Remove the chilies from the pan, let them cool enough to be handled, and break them apart. Discard the stems, seeds, inner veins and any suspicious-looking dark spots. Now grind the pieces to a fine powder in a blender or coffee grinder and, if you are fussy, sieve the resulting particles through a kitchen sieve to remove large, unground flakes. Store the chili powder in a glass container in a cool, dark cupboard to retain its flavor, or place quantities destined for much later use in the freezer, where dried chili keeps indefinitely.

How do you judge a good powder? Like paprika, a superior New Mexico powder smells pungent and a little sweet. A stale one smells unmistakably dusty. The actual hotness of your powder will not be apparent by sniffing it, of course—only by using it in a dish. The taste is liable to so much natural variation that you must judge that personally, particularly so far as sweetness and bitterness go.

Working directly from whole dried chilies: I prefer to cook with powdered chilies because of their convenience so far as measuring goes. It is also easy to add powder in the proportion of hot or mild chilies that you favor for each dish. The aroma of red chilies frying in oil—a basic first step in many recipes I give—has a primitive appeal in Santa Fe cooking. On the other hand, old-fashioned New Mexico cooks often worked directly from the whole chilies, first soaking them in warm water, then massaging the softened pulp until it separated from the skins. After the skins, seeds and veins were discarded, the pulp emerged as a thick chili paste to be used as is or diluted into a sauce with more water.

Here is a modern method along the same lines: Place 10–15 whole dried chilies in a bowl and pour boiling water over them to cover. Steep until the chilies soften, usually about 10 minutes. One by one, remove them from the water, pick out veins and seeds, and pop into the food processor or blender. Process the cleaned chilies to a paste, adding a little of the soaking water if the paste becomes too thick for your machine to handle comfortably. Pass the paste through a kitchen sieve to remove bits of skin that the whirring blades missed.

Sometimes old cookbooks use this paste as the basis for a red chili sauce without so much adornment as salt, but I find that it needs the same flavoring you give any good *salsa*—garlic, onion, oregano, salt and pepper. If you are going to cure meats in the paste, the essential operation for *carne adovada*, you can use it as is or flavor it—the preference is yours. Chili paste will keep for extended periods in closed glass jars in the refrigerator. Since the process of making one is messy, I have as a rule avoided it in favor of using powders, but purists will like to know that paste is always an alternative to powder. In addition, the step of adding chili powder to heated oil along with cumin and black pepper adds a nuance missed with pastes.

Proportions for substituting paste for powder: A dried *ancho, pasilla, mulato* or *chile de ristra* equals approximately 1 tablespoon of powdered chilies. Use that as your guide for substitutions—not the actual quantity of the prepared paste, which can vary according to how much water has gone into it.

To remove red chili stains: Fastidious cooks might well give up on Santa Fe cooking after they see the seemingly permanent stains that red chili and oil make in contact with enameled pans and rubber or nylon spatulas, among many affected implements. I remove them with a weak solution of chlorine bleach and cold water, soaking overnight.

A warning about handling powdered red chilies: When chili powder gets onto your fingertips, it can transmit a burning sensation to your eyes, nose and lips as easily as the oil from green chilies. It is therefore wise not to bring powdered chilies into contact with wooden cutting boards which they might creep into, and be sure to wash your hands thoroughly after exposing them to red chilies. Although the seeds and veins of dried chilies are not nearly so vaporous as fresh ones, be careful about touching them, too. Finally, do not inhale chili powder from a close distance since it can be irritating enough to produce swelling of mucous membranes and even coughing fits.

Chiles chipotles: Chipotles are not a variety of chili but dried *jalapeños* with a distinctive smoky flavor. This is imparted by a special marinade or by smoking and drying. You can buy both the dried and the marinated kind ready-made, the second labeled as *chipotles en adobo* or *en escabeche*. It is easy to become carried away using *chipotles*, so addictive is their smoky, fiery taste. I have given a few recipes where they are specifically called for, but if you want to improvise with them on your own, feel free. It is probably better not to incorporate them into the chili powder you want for everyday use. Like smoked cheese or smoked oysters, *chipotles* lose their savor as an everyday thing.

Hotness scale: Having said that chilies are unpredictable in their hotness, I am nevertheless passing on a scale of hotness, as provided by *New Mexico* magazine, because it is much easier to refer to when you are shopping than a whole essay on chilies. With 1 as mild and 10 as extremely hot, the scale is

1. New Mexico No. 6 and Anaheim
2. Rio Grande
3. Numex Big Jim
4. Hot Ancho
5. Sandia
6. Española and Cayenne
7. Jalapeño
8. Tabasco
9. Santaca and Hontaka (Japanese)
10. Bahamian

I conjecture that several of these names are largely taken from either the chili trade or from agriculture, not from labels you are likely to see in retail stores. In any case, the scale is only approximate. The Española chilies that I pluck directly from a *ristra* in my kitchen are far milder than any cayenne. Somewhere between 1 and 5 on the scale also fall cherry peppers, Italian peppers, the mild *anchos, poblanos, mulatos, güeros*, and *pasillas* of Mexican cuisine. The *pequíns* probably begin at around 7, and get hotter. A bell pepper is too mild even to be rated, although it has a decided flavor of its own.

A Note About Adding Extra Chilies

Theoretically, there is no limit to how hot with green or red chilies a New Mexican dish can be—the only obstacle being when the swelling of lips, running from the nose, sweating on top of the head, pounding in the eardrums and uncontrolled tearing become insupportable. The first American traders to reach Santa Fe before 1850 were said to be so incapacitated by the hotness of the food which greeted them that they were forced to go hungry. No really satisfactory explanation has been put forth for why people in Mexico, India and elsewhere prefer to season their food so painfully. The common or garden explanation—that high seasoning evolved when the basic diet was insufficient—doesn't seem to hold up as well as the one which says that sweating from chilies makes a hot climate more tolerable. The second explanation at least accounts for the rapid conversion to chili of well-fed and even wealthy people after they come south.

But perhaps it is best left unanswered, for Santa Fe, at 7,000 feet above sea level, can be deadly cold in the winter months when the native cooks are still using copious amounts of fresh or canned *jalapeños* or the hot dried flakes called *chile caribe*. Even the milder dishes are accompanied at the table with *picante* relishes or dipping sauces that increase the hotness as soon as you begin to spoon them on.

The decision had to be made whether to make the recipes in this book mild or hot. Since I think it is best for each cook to express his own preferences, and since a dose of chilies is a lazy way to cover up an inferior dish, the recipes are basically mild. Please feel free to add hotness after your own taste. Although the directions for each dish specify the best way to add extra hotness, here are the alternatives at your disposal:

Chopped green chilies: Fresh *jalapeños* and *serranos* now appear year round in supermarkets, making it easy for the cook to chop them as an addition to recipes. The *jalapeños*, being larger, first need to be deveined and seeded before cooking with them; the *serranos* are often small enough simply to chop up directly. For the sake of convenience I usually specify canned *jalapeños* packed in water as a good way to add hotness to a dish—but be sure that you do not buy the kind pickled in vinegar (*jalapeños en escabeche*). One exception is the recipe for Texas-style *nachos* on p. 148. Pickled hot peppers can also be used generally as a garnish at the table, either whole, chopped or cut into thin strips.

Whole dried red chilies: Small *tepíns, pequíns,* and Japanese chilies can be added to preparations with plenty of liquid such as soups, sauces and stews, but be sure to fish them out before serving. They can also be ground in a coffee grinder (not the one you use for coffee, however) if you want to zip up a small quantity of hot chili powder on the spur of the moment.

Cayenne and hot red chili powders: Although I would avoid packaged American "chili powder," which has been flavored with cumin and garlic salt, pure powdered chilies make a good addition to almost any preparation. Make sure that you allow the dish to continue to simmer or braise for at least 15 minutes after you add the chilies, however. Unlike the chopped green chilies, which can be added at the last moment, powdered chilies need a little cooking time to remove their raw and sometimes dusty taste.

Tabasco and other "red hot" sauces: I mention above that Tabasco is not my favorite way to add hotness to a cooked dish since I do not like the sour taste it imparts. However, it and its kin can be good for sprinkling on food at the table. There is even a macho thing about how much Tabasco you can stand on your morning eggs. In New Mexico this varies a little—

the dare is to add green chili *salsa* in enough quantity to impress your buddies.

Uncooked salsas: Uncooked table *salsas*, whether commercial or home-made, do not tend to go well into cooked dishes; their purpose is to be used as a table sauce. If you want to hot up a pot of *frijoles*, for example, it would be better to spoon the *salsa* over the finished dish as you serve it rather than stirring it in at the stove.

Chili paste: For a savory, thick chili agent that adds both hotness and welcome flavor to meat dishes, see the Scorpion Chili Paste on p. 92. It is a good product to keep on hand along with your indispensable can of chopped *jalapeños* and bag of New Mexico chili powder.

Ristras

Once the ripe red chilies are harvested, it is a tra-ditional New Mexican practice to hang them out to dry strung as long chains, or *ristras*. You can spot them under the eaves of houses all through the fall and winter before they are brought inside to be used as decoration and in cooking. Lengths vary from a foot or so—enough to last a small family of nonlovers of chili for a season—up to bristling specimens as long as a man is tall. *Ristras* make such superb kitchen ornaments that they are frequently sold for high prices more befitting bric-a-brac than real, usable food. In-deed, the tourist hankering for local color who buys his authentic Española Valley *ristra* in downtown Santa Fe (or the Albuquerque airport) more likely than not does not suspect that the dried chilies he is bringing home are meant to be plucked from the *ristra* and cooked.

At times it is better he does not know. Time withers and age can stale a length of dried chilies. *Ristras* have even been known to mold in moist climates, and in any climate their progressive wrinkling as time passes tends to rob the chilies of pungency and bite. Dust, however, is not a problem since it can be rinsed off. Shellac, which is applied as a matter of course to chilies, decorative gourds and particolored Indian corn pur-suant to making them into Christmas wreaths, is another matter altogether. Chilies that have thus been preserved definitely should not be eaten.

On the narrow desert road which carries traffic out of Santa Fe and on to Colorado, you see isolated tin-roofed sheds where *ristras* of all types, as well as the shellacked wreaths, are sold for prices that are not too breathtaking. No doubt long-term residents know of sources near Chimayo where *ristras* go for pence. It doesn't matter. It is an experience in itself to walk into these roadside sheds and wander among a forest of *ristras*. You do not wander long, for the smell quickly leads to a burning nose, eyes and throat. The chilies are only partly to blame. There is also the dust—dust of the desert all around, dust of *chile de ristra*, and dust of straw, corn and gourds. And partly it is the shellac.

Once you buy a *ristra* of your own and take it home to hang up, you will naturally want to cook with it. The *chile de ristra* is prepared in any of the ways which this book describes for handling all dried red chilies. As for exactly what kind of *chile*, botanically speaking, you have acquired, natives are content to call them all New Mexico chilies. Some are hot, most are mild, and the taste is not markedly superior to a good imported paprika. But you can always mix the ground *chile de ristra* with hot or pungent chilies of your own selection, thereby making a chili powder not equaled, or at least not duplicated, by anyone else. Even better, you can grind whole cups of this powder and still have many feet of *ristra* left for hanging.

Should you buy a *ristra* for flavor alone? Passionate defenders of New Mexican food detect depth and richness in their homegrown chilies. If you point out to them that much of the appeal of a *chile de ristra* has to do with its romance and not strictly speaking its flavor, they will not be perturbed. The chili farmers of New Mexico work hard at the business of breeding flavor into their product, and if Chimayó chili is perfection to one fancier and Espanola to another, or if this season's crop is half again as hot as last season's, it is all accepted as one of nature's welcome variations. Any New Mexico chili looks handsome on a *ristra* and will find some cook who vastly admires it to cook with as well.

Cooked Sauces

BASIC RED CHILI SAUCE
Chile colorado

This is the everyday sauce of New Mexico cooking, the sturdy, indestructible "red chili" found in every Mexican restaurant throughout the Southwest. Hardly more than a thickened solution of powdered chilies and water, it nonetheless savors of mystique, not so much for its own taste, which is earthy and fairly musty, as for its ability to combine with corn tortillas, meat and cheese. The primal dish made from red chili sauce is the *enchilada*, for it is nothing more than chili, corn and cheese, but this same sauce also plays a part in curing pork, stewing *posole* and saucing diverse dishes from *tacos* and *tostadas* to *chiles rellenos* and *tamales*. Indeed, practically all the food on a Santa Fe restaurant menu comes either with red chili (*chile colorado*) or green chili (*chile verde*), whichever the customer specifies.

Because every cook has his own way with red chili sauce, and because chilies vary in taste from season to season and place to place, there is no danger that *chile colorado* will become monotonous. Nevertheless, it is basically the same, unvarnished thing despite the many names you see for it: chili-powder sauce, red *enchilada* sauce, *salsa de chile rojo, salsa de chile pasilla,* and so on. All of them indicate in some fashion or another that the principal ingredient is dried red chilies. For practical purposes, a sauce which uses the *whole* chilies instead of powdered ones comes under a different heading, since its technique differs in several ways, but the essential taste remains undiluted chili, so powerful a flavor that very little cuts through except for little dynamos like cumin, oregano and garlic.

The basic recipe below is the one to master before you go on to the variations that follow. Good as they are, they depend entirely upon the basic *salsa,* and it in turn depends on the quality of the chilies that go into it. A casual cook can make a good sauce with any mild packaged chili labeled *"chile primero,"* "Espanola *chile,"* "New Mexico *chile,"* or simply "medium-hot *chile."* What you do not want is commercial chili powder, the sort intended for seasoning chili con carne and therefore heavily dosed with garlic salt, cumin and dried oregano. If you want to make up your own powder, please refer to the information about dried chilies beginning on p. 67.

After testing a dozen variations of red-chili sauce, I have considerable confidence in all the versions given here, including the "instant" ones in the following pages. However, a serious Southwestern cook will want to experiment further. Powdered chilies differ so much one from another, palates vary so greatly in their tolerance for hot chili, and recipes dictate such extreme amounts of chili to use (from very little to overwhelmingly too much) that no author can claim to have come up with *the* red chili sauce. It will be a help to you if you read straight through these pages concerning red chili sauces, for then you will have a better feeling for the changes to be rung on a deceptively simple theme.

For about 2 cups:

    2 tablespoons vegetable oil
    3 to 4 tablespoons onion, finely chopped
    1 clove garlic, peeled and finely chopped
    ¼ teaspoon oregano
    1 teaspoon whole or powdered cumin
    2 tablespoons flour
    ½ cup powdered red chilies
    2½ cups water
    ½ to 1 teaspoon salt

Heat the oil over medium heat in a 1- or 2-quart saucepan. Add the onion and garlic and sauté gently for about 5 minutes, or until the onion is wilted, translucent and turning yellow. Stir in the oregano, cumin and flour and cook, stirring constantly, until this mixture (which is like a *roux*) bubbles up and begins to turn a very light brown, about 3 minutes. Remove pan from heat.

In a separate bowl, mix the powdered chilies and water until they are smoothly blended. Pour them into the flour-onion paste, stirring to prevent lumps—a wire whisk helps here. Return the pan to medium heat and bring the sauce to the boiling point. Stir from time to time until you begin to see bubbles. (Since red chilies scorch quite easily, how much you have to stir this sauce depends on the quality of your cookware. Stir constantly and watch carefully the first time out.) When the sauce just begins to show signs of active boiling, reduce heat to low and simmer, covered, for 2 to 3 minutes more. Make sure to stir a few times, reaching thoroughly around the bottom and sides of the pan to catch any lumps beginning to form. When the sauce is thickened, smooth and no longer raw-tasting, add the salt, beginning with the smaller amount. Remove from heat and set aside until needed.

Your finished red chili should be thick enough to nap a spoon heavily; it should have a deep, pungent taste of chili without unpleasant mustiness (a sign of tired chilies) or unpalatable hotness. If it is too bitter or crude for your taste, try other brands of powdered chilies. However, this sauce should not be expected to stand alone. Even if somewhat bitter or sweet, the real test for *chile colorado* is to marry it with tortillas, so plan as soon as possible to make a batch of *enchiladas* with your sauce. You are likely to be surprised, or even amazed, by how much better your red chili is than those served in restaurants.

For a smoother sauce, or if the sauce appears too grainy (a function of the coarseness of the ground chilies), puree the sauce, one cup at a time, in an electric blender. A grainy texture, however, is acceptable and proves that you didn't open a can.

Red chili mellows as it stands and keeps well for a week or more in the refrigerator. Plastic wrap can be pressed directly against the surface to prevent a skin from forming, but this is not mandatory since the skin can be stirred back into the sauce when you reheat it. Be sure to cover the container tightly, though, since the red chili smell permeates other foods nearby. Also, make sure your cooking utensils and storage containers are made of impermeable glass or metal—red chili is notorious for stains. To remove any that slip by you, see the note on p. 69.

VARIATIONS:

Hot Red Chili Sauce: The basic recipe produces a lingering heat at the back of the mouth but not much on the tongue. If you want a hotter sauce, taste it after it thickens, then incorporate cayenne or ground hot chilies (such as *tepíns, pequíns* or Japanese chilies) to taste. If you attempt to add these in powdered form directly to your sauce, it is likely that lumps will form, so first dissolve them in a few tablespoons of water. In fact, if you are cooking an entire New Mexico dinner, it is good to have a teacup by your side half filled with cold water in which you have dissolved a tablespoon of hot red chilies. The concoction can be stirred into any sauce or meat dish that needs added hotness as you go along. Traditionally, New Mexicans of the Santa Fe area were said to like their red chili as hot as possible; a taste for milder stuff develops as you go south to the part of the state under Anglo influence.

Red Chili Sauce with Tomatoes: This mild, faintly sweet version is frankly preferred by most non-Hispanic diners. It is the one many restaurants set out as a matter of course, often considerably thinned if it is to be used as a dipping sauce for *tostado* chips. Add ½ cup tomato puree (or 4 to 5 canned tomatoes reduced to a puree in a blender) to the basic sauce at the same time as the chilies and water go in. For a thinner sauce, suitable for the table as well as for cooking, use 1 to 1½ cups tomato juice instead of tomato puree.

Sweet-and-Sour Red Chili Sauce: Although its taste is not appropriate for every dish (it does not go well with *enchiladas*, for example), the sweet-and-sour tang of this variation makes the basic sauce useful as a table *salsa* to spoon over grilled meat and poultry. In fact, you can also marinate and baste the meat with it quite effectively. Add 2 or 3 tablespoons white or cider vinegar and 1 tablespoon sugar to the basic sauce after it comes to a simmer. You can also add ½ cup tomato puree, as in the preceding variation, if you like a tomatoey sauce. Adding larger amounts of vinegar and sugar is a fairly common practice among some cooks, but I think it changes the red chili so much that in effect it becomes barbecue sauce, albeit a good one.

Red Chili Sauce with Broth: In the more refined styles of Mexican cooking, the liquid used in *salsa de chile rojo* is beef or chicken broth instead of water. Thus refined, the chili can go on the table to serve with roast turkey or capon on feast days. It also makes a good braising liquid for pork shoulder, but watch carefully for scorching, adding extra water to the braising pan as needed. Any red chili used for pot-roasting cuts of beef or pork (such dishes are called *carne adovada* in New Mexico) needs to be thoroughly degreased before bringing it to the table.

Red Chili Sauce with Cream: This might seem like putting chiffon on a cactus, but it is frequently suggested in Mexican cookbooks that you add ½ cup heavy cream to the finished red chili sauce for added richness. After being civilized in this way, the sauce can be used for "Swiss" *enchiladas* and soft *tacos*, or over a festive roast chicken as a table sauce. I have liked it served over *tamales*, which are inherently rich to begin with, but this variation is pretty foreign to the austere spirit of most New Mexican cooking.

RED CHILI SAUCE FROM WHOLE CHILIES

Although the ingredients for this sauce are nearly identical with sauce made from powdered chilies, it somehow acquires a different texture and flavor—the vegetable taste of chili on the vine comes through. The method for making it is as old as the use of chilies. The pods are softened in water until they turn pulpy, then pureed and thickened into the finished sauce. All the variations which apply to powdered chili sauce also apply here.

For about 2 cups:

> 8 to 10 large whole red chilies, such as New Mexico *chiles de ristra*, California red chilies, *anchos*, or *pasillas*
> 2 cups boiling water
> 1 tablespoon vegetable oil
> 1 tablespoon flour
> 1 clove garlic, peeled and chopped
> ½ teaspoon whole or powdered cumin
> ½ teaspoon salt
> Pinch oregano

Pick over the chilies, pulling off and discarding the stems and scraping out as many seeds as possible. Since your sauce will be strained later, it is not necessary to be absolutely meticulous. Place the chilies in a heavy, ungreased skillet over low heat and roast for about 4 minutes. As you shake the pan to prevent the chilies from scorching, you will detect a roasting aroma, but there should be no burning smell.

Transfer the chilies to a bowl and pour the boiling water over them.

Let steep for 10 to 15 minutes. Place the softened chilies and half of their soaking water in a food processor or electric blender, reserving the other half. Puree for about 1 minute, or until the chilies are reduced to a smooth, thick consistency. Add more soaking water, if needed.

Heat the oil in a 1-quart saucepan over medium heat for a few seconds, add the flour, garlic and cumin and stir for about 2 minutes. The oil should sizzle slowly, and the flour-cumin paste turn slightly browner. When the paste is noticeably colored, remove from heat.

Place a kitchen strainer over the saucepan and pour the chili puree through it, using a wooden spoon to push all but the unblended bits of the skin and stray seeds through. Wash out the blender jar or processor bowl with the remainder of the soaking liquid and strain that in also.

Return the sauce to low heat and bring to a simmer, stirring constantly, for about 2 minutes. Add salt and oregano, simmer half a minute more, and taste. The sauce should savor richly of chili and be thick enough to nap a spoon heavily. It may also have a bitter quality, which is not very attractive until paired with the food to be sauced. Set aside until needed or store in the refrigerator.

For a hotter sauce: Although northern New Mexico is noted for its hot chilies, the typical *chile de ristra* produces a mild sauce. After you first taste the sauce, you can hot it up with powdered hot chilies (such as *tepíns* or *pequíns*) or cayenne. To avoid lumps of hot chili powder, first dissolve in a few tablespoons of cold water.

VARIATIONS:

Chili and Tomato Sauce: Unless you are after the raw Aztec taste of chili and nothing but—a taste that is good with only some foods—you can smooth the flavor of the basic sauce with ½ cup of tomato puree (or about 4 canned tomatoes reduced to a puree).

Chili Sauce with Cream and Egg: Add ¼ cup heavy cream with 1 egg yolk whisked into it to the Chili and Tomato Sauce above. This rather refined sauce acquires an interesting dimension by also adding ½ teaspoon of cayenne to it because of the intriguing contrast of hotness and creaminess. With or without the cayenne, this sauce is also very good with *enchiladas.*

ADAPTABLE RED CHILI SAUCE WITH TOMATOES

The basic sauces in New Mexico cooking prove endlessly adaptable to new uses. This one, for instance, can be used in its thick state to moisten meat fillings for *tamales*, to marinate roast pork or barbecued chicken, or to be spooned over the crisp *quesadillas* on p. 150 as they come to the table. Thinned with a little water, it becomes a red *enchilada* or *taco* sauce. Increase the amount of water even more, and the consistency resembles the thin dipping sauces which restaurants present along with the basket of fried tortilla chips. Do not be put off by the quickness of this one—it takes about 10 minutes from start to finish—since the saucing techniques of the Southwest are not meant to be the meticulous, drawn-out affair they are in European sauce making.

For 2 generous cups:

> 2 pounds canned whole tomatoes, drained, or 2 cups canned
>   crushed tomatoes packed in tomato puree
> 1 clove garlic, peeled and roughly chopped
> 4 tablespoons powdered red chili
> ½ small onion, peeled and cut into rough chunks
> ½ to 1 teaspoon cayenne
> ½ teaspoon ground cumin
> ¼ teaspoon oregano
> Salt and black pepper to taste

Place all the ingredients in the jar of an electric blender or the bowl of a food processor and blend until reduced to a smooth puree, about 1 minute. Transfer to a saucepan, bring to a boil over medium heat, stirring once or twice to prevent scorching, and cover the pan. Reduce heat to low and simmer for 10 minutes—the sauce is done when the raw tomato and red chili taste are gone. Once cooled, it will be about as thick as ketchup, suitable to use as a thick meat marinade or to moisten fillings that need to remain fairly stiff (such as the pork filling traditionally employed for *tamales*).

VARIATIONS:

Adaptable Enchilada Sauce: Dilute with ¾ to 1 cup of water and adjust salt as needed. This amount will sauce *enchiladas* for 4 people.

Adaptable Dipping Sauce: Dilute with 1½ cups of water, or as much as it takes to reach the desired consistency for dipping tortilla chips. Adjust salt and simmer with an additional teaspoon of cayenne for a few minutes if you like the hot dipping sauces served in most restaurants.

Red Chili Almond Sauce: Almond sauces are favored in Spanish and Mexican cooking to serve at the table with chicken and fish, although they do not seem to have survived in current New Mexican cooking. This is a very good, easy variation nonetheless. Grind ¾ cup blanched, slivered almonds in an electric blender or food processor until fine, but not a flour. Now proceed with the basic sauce by adding the remaining ingredients to the bowl. You can make the sauce more identifiably Spanish by also adding 2 tablespoons green olive oil and ½ teaspoon each ground cinnamon and cloves to the ingredients list. Because of the thickening added by the almonds, you will need ½ cup or so of water to reach the consistency of a table sauce. Serve warm.

INSTANT RED ENCHILADA SAUCE

This recipe violates all my good intentions about omitting anything with additives or adulterants, for canned *enchilada* sauce is by no means free of them, but it does allow you to begin making *enchiladas* anytime you want.

For about 2 cups:

> 1 can (10 ounces) "hot" enchilada sauce, preferably without sugar and tomatoes (see "Mexican Convenience Foods," p. 52–56)
> ¾ cup tomato puree or about 4 to 5 canned, peeled tomatoes reduced to puree in a blender
> 1 tablespoon powdered red chilies
> ½ teaspoon cumin powder
> Pinch oregano

Mix all ingredients together in a saucepan, bring to a simmer over medium heat, and simmer slowly for 2 to 3 minutes until the chili and cumin lose their raw taste.

BASIC GREEN CHILI SAUCE
Chile verde

First off, the term "green chili" or *chile verde* can mean different things, and knowing one from another is one of those unspoken distinctions that mark an insider. The term applies to (1) a fresh chili picked in its green state before it ripens to red in the fall; (2) a paste made from roasted

green chilies and garlic which is presented at the table to flavor *frijoles*;
(3) a highly adaptable thickened cooking sauce made from green chilies
and sometimes meant to go over *enchiladas, burritos* and the like; and
(4) this same sauce with small chunks of stewed pork added, to be eaten
as a soup with flour tortillas on the side, but often used as a sauce for
bean *burritos.*

The recipe given here is for the *chile verde* sauce (the third option),
but elsewhere I give all the other versions, too. The sauce is what you
receive when you ask for your restaurant *burrito* or *enchilada* with green
chili instead of red. Customarily it tastes much hotter than the red—but
it is not necessarily green in color, since many cooks in the Southwest add
considerable amounts of tomato to their *chile verde*, harking back to
the days when both the chilies and the tomatoes were picked fresh from
the summer garden patch.

This is also the basis for green sauces which incorporate *tomatillos*,
or green tomatoes—and in fact almost any *salsa verde* made in Mexico
is likely to have that ingredient added. In casual usage, if you are zipping
up fresh tomatoes, onion and green chilies into a table *salsa*, you can call
that too a "green chili sauce." It pays to know what an insider knows,
for all the varieties of *chile verde* are equally addictive, however different
from one another they may be.

For 2 generous cups:

    2 **tablespoons vegetable or olive oil**
  ¼ **to ½ small onion, chopped**
    1 **large garlic clove, chopped**
    2 **tablespoons flour**
  ¼ **teaspoon ground cumin**
  ¼ **teaspoon black pepper**
1½ **cups pork or chicken broth (pork broth is obtained after**
    stewing the meat for Shredded Pork, p. 99)
    1 **cup roasted, peeled green chilies, obtained from**
   10 to 12 fresh Anaheim, California or *poblano* chilies
   or 8 ounces canned green chilies (whole, chopped or in strips)
  ¼ **teaspoon oregano**
  ½ **teaspoon salt**
Optional: 2 teaspoons or more chopped, canned *jalapeños* for
    added hotness

Heat the oil in a 1- or 2-quart saucepan over medium heat. Add the
onion and garlic, cover and cook over low heat for about 5 minutes to
wilt the onions. Check halfway through to make sure they are not browning.
Raise the heat to medium again, stir in the flour, cumin and black pepper,
and cook, stirring, for 2 minutes to cook the rawness out of the flour. The

onions will tend to ball up into clumps, but that does not matter. When the onion-flour mixture just begins to color, remove pan from heat and gradually pour in the broth, stirring constantly to prevent lumps—a wire whisk helps here.

Add all the remaining ingredients. Return pan to heat and bring to the boiling point, then cover and simmer over low heat for 30 minutes, stirring occasionally. The finished sauce should be thick enough to nap a spoon—if too thick, dilute with a bit more broth or water. If sauce is not uniformly smooth, puree a cup at a time in a blender or food processor.

The basic sauce is now ready to use or to store in the refrigerator. It keeps well for a week or so, but a skin will form on the cooled sauce, and when cold it will almost solidly congeal. All can be made right again by reheating the sauce as you need it. This *chile verde* is warming but not nearly so hot as almost every native New Mexican likes it. For a hotter sauce, add the optional chopped *jalapeños* at the same time as the mild chilies go in. The upper limit to how hot *chile verde* can be has yet to be determined, but I am nearly positive that no one is reputed to make theirs *entirely* with *jalapeños*.

VARIATIONS:

Green Chili Sauce with Pork: This is the traditional sauce put over bean *burritos*: Cut 4 ounces of lean pork shoulder into ¼-inch cubes and add them to the sauce with the broth and chilies. Often the meat from thin-cut pork chops is substituted for pork shoulder. Many cooks make up this sauce in vast quantity—you see recipes feeding 150 people for feast days— but you can still use the proportions given, multiplying them as you need. If you want to eat the *chile verde* alone with flour tortillas to scoop it up, double the amount of pork and cut it into somewhat larger chunks, about ½ inch square.

Green Chili Sauce with Tomatoes: This is quite a common variation, with or without pork. Add ½ to 1 cup of chopped tomatoes, fresh or canned, at the same time you add the chilies. Putting in tomatoes somewhat tempers the hotness if you happen to be making your green chili with lots of *jalapeño*. A cup of tomato juice can also be substituted for a cup of the chicken broth.

Green Chili Sauce with Cream: This is quite a nice refinement of *chile verde*, particularly if it is intended as a sauce for *enchiladas*. Adding cream to the sauce makes them "Swiss" *enchiladas*, much more seen in Mexico proper than in New Mexico. However, many New Mexican restaurant cooks put some dash of cream into their green chili when the filling for the *enchiladas* is chicken. To make the variation, add ¼ to ½ cup heavy cream or commercial sour cream to the sauce after it has finished cooking. When you reheat the sauce, do not bring it to the boil—that will cause the cream to curdle as often as not. For an even fancier sauce, whisk 1 beaten egg into the hot sauce just as you are about to puree it, then puree very smooth and add ¾ cup heavy cream.

Smoky Green Chili Sauce: This is a personal favorite of mine which is not at all traditional: Add 3 or 4 diced *chiles chipotles* (see p. 69) with the mild chilies (and omit the optional *jalapeños* since the *chiles chipotles* are a variety of *jalapeño* already). The finished sauce will be quite hot and exotically smoky in flavor. Since the taste is so strong, reserve this green chili for plain bean *burritos* or cheese *enchiladas*.

Green Chili Sauce with Tomatillos: Many Mexican cooks and some in New Mexico like the sour, rather odd taste which *tomatillos*, or green tomatoes, impart to green chili. See the note on p. 35 about blanching and processing fresh *tomatillos*. Anywhere from ½ to 1 pound of ripe fruit will do for this amount of sauce, adding their puree at the same time as the chilies. If you are buying canned *tomatillos*, use 1 or 2 of the 7-ounce cans, making sure to drain the liquid thoroughly. With either source, you will be adding between ¾ and 1½ cups of *tomatillo* puree. The name for the sauce is variously given as *salsa verde, chile verde con tomatillos*, or *salsa de tomatillo*—once again, the rules are not binding.

Tomatillos can also be used in place of some of the red tomatoes if you are making the green chili and tomato sauce above. Some cooks make their sauce using 1 cup each of green chilies, red tomatoes and *tomatillos*, and this, too, would be all right. Any of these can be used for any dish calling for the basic green chili sauce.

INSTANT GREEN ENCHILADA SAUCE

This basically uncooked, instant version of *chile verde* bears a respectable likeness to longer recipes for cooked *chile verde*. Its basic component, the canned *enchilada* sauce, must be of high quality, however. The last step in the directions—simmering the *salsa* for a few minutes to mature the flavors—can be skipped if you are proceeding directly to cooking *enchiladas*. The sauce can also be set directly out upon the table for spooning at will over prepared Mexican food.

The addition of the canned *jalapeño* makes the sauce much hotter than the preceding basic green chili sauce.

For a generous 1½ cups:

> 5 canned whole green chilies, drained
> 1 can (10 ounces) green *enchilada* sauce which is not heavily
>   vinegared (refer to "Mexican Convenience Foods," pp. 52–56)
> 1 canned whole *jalapeño* or 3 teaspoons chopped
> 1 clove garlic, chopped
> Salt
> Optional flavorings: 2 tablespoons chopped green coriander
>   (*cilantro*) or ¼ cup chopped scallion

Rinse the drained, canned chilies briefly in tepid running water to reduce their preserved taste. Using an electric blender or food processor, puree all ingredients except salt, including optional *cilantro* or scallion. Salt lightly and taste. The sauce will be quite hot and will turn hotter as it stands—do not rush to test your courage with another canned *jalapeño.*

Although this sauce can be used for cooking as is, its flavor matures if you transfer it to a saucepan and heat to a simmer for 2 or 3 minutes. The finished sauce stores well in the refrigerator closely covered with plastic wrap, but it is not so long lived as red chili sauces.

RANCH-STYLE PAN SAUCE
Salsa ranchera

Improvised pan sauces are so common in New Mexican home cooking that you can never know how to make too many. Here is a typical *ranchero* preparation, though not as hot as many natives would like it—add more *jalapeño* if you share their taste. This sauce takes only a minute or two to whip up with the aid of a processor. Serve it as freshly made as possible over fried eggs (see *Huevos rancheros* on p. 195) or grilled chops and steaks.

For 1 cup:

> 1 clove garlic, peeled
> 1 or 2 fresh *jalapeños*, deveined and seeded
> ½ medium onion, peeled and cut into chunks
> 1 large, fresh Anaheim green chili, seeded and cut into thirds
> 2 tablespoons vegetable or olive oil
> 1 large fresh tomato, seeded, with ½ cup tomato juice or
>   4 canned tomatoes plus ½ cup of their liquid

¼ teaspoon salt
Black pepper to taste
  2 tablespoons chopped green coriander (*cilantro*)
Optional seasonings: ¼ teaspoon cumin, ground coriander
    or cayenne

Turn on the motor of the food processor and drop the garlic and
jalapeños in through the feed tube. When they are chopped, stop the
motor and add the onion and Anaheim chili. If you are using any or all
of the optional seasonings, add them now. Process with fast pulses until
the onions are coarsely chopped. Stop at least once to scrape down the
bowl with a rubber spatula, but do not overprocess.

Heat the oil in a small skillet and add the contents of the processor
bowl. Cover the pan and let simmer for 5 minutes over low heat to wilt
the vegetables.

Chop the tomatoes coarsely with a few pulses of the processor. Uncover the pan, raise the heat to medium, and add the tomatoes along
with their liquid. Simmer over low heat until the sauce is just cooked but
still fresh-looking. Season to taste with salt, pepper and green coriander.

VARIATION:

Pan Sauce with Hot Chilies: A ranch-style *jalapeño* or *serrano* sauce can
be made by eliminating the milder Anaheim chili and substituting 3 or 4
more fresh hot chilies. Although *serranos* are usually small enough not to
need seeding, their pith should be taken out with a paring knife, since it
is the hottest part. This style of *salsa ranchera* will be *very* hot, but it
marries well with fried eggs.

AVOCADO-AND-ZUCCHINI SAUCE

This thick alligator-green sauce looks like *guacamole* and can be used
in the same way, but its content of crisp, grated zucchini makes it more
appealing as a warm sauce, a use not suitable for *guacamole*. The chilies
in it are also quite mild, which means that it can be used along with a
hot red sauce to lavishly garnish a plate of *tamales*. It is an unctuous
complement to chicken *tacos*, too.

For 1½ to 2 cups:

> 1 medium zucchini
> 2 tablespoons olive oil
> 1 large clove garlic, peeled and chopped
> 2 Anaheim green chilies, seeded and cut into thirds
> 3 scallions, cleaned, trimmed and cut into 1-inch lengths
>   (both white and green parts included)
> ¼ cup green or red chili sauce or an uncooked *salsa*
>   that is not sour
> ¼ cup water
> ½ teaspoon salt
> 1 ripe avocado
> Lemon juice to taste

Grate the zucchini by hand on the coarsest holes of a four-sided grater or use the shredding disk of a food processor. Heat the oil in a 10-inch skillet and sauté the zucchini with the garlic over medium heat until the zucchini loses its raw taste but still remains crisp—about 5 minutes. Meanwhile, chop the chilies and scallions, using either a chef's knife or the standard blade of the food processor. Add to the zucchini and sauté another minute.

Place the vegetables in the food processor with the chili sauce, water, salt and half the avocado. Blend until a textured puree is reached; you are aiming for a thick sauce that resembles *guacamole*. (It retains more character, I think, if you do not blend to a smooth puree.) Return the sauce to the heat in the skillet and warm through. Quarter and chop the reserved half avocado into rough ½-inch cubes and add to the sauce. Season to taste with lemon juice.

This sauce can be served warm or at room temperature. If the water is reduced by half, it is also an excellent stand-in for *guacamole* as a dip or chilled salad. Its only fault is that it does not keep—serve within an hour of making it.

Uncooked Sauces (Salsas)

Although the Spanish word *salsa* applies to any sauce, including cooked ones, in common American usage the term has been adapted to mean the uncooked sauces which are used as condiments with Mexican food. To avoid confusion, I will respect this usage and call the sauces in this section *salsas*, but the reader should realize that Hispanic cooks do not make the verbal distinction that we do. Also, certain of these uncooked *salsas* are simmered briefly to remove a little of their rawness, so the rule about not cooking them is not hard and fast, either.

BASIC TABLE SALSA
Salsa fresca, Salsa cruda, Salsa picante, Salsa mexicana, etc.

The various, interchangeable names for this sauce in Spanish give a clue to what it should be like—fresh (*fresca*), raw rather than cooked (*cruda*), and piquant with chilies and onion (*picante*). Presenting a basic table *salsa* is a ritualized habit in New Mexican dining. Tortilla chips are dipped into it before the main dishes come on; spoonfuls of it are dolloped on foods that need extra savor, such as *frijoles*, or which simply benefit from the added zest of fresh chilies; and culinary tradition demands it as the right condiment for grilled meats, just as we use Worcestershire or Tabasco. So fond are Hispanic eaters of fresh *salsa* and its relatives that a whole class of table condiments has sprung up over the years, including raw vegetables pickled with green chilies, marinated strips of fiery *jalapeño*, and all manner of relishes (a few of which are given in the next section of this chapter).

If a Mexican cook makes any of this tribe, it will be *salsa* before anything else, though some Pueblo cooks prefer a mashed relish of green chilies and garlic—refer to the recipe called Green Chilies for the Table (p. 94). So table *salsa* is the first of the uncooked sauces that you, too, need to learn. The method for it is extremely simple. It depends only upon fresh tomatoes, roasted or raw green chilies and onions. In winter, when canned goods have their season, quite a decent *salsa* can still be made. It will not rival the freshness of *salsa* in August, but it will certainly outshine any you can buy in a bottle.

Traditionally, the ingredients for a *salsa fresca* were pounded by hand using a mortar and pestle—large stone ones were standard equipment in Hispanic kitchens—but you can achieve a good result using a chef's knife, a food processor or an electric blender. The texture you want is up to you, since the essence of *salsa fresca* is improvisation, but aim somewhere between a chow-chow relish and a textured puree—you definitely want to see little separate bits of vegetable throughout. If you blend too recklessly and get anywhere near the texture of *gazpacho*, you have gone too far. But at least you will have *gazpacho*.

For 1½ to 2 cups:

> 2 large, firm, red-ripe tomatoes, shaken free of seeds and pulp
> (and peeled if you prefer)
> 1 clove garlic, peeled
> 1 Anaheim or California green chili, seeded and cut into thirds
> 3 green onions (scallions), cleaned and cut into 1-inch lengths,
> or ⅓ cup red onion, chopped
> 4 ounces canned chopped green chilies
> 1 teaspoon olive oil
> 1 tablespoon lime juice or red-wine vinegar
> Salt and pepper to taste
> ¼ cup ice water
> Small handful green coriander (*cilantro*), chopped
> Optional for added hotness: 1 to 3 whole *jalapeños*, fresh or canned,
> which have been deveined and seeded, or 2 to 6 teaspoons
> canned chopped *jalapeños*

Lengthy as the list of ingredients may look, the procedure for making *salsa fresca* takes only seconds. Essentially you have only to chop the fresh vegetables and seasonings until the desired consistency is reached, using either a food processor, an electric blender or a large chef's knife. Here is the technique for each:

Processor: Turn on the motor and drop the small ingredients (garlic, green coriander, green onions, and optional *jalapeños*) into the bowl—they will be finely chopped in a few seconds. Turn off the machine, scrape down the bowl with a rubber spatula, and add all the remaining ingredients except for the water and salt and pepper. Process with brief pulses until you reach a chunky, well-textured puree. Season to taste with salt and pepper and let the *salsa* ripen at room temperature for an hour or longer. At serving time, stir in the ice water—unless you do not like the soupy *salsa* which is traditional, in which case the water can be omitted. Adding ice water to cool the *salsa* is preferable to refrigerating it, since that changes its flavor and texture for the worse.

Electric blender: Follow the procedure given for the processor above, first dropping the small ingredients into the turned-on machine before blending everything else. However, you will usually need to stop the blending process several times to stir up the *salsa* with a spatula, since the blades of a blender tend to liquefy the tomatoes while large chunks of onion still remain. Work at low speed and be patient, for good results are easily possible.

Chef's knife: Starting with the smallest ingredients, first finely chop the garlic, green coriander, and optional *jalapeños*, then lay the Anaheim chili, green onions and tomatoes on the pile and continue to chop. Work the whole mass—cutting through it and gathering it back over and over—until the ingredients are almost pulpy. Now chop in the canned chilies—the softest ingredient—and work a minute longer. Transfer *salsa* to a bowl, add the olive oil, lime juice, and salt and pepper to taste. Allow to ripen for an hour or longer before adding the water at serving time.

VARIATIONS:

These are as extensive as a cook's imagination can reach, for the change of any major ingredient alters the *salsa*. Some cooks like much more onion than I call for, some more garlic; many would use different chilies in season to replace the Anaheim; and there are little extras that stamp a *salsa* with a personal touch, such as ground cumin, fresh or dried herbs (particularly oregano), and red chili powder. I have therefore limited the variations to a few, and they are by no means gospel.

Salsa with Canned Tomatoes: Good-quality plum tomatoes packed in tomato juice or puree can be made into respectable *salsa*. One trick is to use 3 canned tomatoes for flavor and 1 small fresh tomato for texture, even if it is the sorriest grainy wintertime tomato. Cold tomato juice or the liquid in which the tomatoes were packed can be substituted for the ice water if you need the extra flavor. The canned product called "Tomatoes and Jalapeños" (see p. 55) is also very good for making into a zippy, flavorful *salsa* during the months when fresh produce is at a low ebb.

Adding a little extra vinegar or lime juice helps to perk up a *salsa* that relies heavily on canned goods.

Salsa Picante: This, the most common label name for table *salsa*, simply means "hot sauce." Follow the basic recipe but add the optional fresh or canned *jalapeños*—if you don't mind the care it takes to handle them, the fresh are decidedly superior here. Start with one or two *jalapeños* only and increase according to taste and tolerance (the *salsa* will become considerably more *picante* during its ripening period). If you like *salsa* on the sour side, use the chilies packed in vinegar (*jalapeños en escabeche*).

Smoky-Flavored Salsa: An appealing smoky tang is added to the basic *salsa* when you hot it up with the marinated *jalapeños* called *chiles chipotles* (see p. 69 for details about them). Even using just the marinade from the can is enough to add the right touch. The result, however much I like it, is not a traditional *salsa*, though.

Salsa Based on Other Chilies: If you are a gardener, or just lucky enough to patronize a supermarket that caters to chili fanciers, you will enjoy making *salsa* with assorted varieties of chili. The pale-yellow waxy ones called *güeros* are frequently stocked in the West, and in the course of the growing season one sees red-ripe pimentos, dark green *poblanos*, golden Holland peppers, and of course bell peppers. These vary from sweet and mild to tangy and medium-hot, but none are as hot as a *jalapeño* or *serrano*. Use them alone or in combination to replace the Anaheim chili in the basic recipe.

Storing uncooked table salsa: The best advice about storing is don't— fresh *salsa* quickly loses its freshness if left out for more than a few hours and wilts into a sorry melange in the refrigerator. This is one thing you will want to make up new every time. Leftovers need not be thrown out, however. They can be added to bottles of chili relish (such as the sour green chili relish on p. 91) or half-full bottles of commercial *salsa*. Over the course of a week the flavor of the two will blend together—but be warned that the addition of the fresh *salsa* somewhat reduces the keeping qualities of the other product (after all, commercial *salsa* is intended to be semi-immortal).

QUICK TOMATO SALSA

Though called a tomato sauce, the New Mexican style also has chilies in it and in fact is close to being an uncooked *salsa picante* with a higher proportion of tomato added. A quick way to achieve the right result is to combine some fresh or canned tomatoes with an equal portion of bottled *salsa picante* or a green chili sauce with a high tomato content (one sees these also under the label "Green Chile Taco Sauce," but be sure that it is tomato based). Once mixed and heated through, this quick sauce has the correct flavor for *chiles rellenos*, (p. 249), *huevos rancheros*, (p. 195) and most other egg dishes.

For 2 cups tomato sauce:

> 1-pound can of tomatoes, drained
> 1 cup bottled *salsa* containing onion, green chilies and tomatoes, but little or no vinegar

Chop the tomatoes into small pieces in a food processor, but do not liquefy (5 or 8 pulses of the motor). Combine with the *salsa* in a small saucepan and heat through. Serve warm or cold as a table sauce.

VARIATION:

Quick Ranch-Style Sauce: Seeing *ranchera* in a name implies a hot sauce with tomatoes and *jalapeños*, usually cooked up in the same skillet as the meat or eggs which it accompanies. This is a quicker way. To convert the basic tomato sauce above, add 2 to 6 teaspoons canned chopped *jalapeños* as the sauce is heating.

SOUR GREEN CHILI SALSA

This recipe (which is cooked but still tastes like a *salsa fresca*) grew from a home-bottled *taco* sauce that was hot and sour, pure chili green, and almost as thick as chow-chow relish. As duplicated here, it is ideal as a relish to spoon over *tacos* both crisp and soft, but you can also turn it into *salsa* for grilled meats by adding a little water to the portion you are serving. For a milder and more conventional table *salsa*, see the variation that immediately follows—tomato puree is added to soften the taste of the chilies, and the vinegar is reduced by three-quarters. Either version will keep indefinitely under refrigeration, unlike true *salsa cruda*.

For about 3 cups salsa:

> 6 fresh Anaheim green chilies or 3 bell peppers, with
>   seeds and pith removed
> 3 fresh *jalapeños*, seeds and pith removed
> 4 cloves garlic, peeled
> 1 large onion, peeled and cut into chunks
> 1½ cups water
> 1 cup white or cider vinegar
> 1½ teaspoons salt
> 2 tablespoons sugar
> ½ teaspoon cinnamon
> ⅛ teaspoon cloves
> ¼ teaspoon oregano

Chop the seeded Anaheims or bell peppers and *jalapeños* in a food processor until they are finely ground, about 10 seconds, stopping once to scrape down the bowl with a rubber spatula. Avert your face from the machine whenever the top is off. (For a coarser *salsa*, more like pickle relish in texture, process the chilies for only about 5 seconds.) Place the chilies in a 2-quart stainless steel or enamel or coated aluminum saucepan.

With the machine running, drop the garlic cloves into the feed tube and chop fine. Turn off the machine, put in the onion chunks, and process with repeated pulses only until the onion is finely chopped. Stop once to scrape down the sides of the bowl. Add the onions and garlic to the saucepan with the chilies.

Add all the remaining ingredients to the pan, bring to a boil over medium heat, then cover the pan, reduce the heat, and simmer for 15 minutes. Uncover your *salsa* and taste it. If it seems too soupy or the onions are too crunchy for you—they should retain a little bite—boil uncovered for a few more minutes. Otherwise, cover the pan and let the mixture cool to room temperature, then refrigerate in a glass container.

Serve the *salsa* cool but not cold.

VARIATIONS:

Sour Tomato Salsa: For 3½ cups of a milder *salsa*, reduce the water to 1 cup and the vinegar to ¼ cup. Add 1½ cups of tomato puree (or about 12 canned plum tomatoes, chopped) to the saucepan. Cook and cool as above.

Jalapeño-Flavored Salsa: The original version of this sauce was made entirely from *jalapeños*, which will give a different and of course much hotter flavor to the finished product. If you do not wish to seed 16 to 20 *jalapeños*, you can make an extremely hot *salsa* with 4 Anaheim or California chilies and 6 whole *serranos*. These smaller hot green chilies usually do not have to be seeded before you grind them—merely remove the stems. Increase simmering time to 30 minutes, or as long as it takes for the sauce to reach the degree of hotness you think you can tolerate in a table *salsa*.

SCORPION CHILI PASTE

When you are about to bring a chili dish to the table, a last-minute taste can tell you whether or not it is hot enough. If it is not, to sting it back to life, add a teaspoon or more of this chili paste, which you can keep on hand indefinitely as long as you film it with oil and store it in the refrigerator. Small dabs can also be served alongside for barbecued meats. In time you will be able to tolerate it spread on grilled chicken or stirred generously into a *vaquero* stew—two more excellent uses.

For about 1 cup of paste:

>   1 jar roasted red "sandwich" peppers—the sweet Italian
>   style, which usually comes packed in 7-ounce jars (about ⅔ cup)
>   ½ teaspoon cumin seed, whole or ground
>   ½ teaspoon salt
>   1 to 4 cloves garlic, peeled and chopped
>   2 tablespoons vegetable or olive oil
>   4 to 6 tablespoons hottest ground red chilies, or *chile caribe*
>   flakes, or the equivalent in whole chilies (*pequín, tepín,*
>   Japanese) that have been softened in hot water

The procedure for making up this paste is simplicity itself—put all the ingredients at once into a blender jar and whirl until they form a uniform emulsion. A small blender jar is best here; otherwise scrape down the sides of the larger jar from time to time. If you are using whole red chilies, be sure to blend long enough for the seeds to be pulverized. If the paste is too thick for your machine to handle, add a little more oil or water a teaspoonful at a time. The finished product should be as thick as mayonnaise.

Pack the paste into a small jar, such as the one which the red peppers came in, cover with a thin film of vegetable oil and refrigerate indefinitely. The paste can also be frozen, but it really needs to be at hand when the occasion unexpectedly calls for a scorpion in the stew.

About the chilies: These quantities are approximate. Four tablespoons of straight cayenne may be intolerable to you, for instance, and it is impossible to predict how hot your Japanese chilies or *pequíns* might be. Adding a little mild chili powder ground from *anchos* or *chilies de ristra* also improves the flavor. It is a matter of suiting yourself. Packaged chili powders will usually indicate their hotness, and all can be bolstered with a good quality cayenne.

GUACAMOLE SAUCE

Guacamole Sauce is the same thing as *guacamole*, a food so versatile that you are hard-pressed to know how to list it. In this book I have put it with the salads (see p. 171), but it could just as well be called a dip, an appetizer, a filling or a sauce. Any of the versions given may be used as a garnish for *tacos, burritos,* grilled meats, *tamales*—practically any New Mexican dish you can think of. Some cooks do modify it in one of several ways, however, when they use *guacamole* for saucing:

For a smoother texture, process or blend the *guacamole* to a uniform puree. This is common restaurant practice which I do not follow, since I like *guacamole* with texture to it.

For a creamy taste, puree several tablespoons of commercial sour cream (or even whipping cream) into the *guacamole* as you process it.

For a simple sauce you can call *guacamole* in a pinch, simply process the flesh of ripe avocados, adding chopped onion, garlic and salt to taste. Such a preparation is acceptable (to restaurant customers) when it is to go atop a *tostada* or *burrito* already smothered in cheese, lettuce, tomatoes, olives, and so on.

Relishes

All the *salsas* in the preceding section could justifiably be called relishes, too, particularly if you make them well on the chunky side instead of smooth. The several relishes listed below are definitely thicker than any sauce, however. In Mexico proper the number of relishes greatly expands beyond the few I am giving, but in truth you do not find such variety north of the Rio Grande. The primary relish to take note of is "Green Chilies for the Table," simply called *chile verde* in the old *néomejicano* cookbooks. Even more than green chili sauce, it is the agent for bringing the unforgettable taste of roasted fresh chilies into the house.

GREEN CHILIES FOR THE TABLE
Chile verde

Quite a few sauces, both simple and complicated, travel under the unadorned name of *chile verde*, or green chili (see p. 62), but when nothing more than mashed roasted chilies is wanted, the *chile verde* you make is the one below. Its traditional use is for seasoning beans at the table, each diner spooning over as much as he wants—this is done in preference to cooking the beans with chilies. Canned chilies are frequently used for this *chile verde*, but if you roast your own fresh chilies, using either Anaheims, Californias, or the harder to find *poblanos*, it will be all the better. I like the taste a bit more *picante* than ordinary canned chilies give, so some *jalapeño* is also called for. Increase the amount, or eliminate it altogether, to suit your own taste. (For the sort of *chile verde* used as a sauce for *burritos*, *enchiladas*, and such, see the recipes for green chili sauces beginning on p. 80.)

For a generous cup of relish:

> 1 cup whole, canned or fresh home-roasted green chilies
>   (about 6 to 8)
> 1 teaspoon chopped *jalapeños*, fresh or canned
> 1 clove garlic, mashed and chopped
> ½ teaspoon salt
> Optional: 1 tablespoon chopped green coriander (*cilantro*),
>   2 tablespoons chopped onion, plus black pepper, and/or
>   cayenne
> A few drops olive oil

Place the chilies and garlic in the bowl of a food processor and blend for a few seconds until the mixture is pureed but still has some discernible texture. Taste for seasoning, add salt, then add any of the optional ingredients you like—the authentic article more often than not is unembellished except for garlic and onion. Blend the seasonings in for only a second or two so that their flavors and textures will stand out a little. Moisten with a few drops of olive oil for a bit more richness and store in the refrigerator until needed. Serve at room temperature. This sauce keeps well for only 2 or 3 days before staleness or molding occurs.

VARIATION:

Jalapeño Relish: The *chile verde* can be made with great amounts of peeled hot chilies, up to ¼ cup (after which the hotness will be such that few of us could take more than a teaspoon or so without suffering discomfort). Since hot *jalapeño* sauces are usually pickled, add 2 tablespoons white or cider vinegar as well, or, if using canned chilies, look for *jalapeños en escabeche.*

ROASTED GREEN CHILI RELISH

Because you roast your own green pepper—either an unorthodox bell pepper or an impeccably right *poblano*—and mash all the ingredients by hand, this table relish tastes far more appealing than any canned *salsa.* The amount of water used keeps the texture more like a pickle relish than a sauce, but you can add more water, a little at a time, if you want a more liquid result, such as would be good spooned over roast chicken. Hotness can be varied by the amount of *jalapeño* you include; this version is only mildly hot. As with all uncooked sauces of its ilk, the taste of raw onion is quite prominent, though I have kept the amount to a minimum. Scallions can be substituted for the white onion if you prefer.

For about ½ cup:

> 1 **bell pepper or 2** *poblano* **chilies**
> 1 **clove garlic, peeled but not chopped**
> 2 **tablespoons chopped onion, either white or red**
> 2 **tablespoons chopped green coriander (** *cilantro* **)**
> 1 **whole canned** *jalapeño,* **chopped**
> ½ **teaspoon olive oil**
> **Salt**
> **Lime juice**
> 1 **tablespoon water**

Roast the bell pepper or *poblanos* and peel, following the directions given on pp. 64–67. Chop the peeled pepper into small dice.

Place the garlic clove in a small mixing bowl and mash the juice out of it with a fork by pressing against the bottom of the bowl. Discard the pulp. Add the onion, green coriander, *jalapeño* and olive oil. Mash them roughly with a fork, then add the chopped roasted pepper and continue to work the mass into a very chunky relish. (This can also be done in the processor, but the handmade quality is then lost.) Season to taste with salt and a few drops of lime juice, and moisten with 1 tablespoon cold water. Set the relish aside to ripen for ½ hour and taste again. If you want a hotter relish or a soupier one, mash in another *jalapeño* and thin with water, adding only a bit at a time.

VARIATIONS:

Sour Green Relish: A more sour taste may seem desirable to serve with roasted meat and poultry. Add 1 tablespoon cider vinegar at the time you add the water. Taste after ½ hour and add more vinegar if you wish, a little at a time, to reach the desired sourness.

Tomato and Chili Relish: Adding a chopped ripe unpeeled tomato will turn this relish into a very good version of the *salsa cruda* most commonly seen as a table sauce. Chop the tomato roughly or liquefy it in the blender, depending on the texture you want. (If you resort to using a canned tomato, liquefy in the blender.)

SWEET-AND-SOUR RELISH FOR BARBECUE

The delight of any barbecued meat is doubled by dabbing it at the table with this uncooked table sauce or relish. Although it is common for such table garnishes to be quite soupy, this one is so fresh-flavored that it is a shame to thin it too much.

For about 1½ cups:

    ½ cup Roasted Green Chili Relish, p. 95
     1 cup any red chili sauce, including the instant version
        given on p. 80, or canned red *enchilada* sauce
     1 tablespoon cider vinegar, or more to taste
     2 teaspoons sugar, or more to taste
    Salt

Mix the green chili relish with the red chili sauce, add the minimum amount of vinegar and sugar and let the relish sit for 15 minutes. Taste and season with small amounts of salt, sugar or vinegar, if needed. For a more liquid texture, add water a teaspoonful at a time.

VARIATION:

Obviously, before you can make this recipe, you have to have on hand a quantity of homemade green chili relish. If you lack that, make a simpler version, following the basic recipe but substituting ½ cup of canned chilies for fresh. Also, any basic uncooked *salsa* can be modified by adding cautious amounts of cider vinegar and sugar to it until you reach the sweet-and-sour taste desired (see p. 86 for the basic *salsa* recipe).

CHILI VINEGAR

Sprinkled on grilled meats, *tacos*, or even salads, this spiced, salted vinegar is a ranch replacement, Anglo style, for Tabasco.

For 1 cup:

    1 cup cider vinegar
    3 to 10 fresh *jalapeño* or *serrano* chilies
    5 black peppercorns
    1 clove garlic, peeled and lightly crushed
    ½ teaspoon salt

Bring the vinegar to a boil in a covered saucepan (not untreated aluminum). Leave the chilies whole, but trim off their stems and slash them deeply in several places. Pour the vinegar over the chilies and the rest of the ingredients and let stand for a week or so. The pickled chilies keep indefinitely in the vinegar and can be chopped for table relish after this period. Other versions of chili vinegar are made hotter by filling the container as full of chilies as the liquid will cover. A 1-pint jelly jar would hold this amount of vinegar and approximately ⅓ pound of *jalapeños*.

Fillings

The skill of a Southwestern cook in my mind comes primarily from knowing two things: sauces and fillings. The most characteristic specialties of the region, such as *enchiladas* and *burritos*, are literally nothing more than basic methods, to be interpreted by each cook according to the choice of sauce or filling in them. I have given traditional fillings for each method of preparation with its basic recipe. It would be wrong, however, to infer from that that every *burrito* must be filled with refried beans and sauced with green chili, or that *tamales* are somehow ordained to be stuffed with ground pork and sauced with red chili. These are more or less restaurant standards, and it is the pride of every good cook to have his own personal formulas. The variations are the very thing that makes Santa Fe food a matter of individual styles and not the standardized products of restaurant kitchens.

The list that ends this section (pp. 106 to 108) allows you to cross-reference all the fillings, both hot and cold, for which a recipe is given elsewhere in this book. Following each is a suggestion or two about the best use for the filling (discounting the recipe it already accompanies, of course). Please take them only as suggestions, for even scrambled eggs and potatoes, which sound improbable to me as *tamale* stuffings, might turn into a delicious variation under your hands.

HAND-SHREDDED BEEF

To achieve shredded beef, you can start by pot-roasting the meat, or stew it in a Crockpot, or you can follow the technique for boiled pork (p. 99). Pot-roasting will result in shreds one or two inches long; this hand-picked style is often called *machaca* in the Southwest, though Mexican cooks usually reserve that term for sun-dried beef.

The style of shredded beef described below can be used for *tacos* or *burritos* in place of ground meat. Mixed with red chili sauce, it is more or less identical to *carne adovada* in style. Assuming that the bulk of the meat will be refrigerated or frozen, I here give just one simple way to prepare it immediately by moistening with *salsa* and wrapping it in warmed flour tortillas. As with all the simplest ways, it is one of the best.

For 2 to 3 pounds of shredded meat:

   2 to 3 pounds beef brisket or chuck steak (trimmed
      of all excess fat)
   1 onion, coarsely chopped
   1 to 2 garlic cloves, chopped
   1 bay leaf
   ½ teaspoon oregano
   1 teaspoon salt
   ½ teaspoon pepper
   ½ teaspoon cumin, whole or ground
   Vegetable oil

Preheat the oven to 325°. Rub the beef thoroughly with the onion, garlic, seasonings and a little vegetable oil. Wrap the meat in heavy-duty foil and seal the edges all around with tight crimps. Place the meat in a baking dish and bake for about 2½ to 3 hours, or until the beef is tender enough to fall apart. If you hear much sizzling as the meat cooks, turn the heat down.

When the beef is fork-tender, unwrap the top of the foil package, push aside the onions, and place the meat close to a broiler flame. Allow to broil only until the top surface begins to look dry and is starting to brown. Remove from the broiler and let the meat cool. Shred it into long shreds with your fingers, then store them in the refrigerator (for up to a week) or freeze for use as a filling.

VARIATION:

Shredded Beef with Chili: If you want to use some of the beef immediately, mix it to moisten with any red *enchilada* sauce, warm through until bubbling in a skillet, and serve with warm flour tortillas. An even simpler way is to bring the warm shreds of beef to the table with a homemade *salsa* like the *salsa picante* on p. 89. You can also substitute this beef for the jerky in the recipe for scrambled egg with tomatoes and green chilies on p. 203—the result would be a dish that often appears on Mexican menus as *Huevos con machaca.*

SHREDDED PORK

Shredded rather than ground meat is a sign of authenticity when you are stuffing *tacos* or *burritos*, but whether you use shredded pork or beef is often a matter of taste. This is the simplest way to shred pork, providing that you are using a food processor equipped with a plastic pastry blade.

For about 3 cups shredded meat:

> 1½ pounds pork shoulder, trimmed of fat and cut into 2 large pieces
> Lightly salted water, about 3 cups
> ½ onion stuck with 2 cloves
> 2 cloves garlic, peeled
> 5 peppercorns
> ½ teaspoon whole cumin seed
> Pinch oregano

Place the meat in a saucepan, barely cover with water, and add the remaining ingredients. Bring to a boil over medium heat, skim off the foam that rises, and cover the pan. Simmer gently for 45 minutes; do not allow the water to boil. Turn off the heat and let the pork cool in its broth.

To shred the meat, fit the food processor with the plastic blade. Cut the meat into 2-inch chunks and process them, 3 or 4 at a time, until they shred (about 10 seconds). To shred by hand, use two forks, pulling the meat apart as best you can. In either case, store the shreds in the refrigerator, covered, or proceed to make *carnitas*.

VARIATIONS:

Carnitas: This term usually applies to braised pork that is salted, roasted in the oven, and shredded. For this version, place your already shredded pork and 3 tablespoons oil in a heavy skillet over high heat. Season it to taste with salt, pepper, ground cumin, cinnamon and cayenne, starting with about ¼ teaspoon of each spice. Cook, tossing the meat, until the shreds dry out and start to brown just a little. Cool and use in place of unseasoned shredded meat.

Pot-Roasted Pork: The method for post-roasting beef described above also works well for pork. The cuts to use include shoulder, butt, loin and thick-cut chops. Cutting the meat into 1½-inch sections and laying them flat in the pan helps with the broiling process at the end of the cooking period.

SHREDDED TURKEY BREAST

The simplest method for obtaining shredded turkey meat is to poach the breast in shallow water until it is just done but still tender, then to shred the cooled meat in a food processor. The shreds will not be as good as if you pulled them apart by hand—and that is still an alternative, of course—but the results are more than serviceable when you need breast meat for soft *tacos,* green *enchiladas,* or the "Spanish Pie" on p. 160. Leftover meat can be stored for a day or two in the refrigerator or frozen indefinitely.

For 4 cups shredded meat:

Half turkey breast, weighing about 2⅓ pounds
Salted water for poaching

Place the turkey breast, flesh side down, in a 10-inch-wide and fairly deep skillet or a pan that will just hold the meat. Barely cover with lightly salted water, place a lid on the skillet or other pan, and bring the water just to the boiling point over low heat. When you begin to see bubbles, reduce heat and poach the breast for 20 minutes, then turn it over, cover again, and poach 20 minutes more on the other side. Turn off the heat and allow the meat to cool in its broth, still covered. (Make sure, for the sake of keeping it tender, that the breast actually poaches instead of boiling— tiny bubbles around the edges of the pan are enough.)

When the meat is cool enough to handle, peel away the skin and remove the meat from the bone in fairly large chunks, using a paring knife or tearing with your fingers. At this point, if you have time and patience to spare, shred the meat with your fingers; otherwise, shred about a cup of meat at a time in the food processor (see method for shredding pork, p. 100).

SPICED GROUND BEEF WITH RAISINS AND ALMONDS
Picadillo

Spain and most of its colonial progeny cook ground meats with spices, almonds and raisins. Under the name of *picadillo,* this preparation is very common in Mexican homes, but not in Southwestern restaurants, which usually find it expedient to fill their *tacos* or *burritos* with hamburger. *Picadillo* is well worth making in large enough quantities so that you can refrigerate some for later use, for it improves any flour or corn tortilla dish that needs a filling. It is particularly nice on small appetizer tortillas or stuffed into whole green chilies as an alternative to the cheese that usually goes into *chiles rellenos.* Hispanic cooks also serve it on its own as a meat dish, in which case you will want to have warm flour tortillas, shredded cheese and a homemade *salsa* to accompany the *picadillo* at the table. In any case, the *picadillo* itself is not hot, but it usually is served with a *salsa* that lends a nice contrast to its sweet-sour flavors.

For a generous pound of picadillo (enough for 3 to 4 servings as a main course):

  2 tablespoons vegetable oil
  1 small onion, chopped
  2 cloves garlic, chopped
  1 pound ground beef, or a mixture of beef and pork
  1 cup chopped canned tomatoes
  2 tablespoons vinegar
  1 tablespoon brown sugar
  1 teaspoon cinnamon
  ½ teaspoon cumin
  ¼ teaspoon cloves
  ½ teaspoon salt
  ½ cup raisins
  ½ cup blanched, slivered almonds
Optional flavorings: 1 bell pepper or 2 Anaheim chilies, chopped,
    ¼ cup chopped green coriander (*cilantro*), 1 or 2 chopped
    serrano or *jalapeño* peppers, veined and seeded

Heat the oil in a 10-inch skillet, add the onion and garlic, and cover the pan to allow the onion to wilt over low heat, about 5 minutes. Remove the onion mixture to a bowl, raise the heat and sauté the ground meat until it begins to brown. Replace the onion mixture in the pan, add all the remaining ingredients except the raisins and almonds, and bring to a boil. Stir the mixture a few times, cover the pan and simmer gently for 30 minutes. Remove the cover, add the raisins and almonds, and cook over medium or high heat until the *picadillo* has no excess liquid around it but still looks moist. It is now ready to use. If you want to employ any of the optional flavorings listed, add them along with the tomatoes and other ingredients.

Other ways to serve picadillo: Besides eating it on its own with flour tortillas and a table *salsa* (each diner makes his own improvised *burritos*), you can spoon the *picadillo* over hot rice, perhaps the rice with cumin on p. 309. The mixture is also a favorite filling for *tacos*, the folded pastries called *empanadas*, or whole green chilies that are either baked or fried.

It is also quite nice to set your table with *picadillo* and all manner of accompaniments, such as *guacamole*, uncooked *salsa*, shredded lettuce, chopped tomatoes, green olives, chopped scallions and radishes, grated Monterey Jack cheese, pickled *jalapeños*, sour cream and perhaps a cooked red chili sauce. Your guests then take up warm flour or corn tortillas or warm, crisp *taco* shells and contrive combinations to suit themselves. This is at once a convenient and festive way to entertain a number of people buffet style. A pound of *picadillo* fills from 6 to 10 tortillas.

SAUSAGE TO TASTE LIKE CHORIZO

Chorizo sausage is handy for adding to *enchilada* sauce or an omelet, or to lend its particular flavor to soups or *posole*. Its availability, however, is sporadic, and many of the versions you do see marketed are inferior in one way or another. In my experience, the meat in *chorizo* should taste as good as the best *kielbasa*, or Polish sausage, which almost every supermarket carries. So this recipe does a quick change on Polish sausage by flavoring it like *chorizo* and gives you instant access to good-quality sausage. Rather than grinding the sausage up as in most recipes, be careful to stop processing when the meat is still in small, rough chunks. This coarser texture keeps the *chorizo* from disappearing when added to a sauce. The preliminary step of skinning and frying *chorizo* is not necessary with this substitute.

For 1 pound chorizo:

> 2 tablespoons vegetable oil
> 2 tablespoons powdered red chilies, medium-hot at most
>   (e.g., *chiles de ristra* or ground *chile primero*)
> 1 clove garlic, finely chopped
> ½ teaspoon oregano
> ½ teaspoon cumin
> 1 pound *kielbasa* with the ends trimmed

Heat the oil gently in a small skillet, stir in all the remaining ingredients except the *kielbasa* and heat through. Cut the sausage into ½-inch lengths and place them in the food processor along with the chili-and-oil mixture. Process until the meat is reduced to small bits, but stop short of actually grinding it. This will require only 10 or 15 pulses of the motor. Pack the meat into a bowl, cover closely and store in the refrigerator. The "*chorizo*" will keep for a week or so. Use in any recipe that calls for regular link *chorizo*. (Also see the recipe for bulk sausage *chorizo*, p. 205.)

SAGE CHEESE

It would be interesting to work with the moist native white cheese sold around Santa Fe, but in lieu of that, here is a concoction of cream cheese and sage. It is very nice spread between the split halves of the Cheese-and-Chili Puffs on p. 154, baked in *enchiladas* or simply served with wedges of warm flour tortillas. If the flavor appeals to you, refer to the recipe for the Eggs Scrambled with Sage Cheese on p. 103. Also note the variation with piñons, which is good for every use that applies to the smooth version.

For 1¼ pounds cheese spread, or a generous 2 cups:

> ½ to 1 teaspoon powdered sage, depending on its strength and freshness
> 1 teaspoon vinegar
> 1 small clove garlic, peeled
> ¼ to ½ cup fresh parsley
> 1 pound cream cheese
> ¼ pound butter (1 stick)

Generous dashes of coarsely ground pepper
Salt, if needed

Muddle the sage in the vinegar for a minute or two to moisten it. Drop the garlic into the food processor through the feed tube while the motor is running. Add the parsley and soaked sage, along with the vinegar, still using the feed tube. Stop the machine and place the cheese and butter in the bowl, breaking them up roughly into 1-inch pieces. Process until a smooth spread is reached, stopping occasionally to scrape down the bowl with a rubber spatula. (If the finished cheese seems too stiff, thin it with a few tablespoons of milk or cream.) Pepper the cheese to taste, adding up to a teaspoon if you like as much pepper as herb taste, and add salt sparingly if needed. Chill until cool and firm but still spreadable.

VARIATIONS:

Sage Cheese with Piñons: Make exactly as in the basic recipe, but add 1 cup shelled and roasted pine nuts (piñons) at the same time you put in the cheese and butter. This version often does need thinning with 3 or 4 tablespoons of milk, particularly if the processor starts to balk. (If that does happen, the easiest remedy is to process only half at a time.)

Sage Goat Cheese: For this delicious variant, substitute ½ pound of California or French goat cheese for half the cream cheese in the basic recipe. For a really goaty version, use 1 pound of strong goat cheese, such as French Reblochon, and moisten with a few teaspoons of milk to achieve the desired texture.

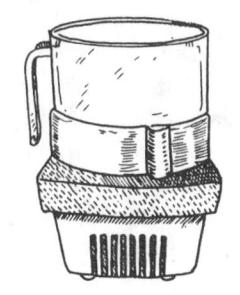

Fillings Based on Goat Cheese or Cream Cheese

Cheese is such an important basis for some of the very best New Mexican food, such as *enchiladas* and *chiles rellenos*, that I do not want to let these special variations slip by in a crowded list. All the recipes in this book, as in most Southwestern cookbooks, tell you to use one or two cheeses for all purposes. If you are already advanced enough to like Monterey Jack cheese in your *enchiladas* instead of Longhorn Cheddar, then you will appreciate the many other possibilities open to you. Cheeses made with goat and sheep milk used to be indigenous around Santa Fe, but there is scarce mention of them in books written after World War II. Here are a few ways to bring back the tangy, musky taste of such cheeses:

Hard cheeses: Genuine imported Parmesan, Romano and similar European grating cheeses are made with goat or sheep milk, which is not usually true of their American counterparts. Grate these cheeses directly onto dishes where a cheese topping is to be melted in the oven, either alone or in combination with your usual melting cheese.

Semisoft cheeses: Certain crumbly goat and sheep cheeses are neither soft nor hard but somewhere in between. These include French *chèvre* (a generic word for goat cheese), Greek *feta* and various blue cheeses. Use them as fillings by crumbling them beforehand and mashing with a bit of cottage or cream cheese to reach a soft consistency you can easily handle with a spoon at stuffing time; large quantities—over a cup—can be smoothed out more easily in a food processor. In the case of *feta*, which is soaked in brine, take into account its extreme saltiness. California goat cheese, now quite fashionable, makes a wonderfully strange stuffing for *enchiladas*, but it is very "goaty" in comparison to most European types. It is also intriguing as a garnish for *tacos* and *tostadas* in place of the usual shredded Monterey Jack. Crumbled blue cheese would be equally unusual and worth trying, but not until you have mastered the more orthodox choices, I think.

Soft cheeses: The softest goat and sheep cheeses often have a very high fat content, making them both expensive and luxurious. An imported French Montrachet, for example, would be rather too lavish to stuff a chili with; on the other hand, its sheer extravagance might appeal to you. Such cheeses are especially good in quiche-like tarts, turnovers (*empanadas*) and *quesadillas*. Commercial cream cheese and its less fattening counterpart, farmer's cheese, are both made from cow's milk. They can be used alone as fillings in place of Monterey Jack or mixed with a little goat cheese for a luxurious texture that is not too overwhelmingly goaty. Cream cheese should be softened to room temperature for easier handling, except in the case of *chiles rellenos*, where firm cubes are definitely what you want. For a lower calorie content, cream cheese can be mixed in the blender or food processor with cottage cheese, using the proportions of 3 or 4 parts cream cheese to 1 part cottage.

Other Cold Fillings

Southwestern cooking runs a bit short of cold fillings because this is country where tradition called for large hot meals early in the morning and late at night, with little demand for luncheon food. There are places, however, where I suggest that it would be good to slice open a *sopaipilla* to make a pocket sandwich, not to mention the times when you might want to improvise your own cold dishes: Why not fill pita bread with a Santa Fe filling?

The cooking of Mexico proper is stronger in this regard than Santa Fe cooking, but no matter. Below are some suggestions to start you off, and I also refer you to the section on salads, particularly bean and lentil salads. One ever-present cold "sandwich" here in the Southwest is the cold *burrito* stuffed with refried beans. It tastes quite bad to me but is absolutely authentic food, albeit it is sold today from vending machines. Unless you are hoeing a row in the afternoon, this specialty sits heavy on the stomach, but you should be aware that cold *refritos* have their place. Other normally hot fillings that conceivably could be used cold are such common items as shredded turkey breast, poached chicken, and even ground meat or *picadillo*.

Here are more suggestions:

Guacamole (pp. 171–74)—for *tacos* and *tostadas* as a main filling; with almost any dish as a garnish.

Sage Cheese (p. 103)—for a sandwich filling; combined with cold chicken as a *taco* or *tostada* filling

The following are sandwich fillings or semi-salads to be eaten with wheat-flour *tortillas*:

Crab or shrimp mixed with a few walnuts, chunks of ripe avocado, dabs of mayonnaise, spiked with green chili *salsa*

Small cubes of Jack cheese and avocado, chopped tomato and chopped Spanish olives, once again moistened with mayonnaise (or olive oil) and a dash of green chili

Chopped cucumber, tomatoes, green onion and fresh-cooked or canned chick peas, held together with mayonnaise or a good homemade vinaigrette. Serve with *salsa* on the side

Chicken or turkey salad of the ordinary kind, but mixed with chopped walnuts and ripe avocado, then flavored to taste with chili *salsa*

Any of the above can be further seasoned with chopped green coriander (*cilantro*)—and a side dressing of *guacamole* would never be amiss.

Other Hot Fillings

In a cuisine where roasts, steaks and chops are rare, their place is taken by all manner of hot fillings, to be endlessly varied in *tacos*, *enchiladas*, *tamales* and so on. Only various kinds of stews rival these fillings in importance. To me, the fillings are the more interesting. Needless to say, the restaurants that restrict themselves to ground beef, cheese, sour cream, chicken and refried beans are giving us barely a glimpse into the possibilities. It is up to us home cooks first to learn the basic methods behind each tortilla specialty, then to go forth bravely to new and untried variations. Such variations are at the heart of every Mexican cookbook, and of any accomplished Southwestern cook.

Because there are so many uses for hot fillings, the suggested ones found here are selected according to nothing more than my taste. For the most part, though, I have remained within the bounds of tradition.

Grated Zucchini with Green Chili (p. 317)—for vegetarian *burritos* or *enchiladas*

Pork Cured in Red Chilies (*carne adovada*) (p. 264)—for almost any use requiring meat, but particularly for *burritos*, *tacos* and *tostadas*

Dry-Cooked Pork with Green Chilies (p. 269)—for *burritos* rolled at the table

Simple *Picadillo* (p. 228)—as a replacement for ground beef in any use, but particularly *tacos*, *burritos* and *tostadas*

Refried Beans in Butter (p. 298)—all uses, but particularly those where ordinary *refritos* are called for

Sage Cheese (p. 103)—for cheese *enchiladas*

Mild Green Chili Dip (p. 156)—for cheese *enchiladas*

Spiced Turkey and Almonds (p. 160)—for *tamales*, *enchiladas* and soft *tacos*

Spiced Shredded Pork (*carnitas*) (p. 100)—for *tamales*, *enchiladas* and soft *tacos*

Pork with Almonds and Orange Peel (p. 240)—for soft *tacos* and *burritos*

Shredded Turkey Breast (p. 100)—for soft *tacos*, *enchiladas*, *tostadas*, or any use ordinarily calling for chicken

Shredded Beef (p. 98)—as a replacement for ground beef for any use, but particularly in *burritos*

Shredded Pork (p. 99)—same as shredded beef, but particularly *tamales*

Spanish Rice (p. 305)—to be mixed with meat or beans as a combination *burrito* or *tostada* filling

Bean Dip with Smoked Chilies (p. 157)—to replace *refritos* in restaurant-style *burritos*

Rice and Potatoes with Cumin (p. 309)—for vegetarian *burritos*

Refried Beans (*refritos*) and variations (p. 296)—all uses, but particularly in restaurant-style *burritos, nachos* and *tostadas*

Turkey Cured in Red Chilies (p. 286)—as a replacement for *carne adovada* (see Pork Cured in Red Chilies)

Pork with Red Chilies and Black Beans (p. 270)—for table-rolled *burritos*

Picadillo (p. 101)—as a replacement for ground beef in any use

Jerky (p. 38)—as a replacement for sausage in any use

Breakfast Sausage (*chorizo*) (p. 205)—as a replacement for ground or shredded meat in any use

Sausage to Taste Like *Chorizo* (p. 103)—for any use calling for meat

Scrambled Eggs and *Chorizo* (p. 202)—for soft or crisp-shelled *tacos*

Fried Potatoes with Green Chili (p. 206)—for vegetarian *burritos* and soft *tacos*

Chili con Carne (p. 257)—to be used alone, or with beans, or thinned to a sauce for almost any dish needing a sauce; traditionally used over *enchiladas, chiles rellenos* and *burritos* in Tex-Mex cooking

Tex-Mex Chili-Meat Sauce—see Chili con Carne (p. 257)

TORTILLAS AND OTHER BREADS

Corn, Cornmeal and Masa for Breads
Hand-Rolled Corn Tortillas (Tortillas de maíz)
Blue-Corn Tortillas (Tortillas de maíz azul)
Flour Tortillas (Tortillas de harina)
Pueblo Indian Tortillas
Sopaipillas
Adobe Bread
Soft Cornbread with Cheese and Green Chili
Blue, White and Yellow Cornbread
Indian Paper Bread (Piki)
Sweet Saffron Rolls (Molletes)
Indian Fry-Bread

ALSO SEE:
Sage-and-Cumin Bread with a Cheese Filling
Breakfast Soufflé Spoonbread
Biscuits

CORN, CORNMEAL
AND MASA FOR BREADS

Corn is so popular in Santa Fe cooking that it deserves a larder to itself. Unleavened cornbread or a simple gruel of corn and water served for many centuries as the daily sustenance of the Pueblos, to be taken up in turn by the Spanish subsistence farmers. When the See of Santa Fe sent out its missionaries to the surrounding countryside, they were expected to live on tortillas and *atole* (the name of the gruel) side by side with the Indians and peasants they ministered to. Now it comes as a small shock to discover that the wheat-flour tortilla has supplanted the ancestral corn among the Pueblos and many of the Spanish-speaking population. However, a great many uses for corn and its products still remain.

Green corn: Fresh corn on the cob, commonly called "green" corn (though it is picked ripe, not green), is used in season by Santa Fe cooks, but the months when it is out of season are far longer. It becomes an event when green-corn *masa*, or dough, is employed for *tamales* in place of dried meal, or when the whole kernels are mixed with fresh zucchini in a dish of *calabacitas*. The local way with corn on the cob is to roast whole ears over a fire, rip off the blistering husks and season the corn inside with butter and lime juice. The New Mexican palate is so used to the flavor of corn slaked in lime water that much fresh corn is made into hominy first before it is used. At other times the kernels are sheared from the cob and made directly into flat breads. A Franciscan missionary father by the alarming name of Torquemada reported in 1610 that the Pueblos hung fresh-corn breads out to dry in the October sunlight of harvest season. The Anglo settlers, many of them arriving via Missouri, relied on traditional American breads made from cornmeal, along with the corn fritters, soups, chowders and relishes produced when green corn could be had.

Cornmeal and flour: Almost all the recipes in this book calling for regular cornmeal are settlers' food, variants on johnnycake and Indian pudding dating from the colonial era and persisting to today. Sometimes the meal acts as a thickener rather than as the main ingredient, e.g., in chess pie or chili con carne. Any conventional cornmeal, whether white or yellow, stone-ground or processed with metal rollers, will do.

Masa: The Hispanic and Indian cooks grind their meal and flour from *nixtamal*, basically the same lime-treated hominy that goes into grits. From this is made the dough, or *masa*, for tortillas. The same word applies to any dough in Spanish, but in Santa Fe it refers specifically to a corn dough or to the basic mix sold by mills for tortilla making. The brand name of tortilla mix sold widely throughout the country is Masa Harina. (Its sister product, Masa Tigro, is used for flour tortillas.) This brand will work well in any recipe for tortilla, *tamal* or similar dough.

Blue corn: From the Indians the Santa Fe cooks learned to work with many kinds of field and flint corn besides what we see on grocery shelves. The most interesting is blue corn (*maíz azul*), which actually looks medium blue-gray after it is made into meal. Sometimes you see it in Mexican groceries as *atole*, meaning that it has been processed to be made specifically into corn gruel. The sort you would want for tortilla making is labeled *harina de maíz azul* and needs to be special-ordered if you want to make blue-corn tortillas from scratch. A good source in Santa Fe is Josie's Best Tortilla Factory, 1130 Agua Fria, Santa Fe NM 87501. El Encanto, Inc., packages a line of blue cornmeal under the Bueno label, which has fairly wide distribution (write El Encanto, Inc., 1224 Airway SW, Albuquerque NM 87105). Be sure not to order *harinilla* instead of *harina* or you will receive the finer grade of corn flour, which is used for corn mush. Making tortillas from blue cornmeal is trickier than from the Masa Harina mix— which makes it *very* tricky—so do not try them as your first tortilla project. For most of us, it would be good to eat as many blue-corn *enchiladas* as we can when we are actually visiting the Southwest—but dedicated cooks will enjoy at least experimenting with the homemade kind.

Although not used for breads, there are a few more corn products worth mentioning here:

Posole and chicos: The whole-kernel hominy, or *nixtamal*, can be used directly for a feast-day stew called *posole*. It is traditionally made in huge quantities on New Year's Day, particularly by Pueblo cooks, who add large amounts of ham hock, salt pork, pork rind and fresh pork meat. On days which are less festive, the pork flavoring is often reduced merely to a chunk of fatback, and then the *posole* is served like a starchy vegetable, the main seasoning being red or green chilies. The best fresh *posole* is sold in the freezer cases of Mexican groceries and Western supermarkets, but you can feel free to substitute canned white or yellow hominy if that is all you can find. Cooking times may have to be shortened to an hour or two in place of the all-day cooking marathons which Pueblo *posole* undergoes, but the results will still be good.

Dried hominy ground into a meal becomes grits, a common food among Anglo settlers in New Mexico who came from a Southern background, but it was not transferred to the native cooking. No doubt many barrels of grits rode down the Santa Fe Trail in the era of great migration a century ago, but as far as I know there is no indigenous New Mexico dish based on it.

Whole dried kernels, steamed but not treated with lime, are called *chicos*; they may be picked up off the ground at harvest time or scraped from whole dried ears stored in the larder for winter. Some Western groceries also carry them, for locals like to cook *chicos* as a variation on *posole*. They are not widely enough available outside the Southwest to bother with, but if you run across a recipe for *chicos* or want to substitute them for *posole*, they should be presoaked and boiled as for dried beans.

Dried corn husks: Packaged corn husks are sold in the Mexican section of supermarkets. They are soaked in hot water until softened and then used to wrap *tamales*. Having looked at a dozen recipes over the years for steaming *tamales* in husks, which is the only authentic way, I noticed that I never carried through by trying them. Traditional *tamal* making stands out as a singularly time-consuming part of New Mexican cooking. So in this book I have recommended that you steam your *tamales* in foil, a surer and quicker method for non-native cooks. If you are bothered by the idea of doing without corn husks, by all means use them.

TORTILLAS FOR THE TABLE

It may seem like belaboring the obvious, but tortillas served as bread need to be kept warm. Supermarkets sell flour tortillas either refrigerated or at room temperature, and corn tortillas either refrigerated or frozen. Whichever kind you want for the current meal should be wrapped in foil—the rest of the package can be kept fresh in the refrigerator by enclosing it in a second polyethylene bag—and then the foil packet warmed in a medium (350°) oven at the last moment. Microwave ovens can heat through a batch of tortillas in a minute, and they need only to be wrapped lightly in paper towels, but the waves do tend to toughen the texture of flour tortillas (a negligible fault, to my mind).

You can imitate Mexican practice and keep your tortillas warm in a covered woven basket made especially for the purpose. Short of that, you will need some kind of insulator or warmer near the table, because tortillas quickly grow cold and stiff as they stand. The quickest solution is a warming tray—simply wrap the heated tortillas in a napkin and place them directly on the tray. If you do not have such a device, the next best thing is to bring out only one shift of tortillas at a time, with a second packet at the ready in a warm, turned-off oven.

HAND-ROLLED CORN TORTILLAS
Tortillas de maíz

If you are a weekend tortilla maker only, it is hardly worthwhile to invest in a mechanical tortilla press. On the other hand, it is no mean trick to roll out a perfectly even, round tortilla without one. Like all but the most dedicated Southwestern cooks, I buy my corn tortillas ready-made, but I have also developed a hand method that produces wonderfully fragrant homemade tortillas, which are flawlessly round into the bargain.

The trick is to cut them out with a sharp-edged pot lid used like a cookie cutter. Indeed, the only thing standing between you and a reputation as a master tortilla maker is the right cutter. It should be 5 or 6 inches across and possess a sharp enough flange to cut through the tortilla dough. (Revere Ware, a popular line of stainless steel pots and pans, provides pot lids that happen to work just right.)

No machines are needed to mix the dough, or *masa*. However, you will need specific bits of apparatus for the rolling out. First is a rolling pin, which can be a straight, dowel-shaped length of wood or one tapered at both ends. Mine is an 18-inch dowel about 1½ inches thick—in other words, a standard French rolling pin—but one sees Mexican pins that are only 8 inches long and an inch thick, especially fabricated for tortilla making (try a sawed-off piece of broom handle). A standard American rolling pin with handles does not give you such a direct sense of contacting the dough, but it too should work.

Next you need 2 sheets of heavy clear plastic film about 8 inches square. Heavy-gauge zip-lock freezer bags are good for this—simply cut out two squares of the size needed, making sure that neither is creased. Anything much thinner will crumple up while you are rolling the tortillas. One way to check the gauge you want is to examine a tortilla press in the gourmet-cookware shops; it will be provided with similar pieces of plastic.

Finally, besides the sharp cutter described above, you will need a heavy skillet or flat griddle for baking the tortillas. (The process is described as baking even though it takes place on top of the stove.)

For 12 to 14 tortillas:

    2 cups Masa Harina (see p. 112 if you are not familiar with this product)
    1 cup plus 2 tablespoons warm water
    Optional: ½ teaspoon salt

Add the warm water and optional salt to the Masa Harina in a mixing bowl and stir with a wooden spoon until the dough forms into a mass and holds together. Tortillas are traditionally unsalted, but that is not law. The dough is now ready to use, and in fact it is desirable to work with it immediately since corn *masa* dries out quite quickly. Heat a skillet or flat griddle over medium heat so that it will be ready to receive your first tortilla.

Divide the dough into 12 parts by first cutting it into quarters directly in the bowl, then lifting out each quarter and dividing it into 3 approximately equal pieces. To keep the *masa* from drying out, either divide the dough into 12 parts, roll each between your hands to form a ball, and place all the balls in a polyethylene bag, or roll out 3 balls at a time, leaving the remaining dough in the mixing bowl covered closely with a piece of plastic wrap. Starting with 3 pieces is better if you are new to working with corn dough. In any case, scraps of dough can always be mixed back into the original *masa*—as can a tortilla which did not roll out right—and extra water can be added if the *masa* gets too dry. Unlike wheat-flour doughs, which are high in gluten, corn dough can be manipulated and reworked without damage to it.

Now you are at the point where you have either 3 or 12 balls of dough ready to roll out. Place one ball onto one of the plastic sheets and immediately cover it with the other sheet. Flatten slightly with the flat of your hand, then run the rolling pin over it 3 or 4 times, working quickly and lightly. In its plastic covering, turn the dough a quarter-turn and repeat 3 or 4 more strokes. Flip the package over and repeat until a ragged 6-inch circle is formed. It is perhaps inevitable that your first tortillas will be oddly shaped at this stage, but try to minimize this by always rolling your pin from the center of the circle of dough, and do not roll quite all the way to the edges. The process is one of rocking the pin across the center of the tortilla and giving quick quarter-turns to round it out.

Now peel away the top layer of plastic wrap from the tortilla. (It does not work to peel the tortilla away from the plastic, however.) Lay it gently back down again, flip the package over, and peel away the other piece of plastic. Cut out a perfectly round tortilla with your cutter and carefully transfer it to the griddle.

If it tears upon being lifted, the dough is too dry or else too sticky, or it may be that you rolled out the tortilla too thin. In any case, knead the failed tortilla back into the scraps you are beginning to accumulate—this leftover dough will be used to make up the last few tortillas. Sometimes if you have difficulty with the dough sticking to the table as you are trying to peel off the second sheet of plastic, it helps to hold it in your hand, tortilla-side down, while you peel. Another good tip, if you have the time, is to let the tortilla dry out for 15 seconds or so after the first sheet has been removed, then turn it over and peel off the second sheet.

CORN TORTILLAS

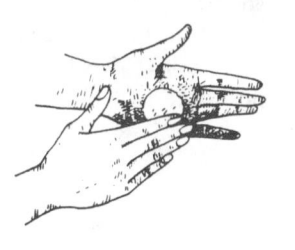
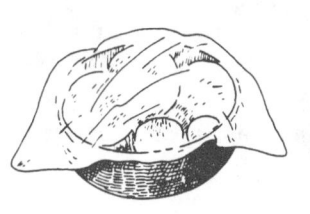

1. Shape each ball of *masa* by hand, leaving the remainder of the dough loosely covered.

2. Roll out 5- or 6-inch tortillas between two sheets of plastic film; then peel away top sheet and cut out a perfect circle with a cutter (see recipe) if tortilla is ragged around the edges.

3. Hold tortilla in one hand and gently peel away the second sheet of plastic.

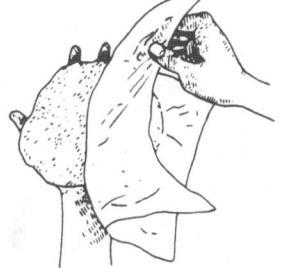
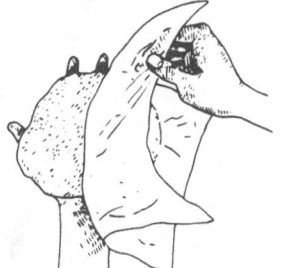

4. Bake quickly on a flat griddle, lowering the tortilla with a slight rolling motion to prevent wrinkling.

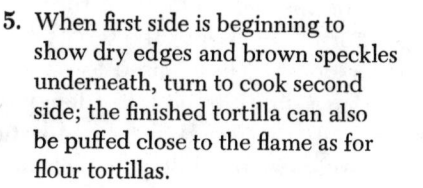

5. When first side is beginning to show dry edges and brown speckles underneath, turn to cook second side; the finished tortilla can also be puffed close to the flame as for flour tortillas.

Baking the tortilla: Whether you are using an authentic Mexican griddle (*comal*), a large skillet or just the griddle plate on your range, it needs to be uniformly hot. Ideally the tortilla is baked in this fashion: lowered gently onto the griddle and not slapped down, the bread cooks on the first side in just under 30 seconds. Flipped over with fingers or spatula, it reveals uniform specks of brown on the cooked side, and its edges have just begun to curl. It now bakes on the second side for a little more than 30 seconds and is flipped again. This time it almost immediately hisses with steam and puffs up, a process which is usually hastened by pressing down firmly with a folded dish towel and quickly lifting it away again. This is done in one quick twisting motion as soon as the tortilla is flipped.

A surer way to puff it, at least in my experience, is to place the tortilla on a cake rack as soon as it has baked on each side and to hold the rack very close to a gas or electric eye turned to high. (Since the cake rack is openwork metal, you will not burn yourself so long as you grasp it by one corner.) Within a few seconds the tortilla balloons up, but if not then, lower it within a ½ inch of the burner. If still no puffing, consider the tortilla a success anyway and go on to the next one.

A tender and perfectly made tortilla is a puffed one, but as long as yours are thoroughly cooked by their time on the griddle, they will be good and usable, if not perfection. The tortillas of beginners tend to come out stiff, either from too dry *masa* or overcooking, but they can be redeemed even then: simply stack your tortillas as they are finished one on top of the other and cover with a plate or large pot lid. This additional period of steaming will cause them to limber up. Baked tortillas can be filled and eaten at once—when they are most delicious—or set aside for use later, in which case they will not really be markedly, if at all, superior to packaged ones. After they cool, store in a plastic bag, either refrigerated for a few days or frozen indefinitely.

Trouble-shooting: After you have gained a bit of mastery over tortilla making, you will acquire added respect for the instinctive skill with which native cooks pat out their corn cakes without benefit of a tortilla press and rolling pin. Should you go so far as to perfect patting them out yourself, an accomplishment which it would be foolish for me to pretend to teach, then by all means invite spectators over for a performance—this is not the sort of skill to hide under a bushel basket.

The rest of us will be trying to correct our mistakes. If your tortilla drastically frays at the edges as it is being rolled, the dough is too dry— add a teaspoon more water to all the *masa* in the bowl, knead for a few seconds and try again. If the tortilla is so moist that it will not separate from the plastic film, it needs more stiffness—knead 1 or 2 tablespoons more Masa Harina into all the dough and try again. If the tortilla wrinkles as you lower it onto the griddle, use a rolling release, first lowering one edge and rolling your hand away from the tortilla more gradually. If the tortillas begin to stick to the griddle, scrape it clean of accumulated particles that build up during the baking. If a finished tortilla is not at all limber, lower the heat under the griddle—it should be about at medium— and reduce cooking time by 15 to 30 seconds. In all likelihood you will achieve at least one perfect tortilla per session, at which time try to capture in your mind's eye *exactly* what you did right.

BLUE-CORN TORTILLAS
Tortillas de maíz azul

Local suppliers of ready-made blue-corn tortillas are rare outside New Mexico, so if you want to produce the impeccably authentic *enchiladas* on p. 220, you will have to persuade a grocer to import packaged blue-corn tortillas for you or, failing that, make your own. I have encountered two products which were said to be absolutely right for making tortillas: the roasted blue cornmeal sold as *atole* and the scarcer New Mexican meal called *harina de maíz azul*. *Atole* is generally available in Mexican sections of the supermarket, unlike the *harina*, which must be mail-ordered (see p. 112.) Unfortunately, the tortillas I produced from *atole* were extremely fragile both before and after cooking. They barely held up well enough to be stacked flat for the layered sort of *enchilada* (p. 219)—a far cry from the tough, gritty blue-corn tortillas indigenous to Santa Fe.

My warning about *atole* notwithstanding, here is my formula for tortillas using either product. This quantity of dough will yield fewer breads than normal since it is difficult to roll blue-corn dough thin without having it tear. If you happen to own a tortilla press, follow the instructions for its use, but expose the tortillas to air for 10 seconds on each side before baking them—this reduces their fragility slightly. In any event, all my blue-corn tortillas turned out too stiff to roll up comfortably, so do plan to use them for flat *enchiladas* and not *tacos*.

For 12 tortillas:

   1 cup Masa Harina
   1 cup *atole* or *harina de maíz azul*
   ¼ teaspoon salt
   1 cup minus 2 tablespoons warm water

Mix all the ingredients with a wooden spoon in a mixing bowl until a corn dough is formed, about 2 minutes. Let stand, closely covered with plastic wrap, for 2 minutes, then proceed with the directions for making hand-rolled tortillas beginning on p. 114.

Since blue-corn tortillas are quite fragile, it helps in handling them always to make sure that the tortillas remain in contact with the plastic film until they reach the griddle. In other words, do not lay them directly on the table or the palm of your hand. In my experience, these tortillas do not puff, but they still benefit greatly in flavor by holding directly over a gas flame for 20 seconds or so. If your tortillas break during their baking, do not despair—large pieces can be stacked into the middle layers of your *enchilada casserole* (p. 215) with no one the wiser. They also can be cut into triangles with a chef's knife and deep-fried as *tostado* chips.

FLOUR TORTILLAS
Tortillas de harina

In Mexico proper, where corn tortillas are the staple bread, the version made from wheat flour—commonly referred to simply as a flour tortilla—was confined to the northern state of Sonora. From there it migrated farther north throughout the American Southwest. By the middle of the 1800s, wheat from the Taos area was abundant and cheap enough so that wheat-based whiskey and flour tortillas, to name two high-demand commodities, were common around Santa Fe, and within a few decades the Pueblos were eschewing corn tortillas as a matter of course.

Flour tortillas are not just corn tortillas with a different starch. They are usually rolled larger, with exhibition-size ones going up to 2 feet across. They are not nearly so aromatic as the corn-based originals, but they are naturally more limber. Still, you find equivalent dishes made from both—rolled wheat *burritos* are like soft corn *tacos*, flat fried ones are like corn *tostadas*, and *burritos* baked in a covering of chili sauce and cheese resemble *enchiladas*.

For the home cook there are good reasons for producing one's own flour tortillas, at least for a festive dinner. They can be made with ordinary all-purpose flour and a rolling pin, eliminating the tortilla press. They can be rolled thick, thin or paper-thin to accommodate personal tastes. Most important, they are incomparably better fresh than store-bought, which cannot always be said for corn tortillas.

The only drawback is that flour tortillas take time and are best made at the last minute (if you want to have the advantage over packaged ones). Once started, the rolling of the dough must proceed directly to baking the bread on a flat surface on top of the stove. However, at certain stages, such as when the dough is resting or after all the tortillas are made, you can relax or turn to other duties. In fact, flour tortillas do not suffer much if they are held under the cover of foil or kitchen towels for up to 6 hours and then reheated, however much you would like to serve the fresh article hot off the griddle.

The best way to speed up tortilla making so that it is enjoyable and not overwhelming is to make only small batches and use the processor for mixing and kneading the dough. This it does in one operation lasting about a minute and a half. From that point, after the dough has rested for 30 minutes, it takes another 15 to 30 minutes to produce 6 homemade tortillas.

For 6 tortillas:

> 1 **cup unbleached white flour**
> ½ **teaspoon baking powder**
> ½ **teaspoon salt**
> 2 **to 3 tablespoons lard or vegetable shortening (many home cooks use leftover bacon fat, in which case the salt is omitted)**
> 4 **to 6 tablespoons water**

Processor dough: Place all the ingredients except the water in the bowl of a food processor (a blender will not do) and process, using the metal blade, for about 10 seconds, or until the mixture is uniform. Pour in 4 tablespoons water and process for 1 minute more. At this point you should have a soft dough that has rolled up into a ball; it will also be warm to the touch. If the dough has not formed into a ball, another tablespoon of water should be sprinkled over it and the dough kneaded for another 30 seconds or so. Repeat with another tablespoon as needed. If the dough feels sticky to the touch, add 2 tablespoons more flour and process for about 30 seconds to incorporate.

Remove the dough and place it in a plastic bag or wrap in plastic wrap. Let sit at room temperature for 30 minutes. This period allows the dough to mature, but it will not rise. Processed dough has a tendency to sweat as it rests, but do not be alarmed if the dough feels moist when you come to roll it out. It needs only to be worked in your hands a few times or sprinkled with a light dusting of flour and kneaded a bit to become workable once again.

Making dough by hand: If you want to mix your dough by hand, which is the ancestral method, then mix the flour, baking powder and salt in a bowl. Add the fat by cutting it into ¼-inch cubes, adding them to the bowl and rubbing them quickly between thumb and forefinger until fat and flour form a coarse meal. Stir in the water all at once, using a fork and tossing quickly. Now begin to knead and press the dough with your hands, adding extra water a teaspoonful at a time to catch the stray dry bits. When the dough can be gathered into a soft mass, turn it out onto a lightly floured board and continue to knead for 5 minutes. Now let the dough rest as directed above.

FLOUR TORTILLAS

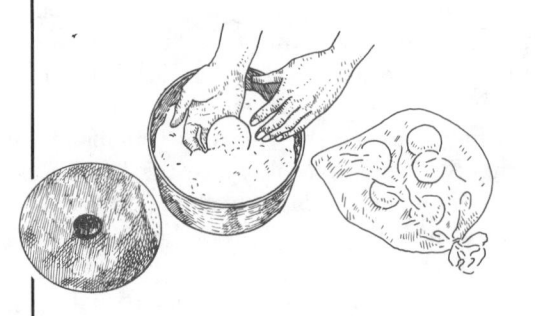

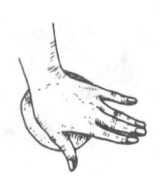

1. Form balls of dough, dredge in flour, and store in a plastic bag to prevent drying.

2. Flatten ball of dough into a disk.

3. Roll out dough 7 inches or larger, working with rapid, even strokes that do not reach to the edge.

4. Lower tortilla onto griddle with slight rolling motion to prevent wrinkles or large bubbles.

5. Turn tortilla when tiny bubbles appear on the upper surface and light brown speckles appear underneath.

6. Immediately puff tortilla on cake rack held close to the flame.

Heat a heavy skillet or a Mexican *comal* or the built-in griddle on your range over medium heat. If you are attempting flour tortillas over 9 inches across, the grilling surface needs to be at least a foot in diameter.

Rolling the tortillas: For 7- to 8-inch tortillas, divide the dough into 6 pieces and roll each one into a ball between the palms of your hands. Store them in a plastic bag so they will not dry out. Place the first ball in your flour canister or a small bowl of flour, dredge it well on both sides, and flatten it on a pastry board, using the palm of your hand, into a flat 3-inch circle.

Roll this pudgy disc with your rolling pin, dusting the board lightly as needed to prevent sticking, until you have a flat, round bread 8 inches across. The technique for rolling the tortilla into a thin circle of uniform thickness is fairly exacting but not difficult to master. Here are the points to keep in mind:

—Since the dough is soft and fairly springy, turn it a quarter-turn and flip it over after every 3 or 4 strokes of your rolling pin. Some cooks leave the board practically free of flour so that the dough grips it; others keep it lightly dusted with flour so that they can keep the dough constantly in motion. Experiment until you find a comfortable way.

—Always roll back and forth in the center of the circle, never all the way to any edge. This is vital if you are to avoid brittle edges in the baked tortilla. It also helps to keep you from shaping breads that look like kidneys or paint splatters instead of perfect rounds.

—Work with soft, pliant dough. Since flours vary from place to place in how much water they need to form a soft dough, it is impossible to dictate exactly how much water you will need. However, if halfway through rolling out your first tortilla you realize that it is just too recalcitrant, mix up a new batch of dough with a little more water. Even quite soft dough will roll out well if you dredge the balls in enough extra flour.

This whole operation is easily learned the first time out unless you have never handled pastry of any kind, and usually only the first few tortillas exhibit a ludicrous misshape. It is normal for the dough to pull back a bit each time you roll it; if it is obviously too rubbery to work with, let it rest another 15 minutes and try rolling again before you give up and mix another batch. Oddly shaped breads can be trimmed into regularity with a sharp knife and no harm done.

Baking the tortillas: It is best to go directly to the baking now. If the rolled tortilla is allowed to sit for any length of time, it is likely to begin sweating again and then will be unmanageable. Make sure your griddle is not fiercely hot, for that tends to produce stiff tortillas, whereas a somewhat too cold one does not do any harm. The way to judge the correct temperature is by eye: lean close to the first tortilla as it bakes on its first side. In 30 to 40 seconds the upper surface will show minute bubbles and a slight change of color, while the bottom will be dry, pale and perhaps sprinkled with brown spots. Your object is to be able to cook the tortilla in 1 to 2 minutes, dividing the time about equally between both sides. If large bubbles swell up during the baking, press them back down with a pancake turner or leave be—they do no harm.

Moving the tortilla onto the griddle in the first place can be tricky, for it is almost as thin as a crêpe and therefore easily wrinkles when you try to lay it down. The knack is to lower one edge first and then roll your hand out from under the dough. Failing that, the dough can first be placed on a plate and then slid gently onto the griddle.

Cook about 1 minute on the first side, making sure to look for bubbles as they appear, then flip and cook for up to 1 minute more. The speckles of brown on the first side will always be prettier than the blotches on the second, so it becomes the public side when you form your *burritos*.

To puff the bread, press down on it with a twisting motion of a folded dish towel as soon as it is flipped onto the second side. Quickly lift up the cloth and watch for swelling up. If none occurs, try pressing and twisting again. If irregular swells appear, press again on the flat sections. I prefer to puff the bread using the improvised cake-rack system described on p. 117: as soon as the second side cooks dry and changes color (about 30 to 45 seconds), transfer it to the rack without flipping and hold over the burner. This action typically causes the bread to balloon quite spectacularly, to your delight and that of all spectators. In any event, any breads that do not puff will still taste perfectly all right, though I find that they lack limberness.

Stack the finished tortillas on a plate and cover immediately with a second plate or a large pot lid—this additional steaming helps to soften them up so that they can be rolled into *burritos*—the main object of homemade wheat tortillas. It is a good idea to do this even when you are baking only 1 or 2 breads. If the stacked tortillas grow cold and stiff waiting to be used, reheat by wrapping in foil and placing in a 275° oven for a few minutes. Tortillas can be refrigerated or frozen for later use, but they will never again taste absolutely fresh. Always reheat old tortillas since cold ones crack if you try to bend them.

The procedure just outlined produces a good, pliant tortilla suitable for eating with beans and chili, and just the right thickness for rolling into *burritos*. However, if you are planning on restaurant-style *burritos*, smothered in sauce and oven-baked, packaged store-bought tortillas will serve the purpose. The usual way to serve flour tortillas is to place one beside each guest, who rips it into pieces as he sees fit, one part scooping up beans, another dipped in sauce or swirled around the plate. Flour tortillas are not traditionally spread with butter, but they are quite good that way. Try lightly buttering the whole surface of the tortilla, roll it up, wrap in foil and heat. The buttery puff of steam that emerges when each diner unwraps his package is delightful.

For thicker and thinner tortillas: For a dough made with 1 cup of flour the thickness of the tortillas is up to you. Thick ones are good as sops for chili sauces and are easier for beginners to roll out and bake. Stop when your circle is rolled to 6 inches in diameter. Bake on a slow griddle for a few seconds more than a minute per side to insure that the inside of the tortilla will not be raw. The signs of a fully baked tortilla are still the same—light brown speckles appearing on the first side at the end of its cooking time, less pretty brown patches on the second side.

Once you are supremely confident, the size and thinness of your tortillas is limited only by the width of your grill. Thin is beautiful in the world of tortillas, and the very best ones are like warm silk to the touch—never stiff. An impressive size that still fits the *comal* is 9 inches. Roll the dough out quickly, making extra sure that you flip it adroitly and keep the board floured. Thin tortillas nick easily at every stage, but a 9-inch one is fairly easy to master. It bakes for only 30 seconds a side, which means you must have the flame rather high in order for the speckles to appear. Bubbles will show up almost immediately, and sometimes the entire bread will puff into a balloon. Press it back down if it does, using the back of your wide spatula—this will help the bottom surface to brown.

Very large tortillas, a foot or more in diameter, become ultra-delicate, easy to tear or wrinkle or pull out of shape. They also cook in a flash over medium-high heat. I encourage you to try them, however, for they are a true novelty of Sonoran cooking and the perfect accompaniment to a simple bowl of red chili and meat.

Using up leftover dough: The dough for flour tortillas keeps perfectly well for a day in the refrigerator and much longer frozen. Shape it into balls just as you would before rolling it out, place in a plastic bag and store until needed. The dishes you can make with the leftover dough the next day are better than plain tortillas, for they take you into the realm of stuffed breads (*quesadillas*) and fritters (*empanadas*), which have always been an endless inspiration to Mexican cooks. In Mexico these are usually wrapped with corn-tortilla dough, but the custom in the Southwest is very often to use wheat flour. For stuffed flour tortillas, see the recipe on p. 237, and for a type of stuffed and fried *quesadilla*, see the recipe on p. 235. Both are delicious and valuable extensions of your skill with flour-tortilla dough, and neither is any harder to make than the basic bread itself. Flour-tortilla dough also puffs up into quite good *sopaipillas*—see the recipe on p. 127.

Using up leftover tortillas: Unlike the uncooked dough, extra baked tortillas are not inspiring, but very often you are left with too many, particularly if the package from the store contained a dozen. Here are some of the best uses for them; all are simple improvisations you can alter to suit yourself or to help clean out a refrigerator where scraps of chili, cheese, *chorizo* or *salsa* are pining:

Burritos: If the tortillas are only a day or two old, they can be reheated and rolled up for *burritos*—older ones will crack apart or may taste too stale. Have at hand the fillings you want to put inside your *burrito*. Refried beans are the most common choice; simply garnish with dollops of green chili *salsa* or any other uncooked relish. Almost anything else does quite as well, however: leftover meat or chicken, which you can moisten with a bit of chili sauce; leftover *carne adovada* or chili con carne; spiced rice with black beans; and *guacamole*. With the exception of *guacamole*, the potential filling should be gently heated in a saucepan while you wrap your tortillas in foil and heat them for a few minutes in a 350° oven. The fresher the tortilla, the hotter you can heat it up again; old ones dry out very quickly, even in foil.

When both components are thoroughly warmed, you are ready for your improvisation. The tortilla is laid flat on a plate, dabs of filling are situated roughly across the middle, extending below the center of the circle rather than above so that you will have room for folding. You then fold the *burrito* in the classic fashion: turn in the right and left sides of the circle to overlap the filling slightly, and next bring up the bottom; then roll up, making a cylinder closed at both ends. (See illus. p. 232.)

This is the point at which old tortillas crack and spill out the filling, but that is not a disaster—*burritos* are eaten catch as catch can anyway, nibbled like a hot dog. The expert *burrito* eater curls his little finger under the bottom to hold it closed and with the other hand lightly spoons *salsa* into the other end after each bite.

These *burritos* are a true specialty of Arizona and of Sonora in northern Mexico. Consumed fresh with large, paper-thin flour tortillas as the wrapping, they are too delicious to equate with the stodgy, unpalatable convenience foods all too often sold as *burritos*.

Tostadas from flour tortillas: Everything that applies to the garnished *tostadas* on p. 230 also applies when you substitute wheat tortillas for corn. But the results of a fried flour tortilla are, in truth, not nearly so good as with corn. Flour *tostadas* have a tendency to turn tough, and they never give off the wonderful aroma which is half the appeal of a simple *tostada*. Of course if the *tostada* is only an excuse for piling up refried beans, hamburger, onion, *guacamole*, olives, cheese, tomato and shredded Iceberg lettuce—what cookbooks call "party" *tostadas*—it hardly matters what is supporting the structure down below. I have seen fried *tostadas* based on flour tortillas that were garnished and labeled as *chalupas*, but that is going a bit far, since a proper *chalupa* is boat-shaped, with a raised rim and invariably made from corn. To make a *tostada* from a leftover flour tortilla, a fairly small one is fried whole in about ¼ inch of oil until browned on both sides—altogether for about a minute or less.

Southwestern quesadillas: In the hands of Mexican cooks, the *quesadilla* is a whimsy, a little fat corn-tortilla package stuffed with anything that comes to mind and then fried to make it all the more savory. In the Southwest, though, it is almost always just a cooked flour tortilla which has been folded in a half-circle over a thin stuffing of shredded cheese and canned green chili strips. These fairly large half-moons are baked in a 350° oven or on a skillet or griddle on top of the stove until the cheese melts, but not so long that the outside completely dries out and stiffens. The finished product is cut into pie-shaped wedges and served hot. Even eaten with the best *salsa* and the best will in the world, such a *quesadilla* is no more than passable, but it does use up leftover flour tortillas.

PUEBLO INDIAN TORTILLAS

Flour tortillas are made fresh for every meal by Indian cooks, three times a day. They are thicker than the ordinary variety, mixed with less shortening and eaten as a sop bread rather than a rollable pancake. An accomplished Indian cook knows her dough so well that she never resorts to measuring spoons and cups. Here is a version only slightly adapted from an account given in the 1950s by a New England woman who came to live in a New Mexico pueblo.

The combination of whole-wheat and white flour is very common in Indian baking. The usual cooking implement is the fixed griddle on top of the stove. If your stove is not so equipped, a heavy skillet will work as well.

These thicker tortillas are not prone to puff and bubble as much as the thin ones, but they are equally good.

For 4 to 6 tortillas:

> 1 cup whole-wheat flour
> 1 cup unbleached white flour
> ¾ teaspoon salt
> 2 teaspoons baking powder
> 1 tablespoon lard or vegetable shortening (leftover bacon grease
>   is also used, in which case the salt is reduced or
>   omitted altogether)
> ½ cup water

Every step in making these tortillas is the same as given in the flour-tortilla recipe on p. 119. The only modification is rolling the dough thicker and baking it longer over low heat in order to thoroughly cook the inside of the bread.

The very thickest tortillas are made by dividing the dough into 4 pieces and rolling each into an 8-inch circle. The result is more than twice as thick and heavy as a normal flour tortilla, so it must be cooked about 1 minute on each side (the normal time), and then turned again and cooked for at least 30 seconds more on the first side. Often that is enough, but it does not hurt to keep flipping the bread for additional baking. The internal moisture will keep even an overcooked tortilla soft, once you cover it on a plate to stay warm. Thick tortillas of this sort are very much like griddle cakes.

A thinner bread, but still twice as thick as the normal one, is made by dividing the dough into 6 pieces and rolling each circle to 8 inches in diameter. Keep the heat a little lower than for regular thin tortillas and cook for a generous minute on each side. Additional flipping once again will not hurt the bread.

For an authentic Pueblo meal based upon this bread, along with pinto beans and mashed green chilies, see p. 19, which describes the pleasures of cooking and eating simply.

SOPAIPILLAS

In most instances New Mexico's cuisine is a stepchild of Mexico's, but that is not true for these delightful little puffed breads, which the state claims as its own. They have now spread throughout the Mexican restaurants of the Southwest, where they are triangular, as a rule, and about 5 or 6 inches across. The usual home recipe tells you to make them smaller, about 3 inches across, triangular or oblong as you wish.

The only real question is the use to which you will put your "sofa pillows." Large ones can be cut open and filled with beans or meat like a pocket bread. Small ones can be used to sop up chili sauce. The common use, however, is to break open the *sopaipilla* and spread it inside with butter and a drizzle of honey and serve it as dessert or even as a side bread—the sweetness is surprisingly compatible with red chili and cheese.

For variety's sake, dessert *sopaipillas* also can be rolled in cinnamon sugar while they are still warm (see p. 334) or served with whipped cream that has been sweetened with honey and lightly spiced with cinnamon. Both ways are good.

The dough given below makes tender, flaky pillows, but the larger ones tend to collapse quickly as they cool. If you want the bread to stay puffed, knead the dough for a minute longer, but you will be compromising tenderness somewhat.

For at least 8 small or 4 large sopaipillas:

> 1 **cup plus 2 tablespoons unbleached white flour**
> 1 **teaspoon baking powder**
> ¼ **teaspoon salt**
> 2 **tablespoons lard or vegetable shortening**
> ¼ **cup plus 2 tablespoons water**
> **Oil for deep-frying**

Making the dough: If you already know how to make biscuits, then proceed as you normally do, for *sopaipillas* are made from the same sort of soft, lightly handled dough. Combine the flour, baking powder and salt in a mixing bowl. Using two knives, a pastry cutter or your fingertips, cut the lard or other shortening into the dry ingredients until a flaky meal is formed. Pour in the liquid all at once and mix the dough quickly with a fork. It will form a uniform mass that is soft, moist and a little sticky. Heavily flour a bread board and turn the dough out onto it. Knead the dough gently by folding it in half, patting it down and folding again. After no more than 10 to 12 foldings, the dough should still be very soft, but no longer sticky.

Cover the dough with plastic wrap and let it rest for 15 minutes.

Divide the dough in half and place one part in a plastic bag while you roll out the other.

Rolling the dough: With the portion of dough in front of you, it is possible to make breads in the following shapes:

2 squares measuring 5 x 5 inches

4 oblongs measuring 5 x 2½ inches

4 triangles with about a 6-inch diagonal.

Large, dramatic square puffs are nice for *sopaipillas* and no harder than the commoner triangles and oblongs. Whatever form you choose, roll out the dough with gentle strokes of a rolling pin, keeping the board well floured. Keep rolling until you have a rectangle measuring about 10 x 5 inches, or somewhat smaller if you prefer *sopaipillas* that are still slightly doughy inside after frying. In either case, using a ruler as a guide, trim the dough into a neat rectangle, then divide it into 2 squares measuring 5 x 5 inches. From this basic division you can proceed directly to frying, or you can cut the squares in half again. Cutting across them produces oblong *sopaipillas*; cutting on the diagonal produces triangles. (For quite small dessert versions, see p. 131.) If you are rolling and cutting a large number of *sopaipillas*, loosely cover the finished shapes to keep them

SOPAIPILLAS

 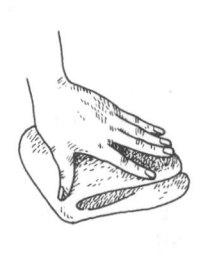

1. Cut fat into dough and mix quickly as for making biscuits.

2. Lightly knead dough by folding into a square and patting down. Repeat several times.

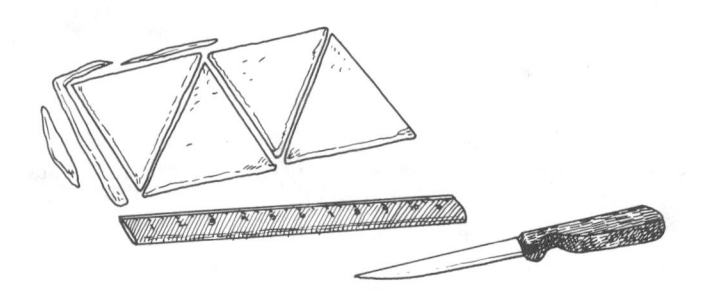

3. Precisely measure and cut rolled-out dough.

4. Use brisk, light patting motions of spatula to help sopaipilla inflate in hot oil.

moist, but do not stack them unless they are very well floured, or they will stick together.

Scraps of dough left over from cutting out shapes can also be fried and puffed just as they are; do not try to knead them into one ball of dough again since, like biscuits, they roll out well only the first time.

Puffing the bread: If you have an electric skillet or deep-fat fryer, heat it to 400°. If, like me, you do not possess this appliance, use a high-sided 10-inch skillet or frying kettle and proceed by educated guesswork (it helps to have a few extra squares around for testing purposes). As you are heating your 1 to 2 inches of oil, drop a scrap of dough into it. The oil is ready when it is hot enough to cause a scrap to bubble hard and puff up as soon as it hits the oil.

When the oil is hot enough, fry the first square of dough. The procedure must be one smooth motion, for the *sopaipilla* will either puff immediately or not at all. Drop the square into the oil and gently paddle it under the surface with a pancake turner or the back of a large slotted spoon. The oil will bubble up hard, and you will feel the *sopaipilla* straining to come to the surface, like a balloon being held underwater. As it begins to puff up all over, release the *sopaipilla* and let it brown on one side—a matter of 10 or 20 seconds—then turn it over to brown on the other.

The initial puffing is really the only precarious step. A failed *sopaipilla* raises a large blister in the center, or several medium blisters, but the corners are left unpuffed. Oil that is too hot or too cold may be the reason, but even a novice can expect 50 percent success. Too-thick *sopaipillas*, by the way, are often not good at puffing, and they can remain bready inside, even though once puffed they will have thin walls and look completely hollow.

Remove the browned squares or triangles and drain on several layers of paper toweling. *Sopaipillas* are served hot. You can keep them warm in a 200° oven while you are frying, or they can be reheated in a 350° oven if you make them ahead. The breads store surprisingly well, so there is no need to make them at the last moment. They even refrigerate respectably, so long as they are thoroughly cooled first.

Stuffed sopaipillas: These are basically stand-ins for *chimichangas*, but they have the virtue of being lighter and easier to handle. Stuff the finished breads with any meat or bean filling you would use for *quesadillas* or *empanadas* (see the list on p. 107). Chili con carne is the most common stuffing, but that is only because in Tex-Mex cooking it is used for practically everything anyway. Cut the *sopaipilla* in half crossways, spoon the filling into the bottom, re-cover with the top half, sprinkle with shredded Jack cheese, and warm in a preheated 350° oven for 5 minutes. Serve with a chili sauce or *guacamole* spooned over; an uncooked green chili *salsa* or even a bottled *salsa picante* is also good. For once, the sourness of the bottled sauce is just right for cutting through the fried taste of the bread. Be sure the *salsa* is at room temperature before using it. The stuffed *sopaipillas* can also be garnished with the familiar array of chopped tomato, shredded romaine lettuce, Jack cheese, olives, sour cream and/or avocado. Do not pour on any sauce until the last minute before eating or the crispness of the dish will be destroyed.

For smaller sopaipillas: If you want the traditional morsels of puffed bread, divide the dough into 3 portions instead of 2, roll each into a 4 x 8 or 6 x 6 inch shape, and go on to cut into small squares, about 2 or 3 inches to a side. These can be fried 3 or 4 at a time in a skillet, depending on its size, but make sure that the oil temperature is not lowered as more squares are added.

Sopaipillas from a mix: If your dough doesn't puff to suit you, resort to Bisquick, which produces balloons that are spectacular, if a bit too salty. The dough seems to work best when a little drier than the package directions recommend for regular biscuits. Begin with about ¼ cup water (no milk) to 1¼ cups Bisquick. Restaurants frequently use such a mix; another of their tricks is to roll out refrigerator biscuit dough (the sort sold in cardboard tubes) and cut it into the desired shapes.

ADOBE BREAD

Adobe ovens, or *hornos*, were adapted by the Pueblos from Spanish designs and made their own. Every village has a baker who turns out traditional round and "bear-paw" loaves from the *horno*, and it is a tribute to the Indians' respect for bread that they cling to so many other kinds— flat tortillas (both wheat and corn), raised loaves, paper and fried breads, and sweet pumpkin bread, to name just some.

Occasionally one sees beehive *hornos* outside the pueblos in the mountain villages, but for all intents and purposes the slow-raised loaves for which the oven is required are beyond our reach. Besides being hand-shaped from native clay, such *hornos* cook in a fashion different from our modern ovens. Wood is burned on the floor of the *horno* until reduced to embers. The baker sweeps these out when he is ready to bake, his raised loaves are slipped right onto the floor in their place, and the door is shut on them for more than an hour. Thus they cook by slowly decreasing heat —and once done, the bread's place is taken by whole pumpkins, corn or other foods that do not need high heat, only prolonged baking.

I have researched recipes for Pueblo bread and tested enough of them to know that the secret of *horno* bread must not lie in the ingredients or the preparation—all of the versions were either unexceptional or else completely unworkable. What I have to offer instead is not true *horno* bread, but a crusty yeast loaf I call "adobe bread" because it is baked in clay. The combination of white and whole-wheat flours is reminiscent of Indian bread, to be sure, and the dense, moist texture of the loaf matches the rustic strength of the food it goes with. Consider adobe bread as a possibility for any menu, such as one with *posole* or green chili stew in it, where you would otherwise automatically serve wheat-flour tortillas.

For 1 medium loaf:

> 2 teaspoons active dry yeast
> 1 teaspoon sugar
> 1 cup warm water (no hotter than 110°F.)
> 1 cup whole-wheat flour
> 1½ cups unbleached white flour (preferably labeled "bread flour," otherwise "all-purpose")
> 1 teaspoon salt
> For salt-water glaze: 1 teaspoon salt dissolved in 2 tablespoons hot water

This is one of the quickest yeast breads you can make, since it is mixed in a food processor, raised only once before baking, and then both raised and baked in an oven that starts off cold. This is not the Indian way, to say the least, but the quickness of the method makes it possible for home cooks who are not dedicated to baking to produce an honest loaf.

Combine the yeast, sugar and warm water in the bowl of the food processor and let proof for 10 minutes—the mixture should foam and begin to smell strongly of yeast. Add both flours and the teaspoon of salt, and process for 2 minutes. The dough will gather into a ball and clump around the inside of the machine a little alarmingly, but most processors have strong enough motors to handle this amount of dough. The dough will also feel warm and sticky to the touch. If it seems definitely too soft to hold its shape well, add another ¼ to ½ cup of white flour, but be sparing— the dough is meant to be soft.

Transfer the bread to a lightly oiled mixing bowl, roll it around so that the top of the dough is greased, then cover the bowl tightly with plastic wrap to exclude drafts, followed by a folded kitchen towel to exclude light. Let sit in a warm place (75° to 85° F.) until doubled in bulk, about 1½ hours. By that time the dough will seem spongy to the touch and two fingers pressed into the top will leave a dimple that doesn't spring back. (The bread can also be raised in a colder room, but the timing is often much longer.)

Remove the dough from the bowl, pat it flat without kneading it, and shape into a rectangle which is just long enough to fit your baking pan.

Roll the dough up from one side into a French loaf and place it, seam side down, inside the pan.

NOTE: Here you have a choice that considerably affects the nature of your bread. If you want a real adobe loaf with a thick, chewable crust, choose an unglazed terra-cotta baking pan. Some models are in the shape of ordinary loaf pans, others fit the long French baguette shape. There is even a *cloche*, or bell-shaped device that fits over a deep, circular pizza pan; if you use that, you will need to double this recipe, for a single portion is too skimpy to fit into the device in the right way. Follow *cloche* directions for forming and baking a large round bread. Assuming that you are using a pottery pan, you also can soak it in water for 15 minutes to achieve a crustier loaf if you wish, but either way the pan needs to be lightly oiled to prevent sticking.

The dough can also be baked in an ordinary metal or glass pan. Perhaps the best alternative to terra-cotta is a dark metal baking sheet. It does not need to be oiled, merely sprinkled with cornmeal. Try the proportions of flour to water given in this recipe, but if your first free-standing loaf baked on a sheet spreads too much, producing a flat loaf, increase the white flour to 2 cups the next time out.

Once the dough is put in the pan, cut a slit down the entire length of its surface, using the sharpest small knife you have, then brush thoroughly with the salt-water glaze. Place in a turned-off oven with the rack in the upper third, turn the heat to 400° F. and bake for 40 minutes. The loaf will not rise dramatically as it cooks, but the finished product will thump hollow on its bottom when it is done, like any yeast bread. Certain ovens fail to brown the top quite enough, so you might want to finish the job by running the bread under the broiler for a last minute or two.

Adobe bread has a dense, heavy texture and a chewy, salty crust, but only a bit of keeping power. You will have to reheat the bread the second day in a hot oven if you want to recapture its original crust. It is so appealing, however, that leftovers are fairly hypothetical. Good as it is when hot from the stove, this bread does not slice well until it is thoroughly cold. Anyway, I prefer to tear pieces off at the table rather than attempt to slice it.

SOFT CORNBREAD WITH CHEESE AND GREEN CHILI

Green chili can be eaten at any meal, including breakfast, as witness this variant of Southern spoonbread. The texture is really more like firm pudding than bread, and its savor is lost if it is not eaten right away. It is delicious served simply buttered in the morning with eggs, or it can be garnished with slices of fresh avocado, dabs of *salsa*, and a sprinkle of chopped green coriander (*cilantro*). You might save such a dressed-up presentation for lunch or Sunday brunch. As a side dish at dinner, serve buttered or with *salsa* only in place of a starchy vegetable.

To serve 4 people:

    ½ cup cornmeal
    ⅓ cup milk
    ½ teaspoon baking powder
    ½ teaspoon salt
     1 large egg
     3 tablespoons melted butter
    Pepper to taste
     1 cup canned cream-style corn
    ¼ to ½ cup canned, chopped green chilies
     1 cup shredded Monterey Jack cheese (about 4 ounces)

Preheat the oven to 400° F. and generously butter a 1-quart casserole, deep and tall-sided, like a soufflé dish, rather than shallow. Combine the first 7 ingredients in the bowl of a food processor and blend into a smooth batter, about 5 seconds, stopping once to scrape down the bowl with a rubber spatula. Add the corn and blend only a second or two more to incorporate it.

Spread half the batter in the buttered casserole, dot with half the chilies and sprinkle on half the cheese. Repeat with remaining ingredients. Bake in the 400° F. oven for 25 minutes. The bread should brown around the edges and set in the middle, but its consistency should remain pudding-like, not dried out. Cut into wedges and serve directly from the pan.

This recipe can easily be doubled and still be made in a standard-size processor. Bake in a 2-quart casserole and increase cooking time to 35–45 minutes.

Blue, White and Yellow Cornbread

Baking-powder cornbread is settlers' food, as opposed to tortillas, but there are versions adopted by the Indians which make it hard to distinguish between pioneer hoecakes and the loaves of Pueblo bakers. Some recipes for New Mexican cornbread are really spoonbread with chili and cheese in them. (One version appears on p. 133.) As for the cornbread recipes that migrated into the state along the Santa Fe Trail, there is no agreement about whether the bread should be salted or sweet, flavored with butter, lard or bacon drippings, moistened with sweet or sour milk.

There is not even a consensus about the color of the meal you should use, but New Mexico has the distinction at least of broadening the argument, for the *harina de maíz azul* or blue cornmeal (also sold in packages as *atole*) is native here. It produces a batter that looks almost identical to dark house plaster, the "blue" of the name being a poetic view of the meal's actual gray color. Once baked, the bread is at first hard to accept as food, but the taste is as good as any cornbread from the Delta. As for the yellow version that follows, it is made from a thin hot-water batter that eventually bakes into a moist, close-grained bread.

Neither of these recipes calls for sugar in the batter, since the Mississippi and South Carolina cornbread of my family had none—sweetened cornbread being a Yankee style—but you can add it to suit your own taste; 2 to 4 tablespoons is recommended for the recipes here.

To complete the color range, see the recipe for corn muffins on p. 210, which uses white cornmeal. White cornmeal also works in these two recipes, of course.

NEW MEXICO BLUE CORNBREAD

For one 8-inch round bread, serving 6 to 8 people:

- ½ cup unsalted butter or margarine, melted
- 1 cup blue cornmeal
- ⅓ cup whole-wheat flour
- ⅔ cup unbleached white flour
- 2 teaspoons baking powder
- ½ teaspoon baking soda
- 1 large egg
- 1 teaspoon salt
- 1⅓ cups buttermilk

Preheat the oven to 425° F. and grease an 8-inch round cake pan by melting the butter in it in the oven. (For a thinner bread with a definite rind, heat a 9-inch iron skillet in the oven and bake the bread in that.) Combine the butter and all the other ingredients except the buttermilk in the bowl of the food processor and blend for 3 seconds or so. Scrape down the bowl with a rubber spatula, pour in the buttermilk, and process for 5 seconds more, stopping once again to scrape down the bowl.

Pour into the prepared pan and bake in the upper third of the oven for 30 to 35 minutes. The dough will rise with a slight hump in the middle and perhaps some cracks. It is done when it is slightly browned and drawing away from the edges of the pan. If, however, the center of the bread sinks soon after you remove it from the oven, it is not baked through—return to oven for a few minutes more. Cornbread is always fragile to cut, so it is best to let it cool for 5 minutes and then serve it in wedges from the pan. This particular bread is rich enough not to need additional butter at the table, although that is customary.

YELLOW CORNBREAD

½ cup melted butter or margarine
2 cups yellow cornmeal
1 teaspoon salt
1 cup boiling water
½ cup milk
2 large eggs
1 teaspoon baking powder

Preheat the oven to 425° F. Melt the butter in an 8-inch round cake pan in the oven. Place the cornmeal, salt and melted butter in the bowl of the food processor and blend for a few seconds. Pour in the boiling water and blend again to make a smooth batter, a matter of another few seconds. Turn off the motor, scrape the bowl with a rubber spatula, then pour in the remaining ingredients and blend for about 5 seconds—the final batter will be quite thin compared to the usual cornbread recipes.

Pour into the prepared cake pan and bake at 425° F. in the upper third of the oven for 30 minutes. The bread is done when the center is firm and the edges draw away from the sides of the pan. To give the cornbread a nice brown top crust, run it under a broiler flame for half a minute after it completes baking. Let cool for 5 minutes before cutting into wedges and serving from the pan, generously buttered. (This bread can also be baked ranch style in a heavy iron skillet preheated in the oven.)

VARIATIONS:

Varying the Color of the Breads: Blue, white and yellow cornmeal can be used interchangeably in the two recipes above. If you like the moistness and close grain of the second version, for example, feel free to turn it blue or white.

Green Chili Cornbread: Add a 4-ounce can of chopped green chilies to either version. Use an extra 2 teaspoons of fresh or canned, chopped *jalapeño* if spicier bread appeals to you. Although formulas for "Southwestern" breads often call for this chili flavoring, I prefer to leave it out to distinguish the bread from everything else on the table.

INDIAN PAPER BREAD
Piki

The Pueblos have the distinction of making what must be the thinnest bread in the world—*piki*. It does rather an injustice to it to call *piki* simply "paper bread," for its layers are at least as thin as tissue paper and often look like they are composed of more air than bread. In the traditional recipe, a thin batter is made from blue cornmeal and water that has been soaked with juniper ashes. The cook sits before a flat stone that has been heated in a fire, armed with no other implement than one whole sheep's brain. This she uses to grease the stone, after which she spreads a thin layer of *piki* batter across the entire surface with a deft sweep of her hand. When the papery sheet of corn batter crinkles and dries, it is lifted off. Three stacked sheets rolled together into a scroll make one *piki*.

As it turns out, *piki* is easy to duplicate at home if you have any size skillet coated with a nonstick surface like Silverstone or Teflon II (a 7- to 8-inch pan is ideal). The batter is brushed onto the pan bottom with a bristle brush (nylon might melt) and lifted off in layers as thin as gossamer. Surprisingly, the procedure is not delicate at all, because however fragile the *piki* looks, it is strongly bound by the gluten in the cornstarch. If you can pour crêpe batter and are adventurous enough to experiment with homemade tortillas and *sopaipillas*, you will have no trouble with *piki*.

For 8 scrolls of bread, serving 4 people:

    5 tablespoons Masa Harina
    2 tablespoons cornstarch
    ⅛ teaspoon salt
    1 cup hot water

Mix the dry ingredients in a bowl, pour in the hot water all at once, and whisk the batter for a few seconds until it is smooth. Arm yourself with a 1-inch bristle brush, preferably a good-quality pastry brush or, failing that, a paintbrush. Heat a nonstick skillet over low heat until it is warm, but do not grease it. The size does not much matter, since small *pikis* and large ones are equally easy to lift once they dry thoroughly. The pan

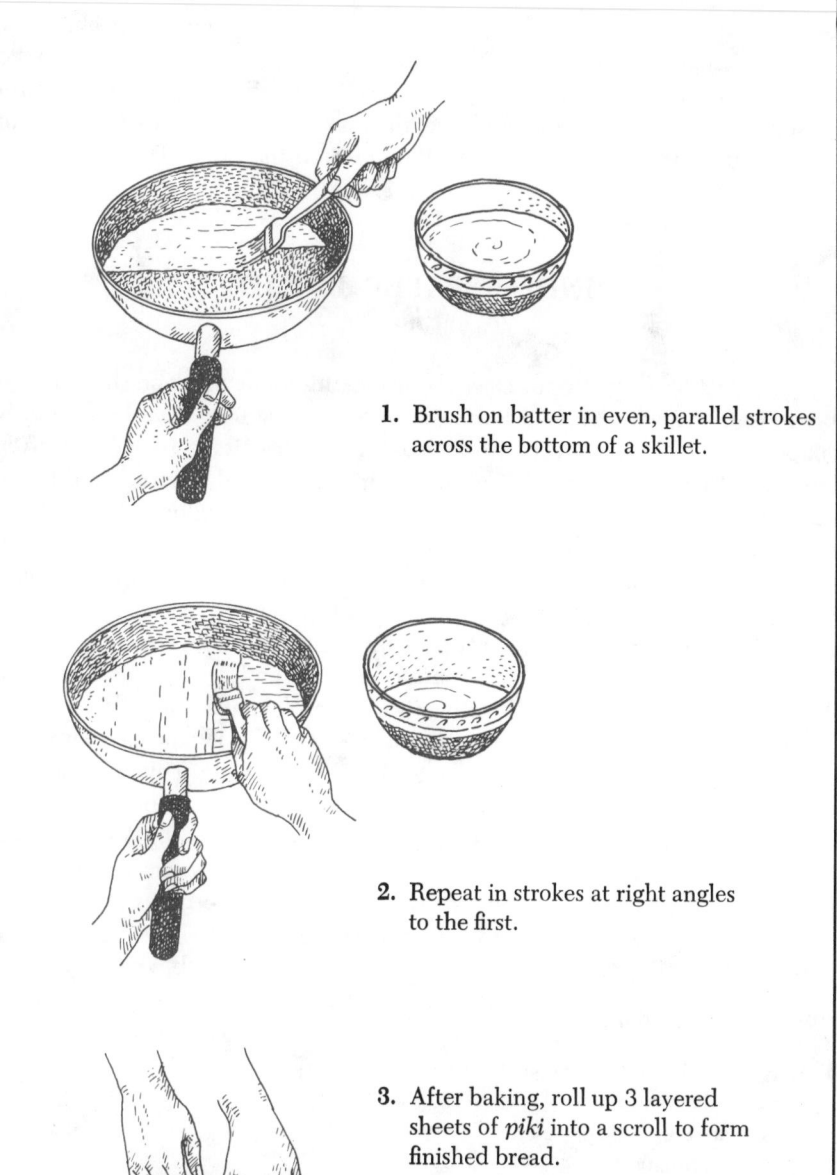

1. Brush on batter in even, parallel strokes across the bottom of a skillet.

2. Repeat in strokes at right angles to the first.

3. After baking, roll up 3 layered sheets of *piki* into a scroll to form finished bread.

should not be made so hot that the batter sizzles when you try to brush it on, for the action of the nonstick material will then cause it to bead up. What you want is a layer of batter spread onto the pan like a layer of paint.

Take the skillet up in one hand and brush on a layer of batter, using broad strokes all in one direction. Immediately apply a second layer over this at right angles to it—in other words, you are painting in a crosshatch. Do not worry about holes in the surface, since even a coating almost imperceptible to the eye will cook into bread. Return the skillet to the heat and cook for about a minute. The batter has to sizzle and evaporate all its moisture before it is done. As soon as the hissing stops and the surface of the bread looks dry and crinkly, peel it off with your fingers by starting up one edge with a table knife, then grasping it by hand and pulling up gently. The layer will peel away quite easily. Lay it on paper toweling or a baking rack to dry completely and proceed to make 3 more *pikis* to lay on top. Do not place the *piki* on a plate once baked, since further steaming causes them to become too sticky—a few moments on paper towels completes their drying out.

Once you have 4 layers, roll them loosely into a scroll and set aside. Cook the breads in this fashion until you have made 2 per person. Serve slightly rewarmed or at room temperature with a good *salsa* and your main-course dish, preferably a Pueblo stew.

NOTES: One small problem about baking the *piki* is that a skillet hot enough to dry out the dough is too hot to brush with more batter right away. It helps to have two pans on hand, one to cool while the other bakes. An ordinary, inexpensive 8-inch aluminum skillet works very well, since it is thin enough to lose heat rapidly. Also, the *piki* dough tends to become gummy on the brush, which needs washing once that becomes a nuisance. Finally, if the batter in the bowl looks too thick at any point, you can dilute it with water or simply make up a new batch.

VARIATION:

Piki in Blue, Yellow and Pink: In ceremonial and festive use, the Indians often color this bread, using blue cornmeal for the blue (actually a gray), ground coxcomb for the pink and safflower for yellow. If you want to duplicate these gay *piki*—who else for a thousand miles around is giving a dinner party with pink *piki*?—the changes to the basic batter are simple. For blue *piki*, make a batter from 3 tablespoons blue cornmeal, 2 tablespoons Masa Harina and 3 tablespoons cornstarch, plus the salt and water in the basic recipe. For pink and yellow breads, simply add a few drops of food coloring to the basic batter as you whisk it up.

SWEET SAFFRON ROLLS
Molletes

In old Santa Fe, the time for chocolate was traditionally four o'clock in the afternoon, the very time when the British and near-British want their tea. Along with the beverage had to come some sweet rolls, or *molletes*. In the mountain villages where such an amenity was a luxury, sweet rolls were a sign of a feast day. The baker's bread dough would have sugar, eggs, a little more lard and a sprinkling of anise added to it for such a treat. Another alternative to anise, the one given here, was to color and flavor the dough with saffron. Lacking the true autumn crocus from which Spanish saffron is derived, the New Mexicans found their own wild safflower and called it saffron. The real thing is asked for here, in a small quantity to avoid the bitterness that comes from an overdose, and the lard is replaced with butter to make a lovely, refined sweet roll.

Serve these neat little rounds at teatime or at breakfast, and be sure to refer to the recipes for *buñuelos*, or bread fritters (see p. 333), which become doubly delicious prepared from this saffron-egg dough.

For 16 rolls:

> ½ cup warm water
> 1 tablespoon sugar
> 1 package active dry yeast
> ½ cup butter
> Scant ⅛ teaspoon saffron threads or powder
> 3 eggs
> 3 cups unbleached white flour, plus another ½ cup if needed for stiffening the dough
> ½ teaspoon salt
> ½ cup sugar
> For glazing: 1 egg yolk blended with 1 teaspoon water

Mix the warm water with the 1 tablespoon of sugar in a cup and sprinkle the yeast over it. Set aside to allow the yeast to proof, about 10 minutes, or until the mixture is bubbly and smells strongly of yeastiness. Melt the butter in a small skillet, let it foam up and drop in the saffron (first crushing it between the palms of your hands if it is in thread form). Take the skillet off the heat and swirl it around, allowing the saffron to turn it a strong orange-yellow color; there will also be a pronounced smell of saffron. Let the butter cool to warm, then beat it into the eggs in a mixing bowl until well incorporated.

Combine flour, salt and sugar in a large mixing bowl with a wooden spoon, then pour in the yeast and egg-saffron mixtures. Begin to stir vigorously until the dough forms a mass and becomes difficult to work. Turn it out onto a heavily floured board and knead vigorously by hand for 5 minutes. Dip your hands frequently in flour to keep them from sticking to the dough. This is meant to be a soft dough, but if it becomes too sticky, start to work in the extra ½ cup of flour by dusting the board with it as you knead. The dough will continue to feel fairly oily to the touch, but it is ready when it has become elastic enough that a dimple poked in it with your finger immediately begins to spring back. If kneading such an oily dough is difficult for you, you can dissolve the saffron in only 1 tablespoon of melted butter, then incorporate the rest (as softened butter) only at the end of the first rising of the dough. Some cooks would also consider that this leads to a more refined end product.

Place the dough in a bowl, cover with foil and then a dish towel over that. Set aside to rise slowly at a fairly low room temperature (65° to 70° F.), allowing a couple of hours for the dough to double in bulk. Even better is to make the dough ahead and let it rise overnight in the refrigerator, in which case you need to cover the bowl with a plate and set at least 2 pounds of canned goods or other weight on top to prevent the dough from overflowing.

When the dough has doubled in bulk, a dimple poked in it will not spring back. Punch the dough down with your fist and allow to rise again. (This is the point at which you can knead in the softened butter, as mentioned above.) The second rising will go faster than the first (unless your dough has been refrigerated) and gives a more delicate bread than if raised only once. However, if you lack time, you can proceed directly with shaping the rolls.

When the dough has doubled in bulk again, preheat the oven to 375° F.

Punch the dough down, turn it out onto a board and knead lightly for a few seconds. Divide into quarters, then each quarter into quarters again. Shape the 16 pieces of dough into balls between your hands and place close together on an ungreased baking sheet. Cover lightly with a dish towel and allow to rise for 30 minutes in a place that is between 65° and 80° F. and free of drafts.

Brush carefully with the egg glaze, making sure that it does not run down the sides and stick to the baking sheet, which would inhibit uniform rising in the oven.

Bake for 12 to 15 minutes, checking after 10 minutes to make sure that the rolls are not browning too much on the bottom (as the saffron and sugar incline to do). If you see signs of overbrowning, slip another baking sheet under the first and lower heat to 325° F. The rolls are done when they sound hollow on the bottom as you tap them—but it is easier to check by tearing one open; its interior should be moist but not at all raw. Serve warm with sweet butter.

Anise-Flavored Rolls: Omit the saffron and add 1 teaspoon powdered aniseed (or Chinese star anise) to the butter—which need not be melted, only softened to the point that it is like stiffly beaten cream. The same flavor can be achieved with ¼ teaspoon anise extract, albeit the old cooks had no such convenience. If you have to powder the anise yourself, the best tool is an electric coffee grinder. If all you have is an electric blender, mix the anise with the ½ cup sugar so that your machine will have enough bulk to work with.

INDIAN FRY-BREAD

Some sort of fry-bread is common among many of the tribes in the Southwest, but a traveler is most likely to meet up with it, as I first did, on Jeep tours through the Navajo reservation—in fact, on the rare occasions when it appears on a restaurant menu it is usually listed as "Navajo fry-bread." Cooked out of doors by shepherd families, where it is hand-patted and fried in Dutch ovens over a juniper fire, the bread is in its true element. It emerges knobby, puffed and heavy in texture, needing nothing more than a bowl of green chili stew to make an outdoorsman's meal.

Transplanted to the kitchen, fry-bread's defects quickly show up. It is oily and too heavy and completely lacks keeping power. The *sopaipilla*, its civilized cousin, is better suited for most purposes. Still, there regularly comes an interlude when you are alone or in the company of good friends to whom a warm kitchen, the smell of frying, and a pot of New Mexican stew are hospitality enough, in which case you have discovered the second-best setting for Indian fry-bread.

The quantity below, which produces 4 servings, is quite enough to manage. Do not plan to have other duties to attend to at serving time and do not invite more friends—the mixing, shaping and cooking of this bread need all the cook's attention. You will mix a soft dough, proceed immediately to shaping it into rounds between your hands and then fry it as soon as it is shaped.

For 4 individual breads:

> 1 cup unbleached white flour
> ¼ teaspoon salt
> 1 tablespoon powdered milk
> 1 teaspoon baking powder
> ½ cup water
> Vegetable oil for deep-frying

Sift all the dry ingredients together into a bowl. Pour the water over all at once and stir the dough with a fork until it gathers into a mass. With the fingers of one hand cupped together and heavily floured, pat the dough and roll it around the bowl, gathering in the loose particles of flour as you do this. Try to make a consistent, soft mass but do not work the gluten in the flour by heavy kneading. The ball of dough will remain sticky inside and coated with flour outside.

Heat 1 inch of oil in a deep skillet—or in an electric wok, in which case you should set the temperature at 350° F. If you have no thermostat, heat the oil until a bit of dough dropped into it begins to bubble as soon as it lands. Temperature is not critical here; you only want to watch the frying so that the center of the bread is done before the crust browns too much.

Cut the dough into 4 pieces. Once again flouring your hands heavily, pick up 1 piece and pat it into a round about the size of your outstretched fingers—5 to 7 inches across. The charm of fry-bread lies in its irregularity, but try to make something regular and flat enough to be presentable. Drop the bread immediately into the oil, press it down at first with a metal pancake turner to submerge the whole upper surface under oil. Fry until browned and puffed on both sides, turning the bread over once. This takes about 4 minutes. At times a fry-bread will balloon exactly like a *sopaipilla*, but it is quite all right even if only various bumps and corners puff.

If at all possible, serve the bread hot, as soon as it has been drained on paper toweling. It will keep for a few minutes in a warm oven, just long enough to let you finish the small batch. Traditionally, fry-bread is brought to the table with butter and honey, the way *sopaipillas* are, but to my taste it is better served as is with green chili stew or chili con carne.

VARIATION:

Stuffed Fry-Bread: Any of the fillings suitable for *tostadas* (p. 230) or *chimichangas* (p. 236) can be paired with fry-bread. Since the bread is usually not cooperative enough to puff completely, it is best not to try to open it up into a pocket to actually stuff it as you would a *sopaipilla*— merely lay it on a plate, making sure it is fresh and hot, and spoon the filling, sauce and garnishes over it. The result is filling and rustic, even more so than the *chimichanga*.

APPETIZERS

Nachos
Melted Cheese with Green Chilies (Chile con queso)
Crisp-Fried Cheese Turnovers (Quesadillas)
Avocados
Ripe Avocado Appetizers
Cheese Puffs with Green Chili
Cream Cheese and Green Chili Dip
Bean Dips
Bean Dip with Smoked Chilies
Sage-and-Cumin Bread with a Cheese Filling
"Spanish Pie" with Spiced Turkey and Almonds
Onion-Cream Tart
Spanish Meatballs (Albondiguítas)
Onion Fritters with Cumin
Indian Piñon Cakes
Piñons, Pecans and Pumpkin Seeds

NACHOS

Nachos long ago outdistanced pretzels and peanuts as the favorite bar food in the Southwest. There is now no stopping the proliferation of fillings that go into them. What started life in northern Mexico as simply crisp *tostado* chips with a topping of broiled cheese has become a production number stuffed with refried beans, shredded meats, chili sauce, chopped onion, sliced tomato and shredded lettuce, with chopped *jalapeño* for the crowning touch. That is a lot for a slender corn chip to bear, and in fact *tostados* quickly turn limp under their burden of moist fillings. I am going back to the pristine and highly authentic version that began all the fuss, followed by one or two simple variations.

Very sturdy, stone-ground *tostado* chips make for a pleasantly gritty *nacho*, as do home-fried chips based upon stale tortillas cut into wedges. Using orange Longhorn Cheddar cheese is the mark of Anglo influence, albeit it has become standard practice throughout the region.

For 4 people as a light appetizer:

> 24 to 36 crisp wedge-shaped tortilla chips (preferably homemade; only the plainest, sturdiest packaged variety will do as well)
> 1 to 1½ cups shredded Monterey Jack cheese
> Chopped, pickled *jalapeños* (sold in cans as *jalapeños en escabeche*)
> Wedges of fresh lime

The procedure is simplicity itself. Crowd the corn chips closely on a cookie sheet or ovenproof serving platter. Scatter the cheese over the chips and place under a broiler until the cheese bubbles and begins to brown (unlike the cheese for *enchiladas*, you want the cheese topping to be very hot and stringy). Scatter the chopped *jalapeño* over the *nachos* according to taste and serve immediately with lime wedges on the side.

VARIATIONS:

Nachos with Beans: These are considered standard in most Southwestern restaurants. Proceed as in the basic recipe, but first dab each *tostado* chip with a bit of refried beans (see p. 296 for a basic *refrito* recipe plus variations, or the more unorthodox beans mashed with butter on p. 298). The melting cheese for this version is usually sharp Cheddar rather than Monterey Jack.

This is also the version that acquires the elaborate garnishing of lettuce, tomatoes, *guacamole*, sour cream and *salsa* that constitutes "deluxe *nachos*." Add as many of these as you like after the *nachos* emerge from the broiler.

If you pack the *tostados* into a circle, leaving no gaps between them, they form a loose kind of bottom crust. Then your garnished bean *nachos* become what restaurant menus like to call a "Mexican pizza."

Nachos with Steak: A hearty Anglo variation found in the cattle country of Texas and eastern New Mexico. Take a thin 6-ounce round steak, pound it flat with a rolling-pin and rub with olive oil and a mashed garlic clove. Pepper heavily and grill or pan-broil to desired doneness. Salt to taste and cut into ½-inch cubes. Now proceed to make the basic *nachos* recipe or the variation with beans, using Cheddar cheese in place of the Monterey Jack. When the *nachos* emerge from the broiler, strew over the warm steak cubes (running back under the broiler for a minute if they have turned cold) and finish with the *jalapeños*.

MELTED CHEESE WITH GREEN CHILIES
Chile con queso

This very popular dish, called *chile con queso* in Spanish, requires a small linguistic note. The Spanish literally reads as "chili with cheese," despite the fact that the cheese outweighs the green chilies in the preparation by at least 3 to 1. In English, we would call it "cheese with chili." Once you understand that the important ingredient often comes last in a Spanish rendition, there is not so much confusion. Chili con carne, for instance, contains by far more meat than chilies. The New Mexicans do make dishes like *carne con chile colorado*; in that case the emphasis at the end indicates that the chili is red—green would be *chile verde*.

As for *chile con queso*, its popularity has spread so widely that it challenges *nachos* as a restaurant appetizer, served with warm flour tortillas to be used as soft scoops or else with crisp *tostado* chips. In tribute to its fame among non-Hispanics, the cheese called for in cookbooks is now almost always bright orange Longhorn or some other Cheddar, but I have reverted to the traditional white cheese, against which more of the green chili flavor stands out. *Chile con queso* needs only a lettuce salad on the side to make a satisfying lunch or light supper.

For 4 appetizer servings or 2 light entrees:

  2 tablespoons butter
½ medium onion
  1 large garlic clove, chopped
¼ teaspoon ground cumin
Generous dashes black pepper
  3 or 4 peeled canned tomatoes, or 2 peeled fresh tomatoes
⅔ cup whole roasted green chilies, drained if canned
  8 ounces Monterey Jack cheese, shredded or cut into small dice
  3 ounces cream cheese, cut into small dice
⅓ to ⅔ cup heavy cream
Flour tortillas

Have the cheeses at room temperature before you begin, since you do not want to heat the *chile con queso* too much after they are added. Melt the butter in a small saucepan, add the onion and garlic, cover and sweat the onion for 5 minutes over low heat. Process the tomatoes, green chilies and seasonings in the processor, stopping when the tomatoes are chopped but not yet pureed. Uncover the pan, add the mixture from the processor and cook over medium heat for about 3 to 5 minutes, or until most of the moisture from the vegetables has evaporated.

Remove the pan from the heat and quickly stir in the cheese all at once. Keep stirring until the cheese melts, then thin with the cream to the consistency you want—*chile con queso* is often as thick as fondue, but can be soupier. Taste to see if the dip is still warm; if not, rewarm very carefully over low heat; even the slightest boiling will cause the cheese to break down and ruin the dish. Serve with flour tortillas that have been warmed in foil in the oven.

VARIATIONS:

The basic recipe can be varied to suit your taste for hotness by adding chopped *jalapeños* (not pickled) along with the milder chilies. Some recipes call for twice as much onion, which would give a crunchy texture to the finished dip; others do away with the tomatoes altogether.

For a creamier dish that is also more stable and less likely to separate, add 1 tablespoon of flour to the wilted onion and cook, stirring, for a minute before adding the chilies. Add ⅓ cup chicken broth with the tomato and chilies and boil for a minute to thicken before the cheese is incorporated.

The taste and texture of fresh chilies are also compatible with the roasted ones already called for: add 1 fresh Anaheim or ½ bell pepper, finely chopped, when you add the tomatoes.

Finally, substituting 8 ounces of French *chèvre* or California goat cheese in place of the Jack cheese gives you *chile con queso de cabro*, a delicious version which should be authentic, even if Southwestern cookbooks fail to mention it.

CRISP-FRIED CHEESE TURNOVERS
Quesadillas

Another snack, or *antojito*, from the enormous repertoire of Mexican cooking, these *quesadillas* are crisp half-moons of corn-tortilla dough filled with cheese and deep-fried. Do not confuse them with two other dishes that go by the same name: one is an egg-and-cheese pie baked in a pastry shell (p. 338); the other is a shortcut restaurant preparation consisting of a flour tortilla folded over a cheese filling and baked (p. 126). In the mind of a Spanish-speaking cook they are all "a little something made of cheese," as the word *quesadilla* implies.

Once you catch on to handling the corn dough (*masa*), one or two dozen *quesadillas* can be turned out in half an hour, so they are not much more trouble than *nachos* or *tostadas*. Like cheese straws, they probably originated as a way to use up scraps of dough, and even now they are whimsies more often found at home than in restaurants. They are crisp enough to reheat well on a paper-towel-lined baking sheet in a 350° F. oven but are best eaten right away with nothing more than the sour green chili *salsa* on p. 91, or any *salsa* with enough tartness to cut the fried taste of the *quesadillas*.

For 15 to 20 turnovers:

Tortilla dough made from 1 cup Masa Harina (p. 114)
About ½ cup shredded Monterey Jack cheese
Several tablespoons canned, chopped green chilies, mild or hot
    or the equivalent in chopped fresh *jalapeños*
Salt
Vegetable oil for shallow-frying

Consult the basic tortilla recipe on p. 114 for making and rolling out *masa*, or corn dough. These *quesadillas* are made in exactly the same fashion, except that you do not need to divide the dough once it has been mixed. Instead, place the dough in a plastic bag and reach in to pull off small clumps of dough around 1 inch in diameter. Roll between plastic sheets, just as for tortillas, and cut into 3-inch circles with a biscuit cutter or a drinking glass. Place a teaspoon of shredded cheese just off center, and dot with a bit of green chili. Using your finger as a pastry brush, moisten the rim of the circle with water. Fold into a half-moon and press the edges together to seal.

As you form them, place the *quesadillas* in a plastic bag or under plastic wrap to keep moist. If the dough begins to crack as you are folding the circles, add a bit more water to the remaining ball of dough, either kneading by hand or whizzing up in the processor.

Heat a scant ½ inch of oil in a small skillet until a scrap of the dough sizzles as soon as it is dropped in. Fry 4 or 5 *quesadillas* at a time until crisp and slightly browned. Depending on the heat of the oil, this takes 2 to 4 minutes. It does not matter how often you turn the *quesadillas* as long as they cook on both sides. Drain on paper toweling and salt lightly. If you are making a large batch at once, keep the first ones warm in a slow oven while you work. Serve with sour green chili *salsa* on the side or the thick version of the adaptable red chili sauce on p. 79.

Avocados

The avocado is a winter fruit, which means it is cheapest beginning in February or thereabouts and expensive in September. The best kind to buy are black ones from California, their skin crinkled enough to justify the old name of alligator pear. Usually bought hard and unripe, they can ripen quite satisfactorily in three to five days if placed in a closed bag and stored in a dark place. You can interrupt the process at any point by putting the fruit in the refrigerator.

Underripe avocados are hard to peel; their flesh is unyielding and soapy-tasting. Ripe ones are easier to peel, aromatic, and buttery in texture —hence the other old name, "Indian butter." If, as often happens, you want an avocado on the spur of the moment and run into those in the supermarket that are mushy to the touch, do not be deceived. They are unripe ones which have been mashed by other inquisitive customers and left to a dismal fate—pulpy, but still not ripe. It is better to do without avocado altogether than to buy those. Cut-rate cooks sometimes carry home the hard young avocados or the squashy unacceptable ones hoping to palm them off in a *guacamole* heavily spiked with onion and garlic. That is a very bad practice best left to restaurants.

Avocado flesh oxidizes and turns brown on contact with air, so it is wise to peel and slice it at the last moment, just as you are ready to garnish a dish. Prematurely cut slices can be kept reasonably fresh by submerging them in ice water—another restaurant practice. Rubbing the cut surfaces with lemon juice, which one sees as the usual cookbook advice, is tedious and mostly ineffective. Half an avocado left over can be preserved by leaving the pit in, wrapping the half in plastic wrap, and pressing the wrap directly onto the flesh so that it is not exposed to air. So protected, the half can be kept in the refrigerator for a few days at most, where it will decline in flavor slightly day by day. Although some may find them tolerable, off-season green avocados from Florida, shaped like smooth gourds, seem to be inferior overall—tougher to peel, slower to ripen, quicker to rot and, because of their lower oil content, ultimately less flavorful even at their best. Frozen avocado spreads are generally watery and without flavor, and not worth their cost.

Once encountered in its ripened state, the avocado easily turns into an obsession. Feel free to embellish practically any soup or main course with it if you are among the addicted. People who are primarily attracted to the "designer" green shade of the avocado sometimes make it into cold avocado soup, avocado mousse or avocado ice cream, recipes for which most definitely do not appear in this cookbook.

RIPE-AVOCADO APPETIZERS

Now that the avocado is permanently established as a fixture in New Mexico cooking, it seems a shame to restrict it to a few uses only. There is more to do with it than make *guacamole* or garnish *tostadas*. Avocados can be capricious about how long they take to ripen once you get them home, particularly if they are late-winter ones, so you may find yourself blessed with two or three perfectly ripe ones a few days after you had planned to use them. Here are some ideas about serving them as an appetizer. I am assuming that one half is enough per guest (an underestimation if the fruits are small or have unusually large pits).

These preparations are meant to show off the avocado itself, so I have not gone into the various garnishes that are possible. However, among the best of the traditional ones are

—boiled shrimp made into salad or simply moistened with *salsa*. (The shrimp are usually placed in the cavity of the avocado.)
—shaved country ham or prosciutto, cut as thin as possible by the butcher.
—raw beef tenderloin, cut as thin as possible by the butcher; moisten with fresh *salsa* or green chili relish. (The meat slices are rolled up and placed on the side. Present with lime wedges on the side.)

All the following avocado recipes are for 4 people.

AVOCADO WITH AVOCADO SAUCE

4 ripe avocados, cool but not chilled
2 tablespoons olive oil
1 tablespoon lime juice
2 small green onions chopped into 1-inch lengths
2 generous dashes Tabasco
Salt and pepper to taste

First cut 3 of the avocados into thin slices in the following way: Halve each avocado, unpeeled, remove the pit, and slice each half in half again. Peel the quarters by slipping your thumb between flesh and skin, just sliding down to separate the two. Now slice each piece into 4 slices lengthwise and gently fan them out on small salad plates. Allot 2 quarters—that is, 8 slices—per person.

Quarter and peel the remaining avocado. Place it in the jar of an electric blender with all the other ingredients. Blend into a smooth sauce, taking time to scrape down the sides of the jar as necessary. Taste for seasoning and spoon a ribbon of the sauce down the center of the avocado slices. Serve cool and as quickly as possible so that the avocado does not lose its fresh taste and color.

This green-on-green appetizer satiates even a fanatic, and the presentation is lovely enough in its simplicity to suit a dinner party.

AVOCADO WITH GRAPEFRUIT DRESSING

Usually the unctuousness of avocados is set off by a sweet or sour dressing, but here the accent is bitter and therefore more sophisticated. The use of grapefruit and Belgian endive takes us leagues away from Santa Fe.

2 ripe avocados
1 tablespoon frozen grapefruit juice concentrate, thawed
   but not diluted
4 tablespoons olive oil
3 tablespoons chopped parsley
Salt and pepper to taste
Fresh grapefruit sections and/or Belgian endive leaves

Place half an avocado, whole or in slices, on small salad plates and garnish with the grapefruit sections and/or small Belgian endive leaves

(3 or 4 per serving). Using an electric blender or whisking by hand, make a dressing from the grapefruit concentrate, oil, parsley, salt and pepper. Drizzle over the avocado and serve cool.

AVOCADO WITH ROASTED RED PEPPER SAUCE

    2 ripe avocados
    2 or 3 roasted and peeled red peppers, either homemade or
      bottled as "sandwich peppers"
    4 tablespoons olive oil
    ½ teaspoon lemon juice
    ½ teaspoon powdered mild red chilies
Salt and pepper to taste

Quarter, peel and slice the avocados as described in Avocado with Avocado Sauce, p. 153. Mix the remaining ingredients in the jar of an electric blender and puree into a smooth sauce, stopping as needed to scrape down the jar with a spatula. Place a ribbon of the richly red sauce down the center of the sliced avocado and serve, cool, as soon as possible. Unlike the other sauces, this one improves if kept for a few hours in the refrigerator, so it can be made ahead if you like.

AVOCADOS WITH SALSA

Quarter, peel, and slice avocados as in Avocado with Avocado Sauce, p. 153, allowing half an avocado per person. Place a ribbon of fresh uncooked *salsa* (p. 86) down the center of each portion.

CHEESE PUFFS WITH GREEN CHILI

Before newcomers to New Mexico begin to explore the local cooking in earnest, they usually discover some hybrids—conventional dishes that simply have chilies added to them. The area supermarkets carry *jalapeño* bread, *jalapeño* jelly and even *jalapeño* bagels. This recipe belongs to that dubious class of food, for it is the classic Burgundian cheese puff called *gougère*, made with cream-puff dough (*pâte à choux*) exactly as it would be in Dijon, but with a dash of mashed green chilies added. It is still one of the best appetizer or cocktail breads you can make, all the better if you split each puff and spread it with a little of the cream cheese and green chili spread on p. 156. The puffs can be eaten either hot, warm or cold, but are best within an hour after baking. If you store them, they tend to turn damp inside, but they can be revived with a few minutes in a 350° F. oven.

For about 30 puffs:

    ½ cup milk
    ½ cup water
     8 tablespoons (1 stick) lightly salted butter
    ½ teaspoon salt
     1 cup unbleached white flour
     4 eggs
    About 1 cup grated Swiss cheese, plus about ¼ cup
        extra for sprinkling on the puffs
     2 tablespoons mashed canned green chilies, made up of 1 whole
        mild chili and 1 *jalapeño*, or any combination of mild
        and hot that you prefer

Preheat the oven to 400° F. and have ready 3 cookie sheets. (If you are short a cookie sheet or two, do not worry. The dough for these puffs can stand and wait, provided it is kept at least lukewarm, and it will still puff.) They will probably require 2 racks in your oven, both in the upper third.

Place the water, milk, salt and butter in a saucepan and bring to a full rolling boil over medium heat. Make sure the butter has entirely melted, remove the pan from the heat and add the flour all at once. Stir for a few seconds to incorporate it, and return the pan to medium heat, stirring constantly, until the dough draws together into one mass. At this point it will also begin to coat the bottom of the pan with a thin film as you are stirring.

Remove the saucepan from the heat and allow to cool for a minute or two. (If the dough is too hot it will cook the eggs and prevent the puffing action.) Break the eggs and stir in one at a time, working vigorously with a wooden spoon. Do not add the next egg until the preceding one is thoroughly incorporated. Eventually all the eggs will be fully incorporated. Stir in the cheese and mashed chilies.

Drop the still-warm dough by tablespoonfuls onto the ungreased baking sheets, leaving about ½ inch between each. Sprinkle a pinch of the reserved grated cheese on top of each puff and place in the oven. Immediately turn the heat down to 375° F. and bake about 15 to 20 minutes, or until the puffs are golden brown. Reduce heat to 350° F. and let the puffs dry out for another 5 minutes or so, but do not overbrown on the bottom.

Stuffed Cheese Puffs: Split the puffs and stuff with the cream cheese and green chili spread below, or puree 6 ounces of cream cheese with a small handful of walnuts, a chopped garlic clove and some ground cumin and black pepper to taste. In this guise, the puffs can be passed during the soup course of a dinner party, though they are still equally good during the margarita hour. Another modest filling would be 6 ounces of goat cheese processed with 2 tablespoons butter, a small handful of piñons, and cayenne to taste.

CREAM CHEESE AND GREEN CHILI DIP

This presto mixture of cream cheese and canned chilies frankly dates from the fifties, the era of labor-free recipes and fad ingredients. Cream cheese is just returning from the no-man's-land of overused foods, so this dip should not be too familiar anymore. It is also extremely useful as a spread (highly unorthodox but delicious is to slice a croissant, spread it with a tablespoon or so of the dip, and heat for a minute in a toaster oven), or combined with shredded turkey breast as a stuffing inside *enchiladas*.

You can, of course, puree in a *jalapeño* or two, canned or fresh, if you want the dip to be hotter.

For about 1½ cups dip:

    ¼ cup blanched, slivered almonds
    1 tablespoon vegetable oil
  12 ounces cream cheese
    1 large clove garlic, mashed
Milk or cream to thin the dip
    4 ounces canned mild green chilies, drained

In a small skillet, sauté the almonds in the oil until they are light brown; set aside. In the bowl of a processor fitted with the standard metal blade, blend the cream cheese and garlic until smooth, thinning with a little milk or cream as needed. Add the almonds along with their cooking oil and the chilies. Process until smooth, stopping at least once to scrape down the bottom and sides of the bowl with a rubber spatula. Serve at room temperature with tortilla chips or sticks of raw *jícama* (see p. 175).

 Bean Dips

There have been successive waves of enthusiasm for Southwestern food since the early fifties and probably before. Each wave brought new discoveries to light, and the passage of time proved which foods were survivors (*guacamole* and *tacos*, for example) or castaways. Apparently the fad for bean dips twenty years ago has left no survivors except for the nearly inedible canned varieties sold in every Western supermarket. I can remember loving them in the past (even the canned ones) and hope to see a revival.

Despite all the concocted recipes for quick bean dips—I give mine below—the genuine article is nothing more than refried beans which have been mashed a little more than usual and cooked a little less dry. Please refer to the *refritos* recipe on p. 296, which is followed by several variations, all of them suitable for bean dips. Also see the beans mashed with butter on p. 298, a delicious variant that lacks only authenticity. Acceptable dips can be based upon canned beans, making sure to drain them and sauté in a skillet with olive oil, onion, garlic and oregano. As you are frying and mashing the beans, add as much of their canning liquid as needed for the desired consistency. Keep the finished dip warm by transferring it to a metal, glass or ceramic bowl and suspending over a pan of simmering water. Always serve warm—cold bean dip congeals and is decidedly unappetizing. Also, despite the current fashion for scooping up dips with raw vegetables, bean dips really go best with tortilla chips, also warm if possible.

BEAN DIP WITH SMOKED CHILIES

Every conscientious Mexican cookbook mentions the smoked *jalapeños* called *chiles chipotles*, but I think they get lost in the multitude of other red and green, fresh and dried chilies, for few cooks realize how available they are. Any good Mexican grocery section sells cans of *chipotles* packed in marinade. Remains of a 4-ounce can last indefinitely under refrigeration, as far as I can tell, and the hot, smoky flavor that the chilies impart to food is exceptionally appealing. Good as the bean dip with butter on p. 299 is, I like this one even more. The *chipotles* enliven the dip and altogether rehabilitate it, for goopy, cold bean dips can be the worst of Southwestern food. Add as many of the chilies as you want, as far as their hotness goes, but make sure that the dip is brought to your guests warm.

For about 3 cups of dip:

> 2 tablespoons olive oil
> ½ onion, chopped
> 2 cups of boiled pinto beans, homemade or canned, with
>   about ½ cup of their liquid
> ¼ teaspoon coarsely ground black pepper
> 2 to 6 canned *chiles chipotles*
> ¼ to ½ cup sour cream
> Salt, if needed
> Crisp *tostados* (fried tortilla chips) for dipping

Heat the oil in a small skillet, then add the onion, cover the pan and allow the onion to wilt over low heat for 5 minutes. Remove the cover, raise the heat to medium and cook until the onion begins to brown well, stirring occasionally to avoid scorching. (The taste of browned onion is strong and distinctive; if you do not like it, simply proceed with the recipe after the onion is wilted.) Remove the pan from the heat and allow the onion to cool somewhat.

Place the onion and its oil in a food processor, add all the remaining dip ingredients and blend until a puree is reached, but before its texture becomes pabulum-smooth. Taste for seasoning, salt as needed and cautiously add more bean liquid or sour cream until you reach the consistency you want.

Unless your beans were already warm, it is likely that the dip is not hot enough. You can heat it through in the same skillet in which you cooked the onion if you are serving it immediately, or you can set it aside in a bowl until a later serving time. To reheat, cover the bowl with foil and place it over a saucepan of boiling water, allowing it to steam for 15 minutes or so. The dip keeps well in the refrigerator, but it should have plastic wrap pressed directly onto its surface to prevent the formation of a skin.

VARIATIONS:

Sour-Cream Bean Dip: For a creamy dip that is neither hot nor smoky, eliminate the *chilies chipotles* and use more sour cream than bean liquid as you thin the dip.

Green Chili Bean Dip: A variation almost as good as the basic recipe eliminates the *chiles chipotles* and adds ½ cup of canned green chilies in their place. The dip can be made hot if you like with 2 teaspoons of canned *jalapeños*.

Bean Dip with Cheese: The basic recipe or any of its variations can be warmed up with 1 cup of shredded Monterey Jack cheese (4 ounces) incorporated just prior to serving. Simply stir in the cheese and steam as directed or add it immediately to the skillet if you are serving the dip straight off. Since the cheese enriches the flavor, the amount of sour cream can be cut considerably or eliminated altogether.

SAGE-AND-CUMIN BREAD WITH A CHEESE FILLING

Some of the pueblos specialize in a quick baking-powder bread strongly flavored with sage. I have adapted it into a flat, round loaf which is not so intensely herbal (sage puts off as many people as it attracts, in my experience). In addition, it boasts a thin center layer of melted cheese and green chili that adds to its interest enormously. Thanks to the food processor, the whole operation of mixing the dough and filling it takes less than 15 minutes. The result is a crusty near-relative of Irish soda bread that is meant to be eaten right away with cocktails or as a regular table bread with stews or chili con carne. I think you will find this a delightful invention, but do not try to save any of it for the following day—it grows decidedly tired after only an hour.

For 6 people as an appetizer, 4 as a table bread:

  3 cups unbleached white flour
  1 teaspoon salt
  2 teaspoons baking powder
  ¾ teaspoon baking soda
  ¼ cup chopped parsley
  ¼ teaspoon sage, or more to taste
  ½ teaspoon whole cumin seeds
  1 large egg
  2 cups buttermilk
  6 ounces Monterey Jack cheese, cut into thin slices
  ½ cup diced, canned green chilies
  4 tablespoons butter

Preheat the oven to 375° F. and place a rack in the upper third. Butter a 10-inch pie plate or a quiche pan or a deep-dish pizza pan with 2 tablespoons of the butter. By far the best choice is a pan made of pottery—it produces an evenly browned, crusty bottom.

Place the first 7 ingredients in a food processor and blend for a second or two. Add the egg and buttermilk and blend for just 4 seconds more. The best method, since you want to avoid any hint of overbeating, is to pulse the dough once, scrape down the sides of the bowl with a rubber spatula and then pulse once more. You need to go only far enough for the dry and wet ingredients just to be blended.

Spread half the dough in an even layer in the pan, then top with the sliced cheese. Try to cover as much of the surface as you can but leave a ½-inch margin around the edges. Dot the cheese all over with the green chilies. Drop the rest of the dough over the filling with a tablespoon. Spread this top layer evenly with a knife, then dot with the remaining 2 tablespoons of butter.

Bake for 40 to 45 minutes. The finished bread will be raised and hollow-sounding when you thump it in the center, and the top should be lightly browned. For a browner top crust, you can finish the loaf by running it under a broiler flame for 1 last minute. Serve immediately, or within half an hour, cutting the bread into pie-shaped wedges directly in its baking pan.

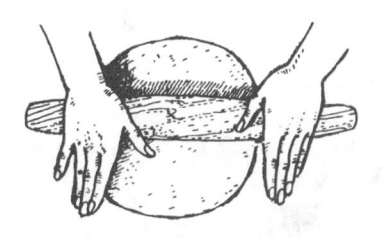

"SPANISH PIE" WITH SPICED TURKEY AND ALMONDS

One reads in Santa Fe history of the lengths to which the wealthy Spanish society along the river went to preserve their Castilian heritage— and their aloofness from the poorer folk who were mixing their blood, their habits and their food with those of the Indians. Here is a European double-crust tart of the kind the richer Spanish settlers might have served at a feast. In deference to the American who once grumbled that the "Spanish pies" of Santa Fe were "more crust than filling," this version has a thin, light pastry, but the filling is still scarcely half an inch thick. It makes up for that by being wonderfully savory—the blend of spices and raisins with the turkey meat is at least as old as the Middle Ages and also reminiscent of the Moroccan influence in Spanish food.

If you are starting the recipe by poaching your own turkey meat, the whole procedure will take you about 3 or 4 hours from start to finish; therefore it is a good idea to have the turkey breast already on hand. To make the handling of the thin top pastry more manageable, it is cut into wedges and laid on the pie in a design like an Aztec sun.

For a 9-inch pie, serving 6 as an appetizer or 4 for lunch:

½ cup blanched, slivered almonds
2 tablespoons confectioners' sugar
½ teaspoon cinnamon
½ onion, chopped
1 or 2 cloves garlic, chopped
3 tablespoons butter
½ teaspoon each cinnamon, allspice, ginger and turmeric,
    plus ¼ teaspoon cloves
2 cups cooked, shredded turkey breast
¼ cup Madeira or dark sweet vermouth
1 tablespoon lemon juice
3 eggs
¼ cup chopped parsley
3 tablespoons raisins
1 teaspoon grated orange peel (the amount from half an orange)
Salt
Pastry for a double-crust pie (see p. 343) or any good tart
    pastry based on 2 cups flour, chilled
Egg wash: 1 egg beaten with 1 teaspoon water

The filling consists of a bed of sugared almonds covered with a layer of spiced turkey and raisins. Despite the long list of ingredients—Spanish cooks reveled in such elaborations—the preparation is simple.

Roast the almonds in a small skillet over medium heat, shaking the pan occasionally, until they turn light brown. Allow to cool somewhat, then transfer to a processor or blender and grind coarsely. Add the sugar and cinnamon, blend for a few seconds more, and set aside.

Sweat the onion and garlic for about 5 minutes in the butter over low heat in a covered medium-size skillet. Add all the spices and stir over medium heat, uncovered, for a minute more. Add the turkey breast, then the Madeira or vermouth and lemon juice, and bring to a boil. Beat the eggs with the parsley in a small bowl and add all at once to the pan. Cook over medium heat, stirring constantly, until the eggs scramble and dry out enough so that they pull away from the bottom of the skillet in definite but still-soft curds.

Off heat, stir in the raisins, orange peel and salt to taste. If you think the filling needs more piquancy, sprinkle on another teaspoonful of lemon juice. Set the filling aside to cool in the refrigerator while you roll the pastry.

Rolling the dough and assembling the pie: Have ready a 9-inch quiche pan, preferably one with a removable bottom, or a free-standing flan ring. Divide the chilled pastry dough into 2 portions and place the one you are not rolling out back in the refrigerator. Roll out a circle of pastry to fit the pan, leaving only a slight margin—about ¼ inch extending above the rim will be enough. Fit the pastry into the pan, pushing gently with your fingers. If cracks appear in the sides or bottom, patch with scraps of moistened dough.

Gently spread the sugared almonds in a smooth, even layer over the bottom of the pie, then spoon on a layer of the cooled turkey mixture, patting it flat and uniform with your fingers. Fold the edges of pastry in over the filling. Chill the pie while you roll out the second circle.

Roll out another thin circle of dough exactly the size of your pie, or slightly smaller. Cut the circle in half, then into quarters. Cut each quarter into 3 wedges. You now have 12 wedges of pastry which will be laid on top of the filling.

Remove the pie from the refrigerator. Glaze the turned-in border with egg wash and proceed to position the wedges of pastry, without overlapping, over the top of the pie, being careful to lay them down so that their points meet in the center. Press the wide ends of the wedges gently onto the glazed pastry border to help hold the pie intact. Now cut a 2-inch circle of dough from the scraps you have left over, glaze its underside and place it, glazed side down, in the center of the pie where the points converge. You now have a Spanish pie shaped like an Aztec sun.

The pie can be baked at once or covered and refrigerated until needed. It is not a bad idea to chill for 15 minutes or so before proceeding.

Preheat the oven to 425° F. with a rack in the upper third.

Glaze the top of the pie with egg wash, allow it to dry for a minute or two, then glaze again. Bake in the oven for 25 to 30 minutes, or until the pastry is nicely browned. If the edges start to brown too much, brush them with water or cover the top of the pie with a loose layer of foil. Serve the pie warm or at room temperature, but not chilled. The baked pie can be kept out overnight, uncovered, to be eaten the next day, or it can be kept in the refrigerator loosely draped with plastic wrap once it has cooled thoroughly.

VARIATION:

For 2 large *empanadas:* The American who grumbled about too much crust in his Santa Fe pie might also have encountered large half-moon shapes called *empanadas.* Making them is considerably easier than forming a double-crust pie. Divide the sugared almonds and the cooked filling in half. Roll half the dough out into a 10-inch circle and carefully transfer it to a cookie sheet. Scatter half the almonds and half the filling over the lower part of the circle, leaving a margin for crimping the edges. Fold the top half down to make a half-moon, crimp a border all around, and glaze twice with egg wash. Repeat with a second circle of dough and bake as directed. Once cooled, finished *empanadas* can be frozen or chilled for a few days. (If your filling seems very moist, prick the top of the *empanadas* with a fork in a dozen or so places after the egg wash is applied—this will let steam escape and help prevent cracks from forming during the baking.)

Naturally, the dough can be subdivided into smaller *empanadas* if you want one for each person. The amount based upon 2 cups of flour would make 12 conventionally small turnovers; they need to bake only about 15 minutes.

ONION-CREAM TART

Onion tarts sound a bit improbable to many cooks, but they are not at all daring if you already are used to filled quiches. The hefty quantity of onions is cooked long enough to remove their rawness and to substitute a sweet, nutty flavor that your dinner-party guests will certainly admire. Dinner-party fare this is, an adaptation of an appetizer served in Swiss restaurants—the Swiss have several kinds of onion-and-cream tarts in their cuisine—but a dose of green chili makes the flavor undeniably South-western. The chilies called for here are mild, but you have the option, as always, of adding diced *jalapeños*. Like any tart based on custard, this one tastes best eaten direct from the oven, letting it cool just to lukewarm.

For 6 people as a substantial appetizer:

Pastry for a single-crust 9-inch pie (p. 344)
   3 tablespoons olive oil
   2 medium-large onions (1 pound total weight), chopped by
      hand or according to processor instructions on p. 49
 ½ cup heavy cream
   3 large eggs
   4-ounce piece of Parmesan cheese
   3 canned tomatoes, coarsely chopped
 ¼ to ⅓ cup canned, diced green chilies
 ¼ teaspoon black pepper
Pinch oregano
Optional: 2 teaspoons diced *jalapeños*, if you want a hotter flavor

Preheat the oven to 400° F. Place a baking sheet, preferably a heavy one made of dark metal, in the middle of the oven and let it get hot. Since the tart filling is placed into an unbaked pastry shell, the preheated metal surface placed beneath it produces a crisp bottom crust, or at least prevents sogginess.

Roll the pastry to fit a 9-inch pie pan or a shallower 10-inch quiche pan.

Line the pan and prick the surface with a fork at ½-inch intervals; chill in the refrigerator while you make the filling.

Heat the olive oil in a large skillet with a cover, add the chopped onions, then cover and sweat the onions for 15 minutes over low heat.

While the onions wilt, process the cream and eggs until they are well mixed and set them aside. Grate the cheese by hand or in an electric blender: you should have about 1 cup of grated cheese.

Uncover the onions, raise the heat to medium, and make sure the onions are cooked through and nutty-tasting. Stir in the tomatoes, chilies and seasonings. Cook for another 10 minutes, or until most of the moisture is gone and the mixture stiffened, but do not let the onions brown. Remove from heat and allow to cool for a few minutes, then quickly stir in the egg mixture and the Parmesan. Pour the batter into the pastry shell, set it on the baking sheet and bake for 50 to 60 minutes, or until the filling is puffed, cooked through and browned on top. Serve as soon as possible, since the tart is at its best warm.

You can also make onion tart the center of a lunch, just as you would a quiche, accompanied by a green salad and white wine. Leftovers are good heated the next day, but neither the crust nor the filling will still be in prime shape.

VARIATION:

Flat Onion Tart: This recipe is adaptable to a Provençale-type flat onion tart made without cream. Spread the dough out in a small pizza pan. Cook the filling as above, but with the following changes in the ingredients: Increase the tomatoes to 6 and the green chilies to ½ cup; omit the cream and eggs. You are aiming at a fairly stiff filling of onions, tomatoes, green chili, and Parmesan. Spread this filling rather thinly over the crust, scatter chopped olives (either black or green) and chopped scallion over the top, if you like, and bake as directed above. This flat tart is done when the top is bubbling and brown and the center of the crust is cooked crisp. It has the advantage over the custard-based version of being quite good after standing for several hours and is arguably just as good tepid as warm.

SPANISH MEATBALLS
Albondiguítas

Hispanic cooks mostly employ their *albóndigas*, or meatballs, in soup, but Southwestern cooks often modify by making them quite tiny for use as an appetizer. This, too, has a European precedent in the form of the tiny meatballs served along with glasses of sherry as one of numerous *tapas*, the Spanish tidbits which often outnumber by tenfold the appetizers we provide at the cocktail hour. The meatball mixture that goes into these *albondiguítas* (tiny shapes always get their own names in Spanish) is the same as the one for the larger versions poached in soup. Both are worth trying. Thanks to the food processor and the electric wok, the time it takes to make 50 or 60 meatballs is less than an hour.

For about 50 small meatballs, serving 4 as an appetizer:

> Meatball mixture from the soup recipe on p. 184
> Oil for shallow-frying—or 3 cups beef broth for poaching
> 3 cups red or green *enchilada* sauce (see the quick versions on
>   p. 80 and 83), or the same amount of the tomato sauce
>   on p. 90

Grind the meat mixture smooth, exactly as you would for the soup, but roll the meatballs only as large as will fit comfortably on the end of a toothpick—about 2 teaspoons or so for each will do. Heat ½ inch of oil in an electric wok to 375° F., or else heat the oil in a 10-inch skillet until it is hot enough for a bit of the meatball mixture to bubble hard as soon as it is dropped in. Shape the meatballs and fry about 8 at a time together until they are well browned on all sides, about 3 minutes. Drain on paper towels and continue until all the meat mixture is used up. Set aside until needed—they will be quite safe at room temperature for a few hours, or they can be refrigerated. (*Albóndigas* also freeze well at any stage of their preparation.)

When ready to serve, heat the red or green sauce in a saucepan, chafing dish, or electric skillet and add the meatballs to warm through, about 5 minutes at a simmer. Serve with toothpicks for piercing the *albóndigas* in their sauce, or present on plates as a first course, in which case a light garnish of chopped green coriander (*cilantro*) makes a nice touch.

Poaching the *albóndigas*: You can poach the *albóndigas* in 3 cups of beef broth (or even water), taking about 5 minutes for a batch of 8 or 10 at a time. Make sure the broth is boiling when the meatballs are dropped in, and poach just below the boil to make sure the pork cooks through. Drain and hold until serving time, then present in a sauce as above. (Strain and reserve the broth for another use.)

VARIATIONS:

Picante Meatballs: If your sauce is a mild tomato sauce, or if you want to present the meatballs with nothing more on the side than a table *salsa*—they are delicious that way—you might want to hot up the *albóndigas* mixture with 2 fresh or canned *jalapeños*. The fresh ones need deveining and chopping before they go into the processor with the meat; the canned ones need only to be cut into thirds.

Hot, Smoky Meatballs: The best *picante* version of these appetizer meatballs is one made with 2 or more *chiles chipotles* added to the processor along with the meat. They add a distinctive hot, smoky savor which is nearly addictive. (For a description of canned *chipotles* in marinade, see p. 69.) Start with 2 *chipotles* the first time out, and either bring the meatballs to the table in a fairly mild tomato sauce like the one on p. 79, or present them with a good uncooked table *salsa* (p. 86) on the side, in which case they will have to be eaten with a fork from a plate.

ONION FRITTERS WITH CUMIN

These are corn puffs stuffed with onion and seasoned with ground cumin. They are savory and light, an excellent appetizer, and they can easily be shallow-fried in a generous ½ inch of oil. Do not attempt to shape them evenly, since the little stray bits of onion are part of their appeal. Serve hot with a sour green chili *salsa* (p. 91) on the side. If you make the fritters small, they can be held in a warm oven for a while, but the larger sizes quickly lose their crispness.

For at least 16 fritters:

> 1 cup Masa Harina or any other corn-tortilla flour
> ¼ cup white flour
> ½ teaspoon baking powder
> 1 teaspoon salt
> 1 teaspoon ground cumin
> ½ teaspoon cayenne
> 1 egg
> ¾ cup milk
> 1 large onion, chopped or sliced into thin rings
> Vegetable oil for shallow frying

With a fork, stir together the first 6 ingredients in a mixing bowl. Blend the egg and milk, then add all at once to the dry ingredients along with the chopped onion. Stir vigorously with the fork until a stiff fritter batter is formed. If the batter is too stiff to drop easily from a spoon, add more milk by tablespoonfuls.

Heat a generous ½ inch or more of oil in a small skillet. Test its temperature by dropping in a speck of fritter batter—it should sizzle immediately but not so much that it immediately browns. Form the fritters by picking up some batter in a tablespoon and pushing it into the oil with a teaspoon. Work close to the surface of the oil so that the falling dough does not splatter. Cook 4 fritters at a time, first browning on one side, turning over to brown the other, then cooking the first side again to deepen the color. Being fairly dense, the batter must brown rather slowly or the interior will not be cooked through. The time needed to thoroughly cook one fritter will be at least 3 minutes; adjust the heat as necessary. Drain the fritters on paper toweling and salt lightly. The first fritters can be held for a short time in a warm oven on a baking sheet lined with paper towels; but all should be served hot and crisp. Accompany at the table with a good, fresh *salsa* (p. 86).

VARIATION:

Crisp Corncake with Onion: If you want a griddle bread to go well with grilled meats, use only ¼ of a small onion and thin the batter with a little milk until it resembles pancake batter. Cook like pancakes on a lightly greased griddle or in a skillet. If the first cake is too thick, thin with more milk. The cakes should be about 3 or 4 inches across. Serve with fresh *salsa* or the cooked sauce that accompanies the entree.

INDIAN PIÑON CAKES

These plain-flavored nut fritters are adapted from a Pueblo recipe, and they exemplify the simplicity of Indian cooking. Their most obvious use is at cocktail time as hot snacks to be dipped into a good uncooked chili *salsa*. The mild but distinctive taste of pine nuts, which is essentially all there is here, soon disappears if you bring in other dishes, so do try to eat the cakes alone and as freshly made as possible.

For 16 to 20 cakes, serving 4 with cocktails:

> 1 cup piñon nuts (pine nuts)
> ⅓ cup powdered milk
> 1 cup whole-wheat flour
> ½ teaspoon salt
> ½ cup water
> Optional: 1 teaspoon ground coriander seed
> Vegetable oil for shallow-frying

The procedure for making these snacks is simplicity itself—merely combine the ingredients in a food processor and blend until a dough is formed, stopping once to scrape the bowl down with a rubber spatula. Heat a good ½ inch of oil in a skillet or an electric wok set to 375° F. or hot enough so that the cakes bubble as soon as they are dropped in. However, do not cook so quickly that they are brown on the outside and still raw inside. Shape the dough into balls, taking up about 2 tablespoons at a time, flatten each one into a disk between your palms, then fry until brown on both sides, turning once. Cooking time should be little more than a minute, but check the first cake to make sure it is not doughy inside. Drain on paper towels.

These cakes are best served immediately, but they can keep for a while in a warm oven. Serve with a homemade chili *salsa* (p. 86) for dunking, or eat plain if you want to enjoy the definite taste of the pine nuts.

PIÑONS, PECANS AND PUMPKIN SEEDS

New Mexicans traditionally contented themselves simply with piñon nuts, which were kept after the autumn harvest for roasting and cracking around a winter fire; but you can make a very good cocktail mix of piñons, pecans and pumpkin seeds. All of them are indigenous to the state, all contribute something different to the mix. The large white pumpkin seeds marketed as *pepitas* in Mexican groceries are not shelled, so I use the smaller green seeds sold in natural-foods stores and supermarkets.

For 3 cups of cocktail mix:

> 1 **cup shelled piñon nuts**
> 1 **cup pecan halves**
> 1 **cup shelled green pumpkin seeds**
> **Generous dashes of cayenne and cumin**
> **Salt**

Toast the seeds and nuts lightly in a large ungreased skillet over low heat (add a teaspoon of butter for flavor if you wish), adding the spices just as the mixture starts to brown. As soon as you can smell the roasting cumin, transfer the mix to a paper bag, salt lightly, and shake to distribute the seasonings. Serve warm or at room temperature with cocktails.

SALADS

Basic Guacamole
Winter Guacamole
Winter Salad of Jícama and Oranges
Radish, Onion and Green Chili Salad
Pinto, Black Bean or Lentil Salad

GUACAMOLE, UNLIMITED

Of the few charmed Hispanic dishes that have reached celebrity status, *guacamole* must be the best known. From its humble beginnings as "Indian butter" through the California-cult era and now into an age of near universality, this simple preparation of mashed avocados has remained cheerfully durable. The only way really to spoil *guacamole* is to use unripe avocados, to leave in large chunks of raw onion as an unpleasant surprise to the innocent consumer, or to make it too far ahead of time. Besides turning brown (a fate that can be more-or-less avoided by pressing plastic wrap directly onto its surface), a *guacamole* left standing for more than 30 minutes loses the delicacy of a fresh-cut avocado. Ideally, it should be made at the last moment and stirred with a light hand.

Guacamole has been the object of unlimited experimentations. Some are time-honored variations, like the *guacamole* with green tomatoes from northern Mexico. Others are obvious shortcuts perpetrated by restaurants. Visitors to Santa Fe quite naturally want to taste this famous specialty of the Southwest, so there is constant pressure for the local restaurants to produce some *guacamole*, any *guacamole*, no matter if avocados are not ripe or tomatoes out of season. The standard recipe of at least one immensely popular restaurant calls merely for mashing an avocado with half a teaspoon of garlic salt! To my mind, that is not *guacamole* at all. Before giving several recipes for *guacamole* and its variants, I have listed nine approaches that turned up in my casual research. By memorizing these, you can instantly settle any passionate arguments over what is true *guacamole*—all of them are. If you are not intrigued, go directly to the recipes that follow.

As for how to serve *guacamole*, it is usually considered a sauce to begin with, but Southwestern restaurants invariably serve it on lettuce as a salad, as a side dish with a combination plate and as a garnish to dollop over *chalupas* and *burritos*. Somewhat less popular, but still encountered, is using it to stuff *enchiladas* or *tacos*. It is mandatory as the topping for *flautas*, crisp-fried little "flutes" made of corn tortillas stuffed with shredded beef or chicken.

Although the word most often applied to the taste of a ripe avocado is "bland," *guacamole* has the ability to mask the taste of almost any dish it is paired with. When the cooks of Veracruz use it to sauce grilled swordfish, they add enough lime juice to make the avocado taste noticeably tart. I think that is a good idea whenever you are serving *guacamole* as a sauce for any grilled meat or poultry.

However you ask it to perform, *guacamole* tastes best when all its ingredients are cool, considerably below room temperature. Do not heat the *guacamole* in the oven with the dish it is to garnish, unless it is the stuffing for *enchiladas*. By all means do not serve it refrigerated, however, a ruinous practice fostered by restaurants.

Now for the styles of *guacamole*:

1. The mainstream style, so to speak, is to mash ripe avocado roughly with chopped tomatoes, fresh or canned green chilies and a fairly small amount of chopped onion. Green coriander (*cilantro*) is optional, as is a dash of lemon or lime juice, or garlic.

2. Same ingredients and texture as the mainstream type, but sour cream is added as a blending agent.

3. The same as number 2, but made even blander by the omission of all chilies.

4. Back to the mainstream version, but leaving out all onion.

5. Again the same as the mainstream version, but given a different texture by not mashing the ingredients together at all, merely roughing them up a bit. The results are more salad than sauce, further pronounced if a crunchy chopped bell pepper is added.

6. A puree of avocado, green chili, onion and a large dash of lime juice. This is sometimes called a Veracruz *guacamole*. It customarily omits the tomatoes.

7. A puree of avocado with only a garlic clove and lemon juice for flavoring. If used for a sauce, a little or a lot of sour cream may also be whipped in. If used as a salad, sliced tomato is placed on top. Popular in many restaurants.

8. Mainstream *guacamole* or one of the close variants to which green tomatoes (*tomatillos*) have been added. This is one of the few approaches that markedly change the taste of the *guacamole*.

9. Pristine puree of avocado. Innocent of any additives except a pinch of garlic salt, this travels in many neighborhods, including downtown Santa Fe, as *guacamole*.

None of the variations with sour cream added are much to my taste, and I recoil if large chunks of raw white onion appear in the mash. It is probably better to let *guacamole* rest on its own merits as produced by each separate cook. As with much else in Santa Fe cooking, the expression of the cook's personality accounts for much.

BASIC GUACAMOLE

For 2½ to 3 cups:

¼ small red onion, cut into chunks
1 tomato, seeded and cut into chunks
2 large avocados (3 if the smooth green variety, which has a large pit), peeled
1 or 2 garlic cloves, mashed and chopped
1 tablespoon olive oil
3 tablespoons lime juice
Salt and pepper to taste
Optional: 1 fresh *jalapeño*, seeded and chopped

Guacamole as a chunky salad is best made with a knife rather than a processor. Cut the onion, tomato and avocado flesh into rough ½-inch chunks, mash them in a bowl with a sturdy fork, then add the remaining seasonings. Made in this way, the *guacamole* is particularly good as a substitute for table *salsa* when the main dish is simple grilled meat or fish.

Produced with the processor, the *guacamole* will be finer grained, but it should not be blended into utter smoothness or the tomato will turn it soupy. If you do use the processor, a good way to control the chopping is first to process the onion and garlic with the metal blade, using repeated pulses until they are finely chopped. Remove them to a bowl and repeat the procedure with the tomato. Remove that in turn and process the avocado with all the remaining ingredients. Add it to the onion and tomato, mix lightly with a fork, and serve immediately. If the *guacamole* must stand, keep it in a cool place, but not refrigerated, with plastic wrap pressed directly onto the surface to prevent discoloring. A well-made summertime *guacamole* is even more refreshing when you skip the tortilla chips and eat it with romaine lettuce leaves or with the aid of *jícama* sticks (see p. 175).

VARIATION:

Gardener's Guacamole: If you are lucky enough to have a vegetable patch, feel free to vary the formula given by adding chopped cucumber, bell pepper, radishes, waxy yellow peppers—whatever will make the *guacamole* lighter, crunchier and more refreshing.

WINTER GUACAMOLE

Guacamole recipes that call for avocado and ripe tomato are rather like asking you to buy pumpkins and asparagus at the same time. Unless you live in California, the only winter tomatoes are pale and mealy, just at the time when avocados are in abundance and at their cheapest. So here is a recipe for a winter *guacamole* without tomato. It is a simple formula, well suited to the bland green-skinned avocados that show up from Florida in December, but also good with the black, wrinkly ones that have a more emphatic and unctuous taste. The chilies called for in the list of ingredients below are decidedly optional. Principally you are after the unadulterated pleasure of the first cheap avocado of the season.

For about 1½ cups of guacamole:

>   2 avocados, halved, the flesh scooped out with a spoon
>   3 tablespoons lime juice
>   1 tablespoon olive oil
>   1 large garlic clove, mashed
> Optional: Any or all of the following—1 mild green chili, roasted
>   and peeled, 1 *jalapeño*, either fresh or canned, veins and
>   seeds removed, ¼ teaspoon cayenne, 2 green onions, cut into
>   1-inch lengths
> Salt and pepper to taste

Combine all the ingredients, including the optional ones, except for salt and pepper, in the bowl of a food processor. Using repeated pulses, blend until you reach a textured puree—about 8 pulses. Continuous processing will give you a smooth puree that can be used as a sauce, but for salads or by itself, the *guacamole* seems better for having some unpureed bits left in. Season to taste with salt and pepper, beginning with only a small amount if the natural sweetness of the avocado appeals to you. Serve immediately or store in a cool place—not the refrigerator—with plastic wrap pressed directly onto the surface of the *guacamole* to keep it from darkening. Some authorities claim that nestling the pit from an avocado into the finished *guacamole* helps to keep it from darkening, so you might also try that.

VARIATION:

Guacamole Sauce: Simply pureeing the preceding mixture until it is smooth gives you a good sauce, but you can adjust it further if you like by adding another 2 tablespoons of lime juice (this tart sauce is good with oily fish like red snapper) or ¼ cup of commercial sour cream, which produces the blander flavor of many restaurant *guacamoles*.

JÍCAMA

Jícama is a tropical vegetable that has little business appearing among New Mexican recipes, but it is very useful cut into ½-inch-thick sticks and arranged around *guacamole* in place of tortilla chips. Its crunchy texture, rather like cucumber, and its mild, sweet taste, are a good match for the typically spicy dips and *salsas* of Santa Fe cooking. The whole vegetable, looking like a very oversized turnip with ugly brown skin, shows up in supermarkets around the country. You have only to peel it with a potato peeler—the skin is fairly tough, but it readily comes off in strips once you have it started—and then cut the flesh into shapes like carrot sticks. A good-sized *jícama* weighing in excess of a pound will yield over 40 sticks. The Mexicans, who eat *jícama* as a streetside refresher on a sweltering day, also sprinkle the flesh with lime or lemon juice. This tastes very good, but it is not necessary for keeping the color white. Unlike apples, pears and celery root, which the cut-up *jícama* resembles, it stays unblemished in contact with air for at least an hour or two.

WINTER SALAD OF JÍCAMA AND ORANGES

To a native Mexican, the combination of *jícama* and oranges evokes not just the time of winter but a specific night, for those ingredients are the basis for Christmas Eve Salad (*Ensalada de Noche Buena*), a festive, complicated affair, which also includes beets, peanuts and pomegranate seeds. The *jícama* and orange salad described here is considerably simpler and much less tropical, but nonetheless refreshing in the dead part of the year when color and crispness are at a premium.

For 4 people:

    2 to 3 cups peeled, cubed *jícama* (about ¼ of a large *jícama*)
    4 oranges, peeled, sectioned, cut into chunks
    4 green onions, chopped
    ¼ cup green coriander (*cilantro*), chopped

DRESSING:

Juice from the salad
    1 tablespoon lime juice
    1 tablespoon vegetable oil
    2 tablespoons sour cream or plain yogurt
Salt

Mix all the salad ingredients in a bowl and allow to chill for several hours. Before serving, remove the salad from the refrigerator and let it come to cool room temperature. Pour off excess liquid into a small bowl or jar. Add the other ingredients for the dressing to this juice, shake or stir with a fork to combine them well, then toss with the salad. Add only a small amount of salt to the dressing since the salad's taste is primarily sweet. The dressing should be put on only at the last minute or it will cause more juice to drain.

VARIATIONS:

Although this salad is appealing and subtle in its own right, you can add to it cubed cooked beets, cucumber, apple, chopped nuts (including peanuts) or even bits of chopped green chilies, hot or mild, according to your taste. A *picante* salad of *jícama* and oranges spiked with powdered red chilies is called "rooster's beak," or *pico de gallo*, in Mexico proper, supposedly named for the pinching action of thumb and forefinger used to eat it.

RADISH, ONION AND GREEN CHILI SALAD

A mild brine takes the sharpness and rawness out of onions and radishes, transforming them into a crisp, summery salad. You can lift the vegetables straight from their pickling broth at the table, in which case they substitute for *jalapeño* strips as a relish, or you can drain them and toss with romaine lettuce for a welcome salad accompaniment for *enchiladas*. Finally, if you shred the romaine first, then add the pickled ingredients with just a drizzle of olive oil over all, the result is a rather special garnish for any *tostada*, *taco*, *enchilada*, *posole* or even green chili stew.

For 4 people:

  1 large bunch radishes, cleaned, trimmed of stems, and
    sliced in half
  4 to 6 green onions, or to taste
  1 red onion, sliced
  2 fresh Anaheim chilies or 1 bell pepper, trimmed, seeded
    and cut into thin rings or strips
  Optional: 1 or 2 cups of peeled, cubed *jícama* (see p. 175)
  Salt
  White or cider vinegar

The pickling is quick and easy. Toss all the vegetable ingredients with a generous sprinkling of salt, then drizzle on one or two tablespoons of white or cider vinegar. Add water barely to cover, then place in the refrigerator for 4 hours or overnight. The vegetables are ready when the radishes have lost their hot, raw taste.

For a sweeter mixture, add the *jícama*, which is a delicious addition, just before serving.

VARIATIONS:

To use in a green salad, toss pieces of romaine lettuce with a vinaigrette, portion onto serving plates, and top with generous amounts of the radish salad, drained from its brine. A New Mexican touch is to sprinkle a few raisins and piñon nuts over the top as well.

If you want a garnish for the *posole* stew on p. 266 or for *tacos* and *enchiladas*, shred the romaine leaves, toss with the radish salad in any proportion you favor, then drizzle olive oil lightly over all. Mix the garnish just at the last minute and serve cool—not cold.

PINTO, BLACK BEAN OR LENTIL SALAD

In Willa Cather's New Mexico novel, *Death Comes for the Archbishop*, gastronomic matters are distinctly placed in the shadow of spiritual ones, but we do learn at least of pinto bean salad. It is Father Latour's first Christmas in Santa Fe, the time is the middle of the last century, and to a civilized Frenchman, the prospects for feasting are decidedly bleak. It takes ingenuity and a 3,000-mile horseback ride just to collect the ingredients for his salad, which contains cooked pintos, diced salt pork (presumably boiled with the beans), chopped onion and a simple dressing of good olive oil, the precious commodity already acquired on the long journey by horse.

A nourishing and quite authentic pinto bean salad can be made exactly this way today, and although by modern standards the pork is dispensable, such an uncontrived dish would go a long way to efface memories of commercial three-bean salad. If you have avoided bean salads, particularly ones made from lentils, which are really the best of all, try the basic recipe given here. The beans are cooked until just done with a warm flavoring of cumin, bay leaf and pepper. They cool in the refrigerator for as long as you wish and are dressed and garnished at the last moment. The result is a far cry from the mushy marinated versions, invariably based upon canned goods, which are usually passed around as Southwestern pinto bean salad. Since the best salad is one you improvise from fresh ingredients, I merely suggest a few garnishes for the basic preparation—ingenious home cooks can easily think up their own, which would be just as good as these.

For 4 people:

> 1 cup dried pinto, kidney, or black beans, or ¾ cup lentils
> 3 cups water
> 1 teaspoon salt
> 1 teaspoon whole cumin seed
> ¼ teaspoon cracked black pepper
> 2 bay leaves
> Olive oil to drizzle over the salad
> Enough lettuce leaves for 4 servings

CILANTRO AND LEMON VINAIGRETTE:

> ⅓ cup olive oil
> 3 tablespoons lemon juice
> ¼ cup, or more, green coriander (*cilantro*)
> Large dash cracked black pepper
> ¼ teaspoon salt
> Optional, but very good: 2 roughly chopped green onions,
>   ¼ cup parsley

Cooking the beans is simplicity itself and so little trouble, once you dispense with a long presoaking, that you will be happy to forget canned beans. Rinse the beans or lentils under cold water in a colander. Combine with all the other ingredients, except the olive oil and lettuce leaves, in a 3- to 4-quart pot—the large size of the pot helps in case the bean water foams up excessively as it boils. Cover the pot and bring to a boil over medium heat. Allow to boil for a full minute, remove the pot from the heat and let stand for 1 hour. If you are using lentils, omit this precooking.

Return the beans to medium heat and boil, stirring occasionally, until the beans are just tender, but thoroughly cooked to the taste. You may need to add extra water from time to time, enough to keep the beans just covered, and if you are cooking black beans, they will need considerable attention to make sure that they do not stick to the bottom and char. As for cooking times, they depend on the age of the beans and altitude above sea level. In general, pintos, kidney beans and black beans take at least 1½ hours. Lentils, however, can take as little as 20 or 30 minutes.

When the beans are done, transfer to a colander and refresh under cold water until they are cooled. Allow to drain completely, then place in a mixing bowl. Drizzle a few tablespoons of olive oil over the beans, toss to coat thoroughly, then set them, lightly covered, in the refrigerator for at least 1 hour, or until serving time. This method is the general one for all cold bean, chick-pea or lentil dishes, so it is well worth having at your fingertips.

Dressing the salad: From this point, you need little more than a good homemade vinaigrette and a bed of lettuce leaves in order to have a delicious preparation. Dressings based upon olive oil and lemon juice are particularly compatible with bean salads, and chopped greens of some sort (parsley, *cilantro*, bell pepper) are always welcome to add color and texture.

Place all the dressing ingredients in a food processor or blender and mix until the greens are chopped and the dressing thoroughly amalgamated. Chill until serving time, then pour over the salad and toss at the last minute. (A prematurely dressed salad will give off water and thin the dressing.)

Garnishes: The simplest bean salad is placed on a bed of lettuce leaves and tossed lightly with a bit of the dressing. Since bean salads particularly take to being fancied up, however, here are some improvisations:

- Chop a fresh Anaheim chili (or half a bell pepper) and 2 stalks of celery. Add to the beans with their dressing.
- For an onion-and-garlic taste, which many Hispanic cooks find absolutely necessary, blend a clove of garlic with the ingredients for the dressing and add half a chopped sweet red onion to the beans before chilling them.
- Along with, or in place of, any of the above garnishes, strips of roasted chilies are good with any bean or lentil. Use canned green chili strips or the sweeter red peppers, which are usually bottled as "sandwich peppers" or Italian *peperonata*.
- Mexican cooks often add cubed beets to their salads—the canned variety (not pickled) is perfectly acceptable, and fresh is even better. A lentil salad garnished with diced beets and cold, fresh-cooked green beans is especially handsome.
- The best known Southwestern bean salad combines three beans— red kidney, chick-pea (*garbanzo*) and fresh green. Use celery, Anaheim chilies, and red onion as your garnishes, but do not get all of your beans from a can if you can help it. I find that fresh-cooked kidney beans and green beans are a must, and they easily disguise canned garbanzos, so those I do not cook up. If you want to prepare your own garbanzos, however, bear in mind that the precooking, as in the basic recipe, is not sufficient—they do need overnight soaking.

SOUPS

CHOOSING A SOUP

The soups chosen for this chapter, good as they all are, are barely representative of the numerous dishes eaten as soup, or *sopa*, in the Southwest. Particularly in the traditional Hispanic culture, there were preparations that we could recognize as soups only by an extension of imagination. A daily *sopa* could be any of the following things:

—clear meat or poultry broth, usually garnished with rice and eaten at the beginning of the meal (*caldo* or *caldillo*)

—meat stews made very thick and usually filled with a diversity of vegetables (*cocido*)

—"dry soups" based on rice or chick-peas with little or no liquid left after cooking (*sopa seca*)

—various creams, purees and other preparations which are not thin enough to be *caldos* or thick enough to be *cocidos*—in other words, all other soups (*sopas*).

As you can see, the culture gives soup a wide latitude, and even though the local restaurant menus do not often reflect it, the home cooks remain dedicated to a long tradition of *posole* (broth with meat and hominy), *menudo* (tripe soup), *cocido* (everyday mixed meat-and-vegetable stew) and, of course, all the soupy variants of meat stewed with green or red chilies. However, when a native speaks of eating *sopa*, he nowadays usually means the dry rice dish we call Mexican rice, that is, rice browned in oil and then cooked with onions and tomatoes. In our eyes, his daily soup is soupless.

This chapter therefore merely opens the door to soups. In deference to customary cookbook organization, the thicker stews, including *posole* and meat stewed with chilies, are placed together with the meat entrees in a later chapter. The "dry soups" are mostly gathered with other rice dishes in the chapter on rice and vegetables. Because it does not appeal to me, I have omitted *menudo*, and because they are little more than broth with rice I have not bothered to give specific directions for *caldos*. However, the soups offered in this chapter do play a part in the local cooking, and by learning them, you will understand the New Mexican way with soup.

MEATBALL SOUP WITH VEGETABLES
Sopa de albóndigas

Every part of Mexico and New Mexico has a version of *albóndigas*, or meatballs, which are invariably cooked and served in their broth. To make a hearty soup, the cook may thicken the broth with a *roux* of flour and lard and then perhaps add chunks of potato to boil along with the *albóndigas*. Even when the broth is thin, it is typical in Mexico to cook some onion and tomato in the pan before adding the broth.

For me, the best kind of meatball soup is based on a clear beef broth without thickeners. Small *albóndigas* are poached with slender strips of carrot, turnip, and zucchini, the whole process taking only 20 minutes from start to finish. Made this way, your soup will be light enough to precede a full spread of main dishes and dessert. If you want your *albóndigas* soup to become a meal in itself, refer to the versions that follow— they produce a pot of soup as sturdy as any *minestrone* or *petite marmite*.

For 4 to 6 people:

MEATBALL MIXTURE:

  1 pound chuck steak, or ½ pound each chuck steak and
    pork shoulder (which makes the *albóndigas* more delicate),
    cut into small chunks
  ⅔ cup matzo meal or dry bread crumbs
  1 egg
  ⅓ cup milk or cream
  1 teaspoon salt
  1 teaspoon ground coriander
  ¼ teaspoon black pepper
  ¼ cup canned green chilies, whole or chopped
  ¼ medium onion, roughly chopped
  1 or 2 cloves garlic, chopped

BROTH AND VEGETABLES:

  3 to 5 cups beef broth, or 1½ to 2½ cups each beef and
    chicken broth

½ cup each, peeled carrots, zucchini, and turnips or parsnips,
    all cut into thin 2-inch strips or batons
Chopped green coriander (*cilantro*) or chopped scallion for garnish

Place the meat into the bowl of a food processor and process until chopped a little coarser than hamburger, about 10 seconds. Scrape down the bowl with a rubber spatula. Combine the matzo meal or bread crumbs, egg and milk in a small bowl and stir with a fork to moisten the meal. Add to the processor bowl along with the remaining 6 ingredients. Process until the meatball mixture is ground smooth, about 10 more seconds, stopping at least once to scrape down the bowl. The meatballs can be formed and cooked immediately, or the mixture can be refrigerated until you need it.

Bring the broth to a full boil in a 3- or 4-quart saucepan. Meanwhile, begin to form the *albóndigas*—5 or 6 for each serving—and drop them in. Although traditionally the meatballs can be as large as small onions, for this lighter version they should be formed from about 1 tablespoon of meat. Shape by lightly rolling the meat mixture between the palms of your hands. When the broth is boiling, drop in the *albóndigas*, add all the vegetables, cover the pot and simmer for about 10 minutes. The meatballs should be done through but not overcooked, and the vegetable batons should still retain some crispness. Serve immediately with chopped coriander or green onion as garnish. The soup looks best in fairly wide, shallow soup plates.

VARIATIONS:

Main-Course Albóndigas Soup: The traditional way with this soup is to make it with a tomato-enriched broth and lots of seasonal vegetables. You will not have to change the ingredients for the meatballs, but here is the new broth-and-vegetable mixture:

For 4 people:

    2 or 3 tablespoons vegetable or olive oil
    ½ onion, chopped
    1 large clove garlic, chopped
    ½ teaspoon oregano
    2 tablespoons flour
    5 large canned tomatoes, chopped, or 1 cup crushed
        canned tomatoes packed in puree
    4 or 5 cups beef or chicken stock (or a combination of both)
    4 to 6 cups assorted fresh vegetables, such as carrots, turnips,
        parsnips, green beans, zucchini, potatoes and celery,
        all cut roughly into 1-inch chunks
    1½ cups shredded white cabbage

Heat oil in the bottom of a 3- or 4-quart pot, then add the onion and garlic. Cover the pot and allow the onion and garlic to wilt over medium-low heat for about 5 minutes. Uncover and stir in the oregano and flour. Stir over medium heat for 3 minutes to cook the flour, then add the tomatoes and stock off the heat and bring the broth to a simmer. Make the meatball mixture and poach it in the broth as directed, but form large *albóndigas* about the size of eggs, allowing 3 or 4 per person. These larger sizes will take about 30 minutes to poach.

At the same time as they are cooking, put in all the vegetables except the cabbage, adding the tender vegetables like zucchini and turnip only in the last 10 minutes of poaching. Taste for seasoning at the end of this period, then add the cabbage and cook at a slow boil for 5 or 10 minutes more. Serve in large soup bowls presented with a homemade *salsa*, which the diners spoon over the soup to make it *picante*.

Albóndigas Without Vegetables: Another traditional version, this one is to be eaten with flour tortillas like chili con carne. Proceed to make the tomato-enriched broth described above but increase the onion to 1 whole onion and use only 4 cups of broth. In addition, many cooks would spice up the soup by adding 1 tablespoon powdered red chilies and liberal pinches of dried mint. Poach the *albóndigas* in the broth as usual, making them large—each one should contain about ¼ cup of the meat mixture. They will need to poach gently for 15 minutes, although native cooks often extend this to 1 hour for the doneness they prefer.

GARNISHED TURKEY-AND-RICE SOUP

Under the Spanish flag, meals in Santa Fe included both liquid and "dry" soups. The liquid ones were commonly thin broths with rice or chick-peas in them. The habit of having first courses of thin soup passed away as a fixture in the modern period, but there have been revivals among lovers of the old ways. One of the staunchest is Sam P. Arnold, who went so far as to build a duplicate of a frontier fort to live in and is an expert on pioneer cooking. His reconstruction of Bent's Fort was turned into The Fort restaurant outside Denver (the original stands in southern Colorado as a government restoration), and in its heyday, fifteen years ago, it inspired anyone who came there with Mr. Arnold's infectious enthusiasm for frontier life.

His courage as a restaurateur makes current Southwestern cooks blanch —he went so far as to import and boil moose noses for unwary customers, and an appetizer called "Broiled Comanche Beef Heart" was a staple. Some of the specialties were outright inventions based upon his wide reading in historic annals. Among them was a garnished rice soup named "Bowl of the Wife of Kit Carson," which I have reproduced after a recipe I jotted down in the restaurant ten years ago. (It is not Mr. Arnold's original, I should mention.) The name is appropriate and evocative, for Kit Carson married a Spanish girl of Taos named Josefa Jaramillo, who doubtlessly served him many a bowl of such *sopa*. The amount of rice and *garbanzos* called for below makes quite a hearty soup, which Mr. Arnold offered as a main course.

For 4 people:

    2 tablespoons butter
    ½ large onion, chopped
    1 clove garlic, chopped
    ⅔ cup rice
    6 cups chicken broth
    ½ teaspoon cumin
    4 whole canned green chilies, chopped (about ½ cup)
Pepper to taste
    2 cups canned or home-cooked chick-peas (*garbanzos*), with
       some of their cooking liquid reserved
    1 whole chicken breast, cooked, then diced or shredded
       or 1 cup cooked, diced or shredded turkey-breast meat
    1 cup Monterey Jack cheese, cut into ½-inch cubes
    2 avocados, cut into lengthwise slices
Optional: 2 tablespoons chopped *cilantro*, green onions or *jalapeño*

Heat the butter in a large saucepan or stock pot of at least 3-quart capacity, then stir in the onion and garlic. Cover the pot and sweat the onion for 5 minutes over low heat. Uncover, raise the heat to medium, and stir in the rice. When the grains start to look milky or opaque, add the chicken broth and cumin and bring to a boil. Boil gently for 25 minutes, or until the rice is quite tender. The soup can be set aside at this point until 15 minutes before serving.

Bring the broth back to a boil and add the chilies, pepper to taste, chick-peas, and the chicken or turkey. When the soup is heated through, but before the chick-peas turn mushy, check the consistency and add chick-pea liquid if it seems too thick—it should resemble a hearty chicken-and-rice soup, not a stew.

Pour into large bowls and bring to the table, garnished at the last minute with the cubes of cheese and slices of avocado. The soup should be hot enough to just melt the cheese, but not cook the avocado. For a bit of variety, garnish with the optional *cilantro*, green onion, or fresh *jalapeño*, but it is delicious without any of them. Present warm flour tortillas on the side if this is a main course.

After writing this recipe, I discovered in a conversation with Mr. Arnold that the secret ingredient in his original, which I failed to detect as a customer trying to guess the ingredients, was a generous dash of *chile chipotle* to add hotness and smokiness to the flavor (1 of the canned kind, chopped, should do; see p. 69 if you are not familiar with *chiles chipotles*).

TORTILLA SOUP

If you cut stale tortillas into strips, fry them until stiffened and then use them as a garnish in the bottom of your bowl, any soup poured over them becomes a tortilla soup. At first blush the addition of tortillas doesn't seem like an improvement. You already might have a good chicken broth with rice, a clear vegetable soup based on beef broth, or a thick tomato soup, to give just three of the most popular ones that Mexican cooks like to use as the basis of their tortilla soups. The combination can be very good, however, and its sheer simplicity has made tortilla soup a staple on restaurant menus throughout the Southwest. However, real ingenuity begins to appear as you draw closer to Mexico itself, where tortilla soup variations are numerous. Northern New Mexico is not really the native ground of this specialty.

Two recipes already given lend themselves well to becoming tortilla soup—the Garnished Turkey-and-Rice Soup on p. 186 and the *albóndigas*, or meatball, soup on p. 184. Eliminate the *garbanzos* called for in the rice soup, and count on either soup to be quite a filling first course.

As for frying the tortillas, allow 1 or 2 corn tortillas per person, preferably stale ones, cut into ½-inch strips with scissors. Heat vegetable oil in a skillet to a depth of ½ inch and fry the strips, a handful at a time, until they are stiffened and beginning to brown. After draining and cooling, these tortilla shreds are simply placed in the bottom of each soup bowl and the soup ladled directly over. It is customary to pass shredded cheese at the table to sprinkle on as a garnish (unless the soup itself already contains cheese).

Also not very much found in the northern reaches of New Mexico, but said to get more popular as you go south, is a "dry soup" based upon tortillas. It is made like Mexican rice, with tortillas used in place of the rice. The *chilaquiles* on p. 239 resembles a dry tortilla soup and is well worth trying. Other versions, which tend to come out like tortilla mush pure and simple, will not be detailed here.

POTATO SOUP WITH GREEN CHILIES

This most simple and delicious of Southwestern soups is really a short-ened form of the green chili stew called a *cocido*. It tastes purely of green chilies, but the mealy potatoes smooth the taste and make it more com-forting than raw chili could ever be. A soup very much like this is served every day at The Shed, the most popular lunch place in Santa Fe, just off Sena Plaza. The variation with sour cream is, if anything, better.

For 4 people:

> 2 or 3 tablespoons vegetable oil
> 1 small onion, chopped
> 1 or 2 cloves garlic, chopped
> ½ teaspoon cumin
> ¼ teaspoon black pepper
> Pinch oregano
> 2 medium boiling potatoes, peeled and cut into small chunks as for vegetable soup
> 8 whole canned green chilies, chopped (about ⅔ cup)
> Optional: 2 teaspoons chopped canned *jalapeños*
> 5 cups chicken broth
> Optional garnish: shredded Monterey Jack cheese or chopped green coriander (*cilantro*)

Heat the oil in a 2-quart saucepan, add the onion and garlic, and cook, covered, over low heat for about 5 minutes so that the onion can wilt. Uncover the pan, raise the heat to medium, and stir in the cumin and pepper. Stir for 2 or 3 minutes, or until the onions start to show signs of browning, then add oregano, potatoes, green chilies, the optional *jalapeños* and the chicken broth. Bring to a boil, cover and simmer slowly for 45 minutes. Serve very hot with the optional cheese or *cilantro* sprinkled over each portion if you like.

VARIATION:

Creamed Potato and Green Chili Soup: The addition of ½ cup of sour cream, stirred in off the heat after the soup has finished cooking, makes it taste richer, and many people would say even better.

CHEDDAR SOUP WITH GREEN CHILIES

As the use of Cheddar cheese shows, this is not an indigenous soup but a modern restaurant invention, a sort of *chile con queso* in soup form which promises to be just as appealing as the original dip. You can, of course, make it with the more traditional Monterey Jack cheese if you like, and there are several other variations possible, some of which I list after the basic recipe. Because of its high cream content, the soup should be served in small cups as a first course, but it is even better as a meal on its own. The only other requirements would be warm flour tortillas on the side and a tartly dressed green salad to help cut the lovely richness of the cream and cheese.

For 4 people as a first course or 2 for a full meal:

    2 tablespoons butter
   ¼ cup chopped onion
    2 tablespoons flour
    2 canned, peeled tomatoes
    3 whole, canned green chilies, well rinsed and drained
 1½ cups chicken broth
 1½ cups heavy cream
    6 ounces sharp Cheddar cheese, shredded
Salt, if needed

Melt the butter in a heavy 2-quart saucepan, add the onions, cover the pan and sweat the onions over low heat for 5 minutes. Uncover the pan and add the flour, stirring for 2 minutes to cook away its raw flavor (but do not allow the mixture to brown). Puree the tomatoes and green chilies roughly in a food processor, stopping while there is still some texture remaining. Stir into the onions for a minute, then pour the chicken broth over and bring to a boil. Stir a few times to ensure that the flour is not sticking to the bottom of the pan, then simmer over low heat for 20 minutes with the pan partly covered. The soup can be set aside at this point to be completed later.

When ready to serve, bring the soup back to a boil, lower the heat to medium and add the cream and shredded cheese. Stir once or twice until the cheese has melted and the soup is heated through, but do not ever let it boil for fear it will curdle. Taste for salt and add it sparingly as needed. Serve alone as a first course, or accompanied by warm flour tortillas if the remainder of the meal is not too filling.

VARIATIONS:

Made as above, this soup is smooth but has bits of chili, onion and tomato floating in it, like *chile con queso*. For a more formal presentation, puree the solid ingredients in a processor just after the soup has gone through its initial simmering. For a meatier meal in itself, add diced, boiled potato and precooked *chorizo* sausage with the cream and cheese, beginning with about ¾ cup of potato and ½ cup of meat. For an even heartier winter pottage, add 1 cup of cooked pinto beans along with the potato and sausage. Add ½ teaspoon cayenne with the flour if you want the soup hot.

ATOLE

Atole is corn gruel, and to us it would taste about as good as it sounds. Mixed from cornmeal and boiling water, it can be as thick as porridge or as thin as, well, gruel. In the mountain villages of New Mexico, the cornmeal used for *atole* is blue, so the dish looks like a thin puddle of poured cement. We are told that it is mainly drunk by invalids and old people, but there is an argument to be made for *atole* as the basic food of pre-Columbian America. The Aztecs sweetened theirs with honey and passed it on to the poor Hispanic farmers throughout Mexico and the Southwest.

It was also employed in a test administered to the Franciscan fathers who first came to convert the Pueblos. The missionary was given a hospitable first meal of *atole* liberally interlaced with sand, a chopped field mouse and the contents of the family chamber pot. If he passed this most horrible example of guest food, the good father was allowed the normal dinner of corn tortillas, jerked meat and dried melon. I will not bother to give a recipe for *atole*, since your measure of hospitality must be your own, but you can begin with about ½ cup of corn meal added slowly to 3 cups of boiling water or milk; add salt or honey to taste.

LENTIL SOUP WITH LIME JUICE

The lentil soups flavored with lemon juice in Middle Eastern cookery are favorites of mine, but few cooks seem to know about that inspired combination; instead, they make the rather stodgy lentil soups from Europe which have salt pork and sausage in them. Here is a light lentil soup made Southwestern rather than Middle Eastern by the addition of green chilies and lime juice. It can be served in summer as well as winter (which can hardly be said of most recipes) and is eminently easy to fix.

For about 6 cups, serving 4 to 6 people:

  1½ cups dried lentils
   6 cups water, and additional water as needed
  1½ teaspoons salt
   ½ teaspoon cracked black pepper
   ½ teaspoon whole cumin
   ½ teaspoon dried mint, thyme, or oregano
   3 bay leaves
   ¼ to ½ cup canned chopped mild green chilies
   1 bell pepper, deveined, seeded and cut into chunks
   1 carrot, peeled and cut into chunks
   ¼ cup lime juice, preferably fresh-squeezed
   2 tablespoons olive oil

Place the first 7 ingredients into a 3-quart pot and bring to a boil over medium heat. Skim off any foam that rises to the surface, cover the pot, and boil gently until lentils are thoroughly soft—this takes anywhere from 30 to 60 minutes. Place the green chilies and 1 cup of the soup into a food processor and process continuously until pureed. Return mixture to the soup in the pot.

Wipe the processor bowl with a paper towel or rinse lightly, then finely chop first the bell pepper and then the carrot in it, using repeated pulses of the motor and stopping at least once to scrape down the bowl with a spatula. Add the bell pepper and then the carrot to the soup. From this point, the soup can be held off heat until serving time, or you can proceed directly to the final step.

When you are ready to serve, bring the soup back to a boil (but do not cook at this temperature for more than a minute since you want the bell pepper and carrot to remain crisp), taste for seasoning and add more water to adjust the texture—the soup should be thick enough to coat a spoon but not porridgy. Stir in the lime juice and olive oil, warm through for a few seconds more and serve.

EGG AND
BREAKFAST DISHES

Ranch-Style Eggs (Huevos rancheros)
Breakfast Burrito (Burrito desayuno)
Green Chili Omelets
Omelet with Whole Stuffed Chilies
Scrambled Eggs with Tortillas
Scrambled Eggs with Jerky
Scrambled Eggs with Sage Cheese
Breakfast Sausage (Chorizo)
Fried Potatoes with Green Chili
Creamed Hominy with Cheese and Green Chili
White Tamales with Cheese Filling
Breakfast Soufflé Spoonbread
Biscuits
White Corn Muffins with Green Chilies

RANCH-STYLE EGGS
Huevos rancheros

The most famous Mexican egg dish in the Southwest is *huevos rancheros*, or ranch-style eggs. Thanks to a proliferation of small changes in the basic dish, the name now means little more than fried eggs, sunny side up, with chili sauce on top. Some directions ask you to cook the eggs in a skillet with the sauce, but that is a little messy if the eggs stick to the pan. The version below calls for a crisp tortilla for the eggs to sit on (you can fry your own in ¼ inch of oil, or simply warm up store-bought *tostadas*). The dish is easier to handle with a knife and fork if you fry the tortilla only to a slight crispness, leaving the interior still pliant. The texture is the same as for soft *tacos* and takes a little getting used to before its chewiness seems appealing.

For 1 person:

> 2 corn tortillas
> Oil for shallow frying
> 2 eggs
> Salt and pepper
> ¾ to 1 cup quick *ranchera* sauce (p. 91) or the basic
> green chili sauce on p. 80
> ½ cup shredded Monterey Jack cheese (about 2 ounces)

Fry 1 tortilla quickly on both sides in ¼ inch of sizzling hot oil, using a skillet just larger than the tortilla. When it is almost crisped, about 30 seconds per side, drain the tortilla over the skillet and set it aside on paper toweling. Repeat with the second tortilla. Pour out all but a tablespoon or two of the oil, let it cool a minute, and fry the eggs without turning them until the whites are set and the yolks still runny. Place the tortilla on a serving plate with the eggs on top and season with salt and pepper. Pour out the oil from the skillet, heat the chili sauce quickly in the same skillet and pour it over the eggs. Top with the shredded cheese, which should just melt from the heat of the *salsa*.

VARIATIONS:

Poached Huevos Rancheros: Warm tortillas in the oven wrapped in foil—some people eat 2 or 3 on the side, so warm up several. Heat the sauce in a 7-inch skillet until bubbling, then reduce the heat, carefully break the eggs directly into the sauce, and simmer uncovered until the whites set. Sprinkle the cheese over, cover the pan and let cook a bit longer until the cheese melts but the yolks are still runny. (If this seems improbable, you can sprinkle on the cheese and run the pan close under a broiler flame for a few seconds.) Transfer the contents of the skillet to a plate and serve with the warm tortillas on the side.

Garnished Huevos Rancheros: It is customary for the sauce on the *huevos* to be fairly hot; some New Mexicans would pour on the hottest *salsa jalapeña* they could find. As a final touch, any number of garnishes to be added at the table are possible. The most common are sliced avocado, chopped scallion, chopped green coriander (*cilantro*), crumbled and sautéed *chorizo* sausage (p. 205) and chopped, pickled *jalapeños*. The basic dish is quite delicious unadorned, however.

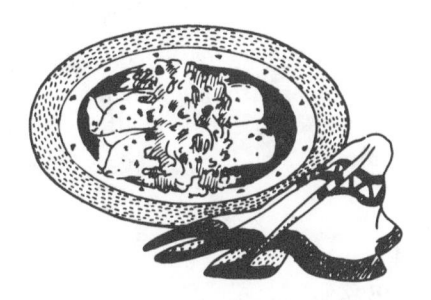

BREAKFAST BURRITO
Burrito desayuno

Any Mexican-style café that caters to the local passion for eating breakfast out in Santa Fe will offer a *burrito desayuno*, or breakfast burrito. These are often quite hot with green chili, but in truth, any of the fillings customary for *burritos* might be served in the morning. Refer to the description on p. 125 to familiarize yourself with the general nature of a *burrito*, and once you have that down, you might try the fillings below. They are typical mixtures found on any morning in New Mexico.

For 2 burritos, serving 1 person:

    2 flour tortillas
Homemade red or green chili *salsa,* such as the sour green chili
      version on p. 91, or red or green *enchilada* sauce, p. 73 and 80
    ½ cup of one of the fillings below

Preheat oven to 300° F.

Prepare one of the fillings listed below, using a small skillet, while warming the tortillas wrapped in foil in the oven for a few minutes. Place 3 or 4 tablespoons of filling in a thick line across the bottom third of a tortilla, spoon over a little *salsa* to moisten and fold in the traditional manner (p. 125).

FILLINGS:

Fried Potatoes with Green Chili Filling: Follow the recipe on p. 206, which yields enough for 6 *burritos*.

Scrambled Egg and Potato Filling: Make potato filling above, stirring in 2 beaten eggs with the green chili. Stir constantly over low heat until the eggs scramble and no liquid remains. The basic recipe will now fill 8 *burritos*.

Egg and Cheese Filling: Scramble 3 eggs with 2 tablespoons butter in a small skillet. Just as they are about to set, stir in 2 tablespoons canned chopped green chilies. When thoroughly set but still tender, remove from heat, salt and pepper lightly and immediately stir in ¼ cup shredded Monterey Jack cheese. Serve at once, since this filling cannot be reheated. For a creamier variation, use 3 tablespoons of the sage cheese on p. 103.

Sausage and Egg Filling: Using the homemade *chorizo* on p. 205, fry 2 sausage patties and crumble them into a small bowl. Scramble 2 eggs and add them to the bowl, then moisten with dabs of *salsa* and proceed to fill *burritos*. Delicious as this basic filling is, it is improved by incorporating half a ripe avocado cut into small dice. Even mediocre late-winter avocados work well here. Some cooks would also add a few diced fried potatoes to the mix.

For burritos that are more picante: If you agree with Santa Feans who believe that a *burrito desayuno* can never be too hot, add 2 teaspoons chopped *jalapeños*, canned or fresh, to any of the fillings above.

Sauced Breakfast Burritos: All the *burritos* above are eaten by hand with a bit of *salsa* inside, but it is also common to see them filled, rolled, and then covered, on an ovenproof plate, with ½ cup or more of green chili, using the recipe on p. 231. It is not necessary to do more than heat these in a 300° F. oven for a few minutes since there is no cheese to melt and both the filling and the *chile verde* are warm to begin with. Once again, the chili sauce is likely to be hotted up with added chopped *jalapeño*.

GREEN CHILI OMELETS

The Mexican way with eggs is more often than not to scramble them, with additional ingredients, such as onion, tomato, potato, chopped chilies, sausage and cheese, usually outweighing the eggs by a considerable margin (albeit a flat omelet in Spain can enclose twice as many potatoes as even Mexican cooks indulge in). The green chili omelets served up in certain Santa Fe cafés are the better for being simple, often nothing more than a plain omelet sprinkled with dashes of hot green chili and cheese. Here are a few variations on a basic theme. All of them are among the most delicious of Southwestern breakfast foods, for green chili, cheese and eggs have a natural affinity.

For 1 omelet:

> ½ cup green chili sauce (see basic recipe on p. 80)
> A few teaspoonfuls sour cream or cream cheese at room temperature
>   2 eggs
> Salt and pepper
>   1 tablespoon butter
> ¼ cup (about 1 ounce) shredded Monterey Jack cheese

Preheat the broiler or set the oven at 425° F.

Warm the green chili sauce and have it ready, along with the sour cream and Jack cheese, so that the cooking and filling of the omelet will take only a minute.

Season the eggs with salt and pepper and whisk them in a bowl with a fork for 30 strokes as for scrambled eggs. Melt the butter in a 7-inch nonstick skillet, then wait a good 5 seconds after its foaming has stopped. Swirl the slightly browned butter around to coat the pan, then add the eggs all at once. Let them sit over high heat for 10 seconds to begin to cook, then swirl them quickly with the flat of a fork, shaking the pan with your other hand. Stop as soon as the eggs coalesce into a flat mass, set on the bottom but still a little runny on top. Plop in a few teaspoons of sour cream or cream cheese, then lift up the pan by the handle to slide the omelet into place for rolling. Still using your fork, carefully lift the back edge of the omelet and flip it over the filling. Rap the farther edge of the pan against the burner to flip over the outer edge of the omelet, or help that along with your fork, too. Holding the skillet in one hand and an ovenproof plate (or small gratin dish) in the other, position them so that they meet in a tight V. With a turn of the wrist, roll the entire omelet onto its plate, and you will have a perfectly folded, finished omelet.

Pour the green chili sauce over the top, then scatter the cheese over. Run the plate or gratin dish close to the broiler flame, or place in the hot

BASIC STIRRED OMELET

1. Briskly stir eggs over high heat as you move your skillet back and forth with the other hand.

2. When the eggs are set but still soft on top, add any desired filling (none is shown here) and use a fork to help bring the edge of the omelet over the center.

3. Tilt the skillet and rap hard on the handle to flip the opposite edge of the omelet over—it can be helped along by a fork, as with the first edge.

4. Holding the skillet and serving plate in a tight V-shape, tilt the omelet out onto the plate in one quick motion, rolling completely so that the folded edges are now underneath.

oven only until the cheese melts. Serve immediately, since a tender, cream-filled omelet soon begins to weep—but that is preferable to one that is tough inside.

VARIATIONS:

Green Chili Omelet with Chorizo: Instead of sour cream, or along with it, fill your omelet with a tablespoon of chopped *chorizo* sausage. The recipe on p. 103 requires no advance preparation, but authentic *chorizo* must be skinned, then the meat crumbled and fried.

Green Chili Omelet with Potatoes: As common as a *chorizo* filling is the one made of diced potato and onion which have been cooked until lightly browned in a little olive oil. Once again, only a tablespoon or so is needed, which makes this a little impractical unless you have a bit of leftover boiled potato or enough people to warrant cooking a whole potato. Combining potato and *chorizo* is also customary, but extremely filling.

Green Chili and Avocado Omelet: In this variation, nearly as good as the basic recipe, the omelet is filled with small chunks of fresh avocado in place of the sour cream. Or, since avocado is really at its best uncooked, you can make the basic omelet, fill and cook it, then scatter fresh avocado in thin slices over the top. A sprinkling of chopped green coriander (*cilantro*) adds another desirable flavoring. Both, however, are reminiscent of the Mexico to the south rather than New Mexico mountain territory.

Flat Green Chili Omelet: The basic recipe, as well as the variations, can be cooked in the Spanish style as a flat omelet, which, by a curious confusion of names, is called a *tortilla*. Stir in any solid fillings as you scramble the eggs. When set, slide the omelet out of the skillet onto its plate but do not fold it. Top with green chili sauce and cheese, then run briefly under the broiler to just heat the topping. Liquid ingredients like sour cream, or fresh ones like avocado and green coriander, are added only after the broiling, when the *tortilla* is ready to serve. Another Spanish touch is to use olive oil in place of butter for cooking the eggs.

OMELET WITH WHOLE STUFFED CHILIES

A whole green chili stuffed with a finger of Monterey Jack cheese is called a *chile relleno*, and it is traditional to deep-fry it. The combination of flavors is so successful that it would be a shame not to extend the ways of using whole stuffed chilies—therefore, this omelet and the variation that follows. They can be served for breakfast or lunch, accompanied with the many garnishes appropriate to *tostadas*, such as shredded lettuce, tomatoes, avocado, olives, sour cream and so on. The bare essential is a good red or green chili sauce. However, a dollop of *guacamole* would be a delightful bonus.

For 1 omelet, serving 1 person:

- 2 whole, roasted mild green chilies, (Anaheim, *poblano*, etc.) either fresh or canned
- 2 finger-length slivers of Monterey Jack cheese
- 2 eggs
- Salt and pepper
- 1 tablespoon butter
- ⅓ cup good tomato sauce (such as the quick version on p. 80) or any homemade chili sauce, red or green

If necessary, review the procedure for making omelets on p. 198.

Preheat the oven to 375° F. and set the tomato sauce in it for a few minutes to warm up.

Carefully open the chilies, lay the slivers of cheese inside, and refold into their original shape. Whisk the eggs together, season them, melt the butter in a small skillet, and proceed to make an omelet. When the time comes to fill it, just before folding, lay the stuffed chilies carefully across the center of the omelet. Fold and transfer to an ovenproof plate. Pour over the sauce, and since the residual heat in the eggs is usually not enough to melt the cheese, slip the plate for a few minutes into the oven.

VARIATION:

Puffy Omelet with Whole Stuffed Chilies: Separate the yolks from the whites of the 2 eggs and beat the whites until they hold soft peaks, using a portable electric mixer. Beat the yolks with salt, pepper and 2 teaspoons of milk until foamy. Fold the whites into the yolks and preheat the oven to 400° F. (and preheat the broiler if you want a browned top on your omelet).

Melt the tablespoon of butter in an 8-inch oven-proof skillet, then spoon in a thin layer of egg. Top with the stuffed chilies, then pour the remainder of the eggs over. Let cook undisturbed until the bottom of the omelet is lightly browned. Transfer the skillet to the oven and bake until puffed and done, but not too stiff. Top with a sprinkling of Monterey Jack cheese and run under the broiler to melt. The cheese is not absolutely necessary, but a good tomato or chili sauce is, since puffy omelets tend to be rather dry. Serve as a brunch or luncheon dish, as you would the *chile relleno* casserole on p. 252.

SCRAMBLED EGGS WITH TORTILLAS

Improbable as it may sound from the title, the tortillas *are* actually scrambled in the pan with the eggs. This is a technique among Mexican cooks, many of whom add tomatoes or sausage to the pan as well, until the proportion of egg is rather minor compared to all the accompaniments. The basic recipe here is at least half egg, but in the variations that follow you can begin adding other ingredients at will. Whether to fry the tortillas crisp or leave them only half-crisp is a question of personal preference—the standard advice is to fry them until only a touch of brown begins to show and the texture remains chewy.

For 1 person:

> 3 tablespoons vegetable oil
> 1 corn tortilla cut into 8 wedges
> 2 green onions, chopped
> 1 whole, canned or fresh green chili, chopped
> 1 tablespoon green coriander (*cilantro*), chopped
> 2 or 3 eggs, beaten together in a small bowl with salt and pepper
> Shredded Monterey Jack cheese

Heat the oil in a small frying pan until quite hot, then add the pieces of tortilla and fry until they are starting to brown and are half-crisp. Pour off all but 1 tablespoon of the oil, then briefly sauté the onion, chili and green coriander with the tortilla. Add the beaten eggs and scramble over low heat until they are set but still moist. Remove from heat, quickly stir in as much cheese as you like, starting with 3 tablespoons or so, and serve.

VARIATIONS:

The basic recipe makes a light, savory breakfast dish which many New Mexicans might consider somewhat insubstantial. You can increase the onion to twice as much, or make the dish hotter with an additional fresh *jalapeño* (deveined, seeded and chopped), or, most common of all, you could add a chopped, seeded fresh tomato to cook along with the other vegetables. For a one-dish breakfast, fry ¼ to ½ cup of *chorizo* sausage in a separate pan and stir it in to cook with the eggs (the *chorizo*-flavored sausage on p. 103 needs no precooking, but be careful not to add salt to the eggs if you use it since it is quite salty in its own right).

SCRAMBLED EGGS WITH JERKY

Scrambled eggs with shredded beef in a pan sauce is a Mexican favorite. Using the air-dried steak called *machaca* is most characteristic; *machaca* refers to the pounding that the meat receives before it is fried with a complement of tomatoes, chilies and onions. The recipe here is for something simpler, the dried beef jerky sold in supermarkets (see p. 38). Since jerky is quite expensive by weight, I call for only a small amount, but you can substitute shredded beef if you like (see p. 98 for instructions), in which case you could allot ½ cup of beef or more. You may be surprised at how much else besides eggs goes into this dish, but it is common for New Mexican cooks to make the eggs subordinate to the meat and sauce. Without the meat, by the way, this sauce is similar to the one that goes over *huevos rancheros*.

For 2 people:

    ¼ cup beef jerky (about 1 ounce)
Water to soften the jerky
    1 clove garlic, peeled
    1 *jalapeño*, deveined and seeded
    ¼ medium onion, peeled and cut into chunks
    1 Anaheim chili, deveined and seeded, then cut into thirds
    2 tablespoons vegetable or olive oil
    2 fresh tomatoes, seeded and cut into chunks, or
      3 to 4 canned tomatoes
    3 eggs, beaten
Salt and pepper to taste
Chopped green coriander for garnish

Cut the beef jerky into ¼-inch pieces and cover with hot water to soften.

Turn on the motor of the food processor and drop the garlic and *jalapeño* in through the feed tube. When they are chopped, turn off the machine, put the onion and Anaheim chili into the bowl, then process in quick pulses until these are coarsely chopped. You will probably need to stop once to scrape down the bowl with a spatula. Heat the oil in a 7- or 8-inch skillet, preferably nonstick, then add the contents of the processor. Cover and sweat the vegetables over low heat for 5 minutes. Chop the tomatoes coarsely in the processor—only 5 to 7 pulses of the motor. Drain the jerky.

Uncover the skillet and stir in the tomatoes and jerky. Stir over medium heat until the sauce boils, then let simmer for 2 minutes or so—it will be reduced but still fairly fresh-looking. Add the eggs and scramble them over medium-low heat, stirring constantly to prevent excessive sticking.

When the eggs are set, remove from the heat, season with salt and pepper as needed (be careful—some jerky is quite salty), and serve with a sprinkling of chopped green coriander (*cilantro*) on top. Accompany the eggs with warm flour tortillas. These eggs are especially good used as a filling for *burritos*, in which case you will also want a homemade *salsa* on the side.

VARIATION:

Fried Eggs with Jerky and Tortillas: Follow the recipe for *huevos rancheros* on p. 195, substituting the sauce above. The fried eggs may be more appealing for those who are not familiar with the thick consistency and orangey color of Mexican eggs scrambled with meat.

SCRAMBLED EGGS WITH SAGE CHEESE

This is a very simple breakfast dish that is also rich enough to replace such brunchtime mainstays in the East as scrambled eggs with smoked salmon. All you need to have on hand already is the easily made Sage Cheese on p. 103.

Take approximately ¼ cup of the sage cheese, either freshly made or chilled, and blend until quite soft in your food processor, then blend in 8 to 10 eggs and season with ¼ teaspoon salt, if needed. Melt 2 or 3 tablespoons of butter in a 10-inch skillet until it foams, pour in the eggs, reduce the heat to low, and gently scramble. Served with fresh parsley on top and a ring of good tomato sauce (or red chili sauce that has a good proportion of tomato in it), this makes a sumptuous breakfast dish for 3 or 4 people. A tablespoon or two of the sage cheese can also be used to fill individual omelets, a delicious variation which does not require the sauce, only a dab of butter to melt over the top as the fresh omelet travels to the table.

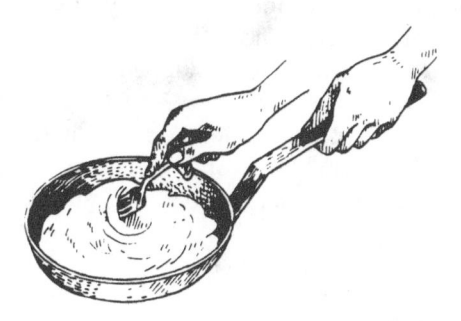

BREAKFAST SAUSAGE
Chorizo

The recipe for patty sausage given here can be used in place of commercial link *chorizo* since it has all the essential flavors of a longer-cured sausage. Besides incorporating it into omelets or fillings for *burritos*, you will find that this mixture makes excellent breakfast sausage, but try to grind it at least a day in advance to give the flavors the benefit of a short curing period.

For 1 pound of patty sausage:

> 1 pound fatty pork shoulder cut into chunks, or
>   unseasoned pork sausage meat
> 1 or 2 tablespoons powdered red chilies
> 1 clove garlic, mashed and finely minced
> 1 teaspoon salt
> ½ teaspoon pepper
> Dashes of ground cumin and oregano
> 1 tablespoon white vinegar

If you are using pork shoulder, place it with all the other ingredients in the bowl of a food processor equipped with the standard metal blade and process until the meat is coarsely ground, stopping at least once to scrape down the bowl with a rubber spatula. (If you begin with preground sausage meat, you will only need to process meat with the flavorings for a few seconds.)

You can achieve coarse bits by using on-and-off pulses of the motor, and a finer-grained sausage if you process continuously for 20 seconds or so, but do not go so far that the meat becomes pasty. Check for seasoning by sautéing a small bit in a skillet—taste and adjust seasonings as desired.

Pack the finished sausage into a bowl, cover closely with foil or plastic wrap, pressing it directly onto the surface of the meat, and allow to cure in the refrigerator for at least half a day. (It will keep in this condition for about a week at most; 3 or 4 days is a more advisable storage time.)

To cook homemade *chorizo*, shape it into thin patties between moistened palms and sauté in a small skillet as you would any patty sausage. Take care to use fairly low temperatures for this, however, because the red chili in the mixture tends to scorch rather easily.

FRIED POTATOES WITH GREEN CHILI

The usual restaurant hash browns are pallid next to this mixture of potatoes, onions and green chili. The chili taste is warming rather than fiery, but you can make it hotter with 2 teaspoons or more of chopped, canned *jalapeños*. A healthy portion of these potatoes is really a working-man's breakfast, but smaller portions go very well in breakfast *burritos*, as described on p. 196, in which case you will not need eggs to fill out the meal.

For 4 people:

> 2 tablespoons vegetable oil
> ½ onion, chopped into approximately ½-inch pieces
> ¼ to ½ cup salt pork, cut into ½-inch dice
> 3 cups boiled potatoes, peeled or unpeeled, cut into ½-inch dice
> Cumin, cayenne and black pepper to taste
> 6 to 8 tablespoons chopped, canned green chilies
> Salt, if needed

Heat the oil in a 10- or 12-inch skillet and brown the onion and salt pork lightly. Stir in the potatoes and seasonings and toss over medium heat until heated through and beginning to brown. Stir in the green chilies, toss a minute more and taste to see if any salt is necessary. Serve quickly and quite hot.

VARIATION:

New Mexican Potato Omelet: The potatoes can be used to fill omelets as soon as they are cooked, allotting about ¼ cup to a 2-egg folded omelet or about ⅓ cup to a 3-egg flat omelet, which a Spaniard would call a *tortilla*.

CREAMED HOMINY WITH
CHEESE AND GREEN CHILI

A Southerner would recognize a familiar taste in this dish, even with the New Mexican additions of Monterey Jack cheese and green chilies—for dried hominy makes grits. This is definitely Anglo breakfast food (a Hispanic version is the white *tamal* described on p. 207), but you can be more native by spooning in a bit of chopped *jalapeño* to add the hotness that many Santa Feans enjoy as a morning ritual.

For 4 people:

> 2 cups canned hominy, either white or golden, drained
> ¼ cup heavy cream
> 3 tablespoons butter
> ¼ cup chopped, canned green chilies or the equivalent in a
>   homemade green chili sauce
> ½ cup shredded Monterey Jack cheese
> Salt and pepper to taste

Combine the hominy and cream in a food processor and blend for about 5 to 10 seconds, or just until the mixture is ground coarsely, but not mushy. Stop at least once to scrape the bowl with a rubber spatula. Melt the butter in a 10-inch skillet, stir in the hominy mixture and the green chilies or green chili sauce and simmer for a few minutes. Remove from heat, stir in the cheese and season to taste. Serve hot with egg dishes at breakfast or in place of a starchy vegetable at dinner, which would carry your meal back to a ranch in the nineteenth century.

WHITE TAMALES WITH CHEESE FILLING

This style of *tamal*, with a dough made from hominy instead of packaged Masa Harina alone, has a taste that anyone who eats grits will automatically associate with breakfast. As it happens, the sweet *tamales* of various kinds are even more likely to be eaten in the morning than these, but no matter. Tossed in melted butter or bathed in a good red sauce like the adaptable chili sauce on p. 79, these fat steamed dumplings are a delightful change from eggs for a hearty breakfast.

For 16 small tamales, serving 4 people:

> 2 cups canned white hominy, well drained
> ½ cup Masa Harina
> ¼ teaspoon salt
> ¼ teaspoon cumin
> ½ teaspoon baking powder
> 4 tablespoons lard or vegetable shortening
> ⅓ cup warm water

FOR THE FILLING:

About 4 ounces of Monterey Jack cheese and a 4-ounce can of
   chopped mild green chilies

To make the dough for the *tamales*, combine all the ingredients except the water in the bowl of a food processor and blend until a smooth paste is formed, about 2 minutes, stopping as needed to scrape down the bottom and sides of the bowl with a rubber spatula. With the motor still running, pour the warm water through the feed tube and process for 10 seconds more. Use this dough to fill, roll and steam your *tamales* in foil as described in the basic recipe on p. 240. This amount is enough for 16 pudgy, rounded *tamales*, and make sure that you twist the foil packages closed at both ends to keep the filling from leaking out—the finished packet will look like a piece of candy twisted in cellophane.

For the cheese and chili filling, first shred the cheese and then toss it in a bowl with the drained, chopped green chilies. Each *tamal* receives a good tablespoon of this filling after a thin layer of dough is spread on the foil, then a top layer of dough is either spooned or folded over it. Steam for about 45 minutes only. Serve hot with a good red chili sauce or just melted butter if you are already having a chili dish for breakfast. If you want to make the foil packets of uncooked *tamales* the night before, they keep very well in the refrigerator, which leaves you with just the steaming in the morning.

BREAKFAST SOUFFLÉ SPOONBREAD

Although billed as a bread, this dish can be baked as soft as custard—certainly there is no possibility of actually cutting it with a knife. The basic recipe below has no chili in it because it is meant to be garnished at the table with sliced avocado, spoonfuls of fresh *salsa* like the one on p. 86, and a sprinkling of green coriander (*cilantro*). The technique of leaving a dish plain and then adding the hotness at the table is more basic to Southwestern cooking than most people imagine. If you do want chili in your spoonbread before cooking it, simply stir in about ¼ cup of chopped, canned green chilies and sprinkle the top of the bread before baking with ½ cup of shredded Monterey Jack cheese: such preparations are often called "New Mexico cornbread."

For 3 or 4 people:

    ½ cup yellow cornmeal
     2 tablespoons butter
    ½ teaspoon salt
    1½ teaspoons baking powder
    Pepper to taste
     1 cup boiling water

3 eggs graded large or extra large
½ cup milk
For the garnish: 1 sliced avocado, 1 cup fresh *salsa*, and a few
    tablespoons of chopped green coriander

Preheat the oven to 400° F. and generously butter a 1-quart casserole, preferably deep rather than shallow.

Blend the first 6 ingredients in a food processor, taking about 5 seconds and stopping at least once to scrape down the bowl with a rubber spatula. Add the eggs and milk and blend for a few seconds more to incorporate them thoroughly. Pour the batter into the buttered casserole. Bake for about 20 minutes, or until the whole "bread," including the center, just sets, but do not allow to dry out. Serve hot directly from the pan, and make sure to scrape some of the outer crust, which always sticks to the sides of the casserole, onto each portion. Serve plain with butter as a side dish in place of a starchy vegetable at dinner, or garnish with avocado, *salsa* and green coriander as a breakfast, brunch or lunch entree.

If intended as the main dish at a brunch, this recipe serves 2 people. It can be doubled, but that requires making the dough in 2 batches (unless you own a very large-capacity processor); increase baking time to 40 minutes for a 2-quart casserole—this is an approximation since exact timing depends on whether your casserole is shallow or deep.

BISCUITS

The only cultural excuse I can offer for putting biscuits in a breakfast chapter is that Southwesterners are the second most likely among us (after Southerners) to still eat biscuits in the morning. My real reason for including them is personal—I travel in hopes of finding a perfect rendition of these most delicate and satisfying of all American quick breads, but I rarely do. There are a few tricks that make them turn out well, the most important being to mix the dough with a fork to keep it light, and to knead it briefly with gentle pats and folding over—never with the pushing and pounding that applies to yeast dough.

Beyond that, almost everything else is secondary and hotly disputed. To my mind, the best biscuits are made with buttermilk and shortening, not sweet milk and butter, and they should be thick, almost twice as thick as the ones carried in the refrigerator section of supermarkets. It should be encouraging to anyone who has not yet mastered biscuits that it takes barely 25 minutes to produce a batch, including mixing, kneading, cutting and baking.

For 8 thick biscuits:

2 cups flour
¾ teaspoon salt
2½ teaspoons baking powder
¼ teaspoon baking soda
6 or 7 tablespoons vegetable shortening
⅔ cup buttermilk

Preheat the oven to 425° F. and place a rack in the middle.

Combine all the dry ingredients with a fork in a mixing bowl and cut in the shortening with a pastry blender or your fingertips, using fast rubbing motions rather than pinching. Add the buttermilk all at once, turning as well as stirring the dough with a fork until you have gathered it into a mass and there is no stray flour in the bottom of the bowl. This should take only about 15 seconds.

Turn the dough out onto a heavily floured board. Knead it as little as possible: simply pat and fold the dough 8 or 9 times until it forms a flat, fairly smooth shape.

Using very light pressure from a rolling pin, roll the dough into a square measuring 5 by 10 inches (it will be about ¾-inch thick). Square the corners with pats from your hands, then cut the dough into 8 square or 10 2½-inch round biscuits. Place on a baking sheet, the biscuits nearly touching, and bake at 425° F. for 15 to 17 minutes. The tops of the biscuits should be browned to a light-blond color, but the sides should remain white.

Split the hot biscuits carefully with a knife as soon as they emerge from the oven and butter generously. Biscuits taste best when eaten immediately. If they must be made ahead for breakfast the next day, they are best split and toasted. Biscuits also make a farmhouse dessert after they are buttered by simply pouring honey or syrup over them.

WHITE CORN MUFFINS WITH GREEN CHILIES

This delicious version of Southwestern cornbread does not have to be served at breakfast, nor does it have to be white—either yellow or blue cornmeal (*harina de maíz azul*—see p. 112) serves equally well. However, in my mind muffins are morning bread. These can be frozen and reheated as you need them, so one morning's labor means bread for another day.

If you want to make this as a pan of cornbread, generously butter a 9-inch round or square cake pan and bake for 25 to 30 minutes at 450° F.

For 12 large muffins, 18 small ones:

- 1½ cups white cornmeal
- ½ cup unbleached white flour
- 1 teaspoon salt
- 1 tablespoon baking powder
- ½ teaspoon baking soda
- 2 eggs graded large
- 1 cup commercial sour cream
- 4 tablespoons melted butter
- ¾ cup cream-style white corn
- ½ cup canned chopped green chilies

Preheat oven to 450° F. with a rack set in the upper third. Generously butter a 12-muffin baking tin large enough for popovers. (If the tin produces small muffins, plan to bake 18 rather than 12 and butter an additional tin.)

Place the first 8 ingredients in a food processor and blend for 10 to 15 seconds, stopping once to scrape the bowl down with a rubber spatula. (Alternatively, mix these ingredients into a smooth batter with an electric mixer—about 2 minutes.) Add the last 2 ingredients to the batter and blend in very quickly with 3 or 4 pulses of the motor (or beat with the mixer at low speed for 1 minute), stopping once to scrape down the bowl again.

Pour the batter into the prepared muffin tin (or tins) and bake for 15 to 20 minutes. Since the finished muffins are very tender when hot, let them cool for 10 minutes before gently easing them out of the pan. Serve warm with sweet butter.

TRADITIONAL SPECIALTIES:

ENCHILADAS, TACOS, BURRITOS, ETC.

Red Chili Enchiladas (Enchiladas coloradas)
Impeccably Authentic New Mexico Enchiladas
*Peanut-and-*Chipotle Enchiladas • Chorizo Enchiladas
Red Chili Enchilidas *with Cream Cheese and Pecans*
"American" Enchiladas
Green Chili Enchiladas (Enchiladas verdes)
Crisp-Shell Tacos • *Three-Way Soft* Tacos
Rolled Corn Tortillas with Carnitas
Tostadas *and* Chalupas
Green Chili Burritos, *Restaurant Style*
Turnovers with Chili-and-Cheese Stuffing
Chimichangas • *Simplest Stuffed Flour Tortillas*
Tortilla Casserole in Minutes (Chilaquiles)
Tamales *with Pork and Almond Filling*
Modest Tamales *with Cheese and Pecans* • Tamale *Pie*
Whole Green Chilies Stuffed with Cheese (Chiles rellenos)

TORTILLA-BASED DISHES

ENCHILADAS

The *enchilada* is the glory of authentic New Mexico food, although it is practically the national dish of Old Mexico, too. In its pristine state it is nothing more than a corn tortilla softened in oil, stuffed with cheese and sauced, but the permutations of sauce and stuffing are endless, and there are even opposing views about how to fold the tortilla—or whether to shape it at all.

The original cheese *enchilada* is a soul-satisfying dish wherever you meet it, but New Mexico cooks are quick to elaborate upon it. The meat-filled version of stacked *enchiladas* (which is also variously called an *enchilada* casserole or *enchilada* torte) is often so substantial that you can easily recognize it as ranch-house food, meant for a one-stop dinner. The practice of placing a fried egg on top, which some would swear is a time-honored custom, may in fact be a rather recent nutritionists' gambit.

Tex-Mex Enchilada Casserole: I am interested here in the basic unadorned *enchilada* with variations, but if you want to recapture the meat-filled *enchilada* of thousands of tourists' memories, here is the way to go about it: Follow the method for basic red chili *enchiladas*, making them in stacks as described on p. 219, but have at your side about 3 cups of any chili con carne. Use this in place of the sauce you would ordinarily nap over each softened tortilla. Bake and serve as usual.

This basic preparation later becomes the expanding *enchilada*, because you can garnish each stack with a fried egg, shredded lettuce, chopped green onion, avocado slices or *guacamole*, sour cream and tomatoes. The fully expanded *enchilada* carries all those ingredients.

RED CHILI ENCHILADAS
Enchiladas coloradas

Like chili con carne, the Margarita and *guacamole*, the simple *enchilada* arouses strong passions about the proper way to prepare it. Yet it is basically peasant food—a corn tortilla dipped in hot oil, then in warm red chili sauce, and rolled around a stuffing of cheese and raw onion. If that is all you need to know about the celebrated New Mexico *enchilada*, skip ahead to the recipe below. You can be assured of a notable success.

But there is much more to say about the *enchilada*. It asks to be assembled with a light, quick hand. The tortilla barely touches the hot fat and the warm dipping sauce; it does not lie around in either long enough to turn sodden. You then immediately sprinkle on a tablespoon or two of Monterey Jack cheese and a teaspoon or two of chopped raw onion. Green onion is a false elegance, for the bite of crude yellow or white onion is what you want. The assembled *enchilada* is now loosely rolled up and placed without crowding in a square baking pan (or any suitably shallow gratin dish). More sauce is spooned over, taking especial care that the ends of the roll, which are apt to dry out, get an extra coat. The last touch before baking is to run a line of cheese down the middle. Since the object is to produce a light texture with no greasiness or, worse yet, crispness, it may also pay to cover the dish loosely with foil and to heat fairly quickly, from 10 to 15 minutes.

Once you have started dipping the tortillas, you must proceed directly to baking. The whole procedure of double-dipping, filling and rolling is messy and time-consuming—you will not have extra time for much else. An *enchilada* that has to wait, either cold or hot, shows its resentment by turning spongy and unappetizing, so do not attempt to manufacture a whole combination-plate dinner with *enchiladas*.

The standard portion is three to a person, which will take about 5 to 15 minutes to prepare once you begin dipping. Rice and bean dishes, which can sit without attention, and a green salad are good accompaniments. It is not customary to garnish *enchiladas* with lettuce, tomato, onions and the rest—in fact, they are at their best simply sprinkled with chopped green onion for color or white onion for bite.

Using blue-corn tortillas is the touch that makes an *enchilada* New Mexican, though you will neither gain nor lose in flavor by choosing these. The only real concern is their availability. In some parts of the West outside New Mexico you can find blue-corn tortillas in natural-foods stores and Mexican groceries, but not very often in supermarkets. Making them from scratch is a possibility, but there is already so much handiwork involved in assembling *enchiladas* that I do not recommend it to beginners (see p. 118 for directions). Besides, the commercial blue-corn tortillas, which are invariably tougher than homemade ones, already have a perilous tendency to fall apart as they are being dipped.

A note about splattering: Any ingredient with appreciable water content will splatter when it comes into contact with hot oil, and tortillas fall into that category. Because you are moving quickly between 2 open skillets of sauce and oil, the use of a spatter guard is out of the question. The best advice is to keep the oil hot enough to sizzle as the tortilla touches it, but not so hot that violent splattering ensues. The suggestion made in Mexican cookbooks that you dip the tortillas into the sauce first and then into the oil (the reverse of what this recipe calls for) leads to a nasty surprise once you try it—a not-so-minor eruption of hot fat and spluttering sauce.

For 4 people:

> 2 cups, approximately, red chili sauce (refer to the various recipes beginning on p. 73; even the instant red chili sauce produces a delicious result)
> 12 corn tortillas, white or blue
> 12 ounces (3 cups), or more, shredded Monterey Jack cheese
> 1 small-to-medium white or yellow onion, chopped
> Vegetable oil for shallow-frying
> Green or white onion, chopped, for garnish

Set up your *enchilada* assembly line first: Using two 7- or 8-inch skillets, place about ¾ cup of sauce in one and heat to warm over low heat. Reserve the remaining sauce, also warm, in a saucepan to the side. Fill the other skillet with ½ inch of vegetable oil and heat it over medium heat (you are aiming for a temperature which will cause the tortilla to sizzle when it first touches the oil). On the counter beside the stove, where assembly will take place, position a plate to hold the tortillas as they emerge from dipping, a baking dish which will receive the rolled-up *enchiladas*, the pile of grated cheese and the chopped white or yellow onion. The baking pan should be large enough to hold all 12 rolled *enchiladas* in one layer—they are not stacked.

Preheat the oven to 325° F.

Now the assembly begins. First, evenly nap, or coat, the bottom of the baking dish with a thin layer of sauce to prevent sticking when the *enchiladas* are baking. Using tongs (the ordinary kitchen variety without serrations) or a large spatula with no sharp corners, lower 1 tortilla into the oil. Hold it on one side for a second or two, flip to the other for another second, and immediately lift out to drain. Next transfer the softened tortilla with your tongs to the chili sauce in the second skillet and repeat the dipping procedure, once again taking only 3 to 5 seconds to moisten both sides with sauce.

ENCHILADAS

1. Handling it quickly and lightly, dip tortilla in hot oil.

2. Quickly dip in warm sauce.

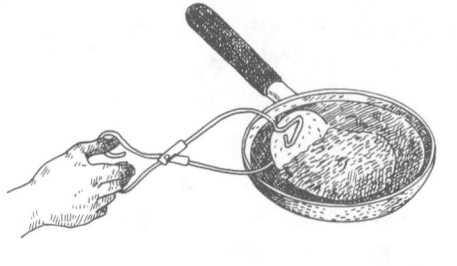

3. Spread cheese or other filling in a line below center of dipped tortilla.

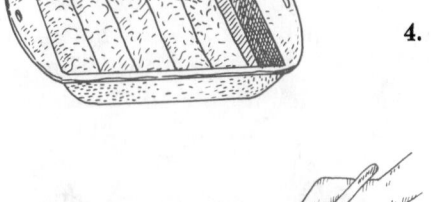

4. Roll tortillas and place seam side down in baking dish.

5. Make sure that sauce covers ends of enchiladas before baking.

NOTE: If this is your first time making *enchiladas*, you will see that the dipping is messy, no matter how carefully you try to keep oil out of the sauce and vice versa. Tortillas are also capable of tearing, creasing and wrapping themselves into unwanted shapes. Proceed anyway, for it does not matter if the tortilla is perfectly evenly coated, so long as you make an effort, and the slightly torn ones can still be rolled up.

Place the dipped tortilla on the plate beside the stove. Sprinkle no more than 2 tablespoons or so of Jack cheese in a line across the bottom half, immediately sprinkle a teaspoon or so of chopped onion across the cheese, and roll the filled tortilla into a loose cylinder. Place in the baking pan seam side down, so that the *enchilada* will not unroll.

Continue in the same fashion with all 12 tortillas, replenishing the skillets as needed. Be frugal with your filling; there should be about ½ of the cheese left for topping. Work quickly, but take time to drain the oil from the tortillas so that they will not be unpalatably greasy.

When the baking dish is full, spoon any sauce remaining in the dipping skillet, as well as the sauce reserved in the saucepan, over the *enchiladas*, paying special attention to coat the ends. If you run short of sauce, moisten just the ends; they are the most prone to drying out. Sprinkle the remaining cheese down the center of the rolls. Place in the oven and bake for 10 to 15 minutes, or until the cheese is melted (but still soft and glossy) and the edges of the sauce bubbling. You can cover the pan loosely with foil for baking, but that is not necessary unless you have run so short of sauce that you are afraid the dish will dry out. (To avert this possibility, you can work with 3 or 4 cups of sauce rather than the 2 cups called for.) Serve immediately, garnished with a sprinkling of green or white onion.

VARIATIONS:

Once you have the basic *enchilada* mastered, you can shape it in any of several ways. Restaurants often do not roll the tortilla after it has been filled, but merely fold it in half. Such half-moon shapes can be quickly run under a broiler (the usual restaurant practice), and of course they are not quite so much work to assemble.

Most often seen perhaps is the stacked *enchilada*, which looks like a short stack of pancakes. For each portion, take a plate which can be heated in the oven, nap it with sauce and proceed to stack 3 dipped tortillas on it, putting a layer of cheese, onion and more sauce between each. Top with cheese and bake at 300° F. for 5 minutes.

Another version, sometimes referred to as an "*enchilada* casserole," is made exactly like the stacked individual *enchilada*, except that one pan big enough to hold 4, 6, or 8 stacks is used. If you try to serve extra people by stacking the tortillas more than 3 deep, the inner texture of the casserole will certainly become heavy and underheated. Tepid *enchiladas* are not worth the eating.

Both the stacked *enchiladas* and the *enchilada* casserole can be eaten with a fried egg on top. In that guise they look and taste like *heuvos rancheros.* The egg garnish, which is not limited to breakfast, is said to meld the flavors of chili, cheese and onion.

Red Chili Enchiladas with Cream Cheese, Farmer's Cheese or Goat Cheese: This makes for rather a long title, but I want to emphasize that in the old culture, New Mexican *enchiladas* stuffed with creamy-textured cheese, often a cheese based upon goat's milk, resulted in a very different taste from what we are now used to. For ideas about such fillings, see p. 105. Thanks to the revival of interest in California goat cheese, diners are becoming accustomed to its strong, somewhat woolly taste, and a positive enjoyment should follow. For a milder, less goaty taste, use European rather than California cheeses. Cream cheese will be rich and bland; farmer's cheese will be bland and unsalty. Allow about a tablespoon to fill each tortilla, but continue to use Monterey Jack as your melting cheese, perhaps augmented with a little fresh-grated Parmesan.

Improbable No-Fat Enchiladas: Skipping the step where you dip the tortillas in hot oil is just not done—but it works anyway. Double the amount of red chili sauce that you warm in the skillet and keep it hot enough so it will soften the tortillas sufficiently for rolling. Because the tortillas absorb extra sauce, the total amount of sauce you need will be ¾ to 1½ cups more than called for in the basic recipe. No-fat *enchiladas* taste perfectly respectable, but they do have a tendency to turn spongy because of the changed method of dipping.

IMPECCABLY AUTHENTIC NEW MEXICO ENCHILADAS

Every part of the Southwest makes its *enchiladas* according to local habit, but this version, using blue-corn tortillas, a chili sauce without tomatoes, and red onion and Monterey Jack cheese for the filling, is honored by time as well as local taste. It could have been eaten in the Santa Fe of the seventeenth century as easily as today, but the cheese would have been a native one, probably marketed in the plaza by farmers who raised sheep or goats in the surrounding villages. If states adopted entrees the way they adopt birds, flowers and songs, these *enchiladas* would be the state dinner of New Mexico. They are as good as they are authentic.

For 4 people:

12 blue-corn tortillas
2 (or more) generous cups red *enchilada* sauce without
  tomatoes (p. 73)
¾ to 1 pound shredded Monterey Jack cheese
1 small red onion, chopped
Shredded romaine lettuce for garnish

Familiarize yourself with the basic method for making *enchiladas* outlined on p. 217. Proceed exactly as in the basic recipe, but with these small changes in the procedure: Soften all the tortillas in the hot oil and stack them on a plate without dipping in sauce. Have ready 4 oven-proof plates. Assemble stacks of *enchiladas*, 1 per person, by first spooning a little sauce in a thin layer on the plate, then adding a tortilla, more sauce just to coat it, and lastly a layer of cheese and chopped onion. Repeat with 2 more tortillas. Make 3 more stacks in the same way. Divide any remaining sauce over the stacks and sprinkle on the last of the cheese. Bake in a 300° F. oven for 10 minutes, or just until the cheese melts and the stacks are heated through. The success of this dish depends on assembling and serving it quickly enough that the *enchiladas* do not turn sodden from standing too long in their sauce. Garnish with the lettuce.

NOTE: As noted on p. 216, the rolling out and baking of your own blue-corn tortillas is rather tricky. You might want to sacrifice a bit in the way of authenticity and use ordinary tortillas made from Masa Harina. If you give way entirely and buy tortillas from the supermarket, the dish will still taste delicious, but the stacks will be a bit tougher in texture.

PEANUT-AND-CHIPOTLE ENCHILADAS

The sauce for this dish, flavored strongly with peanuts and the smoky, hot chilies called *chipotles*, may seem improbable to you, but it has great merits. The flavors blend in an unexpected way, set off by the garnish of fresh green coriander leaves. It is assembled in the same way as the basic red chili *enchilada*. Addictive as the taste of *chipotles* can become, their smokiness is best in small doses. The remainder of the can keeps well in the refrigerator if the contents are transferred to a small bowl and covered with plastic wrap.

For 4 people:

     3 *chiles chipotles,* canned
     2 cups red chili sauce made from powdered or whole dried
        chilies
     ½ cup tomato puree (or 4 canned tomatoes pureed in a
        blender)—omit if the chili sauce already contains tomato
     ½ cup roasted Spanish peanuts
    12 corn tortillas
    12 ounces (about 3 cups) shredded Monterey Jack cheese
     1 small-to-medium yellow or white onion, chopped
Vegetable oil
     4 tablespoons green coriander (*cilantro*), chopped

For the sauce: Using an electric blender or food processor, puree the *chipotles* with ½ cup of chili sauce. Add the rest of the sauce and the tomato puree (if used) and blend thoroughly.

Proceed to use the sauce for dipping tortillas according to the basic recipe on p. 216. Roll the *enchiladas* and place them in their pan for baking, but do not yet cover them with sauce.

Chop the peanuts roughly in a food processor or blender using 4 or 5 quick bursts. Add the remaining *chipotle*-and-red-chili sauce not used for dipping the tortillas. Blend very briefly, so that the peanuts remain coarsely chopped in the sauce, and nap the *enchiladas* as usual. Bake for 10 to 15 minutes in the ordinary way. Serve with chopped green coriander sprinkled over the top.

CHORIZO ENCHILADAS

A red *enchilada* again—but this time the untamed dark red chili, free of any tomatoes or other embellishments, is simmered for a few minutes with chopped *chorizo* (p. 103). The rest of the recipe does not differ in any way from the basic one given for red chili *enchiladas*, albeit the usual meaning of a *chorizo enchilada* in New Mexico is a stacked, meat-filled one to which chopped *chorizo* is added together with ground beef.

For 4 people:

All the ingredients for the basic red chili *enchiladas* on p. 217
     ½ pound chopped *chorizo* sausage, or more if you like

Simmer the chopped *chorizo* in the chili sauce for 5 minutes. Proceed exactly as for the basic red chili *enchiladas*. If you are having trouble dipping your tortillas into this fairly chunky sauce, you can either reserve half the sauce with no *chorizo* in it and use that for dipping or else dip the tortillas in the hot oil only, applying the *chorizo* sauce with a spoon just before you stuff the tortilla. Many cooks, in fact, make a whole stack of oil-dipped tortillas and only apply the warmed sauce as part of the stuffing routine. Bake and serve as usual.

NOTE: The best chili sauce for this recipe is the unadorned chili-powder sauce on p. 73. Its chili-only flavor can stand up to the heartiness of sausage. Any of the other basic red sauces is also appropriate, however.

RED CHILI ENCHILADAS WITH
CREAM CHEESE AND PECANS

In New Mexico cookbooks of the 1940s and earlier, the writers were usually anxious to show that they could make all-purpose American food, not just Southwestern specialties. The result was that more imagination was put into tuna salad and gelatin molds than into varying the traditional, and most delicious, of New Mexican foods. This is one such variation. Although unheard of in a conventional Santa Fe kitchen, this mild, creamy *enchilada* with its cream cheese-and-pecan filling is delicious. It is not for serving to red chili purists, to be sure.

For 4 people:

    6 ounces cream cheese
    ½ cup pecans, coarsely chopped
    ¼ cup green onion, chopped
    2½ cups red chili sauce with cream (p. 77)
    8 ounces (2 cups) shredded Monterey Jack cheese
    12 corn tortillas
    Vegetable oil

Follow the procedure in the main recipe beginning on p. 216 for making red chili *enchiladas*, but fill each tortilla with about 1 tablespoon of the cream-cheese-and-pecan filling below. The Monterey Jack cheese is still sprinkled over the top, however. Bake and serve as usual.

Filling: Put the cream cheese, pecans and green onion into the bowl of a food processor and blend briefly. The texture of the pecans should still be apparent when you finish blending. If your machine has trouble handling the ingredients, thin the filling with milk, dribbled in 1 teaspoonful at a time.

VARIATIONS:

Puree the red-chili-and-cream sauce with 1 egg before warming it, but then be careful not to heat it so much that the sauce curdles—in other words, do not let it approach the boil. The baking time should also be relatively brief, about 10 minutes at 350° F.

This rich filling is also a good candidate for using unusual types of cheese. Replace all or part of the cream cheese with farmer's cheese, ricotta or a mild goat cheese. All of these variations, including the one with egg added to the sauce, are quite unctuous and filling, so do not include other rich dishes in your menu.

"AMERICAN" ENCHILADAS

The traders who first came to the Spanish Southwest reacted with mixed emotions to the cooking that greeted them. Assimilation and rejection were more or less on equal terms, and until quite recently you could see recipes for native dishes that were obviously Anglicized, usually with no warning to the reader, who had no way of knowing that the *enchiladas* eaten on a ranch or farm in southern New Mexico were very much changed from the original.

A Texas chili con carne company, for instance, issued a recipe for "American" *enchiladas* in the forties which I give in general outline: For 4 people, heat 12 corn tortillas in oil or lard and fill each one with a slice of Longhorn cheese, then a dab of ricotta or cottage cheese. Roll up the tortillas and arrange them in a baking dish. Pour over them a generous 3 cups of chili con carne, then a thick blanket of more Longhorn (or any other mild orange Cheddar-type cheese). Bake for 15 minutes at 350° F. and serve topped with chopped onion.

Truck-stop and café cooks from Topeka to San Diego still make *enchiladas* after a similar fashion, and books still state—though with far less regularity—that such dishes are authentic. And so they are, but the tradition is relatively new compared to the antique Spanish bloodline of northern New Mexico cooking. The Anglicized style used to be called Tex-Mex (and it is still in downtown Houston where *burritos* and *enchiladas* come to the table covered with chili con carne *and* beans), but orange cheese or *chile verde* with canned mushroom soup are apt to show up anywhere in the Southwest.

GREEN CHILI ENCHILADAS
Enchiladas verdes

Probably about ten times as many red *enchiladas* are eaten as green, a tribute to the very hot character of *chile verde*, I suppose. In the parts of Mexico where green chili is most popular, there are many variations of it, some made sour by adding green tomatoes, some smoothed with cream and egg added, but almost all extremely fiery. For me the choice between red and green *enchiladas* is no choice at all. I am much more enthusiastic about all the recipes for any kind of red than for the ones below. (On the other hand, *chili verde* seems just right on *burritos*.) You can cook these green ones, however, and come up with authentic Santa Fe dishes. Visitors to Santa Fe almost inevitably are goaded to try the green chili *enchilada* at least once—there is a minor cult about downing the hottest one you can manage.

For 4 people:

> All the ingredients for red chili *enchiladas* on p. 217, but replace the
> red chili sauce with 2 or more cups of the green chili sauce
> on p. 80, or any of its variations. The instant green chili sauce
> on p. 83 will also produce a good result.

Preheat the oven to 350° F.

Follow the same procedure for dipping, filling and baking the tortillas as detailed in the basic recipe for red chili *enchiladas*. The only differences, and they are minor, come in forming and garnishing the tortillas. Green chili *enchiladas* are often folded in half rather than rolled up, and a dab of sour cream is either placed in with the cheese filling or spooned over the top as a garnish after the dish is baked.

VARIATIONS:

New Mexico Stacked Green Chili Enchiladas: Follow the method for stacking red *enchiladas* given on p. 219. The stacked version seems to take more sauce than the rolled, so have ready at least ½ to 1 cup extra over the basic amount. Green chili is also prone to overthickening as it stands. Add a little water if necessary.

Green Chili and Cream Enchiladas: Another traditional style, infrequently seen in New Mexico outside historic cookbooks, is to add ½ cup sour cream or whipping cream to the sauce along with 1 beaten egg. The tortillas are then dipped and assembled in the conventional way, but care is taken not to bake them so long that the egg in the sauce curdles. In the parlance of Mexico proper, putting whipping cream or sour cream in an *enchilada* makes it "Swiss" (*Suiza*). Telling your guests that this variation is a Swiss *enchilada* should arouse some comment.

Green Chili Enchilada Stuffed with Fresh Cheese: The bland sweetness of a fresh cheese is intriguing contrasted to hot *chile verde*. As a substitute for the true Mexican *queso fresco*, use ricotta cheese. It can become both the filling and the melting cheese, or you can mix it in any proportion with the usual Monterey Jack. Also, sometimes the onion is omitted. About 1½ cups of ricotta will fill and top *enchiladas* for 4 people; ¾ cup will do for stuffing only.

CRISP-SHELL TACOS

Santa Fe is one of the few American locales where a *taco* may be something like the Mexican original—a soft corn tortilla rolled around a meat filling, then shallow-fried until the outside is firm but not crisp. Directions for making such "soft tacos" are on p. 228. It is hardly necessary to give a recipe for the crisp-shell version, which has reached the status of franchise food all over the country, except that home cooks are liable to produce *tacos* with cold, soggy fillings. This happens when the kitchen is too preoccupied with frying taco shells, concocting the beef stuffing, grating cheese, shredding lettuce and so on—too much confusion to produce the light, hot snack which is the right thing.

So here is a recipe for a dry beef filling that does not drip out of the *taco* shell, followed by a simple *picadillo*, or spiced meat filling, that also makes a crisp-shell *taco* into truly desirable homemade food. The garnishes are kept to a minimum, since the more ingredients you try to stuff into the shell at the last minute, the colder the *taco* becomes. The shells themselves are store-bought, which eliminates the rigmarole about metal *taco* forms and the like.

For about 12 tacos, to serve 4 people:

> 1 or 2 cloves garlic, peeled
> Optional: 1 fresh *jalapeño* or *serrano* chili, stem and seeds removed
> 1 onion, peeled and quartered
> Vegetable oil
> 1 pound lean ground beef
> Seasonings to taste: salt, pepper, ground cumin, powdered red chili
>   and cayenne
> 1 tablespoon vinegar, any type
> Garnishes (see note on p. 228)

With the processor running and equipped with the standard metal blade, drop the garlic and optional green chili through the feed tube; the machine will chop them almost immediately. Averting your face from the fumes, turn off the processor, add the quartered onion to the bowl and process with short, repeated pulses until chopped. (All of this can of course be accomplished with a chef's knife on a cutting board.) Cover the bottom of a wide-bottomed skillet with a few tablespoons of vegetable oil and heat. Transfer the contents of the processor bowl to the pan. Cover the pan and sweat the onion over low heat for 5 minutes.

Remove cover and crumble in the ground beef. Cook beef and onion mixture together, stirring occasionally, until the meat is crumbly, dry and well cooked—but do not brown it. Add the seasonings to taste while cooking. Do not be reckless with the red chili and cayenne, since the finished *taco* is eaten with a *salsa* that can be as hot as you wish. When the meat is cooked, pour off excess fat, moisten the meat with the vinegar, and stir briskly one last time over high heat to make sure the filling is dry. It is best to proceed directly to filling the warmed *taco* shells, but the beef mixture can be set aside in its skillet if necessary and reheated just before the *tacos* are to be filled and served.

Assembling the tacos: I find that it reduces confusion to stuff the shells with meat in the kitchen, insuring that the basic *taco* is warm and savory when served. So while the beef filling is cooking and just before assembly is to begin, heat 12 boxed taco shells in a warming oven. (These, by the way, tend to be thinner and more fragile than homemade tortilla shells— a maddening trait if you plan to overload your *tacos* with garnish, but a good characteristic for this recipe.) Spoon a generous 2 tablespoons of meat into each shell, working rapidly, and either serve immediately or reheat the batch for a few minutes in the oven if they grow tepid. Pass the garnishes at the table.

Note on garnishes: The only essentials for success are shredded lettuce or cabbage and a table *salsa*. Use either iceberg lettuce, Napa cabbage, or red cabbage and shred it very fine with a chef's knife or the thin-slicing blade of a food processor.

The *salsa* should be homemade, either a *salsa cruda, salsa picante* or a sour green chili relish—recipes for these begin on p. 86. Good varieties of homemade-style *salsas* are carried by specialty stores, particularly natural-foods groceries, but if you must resort to ordinary commercial *salsa picante* or bottled green *taco* sauce, taste for flavor. Rectify with a little chopped green coriander (*cilantro*), chopped fresh green chilies, either mild or hot, to give crunch (the small waxy *güeros*, which are pale yellow in color, are very good), and a little chopped fresh tomato. Once the *taco* is stuffed with meat and lettuce, the *salsa* is spooned over at will.

VARIATION:

Simple Picadillo Filling: Make the basic beef mixture described above, but when the ground beef just begins to look cooked, add ⅓ cup of bottled *salsa picante*. Season as in basic recipe above, then add ½ teaspoon cinnamon, a small handful of raisins, 2 tablespoons chopped green olives and a generous pinch of brown sugar. Cover the pan and let simmer gently for 15 minutes. If the mixture becomes too dry as it cooks and begins to stick to the bottom of the pan, add a little more *salsa* or water, but try to keep the filling almost as dry as ground beef alone would be. For the small amount of trouble that is required to make it, the *picadillo* is far more interesting than the basic beef filling.

THREE-WAY SOFT TACOS

The first surprise for most of us is that *tacos* are made with soft tortillas, if the Santa Fe cook remains close to Mexico in her habits; the second is that almost any soft corn tortilla qualifies. So here are three ways to create *tacos*, depending on the state of your tortillas and the number of mouths to feed. The simple chicken filling is only a suggestion—any of the fillings on p. 107 will also do nicely—but chicken is probably the most common version in the Southwest. The essential thing to bear in mind is that *tacos* are casual food, made with improvised but choice ingredients, and as long as you are sure of the quality of your tortillas, they will be delicious rolled around shredded pork, *chorizo* sausage moistened with red chili sauce, shredded turkey breast or simply the mashed beans in butter on p. 298. One person can easily eat 6 *tacos* at a sitting, so keep your fillings simple and bring them on in quantity.

For every 6 to 8 tacos:

  1 cup cooked, shredded chicken or turkey breast
  3 tablespoons green chili sauce or good commercial green
    taco sauce
  3 tablespoons sour cream
  Salt and pepper to taste
  Grated Monterey Jack cheese
  Green chili relish (p. 91) or a bottled sour *taco* sauce

Mix the chicken or turkey breast, green chili sauce and sour cream in a small skillet and warm thoroughly over medium heat. Season with salt and pepper to taste. Following one of the methods below, fill each *taco* with 1 or 2 tablespoons of filling, scatter a little shredded cheese over that, and then spoon in a couple of teaspoons of *taco* sauce or green chili sauce (the kind to use here is an uncooked type with vinegar, like the one on p. 91).

Method 1: If you have homemade tortillas or good-quality commercial ones, simply warm 6 to 8 of them wrapped in foil in a 350° F. oven for 10 minutes, roll them around the filling described above, salt lightly and eat immediately. This is particularly satisfying when you are alone or have only one other person to share the delight.

Method 2: The procedure followed by Mexican home cooks is to roll each tortilla around its filling and secure the seam with a toothpick— simply stick it straight in. When all the *tacos* are rolled, a scant ¼ inch of oil is heated very hot in a skillet, the *tacos* are placed in the oil, toothpick facing up, and they are fried for a few seconds. The toothpicks are removed, the *tacos* are gently rolled over, and they cook a few seconds more on the seam side. The object is to stiffen the outside of the tortilla and have it change color, but not to get it at all crisp. The finished *tacos* are drained, salted and eaten immediately with table *salsa*.

If this method is used in a restaurant, the *tacos* are reheated in a 350° F. oven as needed and brought to the customer garnished with *guacamole*, sour cream, shredded lettuce and the like. However, they are really better eaten plain with only a sour chili relish and perhaps some sour cream on the side.

Method 3: If your corn tortillas are not freshly made or if the group to be served is large and fanatical about soft *tacos*, the fastest way to produce a batch is to soften all the tortillas you need in oil, just as if you were making *enchiladas*, and stack them up on a plate by the stove as you work. Next fill and roll all the tortillas and line them in a baking pan. Dribble a ribbon of green chili sauce (the cooked version on p. 80) down the middle of the lined-up *tacos* and heat them quickly in a 375° F. oven, watching that they do not stiffen too much (the outside should be resistant to the touch but not crisp). Serve immediately with any of the restaurant garnishes mentioned above. Sometimes a line of cheese is melted on top of the *tacos* as they are baking, and at other times a red chili sauce is substituted for the green, but then the results are very much like *enchiladas*.

ROLLED CORN TORTILLAS WITH CARNITAS

The spiced, shredded pork *carnitas* described on p. 100 are really best, to my mind, stuffed into warm corn tortillas. Garnishing is your choice, and can be no more than a good *salsa*, but here is a delicious combination.

For 4 people:

    3 cups *carnitas* from p. 100
    12 corn tortillas, wrapped in foil and warmed in a 350°F. oven
        for 10 minutes
    Sour green chili *salsa* from p. 91, or any good table *salsa*,
        including bottled *salsa picante*
    2 cups *guacamole* (pp. 171–74)
    Shredded lettuce
    Chopped ripe tomato

As you can tell from the list of prepared components, this is easier for a restaurant to produce than for a home cook, but even if you start from scratch, the *carnitas* take but 1 hour to make, with no work except at the very beginning and end. You will probably already have *salsa* on hand, bottled or homemade.

The dish is one for assembling at the table. Present the *carnitas* warm, the tortillas warm, and the rest at a cool room temperature. Hold a tortilla in the palm of one hand, fill it with *carnitas* in a strip down the middle, and garnish. Roll the tortilla up and eat like a soft *taco*, spooning on extra *salsa* and *guacamole* as you wish.

TOSTADAS AND CHALUPAS

The *tostada* production number is a restaurant specialty throughout the Southwest. What started out as a flat *taco* now supports a small mountain of refried beans, hamburger, shredded iceberg lettuce, *salsa*, shredded Monterey Jack cheese, chopped green onion, chopped tomato, green olives, *guacamole* and sour cream—in that order if you want to build one yourself. These show-biz *tostadas* are one-dish meals along the same lines as the restaurant's *burrito grande*, but smaller sizes are of course possible.

The fillings given for *tacos* on pp. 226–27 work well for *tostadas*, as does the homemade *chorizo* sausage on p. 205—use it in place of ground beef, making sure that it is warm.

Some menus, particularly in New Mexico, call their *tostadas* by the name of *chalupas*. *Chalupa* in Mexico is a canoe for two and also denotes a tortilla shell that has been shaped like the boat. Cooks in New Mexico do not bother with the rather elaborate processes required to shape corn dough in that way, but they call their flat tortillas *chalupas* anyway. Another simplified *chalupa* common in New Mexico is cup-shaped. The soft tortilla is held down in the center while it is being crisped in oil so that the sides flare upwards. I do not think it is worth the trouble; in fact, I do not insist upon frying your own flat *tostadas*, either—whole, flat crisped tortillas sold in boxes work very well.

Assembling a tostada: The operation for assembling one large garnished *tostada* per person is not complicated, but all the garnishes have to be at hand when you begin. Arrange them in little bowls around your work space. The *salsa*, lettuce, tomato, scallions, *guacamole*, cheese, olives and sour cream are served cool, but not chilled. The crisped tortillas (commercial or home-fried) are warmed in the oven, the refried beans are heated in a skillet (a bit of shredded Monterey Jack cheese is stirred in just before assembly time), and the meat filling is warmed in its own skillet. When your guests are ready for them, pull out the warmed tortillas, spread them with a layer of refried beans and a few tablespoons of meat filling, then proceed to garnish with all the cold components. The diners add more *salsa* at the table.

I am not very enthusiastic about the homemade *tostada* because I think it is a restaurant dish that home cooking doesn't much improve upon. There are many better ways to use all the ingredients that go into building one. (*Tostados*, called by a very similar name, are small, fried tortilla chips, served to snack on with a dipping sauce.)

GREEN CHILI BURRITOS, RESTAURANT STYLE

For me, the best *burrito* is the simplest one, nothing more elaborate than a flour tortilla wrapped by hand around a hot filling. Done that way, it keeps fresh for no longer than it takes to eat, so restaurants usually dress their prefilled *burritos* (also called *burros* in other parts of the Southwest) in a green chili sauce, then bake them with cheese in the oven as the customers call for them. Such a presentation is very filling, thanks to the amount of sauce a flour tortilla can absorb, and it is also one of the most popular dishes in any Mexican café. The plate often comes piled high with a mound of lettuce, green onion, avocado, tomatoes, shredded cheese and sour cream—a full-dress parade like the one given to *tostadas*. If you

BURRITOS

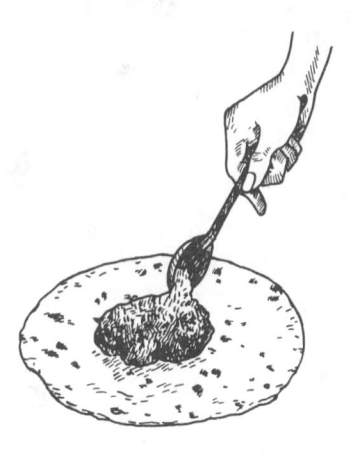

1. Spoon in filling and spread in a broad strip below center of tortilla.

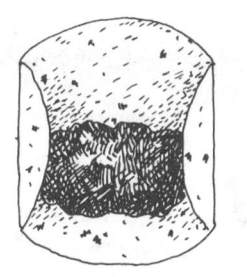

2. Fold in sides to enclose filling partially.

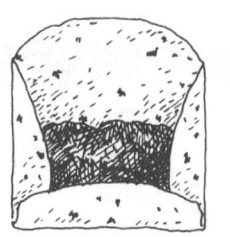

3. Fold up bottom to cover part of filling.

4. Roll to form tight cylinder.

want to try to make the dish on your own, you will find it very simple, but be prepared for assorted busy steps, since the sauce, filling and garnishes must all be readied together for the moment of baking and serving.

Before they became production numbers, the traditional filling for *burros* or *burritos* was simply a few tablespoons of refried beans. Now you can buy large flour tortillas ready to hold half a cup or more of beans, rice, cheese and ground meat, all of which is too much trouble for me. Here then is a method for putting only mashed beans inside the *burrito* with a little pork in the green chili sauce that goes over it. By keeping sauce, filling and garnishes fairly simple, this recipe brings dressy *burritos* into the range of a home cook working without a corps of helpers in the kitchen.

The tortillas can be filled in advance if you like, but do not sauce them until just before baking. All wheat tortillas tend to toughen as they bake, but I find that whole-wheat ones (generally available in a supermarket that already carries fresh tortillas) remain more tender than their white-flour counterparts.

Allow 1 *burrito* per person as a meal in itself, 2 at most. No side dishes are really called for, but a summery squash or rice preparation helps fill out the plate if there has been no first course.

For 4 people:

GREEN CHILI SAUCE:

  ½ pound pork shoulder, trimmed of fat and cut into
      ½-inch dice (sometimes sold precut as meat for chow mein)
Vegetable oil for sautéing
  2 pounds canned tomatoes packed in tomato juice or puree
      (or the equivalent in crushed tomatoes, about 4 cups)
  1 cup canned green chilies, whole or chopped
  2 teaspoons chopped *jalapeños*
  1 clove garlic, minced
Salt, pepper and cumin to taste

FILLING:

  2 cups refried beans, such as the ones cooked in butter on p. 298
      (canned pintos are acceptable, too, after they have been
      fried in oil according to the method on p. 293)
  4 large flour tortillas
  8 to 12 ounces shredded Monterey Jack cheese (2 to 3 cups)
  8 large romaine lettuce leaves, shredded
  2 avocados, peeled and cut into chunks
  4 green onions, chopped
Olive oil

Heat a thin film of vegetable oil in the bottom of a large skillet or 2-quart saucepan (a pan suitable for a small batch of stew) and brown the pork well over medium heat. At the same time, place the tomatoes, green chilies, *jalapeños* and garlic in the bowl of a food processor and blend until smooth but still a little textured. When the meat is browned, pour off the surplus oil and sprinkle with salt, pepper and cumin. Add the contents of the processor to the pan. Dilute with some of the juice or puree in which the tomatoes were packed and bring to a boil. Simmer gently for 1 hour, with an occasional stir until the pork is tender. Dilute with water, tomato juice or beef broth if the sauce seems too thick—it should be quite soupy but capable of coating a *burrito* well—and set aside until needed.

To assemble the *burritos*, fill each tortilla with ½ cup of beans, rolling it up in the classic method as shown on p. 232. Place seam side down and close together in a shallow gratin or casserole baking dish. The pan can be loosely covered and set aside until baking time if you are working ahead.

Preheat the oven to 350° F. and have ready the sauce and shredded cheese. Spread the sauce over the rolled-up tortillas, sprinkle on the cheese and bake for 20 minutes, or until the sauce is bubbling and the cheese melted.

Meanwhile, mix the lettuce, avocados, and green onion in a bowl, drizzle lightly with olive oil and toss gently. Set aside in a cool place until the *burritos* come out of the oven. Carefully lift the *burritos* onto serving plates with a broad spatula—restaurants generally heat them directly on the customer's plate to begin with—scatter the garnish over all and serve immediately. If the baking sauce doesn't seem sufficient, each diner can add table *salsa* to his *burrito* as he likes.

Burrito Grande: The above are by no means the ultimate in *burritos*. Besides being filled with ground meat added to the beans—you could try the fast *picadillo* on p. 228 that originally went into *tacos*—a restaurant's *burrito grande* might advance on the customer with tomatoes, grated cheese and sour cream on top of it, along with chopped olives and a mountain of shredded iceberg lettuce in place of romaine. Such lavishly mounded spectacles are a mainstay of neighborhood Mexican eating throughout the Southwest.

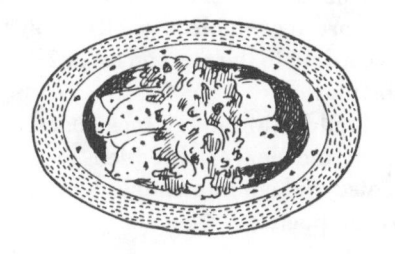

TURNOVERS WITH CHILI-AND-CHEESE STUFFING

You could call these turnoves fried *quesadillas*, for they are rolled out, stuffed and fried in the same way. The only sticking point is that *quesadillas* are made with corn dough and these from the dough that goes into flour tortillas and baked *empanadas*. They crisp and puff up like an old Southern specialty called "fried pies." I have avoided giving them that name because cooks do not like to deep-fry anymore. Do not skip them, though, if you have qualms about frying, for they do not splatter or smell up the kitchen, and you need barely half an inch of oil for the cooking. A small skillet wide enough to hold 1 or 2 turnovers at a time is all the equipment you will need; an electric wok, which cuts down on both oil and splattering, would be ideal. To my mind, these savory turnovers are far easier to make and much lighter than the *chimichangas* served up by restaurants.

For 6 turnovers:

> Flour tortilla dough using 1 cup of flour (p. 119)
> 1 cup (roughly) shredded Monterey Jack cheese
> Strips of canned or fresh green chili, *jalapeños* or *chiles chipotles* (these are best fresh-roasted and peeled, but chopped fresh chili will work)
> Water for sealing the dough
> Vegetable oil to a depth of ½ inch for frying
> Optional: ¼ cup chopped and sautéed *chorizo* sausage, moistened with a little red chili sauce

Familiarize yourself with the procedure for making flour tortillas as detailed on p. 119. Roll out the balls of dough to 6- or 7-inch circles. The turnovers are rolled, stuffed, sealed and fried 1 or 2 at a time. Place a generous 2 tablespoons of shredded cheese, a few strips of green chili and the optional *chorizo* on the lower half of the rolled-out circle, leaving a margin for sealing the folded dough. Dip your index finger into the water and draw a wet line around the perimeter of the dough, then fold the circle in half and seal it all around. Since frying becomes messy if the edges of a turnover open up, make sure your seal is secure by first crimping the edges with your thumb and forefinger, then turning the half-moon over and repeating the crimp once more.

Immediately place the turnover in the ½ inch of hot oil in a small skillet or electric wok. (Deeper fat—the traditional method for frying *quesadillas*—is also acceptable.) The oil should sizzle when you first slide the turnover into it, but it is too hot if it bubbles furiously. Fry on each side for 1 minute, then keep turning the turnover until both sides are an even light brown. The turnover will puff up as it cooks and will also acquire some bubbles if you are shallow-frying it. Prettier ones need oil to cover completely.

Remove the turnover with a slotted spoon and drain on several thicknesses of paper towel. To keep an entire batch of finished turnovers warm, set them in a warming oven at 200° F. while the rest are cooking. If the turnovers have to stand and start to lose their crispness, reheat for about 5 minutes in a 350° F. oven, uncovered.

To serve: Eaten alone as a substantial side dish or a first course, the turnovers need only a sour green chili relish or any good *salsa*. If they form the central interest of the meal, however, they can be covered with warm red chili sauce and garnished like any *tostada* with cheese, *guacamole*, green onion, olives, tomato and shreds of romaine lettuce. An optional *salsa* for the final topping is also possible, but make sure, for the sake of the crispness of the turnover, that all moist sauces and garnishes go on at the very last second. Once soaked through, the dish is not worth eating.

VARIATIONS:

Other Stuffings: A fairly long list of stuffings suitable for turnovers, *quesadillas* and *empanadas* appears on pp. 107–108, but any stuffing which is fairly dry will make a delicious turnover, including any plain leftover cooked meat moistened with a dab of red chili sauce.

CHIMICHANGAS

When a flour tortilla is stuffed, rolled up and deep-fried, the result is called a *chimichanga*—a word which is said to have no meaning in either Spanish or the Indian languages. As served in restaurants, the dish is garnished with the works—lettuce, tomato, *salsa*, sour cream, chopped onion—to make it as impressive as the house *tostada* or "*burrito* supreme." In truth, the frying does no good to the tortilla. It quickly turns tough, and if it has to stand for any period the filling steams and softens the crisp exterior. I recommend that you try stuffing some *sopaipillas*, a far more satisfying operation, as outlined on p. 130.

In case you want to reproduce a restaurant *chimichanga*, however, here is the method: Have ready at least 1 to 2 inches of oil for shallow-frying (restaurants use 4 inches or more), bringing it up to 350° F., or until a scrap of flour tortilla dropped in begins to sizzle immediately but does not bubble madly. Also have ready a filling, traditionally refried beans, plus some meat and cheese for a deluxe *chimichanga*. Use store-bought flour tortillas: unless you are quite expert, it is much easier for a machine to make thin, flexible tortillas than for you to make them by hand. They should be at room temperature or warm, but not cold, when you fill them, or they will crack when you try to wrap up the filling.

For each serving of 2 flour tortillas:

¼ cup refried beans (p. 296)
2 tablespoons beef taco filling (p. 226)
3 tablespoons shredded Monterey Jack cheese
Optional: 2 tablespoons finely chopped green onion

Place a tortilla in front of you and spoon about 2 tablespoons of beans and 1 tablespoon of *taco* filling on it just below the center. Fold in the right and left sides of the tortilla so that they just meet in the center but do not overlap. Fold up the bottom half to cover the filling, and finally fold down the top half to fully enclose it. You should be looking at a package that is closed on all sides like an envelope. Stick in a toothpick where the final seams meet to hold the package shut. Proceed in this way until you finish 2 *chimichangas* per person.

Fry the *chimichangas* 2 or 3 at a time, beginning with the flat side. After about 1½ minutes, pull out the toothpick and carefully roll the packet over to fry on its seamed side. (If you proceed carefully enough and use shallow oil, the filling should not leak out and, more important, the oil will not seep in.) Fry until both sides are crisp and browned.

Remove the cooked *chimichangas* to drain on paper towels, then quickly top with shredded cheese. The residual heat of the fried bread will melt this topping; if it does not, reheat in a 350° F. oven for a minute or two. Garnish with the optional green onion. The *chimichangas* should not wait long after their frying if you want to retain crispness.

Serve with any warm red or green *enchilada* sauce poured over the *chimichangas* and any of the garnishes appropriate to *tostadas*. No side dish is usually necessary except for salad or rice.

SIMPLEST STUFFED FLOUR TORTILLAS

Once you are used to making flour tortillas on your own and feel confident that you can make them 8 or 9 inches across, you are ready to vary your repertoire with stuffed tortillas. These are more or less an improvised dish on my part, although ample precedent exists for such dishes made with corn tortillas. Since cheese and chili are the dominant tastes here, serve with meat dishes that include other flavors—it would be pointless to go to the trouble of making them if you were serving *enchiladas* along with them.

For 6 tortillas:

> Flour tortilla dough using 1 cup flour (p. 119)
> ½ cup, roughly, shredded Monterey Jack cheese
> 1 green chili, roasted, peeled and cut into thin strips—
> a canned roasted chili will do
> 1 *jalapeño*, deveined, seeded and cut into strips (optional)
> Water for sealing edges of tortillas

Proceed with the recipe for flour tortillas on p. 119, rolling out each ball of dough to an 8- or 9-inch-diameter circle. With the dough still on the board, scatter a scant tablespoon of shredded cheese in a thin layer across the bottom half of the circle, leaving a margin for sealing the tortilla into a half-moon shape. Now lay strips of green chili and optional *jalapeño* over the cheese.

Dip your index finger in water and trace a wet line around the outside edge of the tortilla. Fold the dough over into a half-circle, and make a crimped edge all around by pinching with your thumb and forefinger. As long as the filling is quite thin, you do not have to be very careful with the crimped edges—there is little likelihood that the filling will run out onto your griddle. Pat the bread flat and cook as usual on a dry griddle. If 1 minute on each side is not sufficient, keep flipping the bread until it is lightly speckled on both sides. Hold on a warm plate with a cover over it until all the breads are finished.

VARIATIONS:

For a Fatter Bread: Big stuffed tortillas are impressive; but you can make a thicker 6-inch circle if you like, add a little more stuffing (which might include bits of sautéed *chorizo* or chopped *chiles chipotles*) and proceed as above. This bread looks like the baked turnovers called *empanadas*, but baking on a griddle keeps it tender and fresh. The thicker the tortilla, the more you will have to flip it to achieve a thoroughly cooked inside. It even helps to place a domed lid or inverted metal bowl over the bread when you first turn it over for baking the second side. The bowl keeps the heat in effectively; lift it off using pot holders.

Other Fillings: Since this is more or less an invention, you can feel free to stuff the tortillas with whatever appeals to you. The only stipulation is to keep the bread flat, which excludes chunky meat concoctions. You also need a dry filling, since added moisture complicates the baking, and the finished bread is likely to turn sodden in only a minute. Refried beans or a riced or mashed potato flavored simply with a little fried onion, garlic and cumin are good bases for fillings. They can be further enhanced with hot chilies, including the *chipotles* already suggested. If you desire a complicated stuffing, however, it is better to look toward *empanadas* and their kin. Those substantial turnovers are better able to hold a hefty filling.

TORTILLA CASSEROLE IN MINUTES
Chilaquiles

"In minutes" is not an exaggeration, since a casserole of tortilla wedges, *salsa* and cheese takes little more than 5 minutes to assemble and 15 minutes to bake (much less if you use a microwave oven, which is ideally suited to the operation). Such dishes based on fried, stale tortillas are called *chilaquiles*, and they show off the combinatory genius of Mexican cooks. Everything that goes into an *enchilada* also goes into *chilaquiles*, but the entire feeling of the dish is altered due to the layers of chewy tortilla wedges.

Since *chilaquiles* are the perfect solution to a refrigerator stocked with a scrap of this or that, I am giving proportions for 1 person—but they can easily be multiplied. The variety of possible casseroles you can make once you master the basic method is limitless. A few suggestions follow after the basic recipe to get you started. Garnishes make a casserole of *chilaquiles* all the better; feel free to use any bits of *guacamole*, fried *chorizo* sausage, lettuce and tomato, Spanish olives, chopped onion or green coriander (*cilantro*) on hand. This is also one of the dishes which works quite satisfactorily with bottled *salsa*, provided that it is fresh-tasting, a bit rough-textured and not vinegary—the Green Chile Taco Sauce from Ortega, or anything in that style, will be right.

For 1 person:

> Vegetable oil for shallow-frying
> 3 corn tortillas, preferably somewhat stale
> ½ cup *salsa*, either homemade or bottled
> Sour cream
> 2 or 3 ounces shredded Monterey Jack cheese (½ to ¾ cup)

Preheat the oven to 350° F.

Heat a few tablespoons of oil in a small skillet. Cut each tortilla into 8 wedges, then fry 8 pieces at a time in the oil. The usual advice is to stop when they are chewy and half-crisp, but extra crisping does not really hurt the texture of the finished dish. Set the tortillas aside to drain for a few minutes on paper toweling.

To assemble the casserole, arrange 8 wedges of tortilla in the bottom of a small gratin dish or any other casserole of about 2- to 4-cup capacity. Spoon a thin layer of sauce over, followed by a few small dabs of sour cream and ⅓ of the cheese. Continue in this way with the remaining tortillas until you have arranged 3 layers, ending with cheese. Bake in the oven just until heated through and well melted on top, about 10 to 15 minutes. Serve immediately with any garnishes appropriate to *tostadas* (p. 230)—or none at all.

VARIATIONS:

Although *chilaquiles* are seldom made in restaurants, they are an ideal basis for home cooking, especially if the cook likes to improvise. A standard version of the dish calls for cooked, shredded chicken mixed in with the tortillas in the casserole dish, and the sauce is any good green *enchilada* sauce, including the quick one on p. 83. If you want to use a red *enchilada* sauce, you can mix the tortillas with crumbled, fried *chorizo* (p. 205), or the *chorizo*-flavored sausage on p. 103, which demands no precooking. Chopped *cilantro*, green onion or green olives can be scattered into the *chilaquiles*. A very *picante* dish can be devised by sprinkling in chopped, pickled *jalapeños* (*jalapeños en escabeche*). A favorite stuffing like the *picadillo* on p. 101 or the pork with green chilies on p. 269 would also be delicious. If you use them, the sour cream can be omitted.

TAMALES WITH PORK-AND-ALMOND FILLING

The traditional recipes for *tamales* dictate huge quantities, partially because they are Christmas food and the cook should be prepared for a crowd, but also because *tamales* made in the conventional way require time—to soak the corn husks, to stew the filling and to assemble—so that it hardly pays to make only a few. The recipe below, reduced for 4 people, is still a bit involved, but it takes only ½ hour to assemble and 1 hour to steam, assuming that you already have on hand some kind of shredded meat (I call for pork, which is traditional, but you can as effectively use shredded chicken or turkey) and about 2 cups of any red chili sauce. The blender sauce on p. 79 is particularly good for *tamales*. You can use it in its thick state to moisten the shredded pork and then dilute it to spoon over the finished *tamales*.

The filling is from an old recipe—not the usual one for "hot tamales." It contains shredded pork mixed with roasted almonds and orange peel; the almonds are for texture, so the dish will not be of one soft consistency, and the orange peel is an exotic touch. For the guest to Santa Fe in the

1800s who was nostalgic for his faraway Spanish *Navidad,* this filling must have been both festive and evocative.

For 3 or 4 people:

THE TAMAL DOUGH:

1½ cups Masa Harina
  6 tablespoons vegetable shortening (or lard, which is authentic)
  ½ teaspoon salt
  1 teaspoon baking powder
  1 cup lukewarm meat broth (the liquid reserved from braising
      the pork or commercial beef broth)

THE FILLING:

  ⅓ cup blanched, slivered almonds or blanched whole ones
  2 tablespoons vegetable oil
  1 cup *carnitas* from p. 100, or cooked, shredded pork which you
      have sprinkled generously with cumin, cinnamon and
      black pepper
  3 tablespoons red chili sauce, such as the adaptable blender
      sauce on p. 79
  1 teaspoon fresh, grated orange peel
  3 tablespoons raisins
Salt, if needed
  2 cups, or more, red chili sauce for the table

The procedure given here for making *tamales* is a general one, since the size and shape of the *tamales* as well as the filling are up to you. Traditionally, the dough and stuffing are wrapped in softened corn husks and steamed in a kettle which has been lined at the bottom with more husks in order to keep the *tamales* from direct contact with water. Here, aluminum foil and a vegetable steamer are used instead. (Directions for the more colorful traditional way, using the cornhusk wrapping, are on p. 244.)

Processor tamal dough: Put all the dough ingredients except the meat broth in the bowl of a processor equipped with the standard metal blade. Process for about 10 seconds, or until all is amalgamated. Leaving the motor on, pour in the lukewarm broth and process a few seconds more until the dough is stiff enough to spread, rather like a butter-cream icing. (If it becomes too stiff to work with later, beat in a little hot water a tablespoon at a time.) Set the dough aside in a mixing bowl, loosely covered.

Pork-and-almond filling: Coarsely grind the almonds in the processor, about 5 to 7 seconds. Heat the oil in a 10-inch skillet, add the almonds, and sauté over medium heat until they turn very light brown. Add all the remaining ingredients, stirring after each addition, and heat just enough to warm them through. Taste for salt and set aside.

TAMALES IN FOIL

ROUND SHAPE:

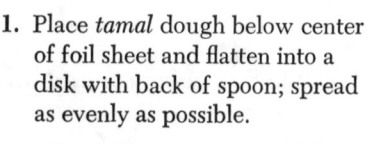

1. Place *tamal* dough below center of foil sheet and flatten into a disk with back of spoon; spread as evenly as possible.

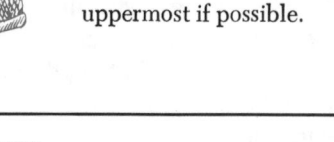

2. Place filling to one side of dough and enclose completely by folding foil over.

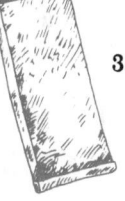

3. Crimp bottom and side of foil tightly.

4. Loosely fold down top and stand in steamer with top uppermost if possible.

LONG SHAPE:

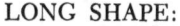

1. Evenly spread an oblong shape of *tamal* dough, placing it below the center of the foil sheet. Place filling in a strip down the center line of the dough.

2. Holding foil packet in one palm, gently fold dough to completely enclose the filling.

3. Tightly crimp bottom and side of foil.

4. Loosely fold over top and stand in steamer with top uppermost.

Assembly and steaming: This amount of dough makes 8 or 9 *tamales*, which, after steaming and saucing, will modestly serve 3 or 4 people as an entree. (If you want smaller *tamales* to serve as an appetizer, see notes on p. 244.) To steam either size, fit a pot of at least 4-quart capacity with a steaming rack—the ordinary 3-legged kind used for vegetables does quite well. Lacking a rack, loosely crumple large wads of heavy-duty foil and lay them in the bottom of the pot, making a layer thick enough to hold the *tamales* out of direct contact with the boiling water. Also cut out 8 or 9 squares of regular-weight foil measuring 8 to 9 inches a side. These are to be used in place of dried corn husks for wrapping the *tamales*.

So now you have within convenient reach the corn dough, the pork-and-almond filling, the foil squares and the steaming kettle. Lay the first foil square in front of you, spread about 3 scant tablespoons of dough over it, fill the center with a generous 2 tablespoons of filling and roll up for steaming. None of this is at all complicated, but there are various choices to make:

For a fat, roundish *tamal*, spread the dough in a circle about 4 inches across, dab the filling directly in the center, and fold the foil from one side to the other, completely enclosing the filling with dough. Crimp the foil along the open side and also the bottom so that excess steam will not leak into the package during the steaming. The top of the package, however, is not crimped but simply folded over; it does not permit leakage since the packet will be steamed standing up.

For a longer, more elegant *tamal* of the kind sold commercially, spread the dough in an even oblong strip about 5 inches long and 3 inches wide. Dab the filling in a narrow line going up and down the oblong but just off center. Fold the package over from side to side, trying to enclose the filling and matching up the sides of the dough as evenly as possible. Crimp the bottom and open side tightly, as above, and fold down the open end.

I find it easier to fold either shape by holding the foil in my hand after the dough is applied, spooning on the filling as if adding relish to a hot dog, and then gently closing the package as if squeezing closed a hot-dog bun. Use the fingertips of your free hand on the outside of the foil to pinch the length of the dough as you are bringing the edges together, and all should be well.

Although it is not easy for a beginner to spread the dough evenly and enclose the filling without missing a little, any way you can manage it is good enough. *Tamal* dough swells quite dramatically as it steams, and as long as the packet is tightly crimped (except for the top), the swelling dough will cover up any sins of assembly. Also, if some of the filling leaks a bit and stains the dough, napping the *tamales* with red chili sauce at serving time will cover up any flaws. In any event, the pudgy *tamales* (call them peasant style) are simple to make even the first time out.

As you finish each package, stand it up on the steamer rack. Try not to overcrowd the *tamales*, and make sure that the crimped bottom edge is facing down. The loosely folded over tops do not have to be absolutely straight up, but at least do not lay them on their sides. Pour about 1 inch of water into the bottom of your steamer (making sure that no part of any packet is actually touching the water), cover and place over high heat. Bring to a boil and maintain it, using medium heat, for 1 hour.

Once steamed, the *tamales* are best eaten fresh, but they can be kept standing for a while, if necessary, in their steamer, keeping the water at a bare simmer.

Serving the tamales: Serve with generous amounts of warmed red chili sauce—you will need about 2 cups—the best sauces for the purpose being those with tomato added, such as the adaptable red chili sauce on p. 79. Be sure to sauce the *tamales* only at the very last minute, as they soak up the warm *salsa* like sponges. It is traditional to apply the sauce over the corn-husk wrapping, but those in foil are naturally unwrapped in the kitchen and then sauced.

No garnishes are required, but passing around bowls of *guacamole* and sour cream makes the *tamales* even more luxurious.

NOTES: If in place of entree-size *tamales* you want to make appetizer-size ones, the amounts of filling and dough given above will produce 12 smaller packets. In case you run short of dough because you find it hard to spread it thin enough, increase the proportions as follows: 2 cups Masa Harina, 8 tablespoons shortening, and 1⅓ cups broth, leaving the remaining ingredients unchanged.

Dried corn husks: Native cooks will use green corn inside their *tamales*, mixing the kernels with green chili and cheese. They then wrap them in the soft green husks and, finally, stand them on corn cobs to keep the *tamales'* feet dry during steaming. Authentic as the husks are, they do not add flavor, and unwrapping them at the table when they have hot sauce around them is pesky to me.

However, should you decide to try them, buy the dried husks sold in the Mexican products section of the market and soak them in warm water for 1 hour to soften. Pat them dry and proceed as above. If you are making the pudgy, informal shapes (see illus. p. 247), roll the sides of the husk around the filling, fold the pointed top end of the husk down toward the wide end, then stand the *tamal* with the open end up. For the longer shape, place two husks side by side to form a square (this means that the pointed ends will face in opposite directions). Roll the husks into a cylinder around the filling and twist the ends closed as if you were sealing a piece of taffy in a wrapper. The twisted ends can be tied with string, but it is more colorful to use thin strips of husk for this. Steam these long *tamales* lying down on the steamer, each propped up slightly by its neighbor.

VARIATIONS:

To complete a batch of *tamales* feels like a triumph, and any cook rolling and steaming a maiden batch can sense the air of a feast day. If you learn to love *tamales*, the repertoire of fillings available to you is endless, for they can be improvised at will. Most of the hot fillings beginning on p. 107 can be adapted to *tamales*. The mashed black beans in butter on p. 298 are particularly delicious, as is the *picadillo* on p. 228 that usually goes into *tacos*. One simple way to make a filling is to begin with a cup of any leftover cooked meat, cut it into shreds or a rough mince, and moisten with your best homemade cooked *salsa*.

Although it is hardly traditional, the meat fillings can be lightened with scrambled eggs, as for the "Spanish pie" filling on p. 160. Cooked, shredded zucchini mixed with grated Monterey Jack cheese and canned green chili would be good for a vegetable *tamal*; boiled potato could be used in place of the zucchini, in which case add a little extra spice and some butter. For sweet *tamales*, a special variety that is unknown outside the Southwest or Mexico proper, see the recipe on p. 248. For improvised (and simpler) breakfast *tamales*, see p. 207.

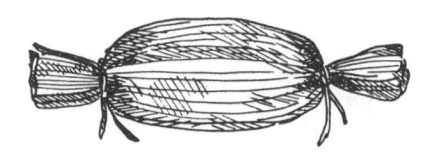

MODEST TAMALES WITH CHEESE AND PECANS

Although *tamales* bring a feast day to mind for a native New Mexican cook, these unstuffed *tamales* are rather modest for that purpose. Their dough takes barely 5 minutes to prepare when you use a food processor, and the results, once steamed, are like the Italian dumplings called *gnocchi*. They should be served as a starchy side dish sauced with the same red-chili-and-tomato sauce that traditionally goes over meat-filled *tamales*. This recipe allows for only 3 small *tamales* per person, but it is very easy to eat twice as many. As with all the other *tamal* recipes in this cookbook, the steaming is done in aluminum foil for the sake of convenience. If you prefer to try your hand at steaming in the traditional corn husks instead, directions are on p. 244.

For 12 tamales, serving 4 people as a small side dish:

>   1 **cup Masa Harina**
>   3 **tablespoons butter**
>   2 **tablespoons lard or vegetable shortening**
>   ¼ **teaspoon salt**
>   ½ **teaspoon baking powder**
>   ½ **teaspoon cinnamon**
>   ¼ **teaspoon cloves**
>   ½ **cup (about 2 ounces) shredded Monterey Jack cheese**
>   ½ **cup pecans**
>   ⅔ **cup warm water**

Place all the ingredients except the water in the bowl of a food processor equipped with the standard metal blade. Process until a uniform coarse meal is reached, about 10 seconds, stopping once to scrape down the bowl with a rubber spatula. With the motor running, pour in the warm water and blend until a smooth, pasty dough is produced, a matter of a few seconds. Scrape down with the spatula and blend a few seconds more.

Proceed to fill foil packets with the dough, following the directions for the basic *tamal* recipe on p. 240. This amount will make 12 *tamales*, each fitting a 6-inch-square wrapping. Steam for 1 hour, as in the basic recipe, and serve hot with a red sauce poured over at the last minute. Or (although this is unorthodox) the *tamales* can be tossed in butter if a red chili sauce is already on your menu to be served with some other dish. A sour green chili table *salsa* would also be appropriate to give these dumplings piquancy.

VARIATIONS:

Tamales in a Casserole: For a generous side dish serving 4 people, double the recipe and shape 20 *tamales* from it. Place the steamed *tamales*, hot or cold, fresh or leftover, in a shallow casserole that just accommodates them. Pour over them about 1½ cups of the adaptable red chili sauce on p. 79, top with 1 cups of shredded Monterey Jack cheese (approximately 4 ounces), and bake at 300° F. until the casserole is warmed through and the cheese melted, about 10 to 15 minutes. This is particularly welcome as part of a vegetarian dinner, further sauced with *guacamole* or the zucchini-and-avocado sauce on p. 85, which is akin to *guacamole*. Serve immediately, for this casserole turns mushy soon after it is heated through.

Sweet-and-Hot Tamales: Once discovered, the *tamal* is hard to abandon. Native Santa Feans do not combine their sweet *tamales*, which are meant

TAMALES IN CORN HUSKS

ROUND SHAPE:

1. Using a single husk, place dough on upper half away from pointed end. Spread dough as evenly as possible and spoon filling into center.

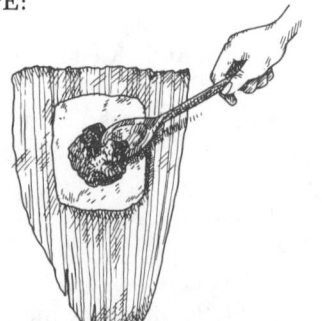

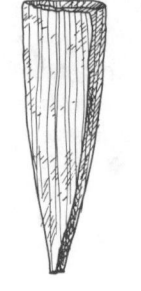

2. Bring in both sides of husk to enclose *tamal* filling completely in dough.

3. Bring up pointed end of husk and stand upright in steamer. Some cooks further seal the husk by folding over the open end or tying it closed with a strip of husk (household string works as well).

LONG SHAPE:

1. Place two husks side by side (points in opposite directions) to form a square. Spread an oblong of dough down the center, then spoon in a strip of filling.

2. Roll in sides of husks to enclose filling completely with dough; then tie ends with strips of husk or string.

for dessert, with hot red chili, but the combination is very nice, as Caribbean cooks long ago discovered.

Make the "modest" *tamales* described above, but with these changes to the dough: Add ⅓ cup brown sugar and ⅓ cup raisins to the processor and increase the amount of warm water by 2 or 3 tablespoons if the dough seems too dry to spread easily on the foil. Then proceed exactly as in the recipe and serve with the same red-chili-and-tomato sauce.

For a larger side dish, you can double the recipe and bake your finished *tamales* in a casserole with cheese, as described above.

Dessert Tamales: In Santa Fe it is more conventional to serve sweet *tamales* like the above at the end of the meal, in which case you want to drizzle with a few teaspoons of melted butter and a few tablespoons of honey—not with a chili sauce. Serve fresh and warm. Guests who are not familiar with Mexican cooking will be surprised by a sweet *tamal*, but they are apt to like it at once.

TAMALE PIE

Tamale pie frequently appears in the pages of Mexican cookbooks; it might well be considered an anomaly there, for as the name indicates, it is an invention of the American Southwest—the correct singular in Spanish for *tamales* would be *tamal*. Although its origins are not clear, tamale pie smacks of the Home Ec mentality, for it is supposed to be an "easy" variation upon *tamales*. Shaping and steaming the *tamales*, the very steps that impart character to them, are skipped. Instead, the dough mixture is spread inside a shallow casserole to form a bottom and side crust, a *tamal* filling is spooned inside, and the remainder of the dough is spread over the top. The casserole is baked at 350° F. for about 30 to 40 minutes, or until the crust is stiffened and barely browned.

If you like tamale pie, use the dough preparation and fillings given for steamed *tamales* in this book, but make a few changes, as follows:

- Heavily butter a shallow casserole or gratin dish with a capacity of about 2 quarts, to prevent the crust from sticking.
- For 4 people, base the recipe on 1½ cups of Masa Harina for the dough, and about 3 cups of filling.
- Prepare a red or green *enchilada* sauce to accompany the pie, since it tends to be dry.
- Melt a layer of Monterey Jack cheese over the top crust during the last 10 minutes of baking—this also helps to counteract dryness.

Some cooks increase the interest of tamale pie by making a more savory dough mixture in place of the plain one ordinarily used for traditional steamed *tamales*. Here is one:

1½ cups Masa Harina
6 tablespoons margarine
½ teaspoon baking powder
¼ teaspoon salt
¼ cup cream or milk
¾ cup hot chicken broth

Combine all the ingredients except the chicken broth in a food processor and mix into a smooth, uniform dough. With the motor still running, pour in the broth and continue to process a few seconds more. Scrape down the bowl with a rubber spatula, then add a few more seconds of processing. The dough should be moist and soft enough to spread in the pan. If it is stiffer than cake frosting, add another few tablespoons of broth.

A successfully made tamale pie is rather like shepherd's pie to those who like it, but even they must admit that it is inedible cold and is really best only right after it comes from the oven.

Tex-Mex Tamale Pie: Tamale pie is frequently employed as a gambit to finish up leftover chili con carne, which should be somewhat thicker than usual for the purpose. Some cooks add chopped green olives to this filling, while others use only a top layer of dough; for that, spread 2 to 4 cups of the filling out in a shallow baking pan (9 by 9 inches or 9 by 13 inches, depending upon how much leftover chili you have), then top with *tamal* dough and bake as directed above.

WHOLE GREEN CHILIES STUFFED WITH CHEESE
Chiles rellenos

While vocal fanatics over Tex-Mex cooking argue about the perfect chili con carne, the quieter devotees of Southwestern food hunger for the perfect *chile relleno*, a good example of which can make a cook's reputation. In truth, these stuffed chilies are rather tedious to make, since they involve several delicate steps, and the finished product must be served quickly in order for the crisp batter coating not to turn soggy. All this fuss makes *chiles rellenos* a restaurant dish by and large, but they are well worth trying at home, particularly if you have an electric wok or similar utensil to make the frying easier and more controllable. I give the classic version first, then a few other fillings to consider besides cheese. Last of all is a method for baking the chilies, making them far easier to handle, if not the stuff to engender fanatical devotion.

For 8 or 12 stuffed chilies, serving 4 people:

> 8 or 12 whole roasted and peeled chilies (at harvest time these are fresh, home-roasted *poblano* chilies; any other time, they are canned)
> 6 ounces, approximately, Monterey Jack cheese
> Flour for dredging

BATTER:

> 2 eggs, separated
> ⅔ cup milk
> ⅔ cup flour
> ½ teaspoon salt
> 1 tablespoon vegetable oil
> Vegetable oil for shallow-frying
> 3 cups tomato sauce, such as the quick one on p. 80

Mix all the batter ingredients except the separated egg whites in a food processor and blend into a smooth batter. Let sit to ripen for 20 minutes, then blend a second or two more. Beat the egg whites until sitff but not dry, then fold in the processor mixture with a rubber spatula.

While the batter ripens, stuff the chilies. If you have roasted and peeled your own Anaheim, California, or *poblano* chilies, try to keep them whole, with only the tops removed. (Native cooks leave the tops on to show that they have troubled to prepare their own chilies, in which case the cheese filling is inserted through a slit in the side.) Cut the cheese into small finger shapes and insert them into your chilies. If you are using canned whole chilies, as will almost always be the case, you will find them exceedingly fragile. Sometimes they fall into shreds the instant you try to open them up; sometimes they cooperate and allow you to open them flat, lay in a couple of narrow slices of cheese and fold them back into their original shape. However frustrating it may be, fold the chilies around 1 or 2 slivers of cheese, even if it requires rolling them up like anchovies afterward—you will be losing only the elegant, pointed shape. Set the chilies aside.

Frying the chilies: Heat a good ½ inch or more of oil in a medium-size skillet or electric wok, setting the temperature at 375° F., or heat until a drop of batter bubbles and starts to puff as soon as it hits oil.

CHILES RELLENOS

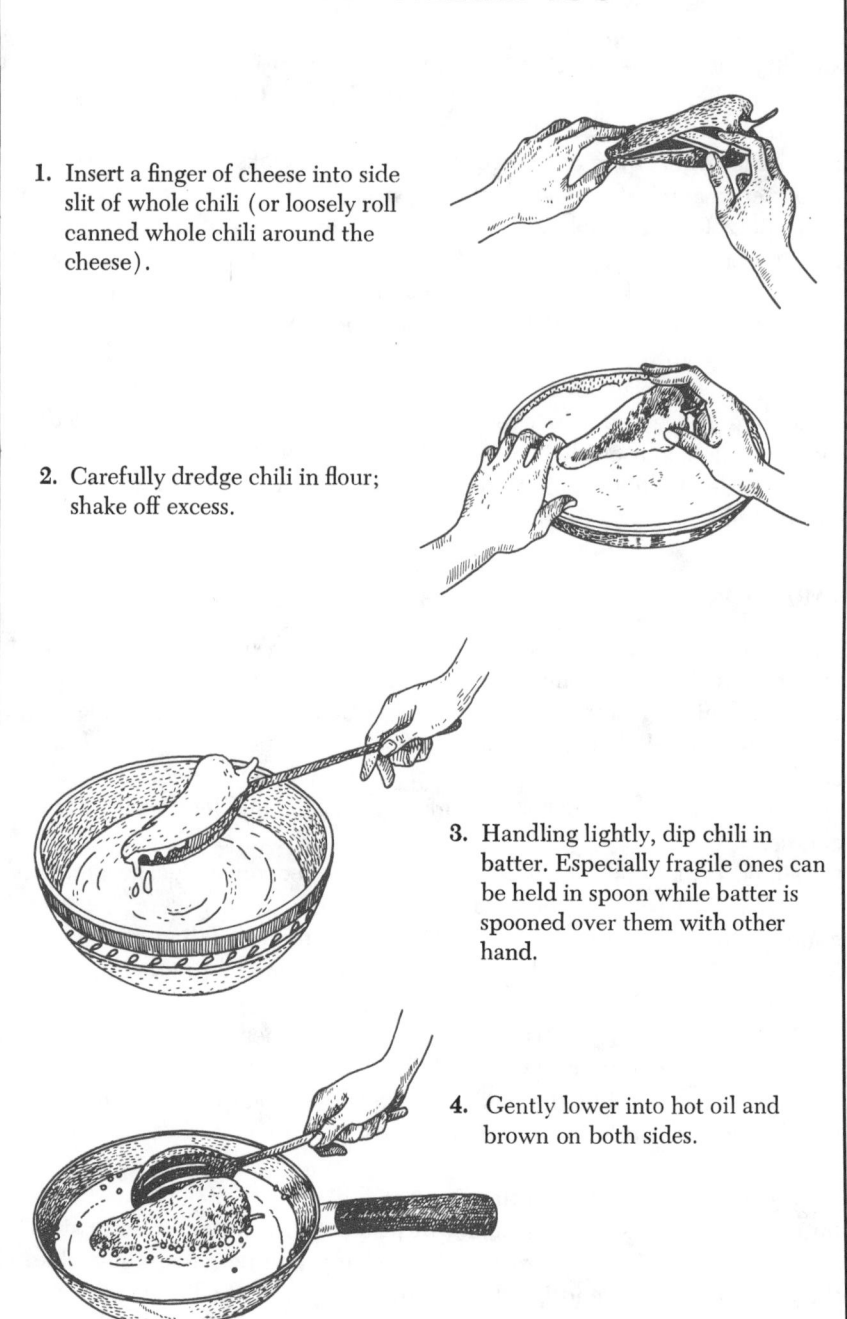

1. Insert a finger of cheese into side slit of whole chili (or loosely roll canned whole chili around the cheese).

2. Carefully dredge chili in flour; shake off excess.

3. Handling lightly, dip chili in batter. Especially fragile ones can be held in spoon while batter is spooned over them with other hand.

4. Gently lower into hot oil and brown on both sides.

Carefully pat the chilies dry with a paper towel, then turn them over and dry the other side. Handling a chili gently in your fingers, dredge it lightly in flour and drop it softly into the batter. Turn it over to coat the other side, using a slotted spoon, then place the coated chili in the oil—it is quite all right if the chili is coated with what looks like a thick covering of batter, making it appear double in size. Fry for just a minute or so on each side, letting the batter puff, brown and crisp all over. Drain the finished chilies on paper towels and keep warm in a 200° F. oven while you complete the frying. The amount of batter given above will coat up to 12 chilies, but for the sake of keeping them crisp, you may want to fry only 8 in one go.

Serve hot as a main dish or as a first course, with a generous amount of tomato sauce spooned over at the last moment. The *chilies rellenos* also taste delicious on their own, with nothing but a good homemade *salsa* on the side. Leftover chilies turn soggy and cannot be rewarmed very successfully.

VARIATIONS:

Other Fillings: Almost the only filling encountered in Santa Fe restaurants is the classic one of cheese alone, sometimes sprinkled with a bit of chopped onion. Home cooks, however, often use the ground meat-and-spice mixture called *picadillo* (a simple version appears on p. 228 as a *taco* stuffing). That demands that you roast your own *poblano* chilies, however, since canned ones cannot stand up to anything bulkier than a sliver of cheese.

Home cooks also like to cook some chopped onion, garlic and fresh tomato until it is thick, then, off the heat, mix it with cheese, green coriander, and a pinch of oregano. This fresh tomato filling reminds any Southwestern native of high summer when the tomatoes and chilies are at their best.

The third alternative is *refritos*, or refried beans (the version with butter on p. 298 would be delicious). These work well even if only canned chilies are at hand, but the baking method described below is the recommended cooking style for this version.

Chiles Rellenos in a Casserole: Preheat the oven to 400° F. and heavily butter a shallow casserole which will just hold the stuffed chilies side by side. Stuff the chilies with the cheese or any alternative stuffing, dredge them lightly in flour, and lay them in the pan. Make the batter as directed, allow it to rest, then dollop it generously over the chilies. Bake for 10 minutes, then run under the broiler for a few seconds to brown on top. You can also sprinkle more cheese on the casserole prior to broiling. Serve with the same tomato sauce as for fried *rellenos*, or leave the chilies un-sauced and use as a vegetable alongside grilled meats.

A Luncheon Casserole of Chiles Rellenos: This is made exactly as for the large casserole above, but place only 2 chilies per person in individual gratin dishes, then top with a layer of batter. Bake as directed, top with cheese, and run under the broiler to brown. Garnish as decoratively as you would a *tostada*, with sliced avocado, green onion, tomatoes, lettuce, olives, sour cream and so on. Or dollop on a few spoonfuls of *guacamole*. Bring the individual casseroles to the table with the tomato sauce on p. 79, or any good green chili sauce.

Chiles Rellenos with Spoonbread: For a terrifically good brunch dish, make a casserole of stuffed chilies and the breakfast soufflé spoonbread on p. 208. The technique is to make the spoonbread batter and stuff fingers of cheese into 8 whole chilies, as above. Now nap a thin layer of batter in a buttered casserole, lay in the stuffed chilies and top with the remaining batter. Bake at 350° F. for 30 to 40 minutes. Serve warm—to vast acclaim —with a tomato sauce or fresh *salsa*.

"Stuffed" Chilies Without Stuffing: To save the bother of slitting and stuffing whole chilies, native cooks often prepare a *relleno* that needs no stuffing. The method is first to cook a batch of *picadillo* (p. 101), allow the meat to cool, and mix with 1 cup of chopped, roasted green chilies, canned or fresh. This mixture is then rolled with floured hands into meatballs about the size of ping-pong balls. They are dipped in the same frying batter as for regular *chiles rellenos*, then deep-fried until the coating is puffed and crisp—the interior is already cooked, of course.

In this way the cook has achieved an admittedly bulky *relleno* which, however, duplicates the flavor of one that had to be laboriously stuffed. Rather than serve these with tomato or red chili sauce, the custom is to present the same warm, sweet sugar syrup with raisins that accompanies *buñuelos* for dessert (p. 333), but you can substitute a chili-based sauce as you please.

MEAT, POULTRY, AND FISH

Chili Con Carne • Son-of-a-Gun Stew
Pepper Steak with Green Chilies
Charcoal-Broiled Steak with Green Chili and Guacamole
Vaquero Stew • Pork Cured in Red Chili (Carne adovada)
Posole • Dry-Cooked Pork with Green Chilies
Pork Stew with Red Chilies and Black Beans
Pork Spareribs with Chipotle-and-Peanut Sauce
Green Chili Stew with Lamb or Pork
Barbecued Leg of Lamb
Chicken Braised with Rice (Arroz con pollo)
Chicken Braised with Rice, Tomatoes, Saffron and Peas
Lemon-Broiled Chicken with Green Chilies
Stuffed Turkey Breast with Pumpkin-Seed Sauce
Turkey Cured in Red Chilies (Turqué adovado)
Mountain Trout

CHILI CON CARNE

The Mexican stew called *carne con chile*, a northern specialty which gave rise to American chili con carne, is hardly ever sweet, tangy or full of tomatoes. "Chili" (to use its familiar nickname) can be all of these, and it often sports many another odd ingredient—see the list following this recipe. Purists who like their Tex-Mex food to be as close as possible to its origins object to making chili with ground beef. They say it should be made in true Mexican style with small cubes of meat, sometimes boiled before the red chili powder is added, and they are particularly vocal about omitting tomatoes or beans from the pot.

Really, the choice is yours, for chili has migrated into every part of the country and transformed itself to fit every taste. Since the New Mexican version of *carne con chile colorado* is already included elsewhere in this cookbook (p. 21), I have tailored this recipe for chili con carne to be savory of kidney beans, tomato, sweet green pepper, and even vinegar, all ingredients that Hispanic cooks do not usually put together in their simpler chili-powder stews. On p. 259 is a fairly extensive guide to garnishing chili at the table, but it will be good enough served plain with sourdough bread and cold beer.

A note about the amount of powdered red chilies to use: The quantity called for below will not make your chili too hot, assuming that you are using the mild New Mexico red chilies. If you know your powdered chili is hot—if, for instance, it has a large amount of *chile caribe* or *pequín* in it—reduce the amount to 4 tablespoons and make up the rest with a good-quality paprika. In any event, avoid premixed "chili powder" which is filled out with cumin and garlic; it is inferior for use in a decent home-made pot of chili.

Since chili improves overnight, it is best made in advance. Chili can also be used again as a Tex-Mex meat sauce or as the filling for a tamale pie (p. 248).

For 8 servings:

    2 to 3 pounds beef round or chuck steak
    3 tablespoons vegetable oil
    2 medium-large onions (1 pound, about), chopped
    ¼ cup flour
    2 to 4 cloves garlic, finely chopped
    ½ of a 6-ounce can tomato paste
    3 cups crushed tomatoes, or the equivalent in whole
       canned tomatoes, roughly chopped
    5 cups beef broth, or the equivalent in beef broth and water,
       mixed to desired proportions
    6 tablespoons powdered red chilies
    2 teaspoons whole or ground cumin
    1 teaspoon oregano
    ½ teaspoon black pepper
    2 teaspoons salt
    3 tablespoons cider vinegar
    1 bell pepper, chopped
    4 cups red kidney beans, home-cooked or canned
 Optional: 1 or 2 chopped *chiles chipotles*
       (see p. 69 for description)

If your guests are at all touched by chili snobbery, they may expect you to cut up the meat for your chili by hand, in which case cut it into ½-inch cubes. For less demanding guests, grind the meat, coarse or fine as you choose, using the standard metal blade of the food processor. Grind only ½ pound at a time and be sure not to process for more than a few seconds since tender supermarket beef is quickly ground to a paste. Some aficionados like the texture produced when half the beef is cubed and the other half coarsely ground.

Heat half the oil in a large skillet and brown the beef thoroughly in 3 or 4 batches—larger quantities are likely to crowd the pan, which will cause them to steam instead of sauté. As each batch is finished, transfer it to a 4- to 6-quart pot or Dutch oven.

When all the meat is browned, make sure there are at least 2 tablespoons of fat left in the skillet, and add the onions. Cover the pan to sweat them over low heat for about 5 minutes. Remove the lid, raise the heat to medium, and stir the onions until they are uniformly light brown but not at all charred. Sprinkle the flour over the onions and continue to stir for a minute to incorporate it and cook the mixture through. Transfer the onions to the pot with the beef.

Add all the remaining ingredients except the bell pepper and the beans to the pot—including the optional *chiles chipotles*—and place over medium heat. Stir thoroughly, bring to a simmer, and cook gently, covered, for 1½ hours. The chili will need little attention as it cooks except for an occasional stirring to keep it from sticking to the pot. Add up to 1 cup of water to the mixture if it seems too thick.

At the end of the simmering time, degrease the surface of the chili if necessary and add the chopped bell pepper. Simmer another 15 minutes, then add the beans (including some of their liquid if the stew needs further thinning) and simmer barely 5 minutes longer. The chili can be served immediately or held; it is said to be better on the second day by those who make it their business to know all about chili. Bring to room temperature before reheating and serve with sourdough bread, biscuits, cornbread or flour tortillas.

Many chili eaters, especially in California, like to spoon table garnishes over their chili. Besides the apparently mandatory grated Cheddar cheese, one sees a multitude of other toppings—sliced black olives, sour cream, squirts of lime juice, chopped green coriander (*cilantro*), red pepper flakes, and chopped scallions or red onion. This chili is robust enough on its own not to need any of these extras, but they certainly dress it up.

VARIATIONS:

These are beyond numbering. The first thing home specialists usually strive for is a "secret" ingredient. It is this that makes anyone's pet chili personal, and thanks to several "world championships" of chili making, there is forever a temptation to fool the judges with unanticipated strokes of brilliance. If you want to explore this dark area of chili, the most common "secret" additives are listed here, with the special warning not to try all at once. In no order of preference, the additives include celery seed or celery salt, caraway seed, red wine, whole-kernel corn, Dijon or powdered mustard, bay leaves, brown sugar, Worcestershire sauce, Chinese chili paste with garlic (a bottled product sold in Oriental groceries) and all forms of dried red chilies, such as *ancho, pasilla* and the small, very hot *tepins* and *pequins*. To those purists who think of simple aboriginal chili as the real thing (consisting of little more than meat, red chilies, and water) such unwritten embellishments are an abomination.

Texas Chili: To make your chili more passable to the Texas branch of higher appreciation, omit the tomatoes, tomato paste, bell pepper and beans. Your stew will contain a greater proportion of meat, which is also the Texas taste. Diluted with a little more beef broth, such a chili becomes a Tex-Mex meat sauce, to be ladled over *enchiladas* instead of other red chili sauces. One also sees it used over *chiles rellenos, burritos* and *tamales*. Use it in any of these ways as you like, announcing that they are Texas style. Eaten out of a bowl, such chili may be permitted to have beans in it.

Chili with Vegetables: Thanks to the combined influence of California, nutritional caution and widespread vegetarianism, you often find chili with vegetables in it. Besides the chopped bell pepper already called for, feel free to add chopped celery, carrots and California black olives to your pot, putting them in for the last 15 minutes of cooking time to preserve their fresh texture. About ¾ cup of each would be a good start, chopping them into ½-inch dice or smaller, as you like. Less often encountered in a bowl of chili, but good nevertheless, are whole-kernel corn, zucchini, hominy and chick-peas. For true vegetarian chili, add all of these and omit the beef. A cup of bulgur wheat is sometimes added to duplicate the texture of meat. With or without it, such a vegetarian chili needs to cook for no more than an hour, and the softest ingredients, particularly zucchini or canned beans, require a bare 10 minutes or less of simmering.

SON-OF-A-GUN STEW

Here is food that once sustained a way of life, but now is nearly forgotten. Cowboys, farmers and Western workingmen in general all knew of son-of-a-gun stew and ate it with gusto (but also complaints). One recipe that I have seen instructs the cook to slaughter a beef—in fact, the most usual animal was a calf—and cut only its liver, heart, brains, sweetbreads, kidney and marrow gut (a tube connecting two of the cow's stomachs) into ½-inch dice. The meat itself went for another purpose. Salt and chili were tossed in for savor, along with a chunk of fresh suet, and then the pot was stirred for several hours to reach the final result.

Although the name needs no explanation (it was less discreetly called "son-of-a-bitch" stew and more pointedly "boss's" or "foreman's" stew), the origin of the dish is vague. It helps to know another bit of lore, which is that the Plains Indians hunted their game not for the muscle meat, which was left behind for the scavengers, but for exactly the vital and symbolic innards, the givers of strength, that the cowboys learned to put into their own son-of-a-gun stews.

PEPPER STEAK WITH GREEN CHILIES

Home cooks who are familiar with Southwestern food invariably begin to tinker with other styles of cooking—hence all the spoonbreads, omelets and corn muffins with green chilies added to them. In this case, the dish is steak *au poivre*, already altered from the original by using green peppercorns instead of cracked black pepper, now pushed a step further by including chopped green chilies and *cilantro* in the pan sauce. The preparation is rather like a steak Diane.

Following the basic recipe is a variation using hamburger steak. Please do not skip it out of the notion that it will be too plebeian. If you use chuck or round steak and grind it at the last moment in a food processor, the taste is delicious.

For 4 people:

>   2 tablespoons butter
>   1 tablespoon olive oil
>   4 tenderloin or loin strip steaks, weighing 6 to 8 ounces each
> Salt and pepper to taste

FOR THE SAUCE:

>   2 tablespoons butter
> A finely chopped mixture of 2 green onions, 2 whole canned
>   green chilies, and 2 tablespoons green coriander (*cilantro*)
>   1 tablespoon green peppercorns
>   ½ cup white wine or dry white vermouth
>   ¾ cup heavy cream
> Salt to taste
>   1 tablespoon butter for enriching the finished sauce
>   2 tablespoons additional *cilantro* for garnish (optional)

Heat the 2 tablespoons butter and the olive oil in a 10-inch skillet until foaming, add the steaks and sauté quickly, turning once, until they are done to rare or medium rare—this should take only 3 or 4 minutes per side if you keep the heat at medium or somewhat higher. Season with salt and pepper. Set the steaks aside in a warm oven with the door ajar to help prevent any further cooking.

Working quickly, pour all the remaining fat from the pan and discard it. Melt 2 tablespoons of butter, then add the chopped green onions, chili and *cilantro*. Sauté for only a few seconds, then add the green peppercorns and wine. Raise the heat to high and boil down until most of the wine is evaporated and the sauce is syrupy. If you want a smoother-textured sauce, mash the solid ingredients with the back of a large slotted spoon at this point.

Add the cream and continue to boil rapidly until the sauce is thick enough to coat a spoon—but do not let it go so far that it begins to look pasty. Remove from heat, salt to taste, and swirl in the additional tablespoon of butter. Pour the sauce over the steaks, garnish with coriander, if desired, and serve immediately.

VARIATION:

Hamburgers with Green Chilies: Instead of the steaks, have about 1¾ pounds of chuck or round steak trimmed of fat, then cut into rough chunks. Chop in a processor until the meat is coarsely ground—it will take 20 seconds or less—then shape it into 4 thick oval patties. Dredge each patty lightly in flour and proceed as with the basic recipe. These are best when quite rare, so do not cook more than 3 minutes or so on each side, keeping the heat high enough to brown them well.

CHARCOAL-BROILED STEAK WITH GREEN CHILI AND GUACAMOLE

A thick charcoal-broiled beefsteak is still wonderful food, even after the passage of various sophisticated trends in American cooking. The appearance of the kettle barbecue has made it taste even better; the smoky flavor imparted to the meat needs no other complement than salt and pepper. Having said that, I still would venture to improve upon perfection by giving this recipe. The broiled steak is taken off the grill and spread first with a light coating of green chili paste, then with a generous ribbon of *guacamole*. The result is a gussied-up dish by the standards of primordial beef eaters, but it is extraordinarily delicious. Be sure that the *guacamole* is not refrigerator-cold, for that detracts from the dish.

For 4 to 6 people:

> 4 to 6 thick rib-eye, strip sirloin or similar steaks
> Olive oil
> Salt and pepper
> Green Chilies for the Table (p. 94)
> *Guacamole* (pp. 171–74, any version)

Have the barbecue coals white-hot. Rub each steak with olive oil and score the fat with a knife to prevent the meat from curling as it grills. Sear the steaks quickly for about 5 minutes on each side, then place the cover on the barbecue kettle or raise the level of the grill if your barbecue is not the type that can be covered. Cook for as long as it takes to reach the stage of rare or medium rare, usually from 5 to 15 more minutes, depending on the hotness of the coals.

Have ready at your side the green chili paste. When the steaks are done to the desired degree of pinkness, remove from the fire, season with salt and pepper and arrange on a platter. Spread each steak lightly with a tablespoon or more of the green chili. Bring to the table, where your guests are presumably waiting in eager anticipation, and make them wait the few seconds longer it takes for you to decorate each steak with a broad ribbon of freshly made *guacamole*. As older cookbooks used to say, "Eat with relish."

VARIATIONS WITH VEAL AND CHICKEN:

Spanish cooks are very fond of grilling thick veal chops, often as big as our rib-eye steaks. Usually the meat is not very young; it is closer to what butchers call "baby beef." Although a bit unusual in texture—I think of beef at this age as a little slick—such chops are delicious when treated in the manner described above. Have your butcher cut the shoulder or loin chops about an inch thick and grill them at least to the medium stage, which is not so soft-textured as the rare. Squeeze a few drops of lemon juice over the finished chops before adding the chili and *guacamole*.

Quartered broiler chickens are also delicious made in this way. After searing them, cook bony side down for at least 15 minutes; the parts are done when no pink juice runs from an incision you poke right where the thigh meets the body of the chicken. Breast parts are generally cooked about 5 minutes earlier. Sprinkle with lemon juice, as for the veal, and smear with the chili. Since the diners will have to carve around the bones, it is probably more convenient to present the *guacamole* on the side rather than on top of the pieces. One large quarter per person is an adequate serving if there are hearty side dishes. If chicken is the focus of the meal, broiler halves from 2- to 2½-pound birds would be sufficient.

Scorpion Steak with Guacamole: If you have the palate for extremely hot foods, substitute the Scorpion Chili Paste on p. 92 for the green chili in any of these versions. The fiery taste of the red chili offset by the cooling taste of *guacamole* is very appealing with grilled meat, but this is not a dish to spring on the fainthearted.

VAQUERO STEW

In Spanish-speaking New Mexico, the cowboys were called *vaqueros*, and their proper territory was the high-plains country east of Santa Fe, adjoining west Texas. It was a harsh, unforgiving place to work, and annals of the old times reveal that the food was more or less the same bare stuff as other cowboy food, except that the ever-present stews, including the son-of-a-gun stew on p. 260, would be liberally dosed with red chili. The dish that has come down to us as chili con carne probably began life as a *vaquero* stew.

The choice of meat used in cowboy stews depended on the season. Christmas and New Year's coincided with the calving season, and therefore the choicest newborn veal could be used. If the weather was so forbidding that calf slaughtering was out of the question, then the meat might be jerky or the cured *carne adovada* described below, using flanked beef instead of pork. Range-fed beef, eaten the rest of the year, tended to be tough and sinewy, so it was either pounded well before the chilies were added or else stewed from sunup to dinnertime. In any event, the pot would have held as much innards as flesh, for there was no question of wasting the liver and lights.

Any of the stewing methods given in this chapter can be adapted to *vaquero* stew by simply using chuck steak cut into 1-inch cubes and braising it for 2 hours before adding vegetables. However, if you want *real* cowboy stew, follow this method:

Heat ¼ inch of lard until smoking in a cast-iron Dutch oven. Stir in gristly chuck steak, untrimmed, allowing ½ pound per person. Brown well over a fiercely sizzling flame, meanwhile cutting in chunks of onion and roughly chopped garlic. When the meat and onions are brown, stir in powdered red chilies (from 4 tablespoons to ½ cup), making sure that a good proportion of it is cayenne or hot *pequín.* At the same time, sprinkle the meat with salt, black pepper and a light coating of flour or cornmeal, and keep stirring. When the chili and flour are incorporated, cover the meat with water and simmer, uncovered, until the cows come home (at least 4 hours). When you are within half an hour of eating, cut in chunks of peeled potato, allowing 1 or more per person, and raise the heat to boiling. Cook, adding more water as needed, until the potatoes are done. Serve hot with sourdough bread or flour tortillas, making sure not to skim any grease from the pot.

PORK CURED IN RED CHILI
Carne adovada

The local name for this preparation is *carne adovada,* or pickled meat, indicating that the cured strips of freshly slaughtered pork were to be saved for later consumption. In the village economy, pig slaughtering was seasonal, and there had to be a quantity of meat suitable for stewing or frying in the intervening months. In the modern versions encountered in Santa Fe restaurants, the "pickled pork" is really just a stew of pork chops or shoulder marinated in the standard red chili sauce. If you want to proceed that way, then simply cover your pork cuts with 2 cups of a good chili sauce (p. 73) for at least a day, then make a stew, adding water and more sauce as needed to keep the meat moist.

In the recipe below, the pork is treated as though cured meat was being taken out of storage for a family meal. The results are not a stew— and in fact the best use for the cooked *carne adovada* is to stuff it into wheat or corn tortillas or to arrange it as part of a larger plate of beans, rice, vegetables and other simple dishes that need to be combined to amount to something better. On its own, this is quite plain food.

For 4 people:

12 thin-cut pork chops (about 3 pounds) trimmed of fat
2 onions, peeled
4 tablespoons powdered red chili, or flaked *chile caribe*, which is quite hot
1 teaspoon cayenne, if needed for extra hotness
1 teaspoon salt
½ teaspoon oregano
1 tablespoon sugar
2 cloves garlic, peeled
1 tablespoon vinegar
Optional: ½ teaspoon ground cumin and ¼ teaspoon cloves
⅔ cup water

The modern cut of meat for *carne adovada* is usually the thin-cut pork chops called for here, but it is worth knowing that Hispanic cooks cut their meat strips with the grain, not against it—in this way, they claim, the meat acquires more flavor while it cures.

Have ready an oven dish or casserole that will hold the chops snugly in one overlapping layer.

Cut 1 onion into 8 slices, then cut 4 more slices from half of the second onion. Roughly chop the remaining half onion and then combine it with all the remaining ingredients except the water in the jar of an electric blender or the bowl of a food processor. Blend to a puree, adding the water only after the process is well along—it works best to pour it in through the hole in the blender cap or the feed tube while the motor is still running. Taste the chili sauce for hotness; many Santa Fe cooks would make it too hot for a novice to tolerate, so be guided by your preference. In any case, the texture of the marinade should be thick, almost pasty.

Assemble the meat for curing by coating all the chops with the chili marinade, covering both sides, then making overlapped layers of chili-coated meat and onion slices in the baking pan. Scrape any remaining sauce over the whole assembly once it is laid out, cover with foil and refrigerate for 24 hours or longer.

Cooking the meat: Preheat the oven to 325° F. (One is often told to pan-fry *carne adovada* in oil, but that has drawbacks if you are fastidious about sputtering grease.) Arrange the meat in a single layer in a casserole, spoon the marinating liquid over it and bake for 1 hour. After this time the liquid will have evaporated and the meat will have started to brown. Serve with or without the onion slices that cooked along with the meat. For a moister result, add ½ cup water to the casserole, cover with foil and bake for 1½ hours or until very tender.

A second method is to barbecue close to the charcoal. Being thin, the chops are grilled only 5 minutes or less to a side. If they are still pink near the bones, place the chops directly onto a warm serving platter and cover them; they will cook a little more in a few minutes in their own heat. The onion slices can also be grilled if they are still manageable.

Since these versions of *carne adovada* are dry, they go well with sauced vegetables like the *calabacitas* with cream on p. 318.

VARIATIONS:

Cured Meat for Stuffings: Rather than curing the pork to cook as is, you can preserve miscellaneous bits of meat in red chili with the intention of sautéing them later, then chopping or grinding the cooked meat for stuffings. Chunky pieces of meat also can be shredded in a food processor using the method outlined on p. 99. Even after a short period of curing, the *carne adovada* is strong-flavored, and it has the advantage over leftover stew of not being soupy.

POSOLE

One old cookbook doesn't put too fine a point on it by calling *posole* "hog and hominy." The main difference between everyday *posole* and feast-day *posole* is how much of the hog gets put in. Your stew can be nothing more than a cup of hominy, a little salt pork and a scattering of crushed red chili pods—which makes it daily fare in New Mexico and quite rustic. The feast-day version, particularly popular in the pueblos, calls for cooking pounds of hominy with a pig's head, feet, ribs and salt rind until a vast, fatty stew of corn, pork and chili has been cooked up. It is customarily eaten for good luck on New Year's Day or to celebrate the patron saint's day of the pueblo. As with Texas barbecue, making *posole* in legendary quantities is half the ritual.

The recipes I give below are comparatively modest and much less fatty. The basic recipe is really a green chili stew with the *posole* added as a starchy vegetable, and it is meant to be approached with as little fuss as Irish stew. The Mexican way with *posole* (in Mexico spelled *pozole*) is to present the hominy and pork in a clear broth; it then acquires color and savor from the numerous garnishes applied at the table. Since this treatment is sometimes still encountered in home cooking around Santa Fe, I give a recipe for it among the variations that follow the basic recipe. An array of fresh garnishes not only brightens up *posole*, it makes it more digestible. (For an uncomplicated *posole* which is cooked without meat and meant to be served as a side dish in place of rice or beans, see the vegetable section, p. 315.)

Traditional recipes for *posole* called for hours of cooking, particularly if dried hominy from the winter-storage bins was used. I find that the modern frozen *posole* needs only an hour or two all told to cook perfectly well; make that half an hour if you use canned hominy.

For 4 people:

    1 onion, chopped
    2 cloves garlic, peeled and chopped
    2 tablespoons vegetable oil or lard
    ½ teaspoon each black pepper, ground cumin, cloves and cayenne
    1½ pounds pork shoulder, cooked as for the shredded pork
        on p. 99, then cut into 1-inch cubes
    2 or 3 cups frozen, precooked *posole* (see "Preparing" below),
        or canned white or yellow hominy, drained and rinsed
    3 to 5 cups pork broth, degreased and strained
    1 cup canned chopped green chilies
    2 whole *jalapeños*, canned or fresh, chopped (to be omitted
        if you want milder *posole*)
Salt, if needed
Optional: garnishes described on p. 268, arranged on the table
    in small bowls

Preparing frozen posole: Packages of fresh-frozen *posole* can often be found in supermarkets that are well stocked with Mexican foods. The golden or white hominy in the packages has already been treated in lime water and the skins removed from the kernels; sometimes it has also been pre-seasoned. For use in *posole* stew, it only needs to be precooked (although the native cooks often add it directly to the pork as it is stewing and cook them together for 3 or 4 hours). Slightly defrost the *posole* so that the frozen mass can be broken apart, add it to 2 quarts of lightly salted boiling water in a 6-quart pot and boil for 45 minutes, or until the kernels swell and pop open. It is quite all right to cook the *posole* for much longer than this, as most recipes require, but I find that the shorter time is usually sufficient. For the 2 to 3 cups of cooked, drained *posole* needed in this recipe, begin with 1 cup of frozen. Unused portions, whether still frozen or precooked, should be quickly refrozen to prevent souring.

Sauté the onion and garlic in the oil or lard until they wilt and begin to take on a little browning. Add the spices, stir for a minute, then stir in the pork, precooked *posole* or canned hominy (without liquid), pork broth, green chilies and the *jalapeños*, if you are using them. Cook at a simmer, covered, for 45 to 60 minutes—the meat and hominy should be tender and the chilies and onions well amalgamated into the broth. If the *posole* seems at all unfinished, continue to cook for up to 60 minutes longer.

Degrease the stew, check for salt, and serve in wide soup plates. There should be a generous amount of broth for each portion, so add water as needed to keep the pork covered in the final minutes of stewing. Each diner garnishes his own *posole* at the table (see the variation with clear broth, below). If you are eating this stew as a plain daily meal, no accompaniments are necessary beyond warm flour tortillas and a good uncooked *salsa* (p. 86).

VARIATIONS:

Posole with Red Chili: The huge feast-day *posole* that uses many pig's feet and pounds of hominy is generally flavored with handfuls of crushed red chili pods that cook in the stew for hours. However, you also see versions cooked with red chili powder or with no chili at all—in that event, a red chili sauce (such as the one made from whole chili pods on p. 77) is passed at the table. You can flavor the basic recipe by adding 2 to 4 tablespoons powdered red chilies in place of the green chili called for in the basic recipe; simply stir them into the onions along with the other spices. Although it is not traditional, you can also add tomato to this variation with delicious results—stir in 1 cup crushed tomatoes packed in puree when you add the pork broth.

Clear Broth Posole: The thinnest *posole*, leaning heavily on its garnishes for interest, is made without any chilies; it contains just the hominy, the braised pork and the pork broth. Put in the onion and garlic whole so that they can later be removed, and add any seasonings (whole black peppercorns, leaf oregano, whole cumin, whole red chilies) tied in a cheesecloth bag so that they too can be removed.

When served, each soup plate should contain generous amounts of clear broth along with meat and hominy. Whether the broth is impeccably degreased or left with some dots of fat is according to taste.

Garnishes: The table garnishes for this clear-broth *posole* should be elaborate, for it recalls to mind the traditional Christmas dinners of the old culture. Pass homemade *salsa* (cooked or uncooked, red or green), finely shredded lettuce or cabbage, thinly sliced radishes, chunks of ripe avocado, chopped tomato (if in season) and lime wedges. If eaten in fairly small portions, this is about the only version of *posole* light enough to serve as a first course and still be followed comfortably by main dishes. If eaten alone, however, add shredded Monterey Jack or grated fresh Parmesan cheese to the garnishes and accompany with warm flour tortillas.

DRY-COOKED PORK WITH GREEN CHILIES

The pork in this recipe is actually stewed, but it is called "dry" to denote that it can be used to stuff *burritos* or *tacos*. Since those are essentially off-the-cuff foods, it also helps that this dish takes only about 20 minutes to make, just long enough for the sautéed cubes of meat to cook through with their green-chili flavoring. To someone unfamiliar with Southwestern cooking, it may come as a surprise that this simplest of stews, rolled up in warm flour tortillas and garnished with table sauce, can be so utterly satisfying. In northern New Mexico, the meat traditionally used would have been mutton, but cubed shoulder of lamb is a good substitute when you want a change from pork. Do make sure that you enclose this preparation in the freshest, largest and thinnest wheat tortillas you can lay hands upon, and blend your table *salsa* only about an hour before you cook the meat, as directed on p. 86.

For 4 people, 2 burritos each:

> 1 small onion, peeled and quartered
> 2 cloves garlic, peeled and chopped
> Optional: ¼ cup chopped green coriander (*cilantro*)
> 1 pound pork shoulder, trimmed of fat and cut into ¾-inch cubes
> (or 1 pound lamb shoulder)
> 2 tablespoons olive oil
> 1 teaspoon ground cumin
> ½ teaspoon black pepper
> Salt to taste
> ¼ cup tomato puree, or about 2 canned tomatoes, chopped
> ½ cup green chili sauce (p. 83)
> 1 or 2 teaspoons canned, chopped *jalapeños*, if your chili sauce is
> not very hot

Chop the onion, garlic and optional *cilantro* fine in a food processor. Brown the pork in the oil over medium heat, adding the spices, salt and the onion-garlic mixture from the processor when the meat is about half done, or just beginning to brown. Add the tomato puree or chopped tomatoes, the green chili sauce and the *jalapeños* to the sauté. Bring the mixture to a boil, immediately reduce heat, and simmer gently with the cover on for about 10 minutes, or until the pork is cooked through and most of the sauce is thickly coating the meat. Raise heat and cook off excess liquid, if any. The dish should be finished from beginning to end in about 20 minutes without the meat giving off all of its moisture and drying out.

Bring the pork to the table with 8 warmed flour tortillas and a bowl of *salsa*. Each guest rolls his own *burritos* according to the traditional method on p. 125. This preparation is a good one to know by heart in case the urge for green chili *burritos* attacks at midnight and someone must be the hero of the moment stoveside.

PORK STEW WITH RED CHILIES AND BLACK BEANS

For this dish, pork is braised with red chilies as in the classic Southwestern *carne adovada,* but it is finished differently by adding several cups of black beans, which became popular in the Santa Fe area only in recent times. The thickening of the stew with corn meal is an Indian practice, making this an eclectic though simple dish. The consistency of the finished stew is thick enough to serve spooned over rice, a presentation that helps relieve the hotness of the chilies. Warm flour tortillas would also be offered on the side so that each guest can improvise his own *burritos* filled with the pork, beans, rice and a dab of homemade *salsa*.

For 4 people:

    1 cup dried black beans
    4 cups water
    ½ teaspoon salt
    2 bay leaves
Generous pinches of oregano, black pepper and whole cumin seed
    2 or 3 *jalapeños*, deveined and seeded
    2 cloves garlic, peeled
    1 onion, peeled and cut into rough chunks
    3 tablespoons ground red chilies
    2 tablespoons cornmeal
    2 tablespoons vegetable oil
    1 to 1½ pounds pork shoulder, trimmed of fat and cut into
        ½-inch cubes
    2 tablespoons honey
    1 teaspoon cumin
    1 teaspoon cinnamon
    ½ teaspoon salt

Wash and drain the beans several times under running water, then combine with the water and seasonings (through the cumin seed) and boil until tender—about 2 hours—adding more water if necessary to keep them covered. Black beans have a tendency to foam up, so be sure to keep the lid on your pot ajar, and stir occasionally to prevent scorching. Set the cooked and drained beans aside until you need them. Reserve their cooking liquid. Meanwhile, prepare the meat:

Chop the chilies and garlic in a processor by first turning on the motor and dropping them through the feed tube. Stop the machine, add the onion and chop it with several quick pulses of the motor, stopping once to scrape down the bowl with the spatula. Remove and set this mixture aside and place the ground red chilies and cornmeal in the processor. Blend them to a smooth paste with ½ cup or so of the bean-cooking liquid. Set aside.

Heat the oil in a 3-quart pot or a large skillet, then brown the pork cubes over moderate heat, adding the honey, cumin, and cinnamon to the pan in the later stages of the browning. Without removing the meat, add the onion mixture and sauté for a few minutes more over low heat to wilt it, then add the red chili-cornmeal paste. Stir up the brown bits from the bottom of the pan and add the rest of the bean-cooking liquid, plus enough added water to make 2 cups. Bring to a simmer, cover the pan, and cook for 30 minutes without allowing the mixture to boil. When that time is up, add salt to taste and the cooked black beans, and simmer for another 30 minutes. The stew should have a thickened sauce, but add more water as needed if it becomes too dry.

The stew can sit for as long as necessary before it is to be served. If the pork was well trimmed, the finished dish should need no degreasing before being gently reheated and served over steamed rice. Warm flour tortillas and a good table *salsa* are also appropriate.

VARIATION:

Leftover stew and rice can be mixed together to make a delicious filling for *burritos*. Reheat the mixture in a skillet over low heat, then spoon directly into flour tortillas with a little extra *salsa* to moisten the filling. Filled this way, the *burritos* make a good informal lunch or just a nice next-day reward for the cook.

PORK SPARERIBS WITH
CHIPOTLE-AND-PEANUT SAUCE

The special flavor of this oven barbecue comes from smoky *chipotle* chilies, which you can buy canned in large supermarkets or Mexican groceries. The peanuts are a perfect complement to red chilies, although the pairing of them in Mexican stews and sauces is not much known in the U.S. outside the Southwest. The recipe requires that you cut up the spareribs into short lengths to serve as an appetizer. You can serve them as a main course as well, which only entails separating the slab into 2- or 3-rib sections.

Devotees of ribs will notice that these are not marinated or even basted, but I don't think they suffer from it. If you follow the simple method given, the rib pieces will be glazed, fully flavored and chewy. If you like spareribs that fall off the bone, then add all the sauce when they first go into the oven and bake with a foil covering over the pan to promote braising action. The resulting sauce, degreased, will be thin enough to use as a dipping sauce.

For 2 to 3 people as a main course, 4 to 6 as a large appetizer:

    1   slab pork spareribs weighing 3 to 4 pounds
 1½   cups red chili sauce (p. 73)
    ½   cup tomato puree, or about 4 canned tomatoes, pureed
    4   *chiles chipotles* (see description, p. 69)
    2   tablespoons brown sugar or honey
    2   tablespoons cider vinegar
    ¼   cup roasted Spanish peanuts
Green coriander (*cilantro*) chopped, for garnish

Cutting up the spareribs: A slab of spareribs is simple to cut up at home after the butcher has separated it from the spine, or chine bone. Have him do this and include the chine with your ribs, cutting it into 2- or 3-inch lengths.

The procedure for cutting up the ribs is first to trim off and discard the small flaps of fat, then trim off the skirt of meat on the back side of the slab—do not mistake this for fat because it is filmed with a white membrane. Cut up these scraps of meat into bite-size squares or triangles. Now separate the individual ribs by slicing down between them with a heavy chef's knife. The short, soft ribs at one end can be cut into halves or left intact. The long, bony ribs usually have a cartilaginous hinge at their thick end. Wiggle it with your fingers until you find the spot where the hard bone joins the cartilage and cut there—you will have separated it into one long sparerib and a shorter fleshy stub.

Cooking the ribs: Preheat the oven to 375° F. Place the trimmed ribs, the stubs, the pieces of chine bone and the meat scraps in a 10- by 13-inch roasting pan, or any ovenproof pan which will hold the meat in 1 layer. Salt and pepper the meat and bake uncovered for 1 hour.

Meanwhile, prepare the sauce by combining the red chili sauce, tomato puree, *chipotles*, sugar and vinegar in a blender. Blend at low to medium speed until the *chipotles* are incorporated (this is sometimes easier to do if you puree them first with ¼ cup of sauce, then add the other ingredients). Do not salt.

At the end of the hour, remove the spareribs from the oven and raise the heat to 425° F. for glazing them. Take the ribs out of the pan with a slotted spoon, transfer them to a large mixing bowl and pour the sauce over, reserving ½ cup. Discard the fat in the baking pan, put the ribs back in, tossing them a little to coat completely with sauce, and bake at 425° F. for 20 minutes more.

Serving the ribs: Once again, transfer the ribs to the large mixing bowl and let them stand, warmed by their own heat, while you finish the sauce. Degrease the baking juices in the pan and add the reserved ½ cup of sauce. Stirring over low heat, scrape up the cooked bits that cling to the bottom of the pan. If the sauce is not thick enough to coat the ribs, turn up the heat and boil for a few minutes—this is rarely necessary, however. Grind the peanuts coarsely in a processor or blender and stir them into the sauce. Season with salt and pepper to taste. Pour the sauce over the ribs and transfer them to a serving platter. Garnish with a liberal sprinkling of *cilantro*.

VARIATION:

This trouble-free method of making spareribs should not be missed just because you cannot find *chipotles*. Canned or fresh *jalapeños* can be substituted, in which case begin with only 1 and work your way up to the hotness you like. The sauce can be made more natively New Mexican by omitting the tomato puree and increasing the amount of red chili sauce to 2 cups; in that case, add a pinch of oregano.

Barbecuing on the Grill: To adapt this recipe for an outdoor barbecue grill, cut the slab of ribs to make 2 or 3 large pieces that can be easily handled with tongs. Rub the slab with olive oil. Grill over medium coals under a closed lid for about 1 hour, basting each side 2 or 3 times with the prepared sauce. Remove the cover and grill 15 minutes more, basting each side once, if the meat has not crisped yet. Keep ½ cup of the sauce reserved to reheat, mix with the ground peanuts and coat the ribs as they are served.

GREEN CHILI STEW WITH LAMB OR PORK

A simple chili stew, or *cocido*, can be strikingly good and certainly better than you might think if you are used to the common or garden variety of American stew. When a fairly large number of green chilies are added to the broth, they thicken it and add a warming savor at the same time—the point is not merely to make the stew fiery, although many New Mexican cooks do prefer their *chile verde* quite hot. This particular stew is based on the simple, delicious green-chili-and-potato soup on p. 189. Little more than the addition of meat turns it into a main course. It is traditionally eaten with a generous number of warm flour tortillas placed in the center of the table. No side dishes are needed at all, but in an authentic New Mexico meal a course of beans would follow.

The kind of meat you put into the stew is up to you. Beef, which is least likely to be used in northern New Mexico, would suggest a cowboy or *vaquero* stew. Lamb is the most common, and is the invariable choice of Hispanic or Pueblo shepherds (actually, they usually cook mutton, but supermarket lamb is old enough to stand up to stewing). Pork implies a more Mexican touch, but it is often seen in restaurants throughout the Southwest as well.

For 4 people:

> The green chili-and-potato soup on p. 189
> 2 to 4 teaspoons canned, chopped *jalapeños* if you want the
>   stew more *picante*
> 1½ to 2 pounds lamb or pork cut into chunks for stewing
> Green coriander (*cilantro*) for garnish

Consult the procedure for making the green chili-and-potato soup. Pork and lamb really only require about 45 minutes of simmering, assuming that you are not actually boiling them, for that would cause toughening and would require another hour or so of cooking. Add either of these meats along with the potatoes.

Traditionally, though, New Mexican cooks like to simmer their stews for quite a long time—long enough so that the meat is spoon-tender and separated into strands. If that is what you prefer, too, cook the chilies, broth and meat for 2 hours, then add the potatoes, along with any optional vegetables, so that they can cook for only as long as they need. (See variations below for some other vegetable possibilities.) Serve any version of the stew in soup bowls with warm flour tortillas on the side, allowing at least 3 per person.

Green Chili Stew with Vegetables: You should feel free to add vegetables to your green chili as you like, particularly if you are fortunate enough to have your own homegrown produce. A Pueblo garden would certainly yield zucchini, corn and tomatoes in high summer. The Indian method, more often than not, is to brown the onions, meat and green squash before the broth is added; the cooking time, even for tomatoes and corn, would be long enough so that the meat was cooked to shreds. Time your own additions to suit the nature of the vegetables you have. Tomatoes can go in with the meat, but zucchini and corn really should be dropped in only 5 or 10 minutes before the dish is completed so they will not be overcooked.

Winter Stew: This has *posole* or hominy added. Frozen *posole* can take as much cooking as you give it (the minimum is 45 minutes), but canned hominy needs only to be heated through. Summer squash is still available in the winter—it was traditionally stored in dried form through the long Santa Fe winters—and although truck-garden vegetables were not common then, you can put in carrots, turnips, yellow squash, parsnips and even mushrooms. Your green chili stew will have lost something in authenticity, but it will be *yours*.

BARBECUED LEG OF LAMB

Of all the collaborations between the Indian and Spanish styles of cooking, barbecue is certainly the most famous. As widely as it has infiltrated the rest of America, the barbecues of legend remain in the Southwest. Barbecuing can mean either pit-roasting (the Indian method) or roasting on spits (the Spanish method), but when it comes to a massive, day-long affair, as in a Texas barbecue, the event invariably begins with digging a trench and lining it with white-hot coals. The cooking involves literally gallons of red chili sauce, a whole kid goat, large beef briskets and fat link sausages (and a gored ox if the pit is big enough). To really appreciate such an event, it is good to do a heavy day's work first and then allow several hours for eating and drinking—this is trencherman's food.

That is but one style of barbecue, however. Before Texas chili came into the picture, the Spanish cooks of New Mexico took a Mediterranean approach by rubbing the meat, preferably very young lamb or kid goat (*cabrito*), with olive oil, garlic and wild herbs. Whether pit or spit-roasted, the meat was cooked without barbecue sauce so that the diners could best appreciate the tenderness and flavor of a spring-slaughtered animal. For the Pueblos, the roasted meat would have been wild game, particularly venison, and was cooked with no seasoning, not even salt.

The recipe below captures this more pristine style of barbecue, and it combines the best of pit and spit cooking because you use a modern kettle barbecue, thus allowing you to sear the lamb over hot coals, then finish its cooking under the slow, smoky heat of the covered kettle. Kid goat would be as delicious and authentic as the butterflied leg of lamb called for. It can be substituted if you live in a city where there are Hispanic butchers, or if you live in the Southwest and can locate a government-inspected source of goat (they are few and far between, however). Look for the *cabrito* to be available during February and March, the traditional slaughtering months, and have a leg butterflied to be cooked exactly as lamb is cooked.

Whichever meat you use, serve it with fresh uncooked *salsa* (p. 86) and warm flour tortillas. Rice, vegetable and salad are enough to complete the menu, choosing the pureed *garbanzos* on p. 303 if you want to keep the Spanish flavor, and the *calabacitas*, or zucchini, on p. 318, for their freshness.

The size of leg you need depends on the number of people you want to serve. For 8 people or more, have the butcher bone an entire 7-pound leg. For 4 people, have him cut a 3-pound section from the loin end, or a 4-pound section from the shank end (which has comparatively more bone than the loin).

For 4 people:

- 1 piece boned leg of lamb (see above for quantity)
- 2 or 3 large cloves garlic, peeled
- 1 teaspoon oregano
- 1 teaspoon coarsely cracked black pepper
- 1 teaspoon salt
- 4 tablespoons olive oil
- 1 tablespoon lemon or lime juice

A few hours before you start the coals, prepare the lamb by trimming it of excess fat. If you are fastidious, shave off the outer membrane, or fell, on the outside of the leg, using a very sharp paring knife, or at least shave the part stamped with the USDA inspection seal. Using a mallet, a heavy rolling pin or the flat of a cleaver, flatten the meat into butterfly shape. At this point I proceed to the marinade, but some cooks find the butterflied leg too floppy to handle comfortably. To make a more secure piece of meat, stick 2 or 3 long metal shish-kebab skewers through the leg from side to side, or else plan to grill the lamb inside a large, hinged meat rack made especially for barbecuing.

To make the marinade, combine all the remaining ingredients in the jar of an electric blender and blend until pureed but still somewhat textured. The marinade can also be made in a mortar and pestle (the traditional way) by first mashing the solid ingredients to a pulp and then drizzling in the oil and lemon juice. A third method is to work by hand using a chef's knife, first mincing the garlic as fine as possible, then grinding it to a paste under the flat of the knife with the salt. Transfer the garlic mash to a small bowl and work in the remaining ingredients with a fork.

When the marinade is ready, slash the lamb ½ inch deep in a dozen places on either side, then thoroughly rub the marinade into the meat, paying special attention to getting it into the slashes. (If you are a garlic lover, extra slivers of garlic can also be inserted into the slashes.) Transfer the lamb to a shallow pan, cover with plastic wrap and allow to sit at room temperature for 1 hour or more. If you are preparing the meat to this stage well in advance—more than 6 hours—set the lamb, covered, in the refrigerator and bring back to room temperature half an hour before grilling.

Grilling the lamb: Light the coals in a kettle barbecue with the rack set close. When they are white-hot, grill the lamb on both sides to sear it well, then close the vents and continue to grill with the cover on until the lamb is rosy-pink in its thickest part but no longer squishy to the touch. Timing is hard to specify, but the advice from one manufacturer of kettle barbecues is to cook 22 minutes per pound for rare lamb (140° F. internal temperature) and 28 minutes per pound for well done (170° F. internal temperature).

For somewhat more controlled timing, I like to first sear the meat well over the coals, then transfer it to a preheated 350° F. oven, allowing about 45 to 60 minutes more cooking, or until a thermometer inserted into the thickest part of the leg reads 150° F. At this point the thinnest edges of the leg will be medium and the very center rare.

Transfer the lamb to a carving board, allow to rest for 10 minutes, then cut into slices crosswise and at an angle. (If you have used the oven to finish roasting, you may have some pan juices—spoon them over the slices after carving.) Serve with *salsa*, warm flour tortillas, and perhaps *guacamole*, the best of all Southwestern accompaniments to grilled meat. Leftovers are delicious eaten cold with *salsa* and tortillas the next day, if you make sure the meat is brought to cool room temperature.

CHICKEN BRAISED WITH RICE
Arroz con pollo

Every Spanish-speaking country must possess a version of *arroz con pollo*, but few of them could approach the starkness of the one traditionally made in Santa Fe. Stripped of garnish, it consisted of onion and rice browned in bacon fat, to which a cut-up fowl and a dash of wild "saffron" (actually safflower) were added—only the richer folk would have had authentic Spanish saffron. The cooking time depended not so much on the rice as on the bird, which probably reached a respectable age and toughness before being relegated to the pot.

If you think of *arroz con pollo* as a dressed-up dish, the one given here will surprise you. The bacon fat, the "saffron" and browned rice are all gone, but its basic flavors of onion, rice and chicken remain—and it is very good. Most recipes instruct you first to braise the browned chicken in water and then add the rice in the final half-hour or so of baking. My directions are more finicky since they require that you precook the chicken and rice in separate steps, but the advantage of taking this extra trouble is that you will not find yourself with too little or too much cooking liquid, and the braising broth can be degreased rather than left with a layer of strong-tasting chicken fat.

Despite these little refinements in technique, this is by any measure still an everyday *arroz con pollo*. The variation following the basic recipe adds a typically Spanish garniture of potatoes, chick-peas and green peas. The recipe following that is grander still, a full-dress offering for company.

For 4 to 6 people:

    4 tablespoons olive oil
    1 medium-to-large onion, chopped
    1 large garlic clove, chopped
   12 chicken pieces, mixing fryer thighs, breasts and drumsticks,
      or 6 chicken quarters
    4 tablespoons flour
    1 teaspoon oregano
    1 teaspoon ground cumin
    1 teaspoon black pepper
Salt
    4 tablespoons vegetable oil
    4 cups chicken stock or canned chicken broth
    2 bay leaves
Optional: ½ teaspoon turmeric, for color
    2 cups long-grain rice
Optional garnish: small handful green coriander (*cilantro*) and
    small handful scallion greens, both finely chopped

You will need a large frying pan for browning the chicken pieces and a Dutch oven, casserole or roasting pan large enough to hold the chicken and rice comfortably as they bake—a 6-quart capacity would probably be the safe minimum. A wide, shallow *paëlla* pan would be ideal if it can be covered with a lid.

Heat the olive oil in the large frying pan over medium heat and add the chopped onion. Reduce heat to low, cover the pan and cook for 5 minutes, or until the onion wilts. Uncover, raise heat to medium again, and add the garlic. Continue to cook, stirring occasionally, until the onions turn yellow with a little browning at the edges. Scrape onion mixture into the casserole or roaster.

Place half the chicken in a sturdy brown paper bag and sprinkle half the flour, oregano, cumin and black pepper into the bag. If you are using chicken pieces, they need no further trimming except to pull off pockets of chicken fat with your fingers. If you are using chicken quarters, trim away the wing tips and, if you want to be meticulous, the bony parts of the back, tail and breast. Salt the pieces in the bag lightly—very lightly if the chicken broth is salty already—close the top of the bag tightly, and shake vigorously until the chicken is evenly dusted with flour.

Heat the vegetable oil in the frying pan over high heat and add the chicken parts. Sauté for about 5 minutes on both sides until the pieces are well browned. If you are using chicken quarters, the skin side will brown much more evenly than the bony, but that is not important. As you near the end of the browning, repeat the flour-dusting operation with the remaining half of the chicken (or work with two frying pans at once if you like). Place the browned chicken in the casserole or roaster with the onions and proceed to brown the rest of the pieces.

When all the chicken has been transferred to the casserole, pour in 1½ cups of chicken stock, or enough to come up about 1 inch in the pan. Toss in the bay leaves and optional turmeric (and trimmed wing tips if they are available), cover the casserole, and bring to a boil over medium heat.

Preheat the oven to 350° F., place the bubbling casserole inside, and bake for 20 minutes, or until the chicken is almost done. At this point the dish can be set aside to be finished later, or you can proceed directly to the final cooking, which will take about 30 minutes.

When you are ready to proceed, remove the chicken from the pot and set it aside. Using a large kitchen spoon, carefully degrease the surface of the braising stock. Add to it all but ½ cup of the remaining chicken stock. Place the casserole over high heat, bring to a rolling boil and add the rice. Cover and bring to the boil again, then place in the oven. Reduce temperature to 300° F. and bake for 10 minutes. At that point, when the rice is half-cooked, add the reserved chicken and continue to bake until the rice is tender, the stock is completely absorbed, and the chicken pieces are done, about 15 to 20 minutes more. If the rice seems underdone at the end of this time but all the stock has been absorbed, add the remaining ½ cup of stock, which you have first brought to a boil. If pink juice runs from any of the chicken pieces when you pierce them with a fork, bake another 5 to 10 minutes.

Serve the *arroz con pollo* directly from the pot or arrange the rice on a platter with the chicken on top. Sprinkle with the *cilantro* and chopped scallion greens if you like and make sure that there is a good homemade table *salsa* already waiting, such as the basic uncooked *salsa* on p. 86.

VARIATION:

Chicken Braised with Potatoes, Chick-Peas and Green Peas: The three additions that make the basic *arroz con pollo* more elaborate all go in while the rice is cooking, but not at the same time. Have ready 1 pound of pink or yellow boiling potatoes, peeled and cut into 1-inch chunks or cubes. Drain' a 15-ounce can of chick-peas (about 1½ cups). Defrost a 10-ounce package of frozen baby green peas. When you reach the step that calls for adding the rice to the boiling chicken stock, add the potatoes at the same time. When it is time to add the reserved chicken pieces, add the chick-peas. Five minutes before the entire dish is done, add the green peas, which barely need to be heated through. Although all this coming and going of ingredients sounds rather complicated on paper, the entire operation of making *arroz con pollo* is not at all tricky in practice, and minor timing variations do not harm the finished product.

CHICKEN BRAISED WITH RICE, TOMATOES, SAFFRON AND PEAS

A Spaniard would feel very deprived if his *arroz con pollo* came as naked as does the basic recipe given above. It was a fact of life in New Mexico that many people did eat this dish without much adornment, but there were festive versions as well. Here is one that I particularly like. It uses the authentic garniture of saffron, tomatoes and green peas, but in an untraditional way. Instead of baking with the chicken and rice, these ingredients are sautéed separately and added to the casserole only for a few minutes of final cooking, just enough to marry the flavors. The result is fresh and reminiscent of spring, not at all like the greasy *arroz con pollo* of restaurant notoriety, a dismal combination more often than not of dried-out chicken and Mexican rice. The addition of green chilies to this recipe stamps it as New Mexican since these take the place of the traditional Spanish olives.

For 4 to 6 people:

Basic recipe for chicken braised with rice, p. 278
    4 fresh, red-ripe tomatoes, seeded and chopped, or 2 fresh
      tomatoes and 3 canned tomatoes
    2 tablespoons butter
  ¼ teaspoon saffron threads
    1 10-ounce package baby green peas, defrosted
    1 bell pepper, seeded and chopped
  ¼ to ½ cup canned chopped green chilies

Make the basic recipe as given, and be sure that you have the *cilantro* and scallion garnish at hand. Proceed to the point that the entire dish is within 10 minutes of being finished. At that point prepare the tomato-saffron-green pea addition as given below—this takes only 5 minutes or so—and add it to the casserole for the last 5 minutes of baking.

If you have good-quality fresh tomatoes, they need no preparation beyond being seeded and chopped. If you are stuck with fair-to-poor tomatoes, then first seed and chop into rough chunks, then place in a food processor with the canned tomatoes. Process with a few brief pulses until the tomatoes are finely chopped but not reduced to a puree.

Heat the butter in a medium-sized frying pan until bubbling. Crumble the saffron threads between your palms until no whole threads remain and add to the butter. Swirl the pan around for 30 seconds to soften the saffron, taking care that the butter does not brown, then add the tomatoes. Raise heat to high and cook until the tomatoes begin to bubble. Add the peas, bell pepper and chopped green chilies and stir thoroughly. Cook over high heat for a minute or two longer so that the mixture heats through.

Remove the *arroz con pollo* from the oven, take out the chicken, and stir the contents of the frying pan into the casserole. Even if the rice appears dry at this point, do not add extra liquid—the tomatoes will furnish enough moisture to finish the rice. If the chicken is already done, set it aside where it can be kept warm; otherwise, return the chicken to the casserole, cover and bake another 5 to 10 minutes.

To serve, arrange the rice on a platter, place the chicken on top, and sprinkle on the *cilantro* and scallion garnish. Because this dish lacks hot chilies, it is one of the few New Mexican specialties that is complemented by wine—either a light-bodied Spanish Rioja, a California Zinfandel or any noble Chardonnay would be delicious. For a vegetable, good choices would be the pureed chick-peas on p. 303 or the zucchini with green chili and corn on p. 318.

LEMON-BROILED CHICKEN WITH GREEN CHILIES

Since the traditional cooking of the region has a shortage of light, summery dishes, this modern Southwestern adaptation of broiled chicken is very welcome. Marinating the chicken quarters in lemon juice, olive oil and green chilies makes them taste fresh and tangy; the only other attention this simple preparation requires is a close eye near the end of the broiling time to see that the lovely crisp skin does not char.

For accompaniments, you need nothing more than a green salad and the summer rice on p. 307. If you add to your menu with *guacamole*, a bowl of pinto beans and warm flour tortillas on the side, you could easily cut each portion of chicken to a quarter instead of a half.

For 4 people:

    1 or 2 cloves garlic, peeled
    2 or 3 canned, whole green chilies, or about ¼ cup chopped
    1 fresh *jalapeño*, deveined and seeded
    2 tablespoons parsley or green coriander (*cilantro*)
    3 tablespoons olive oil
    3 tablespoons lemon juice
    ½ teaspoon cumin
    ¼ teaspoon black pepper
    4 chicken broiler halves, or 8 quarters
  Salt to taste

Place all the ingredients except the chicken and salt in the jar of a blender and puree until quite smooth—try not to leave large specks of solid matter which will char under the broiler. Chop off the last two joints of the chicken wings, then rub the chickens with the marinade and let them sit at room temperature for 1 hour. (If you are preparing the dish more than an hour in advance of broiling it, cover the marinating chicken with plastic wrap and place in the refrigerator. Bring the chicken back to room temperature before broiling.)

Preheat the broiler with a rack about 6 inches from the flame. Drain excess marinade from the chicken and reserve. Place the pieces bone side up in a shallow broiling pan lined with heavy-duty foil and a rack. Broil for 30 minutes, allowing about 8 minutes per side before turning the chicken, and winding up the last 6 minutes with the skin side up.

At that point, if the chicken shows signs of charring, brush with more marinade and finish the broiling more than 6 inches away from the flame. Conversely, if the chicken seems too pale, brush with marinade and place 4 inches away from the flame. Your aim is to achieve a crisp-browned skin just as the meat of the thighs is cooked.

Let the finished chicken rest at room temperature for 5 minutes to absorb its juices and continue to cook a bit, then salt to taste and serve. This dish is delicious cooked over a barbecue flame, and the cold leftover portions are, if anything, better than when the bird is hot from the broiler.

STUFFED TURKEY BREAST WITH PUMPKIN-SEED SAUCE

In the main, I have kept away from what we think of as refined dinner-party food in favor of the earthier cooking that is truest to Santa Fe, but a few dishes should mirror the city's newfound status as a pleasure retreat. In this casserole of layered turkey breast with a rice-and-onion stuffing and a mild sauce flavored with ground pumpkin seeds, we are not far from the stuffed and reshaped roasts of French cuisine. This particular version, in fact, owes its origins to Turkey Orloff, a delightful variant on Veal Prince Orloff which Julia Child invented and for which she published the recipe a few years ago.

Despite the content of green chilies in the sauce, it is not at all hot, and the unctuous, luxurious textures throughout make it suitable for formal occasions—it is reminiscent of the millionaires' food served every night along Canyon Road during Santa Fe's high summer season. This is an excellent dish to show off your skills at a dinner party, for the results look elaborate when presented at the table. Impressive as it is, however, nothing in the recipe is beyond the reach of a novice cook.

For 4 people:

    8 slices of raw, precut turkey breast, each about ½ inch thick (total approximately 1¾ pounds); if presliced turkey is not available, see the instructions below for cutting the slices yourself

Flour for dredging
Vegetable oil for sautéing
Salt and pepper

RICE-AND-ONION STUFFING:

    3 tablespoons rice, either long grain or converted
    1 large onion (or 2 small ones) weighing a generous pound
    4 tablespoons butter
    1 clove garlic, finely minced
Dashes of pepper and ground cumin
    ½ teaspoon ground red chilies, or more to taste
    ¼ teaspoon salt
    ¼ cup cream

PUMPKIN-SEED SAUCE:

   1 cup chicken broth
   1 cup canned green chilies, whole or chopped
  ½ cup shelled green pumpkin seeds
   1 tablespoon butter
   1 egg, beaten
Extra broth or cream to thin the sauce
Salt and pepper
   6 ounces Monterey Jack cheese, shredded
   2 tablespoons additional butter

If turkey breast is presliced, this dish can be prepared in an hour, assembled and kept in the refrigerator until you need it. Cutting your own slices from a half turkey breast, bone in, as described below, will add about 30 minutes to the preparation time.

Spread a thin layer of flour on a plate, dredge as many turkey slices as will fit in a medium skillet (about 4 at a time) and shake off the excess flour. Heat a thin film of vegetable oil in the skillet, then sauté the turkey quickly on each side until just firm and touched with brown—only 4 to 5 minutes at most. Do not actually cook the turkey through at this stage. When all the slices are done, salt and pepper them and set aside. Also set aside the skillet.

Preheat oven to 325° F.

To make the stuffing, drop the rice into boiling, salted water and parboil for 5 minutes. Drain and set aside. Chop the onions fairly fine with pulses of a food processor. Melt the butter in a 2-quart saucepan or an oven casserole that can also be heated on the top of the stove. Add the onion and the drained rice. Stir in all other stuffing ingredients except the cream, cover and set in the oven for 45 minutes. Stir in the cream, scraping down the sides of the rice if they are beginning to brown, and return to bake, covered, for 15 minutes longer. The finished stuffing should be quite soft, but the rice grains will still be separate. Taste for salt and set aside until assembly time.

Making the sauce: This can easily be done while the rice and onions are baking. Pour the chicken broth into the skillet which was used for browning the turkey, stirring over medium heat to incorporate the nice browned bits from the bottom of the pan. Put the chilies and pumpkin seeds into a food processor or electric blender and process until smooth, about a minute or so. Add this mixture to the chicken broth, bring to a boil, then add the butter. Cover and simmer gently for 20 minutes. Remove the sauce from the heat and immediately whisk in the egg. If the sauce is thicker than half-whipped cream, dilute it with more chicken broth or heavy cream. Season to taste with salt and pepper.

Assembling and baking the casserole: Use a shallow gratin or baking dish at least 9 inches square, large enough so that the turkey slices fill it in one layer, slightly overlapping. Spoon a thin layer of sauce over the bottom of the dish, then add the turkey slices, placing a portion of the rice-and-onion filling in between the overlapping sections. Spread any left-over filling over the top, then pour the remaining sauce over. Sprinkle on the shredded cheese in an even layer and, finally, dot the top with bits of butter. The casserole can be covered with foil at this stage and kept re-frigerated for up to a day, or frozen until you are ready to bake it.

To bake, preheat the oven to 350° F. Bring the casserole to room temperature, uncover and bake in the middle of the oven for 30 minutes. The sauce should be bubbling, but if the cheese starts to brown, drape foil loosely over the pan during the last few minutes of baking. Serve as a main course with warm flour tortillas. If your meal is not altogether New Mexican, accompany with French bread, a vegetable and a green salad, as you would any choice European stuffed roast.

Although it needs no garnishing, you can strew chopped green cori-ander (*cilantro*) and sliced avocado over the casserole before bringing it to the table—it will be all the more lavish and considerably more Mexican in tone.

To bone and slice a turkey breast: If you do not have presliced turkey breast on hand, and your butcher is not willing to skin, bone and filet one for you, buy a half-breast weighing about 3 pounds. Chill it to make it easier to work with. Peel off the skin by pulling it with your fingers gripped in paper towels. It should come off in one piece, but you may need help with a paring knife here and there to free skin that is close to the bone. Now cut the meat away from the breast bone exactly as you would a chicken breast, inserting your paring knife along the whole length of the breast bone and cutting along the ribs, always working with the blade pointed away from you and into the bone. Keep slicing and tugging the meat until you have entirely freed it. The trickiest part is at the wing and wishbone joint, but there it will not matter if your cutting is a bit ragged.

When the meat is off the bone, you will find that it separates naturally into two pieces. One part, the larger, lies on top of the second, smaller *filet mignon,* once again like the two pieces of a half chicken breast. Keep-ing the blade of your knife away from you, scrape the long white tendon out of the filet piece—you can grip it in a paper towel to keep it from slipping—and discard it. Now you have two whole pieces of turkey breast ready to cut into scallops.

Slice the thick end of the large piece into ½-inch-thick slices until it starts to taper off. At that point, turn the knife blade level with the table and begin to slice the meat on the diagonal, making flat ½-inch cuts. The small filet piece is also cut with a flat slice into 2 approximately equal scallops. All slices should be about equal in size, and you should have at least 8 scallops when you finish (if you have more, they can easily be stuffed and sauced in the casserole along with the others). To make this dish even more elegantly tender, pound the scallops of turkey flat between two sheets of waxed paper, using either a mallet, rolling pin or the flat side of a cleaver. The meat will spread out to about ⅓ larger in size and will end up about ¼ inch thick. Proceed to dredge, sauté and season the turkey meat as above.

TURKEY CURED IN RED CHILIES
Turqué adovado

When New Mexicans marinate meat in red chili sauce for a day to make their *carne adovada*, they ordinarily use thin strips of pork, but there is ample precedent in Spain for treating turkey in much the same way. The recipe below gives you a virtually no-fat alternative to pork for filling *burritos* or *tamales*, and the texture of the meat after its braising time is quite close to the traditional stew. In fact, if you do not want the drier *carne adovada* of the recipe on p. 264, you can also cook pork shoulder using the method below. Any meat you use will be considerably hotter than most of the dishes elsewhere in this book.

For a simple dinner centered on this *turqué adovado*, serve with warm flour tortillas, a bowl of pinto beans with green chili *salsa* on the side, and either a green-bean salad or another vegetable. Each diner spoons the turkey into a tortilla and rolls his own improvised *burrito*.

For about 1¾ pounds of filling:

  2 turkey drumsticks, weighing 2¾ pounds total
  ½ onion, peeled and cut into chunks
  2 cloves garlic, peeled
  Generous pinch oregano
  1 tablespoon vinegar
  1 tablespoon sugar
  6 tablespoons powdered red chilies (less if your mix is more than medium hot)
  ½ teaspoon salt
  1 cup water

You have a choice of marinating and stewing the turkey drumsticks whole or taking the meat off the bones before marinating it. Here is the way to prepare the turkey for the second method: Peel the skin from the drumsticks by pulling it away with your hands, helping to free stubborn spots with a paring knife. Cut a line down the length of the drumstick with your knife, penetrating all the way to the bone. Repeat on the other side, then begin to cut away chunks of meat, starting at the wide end of the drumstick. You will find the turkey tough and full of tendons leading to spiny, flat bones. Scrape these away with the edge of your knife, but do not worry too much about being thorough, since the long cooking will make it easy to remove them later. When you have the bone well stripped, cut the meat into 1-inch cubes.

For the marinade, chop the onion and garlic in a food processor, then add the remaining ingredients and process until a smooth paste is formed. Mix the meat and marinade together in a glass or stainless-steel bowl, cover with plastic wrap, and marinate in the refrigerator for 24 hours. At the end of that period, you can cook any or all of the meat—it will keep well in its marinade for at least 3 days.

To cook the turkey, place it in a saucepan together with the marinade and any accumulated juices. Bring to a boil and simmer for 2 hours. You will need to add up to a cup of extra water during the cooking time to insure that the meat does not dry out. If you want a little sauce around the meat, add enough water during the last few minutes of cooking to produce a thick sauce. For drier meat, uncover the pan and boil vigorously until the liquid around the meat evaporates, watching carefully at the end to avoid scorching the chili. When the turkey is fork-tender, use it as a filling for *burritos*, *tacos*, *enchiladas* or *tamales*.

Here is an appealing way to use the turkey after it has cured:

Turkey Tamales: Turkey is a delicious substitute for the common pork filling in *tamales*. You will need a generous cup of filling for 8 to 12 *tamales*, following the recipe on p. 240. Be sure to cook the meat dry so that liquid will not seep out during the steaming time, then grind it to a coarse texture with a few pulses of a food processor. Adding orange peel and the other additions which go into the meat filling on p. 241 would be all to the good, but you can make quite a good *tamal* stuffing simply by throwing ¼ cup of blanched almonds and a few tablespoons of raisins into the processor while you are grinding the turkey.

MOUNTAIN TROUT

The Southwest seems as poor in fish recipes as Mexico itself is rich, and there is no overcoming the physical facts behind that—this is arid country far from the sea. New Mexico's high, frigid streams and lakes do provide the home cook with trout—assuming that they are not cooked outdoors as they are caught. Even the Spanish talent for using salt cod in a hundred clever ways did not transplant itself across the Atlantic, for traditional *néomejicano* cookbooks do not mention it at all. The Pueblos had no ways of cooking fish to pass along, since catching fish, which were like water spirits, was prohibited by their religion.

So Santa Fe restaurants often make do with no fish at all, following the lead of the local cooks. Anything they do serve in the Mexican style, like shrimp cocktail or red snapper Veracruz, has been obviously borrowed. The rainbow trout, which one automatically identifies with Rocky Mountain fishing, is also an importation, by the way, planted to supplement the native and even smaller cutthroat trout. However, the cook who confronts a mountain trout, either streamside or in the market, will find it delicate and rewarding to prepare, particularly if the cooking is kept simple.

Pan-Fried Trout: Pioneers, miners and sportsmen all fried their trout freshly caught. This has the advantage of needing only a frying pan and a lump of fat, and perhaps some cornmeal to bread the fish with. As someone who ate freshwater fish this way throughout his childhood, I speak with a little feeling when I say that the crunch of cornmeal and the coarse taste of bacon fat are not helpful in bringing out the pristine taste of a mountain trout. I wonder how many cookbook writers, blithely passing on the recipe yet again, have actually tasted it?

Grilled Trout: This is more delicious than the traditional pan-fried. Heat a charcoal fire with the grill set near the flame and grease the grill if you find that it helps to prevent sticking. Take 1 whole trout per person and rinse it free of sliminess—this also helps retard sticking to the grill—then rub lightly with vegetable oil. Score the fish skin on both sides with several diagonal slashes so that the trout will not curl up as they cook, then lay them over the white-hot coals. Cook for about 5 minutes a side, or until the skin is charred and the flesh just cooked. You can brush the trout with butter as they grill, but it is not necessary. Salt and pepper them as they come to the table, and let each guest squeeze fresh lemon over his portion. Thanks to the simple bone structure of trout, diners will have no trouble lifting the filets away from the spine. Pass some parsley butter on the side.

Poached Trout: If the trout you are cooking actually is fresh-caught, it will taste freshest after being poached. Either beside the stream or at home, the requirements are simple: merely an inch of salted water (or water combined with white wine) which you bring to a simmer and cover for the 5 minutes it takes the fish to poach. The home cook will also have ingredients at hand to flavor the poaching liquid, such as a chopped carrot, half an onion, some whole peppercorns, a bay leaf and a sprig of parsley. Be careful when lifting the fish from its liquid—there is no tenderer fish than trout—and allow to drain for a minute before fileting. Once again, the only embellishment needed is melted parsley butter and a lemon wedge.

Trout with Mint: It has been written that the traditional herb for Rocky Mountain trout is mint, or *yerba buena* in its wild state. I have seen recipes that call for stuffing the whole fish with fresh mint sprigs, then trussing it up in raw bacon strips and toothpicks before broiling. I cannot vouch for this method personally, but it was a notably popular specialty at The Fort restaurant in Denver when it was operated by Sam Arnold, an authority on the cooking of the early West. In any event, you do not have to use bacon. It is very easy simply to slip some mint inside the trout before grilling it over charcoal. Another sprig or two can be bruised and placed in melted butter to infuse its flavor. Use this at the table after fishing the mint out of the butter.

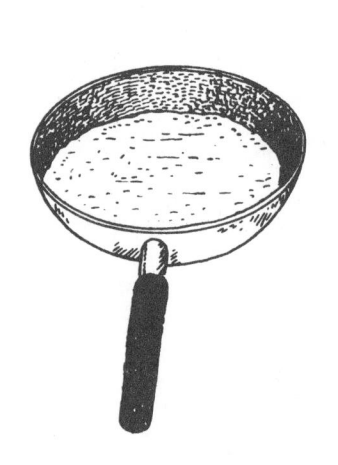

BEANS, RICE AND VEGETABLES

Dried Beans, Lentils and Chick-Peas
Two-Day Pinto Beans (Frijoles de olla)
Refried Beans (Frijoles refritos)
Refried Beans in Butter • Chili Beans
Pinto Beans with Green Chilies and Tomatoes
Pureed Chick-Peas
Spanish Rice • Summer Rice
Rice and Potatoes with Cumin
Potato Gratin with Green Chilies
Baked Whole Green Chilies
Green Corn with Lime Butter
Corn Off the Cob
Blue Cornmeal Mush (Chauquehue)
Posole as a Vegetable
Steamed Vegetables with Green Chili Butter
Grated Zucchini with Green Chili
Zucchini with Green Chili and Corn (Calabacitas)

DRIED BEANS, LENTILS AND CHICK-PEAS

Indian and Spanish cooks in the old Southwest all relied on large amounts of various dried beans, and, in fact, there are fewer varieties of beans in the modern Santa Fe diet than in the past. As you get closer to Mexico proper, the larder of beans includes pink beans, black beans, red kidney beans and sometimes broad beans and lima beans. In Santa Fe the common choice is the pinto bean. Its name means "painted" in Spanish, referring to the mottled brown-and-tan coloring of the raw bean; when cooked, the color changes to a uniform pinkish tan, not nearly as striking as the darker shades found in kidney and black beans. There is also a small boiling bean, about the size of a large pea and the color of milk chocolate, which Santa Feans call a *bollito*. Because it never became a modern commercial crop, its use is now quite limited; it may still be employed as an ingredient in salads, according to some local cooks.

Unlike what you encounter in Mexican restaurants, where only beans are generally used, the Hispanic cooks of New Mexico retained an inherited Spanish allegiance to *garbanzos*, or chick-peas, and brown lentils. This came directly from the conquistadors, along with the "dry soups" in which *garbanzos* and rice are cooked together. However, despite this varied heritage, the pinto seems now to have gained the upper hand in almost every preparation calling for a bean of any sort.

New Mexican food employs cooked beans frequently, so most cooks buy their pintos or kidney beans canned. You can do the same, rehabilitating them by cooking some onion, garlic and oregano in a little oil, then adding to these the canned beans with their liquid. Butter instead of oil is also good for reviving canned beans, although it is not so authentic.

Cooking Dried Beans

To boil up your own dried beans, it is not necessary to soak them overnight as our grandparents used to do. Simply place the beans in a saucepan large enough to hold them after they swell up—they usually expand to about 3 times their uncooked volume—and add water to cover. With the lid on the saucepan, bring the beans to a boil over low heat, let them boil for exactly 1 full minute, then take the pan off the heat to sit, still covered, for 1 hour.

Given this precooking, an ordinary batch of beans will be cooked after about another 2 hours of boiling. But all the beans used in Santa Fe cooking—pinto, kidney or black—can be stubborn, so allow extra time, and be sure they really boil. Keep them covered at all times with at least 1 inch of water above the beans; prevent boiling over by leaving the pot lid ajar for steam to escape, and do not salt until the last half-hour of boiling. As for flavoring, a bay leaf, half an onion, and a clove or two of garlic will do. A nice extra touch is to throw in a generous pinch of whole cumin seed and another of coarsely ground black pepper. Leftover beans should not be allowed to sit around for long, since they turn sour rather quickly.

TWO-DAY PINTO BEANS
Frijoles de olla

The title does not mean that it takes two days to cook pinto beans— merely that you should make enough for another day. That next day, when Mexican cooks refry their *frijoles*, raises an everyday pot of beans to something special. Calling them "refried" is misleading, by the way, for the frying only occurs once, and contrary to what one may think, the actual amount of fat is so small as hardly to constitute frying at all— barely 2 tablespoons for every 2 cups of pintos.

The Tex-Mex specialty called "chili beans" has also led non-natives to think that all Southwesterners eat their beans heavily flavored with chili powder and tomato sauce, when in truth the beans are usually cooked quite simply. Chili is added in the form of mashed, fresh green chilies or some other form of *salsa* at the table. Humble as they are, *frijoles* really are a minor glory of the Mexican kitchen—some would say not so minor, since they are the mainstay of a subsistence diet. The small variations of adding cheese, chopped *chorizo* sausage, sour cream or even just extra onion all result in a new dish from the original pot. Cooks go so far as to know three or four different ways to mash the *refritos*, since texture is nearly as important as flavor.

This recipe outlines the commonest way to cook pintos. The second, followed by variations, is for the second-day refried beans, when they really come into their own.

For about 6 cups of cooked beans, serving 4 people at two meals:

    2 cups dried pinto beans
    Water to cover
    1 small onion, chopped
    2 or 3 cloves garlic, chopped
    4 thin slices salt pork (about ⅓ cup)
    1 teaspoon whole cumin seed
    ½ teaspoon cracked pepper
    ½ teaspoon oregano
    1 teaspoon salt

To precook the beans, bring about 2 quarts of water to a boil, drop in the pintos and bring back to the boil, uncovered. Boil for exactly 2 minutes, remove the pan from heat, cover it, and let stand for 1 hour. At that point, the pintos can be cooked immediately or left to wait. My practice is to lift the pintos out of their soaking liquid with a slotted spoon to cook in fresh water, for no amount of cleaning and picking over quite removes all the grit that accompanies dried beans.

When you are ready to cook them, put the beans and all the remaining ingredients in a pot, cover with 2 inches of water, and bring to a boil. Cover the pot and allow the beans to boil for as long as it takes until they are cooked through and tender. This can take as long as 4 to 6 hours, but altitude and the age of the beans make any exact time hard to estimate. After 2 hours, the pintos are usually cooked insofar as their proteins no longer taste raw, but it takes at least another hour before they are soft enough to mash well the next day.

Although a pot of pintos is as easy a dish as one could imagine, there are a few things to look out for. If foam appears when the beans are brought to the boil, skim it off and leave the lid of the pot slightly ajar to avoid any danger of boiling over. Stir the cooking beans up once every hour and add extra water as needed, keeping it level with the pintos as they near completion.

Putting salt in at the beginning of the cooking time is said by some cooks to toughen the beans but on the other hand it raises the temperature of the boiling water—a necessity at high altitudes. If a pot of beans seems very stubborn about not getting tender, do not raise the heat to a furious boil—this will only expel water from the inside of the beans—and do not mash, blenderize or process the beans, hoping that the raw taste will go away: it won't. Only long, patient cooking produces what you want: a pinto that is soft inside with a tender skin and milky, slightly thickened cooking liquid.

Pintos in a Crockpot: Without precooking or soaking the beans, place them in a Crockpot or slow cooker along with about 5 cups of water and the other ingredients. Bring to a boil over high heat, then cover the pot, reduce the heat to low, and cook overnight, up to 16 hours, or cook on high for 8 hours. Test for softness and cook further over high heat if liquid needs reduction.

Serving: Assuming that you are making *refritos* on the second day (nothing is stopping you from refrying them immediately if you want), you will be eating the pintos whole in their pot liquor the first time around. You can of course simply spoon them onto a plate, but usually a thickened liquid is appreciated. You arrive at this by mashing or pureeing some of the beans. The easiest way is to ladle out half a cup of beans along with the same amount of liquid, puree them in a processor or blender and stir them back into the pot. Some cooks go so far as to mash almost all the beans at this point, using a potato masher or a slotted spoon.

Although whole pintos are cooked plain most of the time, you can add 1 tablespoon of powdered red chilies to the portion to be served— that is, 3 cups of pintos plus their cooking liquid—and simmer another 20 to 30 minutes. Just as traditional, and better to my mind, is to bring the pintos to the table plain and then pass around a homemade green chili relish like the one on p. 94. Boiled pintos with green chili and wheat-flour tortillas has been daily fare among the pueblos and villages for a long time.

REFRIED BEANS
Frijoles refritos

On the second day you will have 3 cups of pintos left with their pot liquor, enough for 4 people. There are at least a dozen ways to revive the leftovers, all involving frying in a small amount of oil or fat, and all considered to be better than any pot of first-day beans. It is *refritos*, not beans in the pot, that attracts the fanciers and the praise.

Simplest refried beans: Heat 3 tablespoons of bacon fat, lard or vegetable oil (the first two are the most authentic) in a wide, heavy skillet. When the fat is close to smoking, spoon in the beans, and their liquid, 1 large spoonful at a time. Mash them thoroughly with a potato masher until all the beans and liquid have been incorporated. You can mash everything smooth or leave some beans half-intact for a more interesting texture, but however you do it, the pintos will absorb from 1 to 4 cups of pot liquor, becoming rich and savory. Some cooks now turn the heat low and let the beans cook until the edges of the mass start to crisp and brown, but this is not really necessary. If the spattering of fat and beans is too messy for you, you can mash the beans in the skillet off the heat, then add the oil and warm through. You won't really have fried the pintos in any sense, but the taste is still good.

Refried beans from a can: Since the point to frying is to revive the beans, taking them out of a can already mashed defeats the purpose of *refritos*—unless of course you intend to re-refry them. Most restaurants resort to canned refried beans in a pinch, or even as regular practice, but it helps the flavor if you at least buy canned whole pintos or kidney beans. These are of passable texture and can be mashed in a few tablespoons of oil (allow 1 tablespoon per cup of beans, plus ½ to 1 cup of liquid from the can). Canned beans usually have little extra flavoring, so you can also add powdered cumin, chopped onion, oregano and garlic to good effect, allowing about ¼ of a small onion for every cup of beans, the other ingredients to taste.

VARIATIONS:

Refried Beans with Onions: This, the most common method, involves sautéing half a chopped onion in the oil until it wilts, then going ahead with the beans. Often extra oregano is also added at this point, starting with a scant ¼ teaspoon. (For a luxurious version using butter, see p. 298.)

Refried Beans with Cheese: Proceed with either the basic methods or the one with onion above, then scatter ½ cup or more shredded Monterey Jack cheese over the finished beans. This can be stirred in or simply allowed to melt over the surface of the *refritos*, a method the restaurants almost always follow when they warm an entire combination plate in a hot oven before it comes to the customer.

Refried Beans with Cracklings: Remove the slices of salt pork (included in the basic recipe on p. 294) from the bean pot, cut them into ½-inch pieces, and sauté in 3 tablespoons oil with half an onion, chopped, as above. Since they have absorbed water in their boiling, these cracklings will spatter quite a lot, so begin with the heat low and the cover on. When the spattering noises subside, take off the cover and continue to sauté over medium-low heat until the pork browns and begins to crisp; then proceed to refry the beans in the oil and rendered fat.

Creamed Refried Beans: Stirring half a cup of sour cream into the basic refried beans or the version with onion is quite delicious—and very rich.

Mexican cooks also sometimes stir in milk or sweet cream. In all these variations, it seems to save the dish from too much unctuousness if you leave quite a bit of texture in the mashing.

Refried Beans with Chorizo Sausage: Skin a 4-ounce *chorizo* and crumble the meat or use half a cup of the *chorizo*-flavored sausage on p. 103. Sauté the sausage until it begins to brown, using the same skillet that will be used for the beans. Proceed to mash the beans directly over the sausage, adding a tablespoon or so of extra oil if the *chorizo* does not render much fat. For a delicious smoky variation, mash in 2 *chiles chipotles* with their canning marinade (see p. 69 for a description).

Refried Beans with Green Chilies: This, one of the very best variations, is quite flexible. You can serve the basic *refritos* with a green chili *salsa* on the table. You can stir in green chili just after the beans are cooked, starting with ¼ cup of canned, chopped chilies or the equivalent in home-made green chili sauce. For the hottest *refrito* of all, make the version with the onion above, adding strips of fresh *jalapeños*, trimmed and seeded. Cut up 1 or 2 chilies to start, making the strips as thin as matchsticks, and sauté until they just begin to wilt. They will still be crunchy when done. An easier way to obtain chili hotness is simply to add 2 teaspoons of chopped, canned *jalapeños*.

Storing note: A pot of cooked beans refrigerates well for 2 or 3 days, after which it may begin to sour; frozen, it keeps indefinitely but changes in texture rather unpalatably. Refried beans keep well in the refrigerator a little longer and are reheated by re-refrying them in a few tablespoons of oil. You can also put them in a casserole, sprinkle Monterey Jack cheese and some chopped onion over the surface, and bake at 350° F. until the cheese melts and the beans are warmed through.

REFRIED BEANS IN BUTTER

This recipe is not faithful to the spirit of *refritos*, which are consider-ably more austere—basically, little more than boiled kidney beans or pinto beans mashed in hot lard and onions. Directions for making the real thing are on p. 296, but this version is so good that I urge you to try it, too. Because the beans are roughly mashed with a slotted spoon, the texture is not the baby-food puree of commercial canned *refritos*. The color, how-ever, is still a bland gray-pink if you use pinto beans. I therefore call for black beans here, readily available in almost any supermarket or natural-foods grocery. Kidney beans, another good alternative, produce a ruddy dish that is just as appetizing. Do not feel that you are taking a shortcut in resorting to canned beans, by the way, since the difference between them and homemade is negligible in this dish.

Please do not overlook the recipe that follows for black bean dip, for the simple step of pureeing this dish in a food processor creates a dip that is infinitely superior to any you can buy and almost as superior to the tricked-out recipes that call for sour cream and bacon bits.

For roughly 3 cups of cooked beans:

> 3 cups cooked black kidney, or pinto beans, plus cooking liquid
> (a 27-ounce can, approximately)
> 1 onion, chopped
> 2 cloves garlic, chopped
> 4 tablespoons butter
> ½ teaspoon cayenne
> ½ teaspoon coarsely ground black pepper
> ½ teaspoon ground cumin
> Wedges of lime for garnish

Drain the cooked beans and reserve the liquid. Combine the onion, garlic, butter and seasonings in a 10-inch skillet, stir over medium heat, and cover to allow the onion to wilt, about 5 minutes over low heat. Uncover, turn heat up to medium, and add the beans. Using a large slotted spoon, roughly mash the beans as you are heating them, but not to the point that the beans lose all their shape. Thin out if necessary with some of the reserved liquid. Serve garnished with wedges of lime to squeeze on as the guests are served.

These beans are excellent as a side dish, as a filling for *tostadas* or any other tortilla dish that calls for refried beans, but best perhaps on their own, spooned into warm flour tortillas. See the recipe for *burritos* on p. 125, which gives the traditional way to eat beans and tortillas.

VARIATIONS:

Black Bean Dip: The beans become a dip simply by pureeing them with the reserved liquid, half a batch at a time, in a food processor. Leave a little texture in the dip, serve warm with fresh lime wedges and perhaps a sprinkling of green coriander—no better way to fuel the cocktail hour can be imagined. The dip is eaten with *tostados* or any suitable corn chip.

Mashed Beans with Cheese: One of the customary ways to prepare refried beans is to stir in ½ cup or so of shredded Monterey Jack cheese a moment before serving. A further elaboration is to spread this mixture on an oven-proof plate, scatter more cheese over the top, dot with pieces of mild or hot green chilies (canned are all right) and heat in a 350° F. oven for about 5 minutes. The dish can be eaten with chips like a dip, which makes it a kind of *nachos*, or it can be brought to the table along with the main dish. In that case, a traditional garnish around the edge of the plate would be shredded lettuce and slices of radish. Such incremental changes are among the beauties of Southwestern cooking.

𝕮𝕮𝕮   Chili Beans   𝕯𝕯𝕯

Chili beans are a cowpuncher or ranch-house dish adapted from a Mexican original. Since the hybrids have become popular outside the Southwest quicker than the originals, pinto beans with tomatoes and chili powder are thought to be mandatory. So it comes as a minor shock to find that the Hispanic cooks prefer to boil their *frijoles* with little extra flavoring, if any at all, leaving the chili to be added at the table in the form of a homemade *salsa*. It would be wrong to deny chili beans their place, though, given all the publicity and genuine affection for Tex-Mex cooking.

There are two distinct ways of cooking the beans. In the first, nothing but tomato and red chilies is added. Indeed, this is a way that could be called indigenous—something like it was eaten in the Santa Fe of the *conquistadores*. The second recipe, which I found in a collection of historic recipes under the name "Spanish Beans," was clearly devised by a cook who knew how beans were baked in Boston and wasn't about to abandon them just because a chili or two hove into sight. Either version can be found today in the Southwest, particularly if you sign up for chuckwagon dinners at your dude ranch.

CHILI BEANS I

For 4 people:

  The recipe for boiled pinto beans on p. 294, about 6 cups
  1 cup tomato puree or crushed tomatoes
  3 to 5 tablespoons powdered red chilies
  1 teaspoon cayenne (if you want the beans hotter)

The pintos are the basic beans in a pot (*frijoles de olla*) of Mexican and New Mexican cooking. You may substitute kidney or pink beans for the pintos if you like; they are cooked exactly the same way. When the beans have boiled until they are done, but not so tender that you can mash them (after about 2 hours, that is), transfer them with their liquid to a covered casserole.

Preheat the oven to 325° F. Stir the tomato puree and powdered chilies into the beans, cover the casserole and bake for about 45 minutes to 1 hour, or until the pintos are tender and the liquid thickened to a sauce. Serve in place of Mexican *frijoles*.

VARIATIONS:

Chili-Bean Casserole: You can elaborate on the basic treatment by adding more ingredients to your casserole: 1 bell pepper, chopped; 1 small onion, chopped; 2 cloves garlic or 2 fresh, seeded *jalapeños*, chopped. The most common meat addition is the salt pork that originally flavored your pot of beans, chopped; or allow about 4 ounces of precooked bacon or as much as ½ pound of cubed, browned meat. If you add cubed beef to the casserole, increase the baking time to 1½ hours and add water as needed to prevent drying. At the end of that time, uncover the dish, scatter on a thick layer of shredded Monterey Jack cheese (orange Longhorn or American cheese is the more usual Tex-Mex style, however) and let it melt as a topping for the casserole.

Cornbread Tamale Pie: Another way is to stew the meat and beans together (see variation above) until both are done, then spread on a ½-inch layer of any cornbread batter. Bake at 375° F., uncovered, for 20 to 30 minutes. The result is a kind of tamale pie.

CHILI BEANS II

For 4 people:

The recipe for boiled pinto beans on p. 294, about 6 cups
Salt pork from the beans, diced
  1 onion, chopped
  ¼ cup cider vinegar
  3 tablespoons brown sugar
  1 bay leaf
  ½ teaspoon thyme
  1 teaspoon dry mustard
  ½ teaspoon salt
  2 cups tomato puree, or the equivalent in canned tomatoes
  4 tablespoons powdered red chilies
  ½ cup double-strength coffee

Once again, the beans can either be simmered in a pot on the stove or baked in a 350° F. oven. Combine the beans, their cooking liquid and all the other ingredients in a casserole. Bring to a boil if the casserole is flameproof; otherwise, stir well and place in the oven to bake for 1 to 2 hours, or until the beans are tender and the liquid reduced to a thick sauce. Serve in place of Mexican *frijoles*.

PINTO BEANS WITH
GREEN CHILIES AND TOMATOES

One sign of the spareness of New Mexican cooking is that mashed beans (*frijoles machacados*) are usually flavored with nothing more than a little extra onion. In this version, however, the beans are enriched with green chilies, onion, garlic and tomatoes, the specific purpose being to revive canned beans on those occasions when there isn't time enough to boil up a fresh pot.

For 4 people:

> 2 or 3 cups canned, whole pinto beans
> (red kidney beans or black beans work equally well)
> ½ small onion, chopped
> 1 clove garlic, chopped
> 2 tablespoons vegetable or olive oil
> 1 fresh, peeled, seeded and chopped tomato or 2 canned tomatoes, chopped
> ¼ cup canned, chopped green chilies
> ¼ teaspoon ground cumin
> Salt and black pepper to taste

Bring the beans and their liquid to the simmer in a saucepan. Place the onion and garlic in the oil in a separate small skillet, then cover and cook for 3 minutes over low heat until the onion is wilted. Raise the heat and stir in the remaining ingredients. Simmer over medium heat, stirring occasionally, for 2 minutes.

Place about ½ cup of beans and an equal amount of their liquid in the bowl of a food processor and blend until pureed, about 5 seconds. Add the pureed beans and the contents of the skillet to the saucepan, simmer slowly for 5 minutes more, and serve.

VARIATION:

Pintos with Fresh Hot Green Chilies: In place of the mild chilies, trim the stems from 1 or 2 fresh *serrano* or *jalapeño* chilies. Cut in half lengthwise, remove the pith and seeds, then cut the chilies into matchsticks. Add to the beans as they first begin to simmer and do not cook so long that the chilies lose their crunchy texture entirely. If you do not like this raw chili taste, substitute 1 or 2 teaspoons of canned, chopped *jalapeños*, or simply spoon on a hot green chili sauce at the table.

PUREED CHICK-PEAS

This is a quick-and-easy side dish on the lines of refried beans. The use of chick-peas, however, makes for a drier, lighter consistency and a taste more identifiably Spanish than Mexican. Although I call it a puree, the chick-peas retain a coarse texture—one that Mexican cooks call *machacado*, or mashed. This is achieved by using brief pulses of a food processor when pureeing the chick-peas. If you want a smoother result, run the machine continuously and add sparing amounts of water until you reach the desired texture. Canned chick-peas are usually sold as *garbanzos*, their Spanish name. I indicate canned chick-peas in this recipe because they are close in taste and texture to the home-boiled. You can always boil your own, of course, but make sure you have plenty of time to spare in your cooking schedule—dried chick-peas require overnight soaking and then at least 3 hours of boiling the next day—very dry ones may need as much as 6 hours of boiling. To get the 3 cups of boiled chick-peas required below, start with 1 cup of dried if you are making them from scratch.

For 4 to 6 people:

    4 tablespoons olive oil
    1 medium or large onion, chopped
    1 large clove garlic, finely chopped, or 1 teaspoon commercial
        garlic puree
    ½ teaspoon oregano
    ½ teaspoon whole or ground cumin
    ½ teaspoon black pepper
Salt to taste
    2 14-ounce cans chick-peas, drained (about 3 cups)
    ¼ to ½ cup canned chopped green chilies
    ¼ cup whipping cream or half-and-half
To garnish: small handful of green coriander (*cilantro*) and
        scallion greens, both finely chopped; lime wedges or
        bottled lime juice

Heat the olive oil in a medium or large frying pan over medium heat. Add the chopped onion, lower heat, and cook, covered, for about 5 minutes or until the onion wilts. Remove cover, raise heat to medium again, and stir in the flavorings—garlic, oregano, cumin, pepper and salt. (The amount of salt will depend upon your taste and the saltiness of the chick-peas to begin with; proceed cautiously.)

Leaving the onions to cook with their seasonings, place the chick-peas in a food processor and puree with short, repeated pulses. The texture you want will look like oatmeal flakes rather than a puree as smooth as mashed potatoes. Lacking a processor, puree the chick-peas with a potato masher, a vegetable mill fitted with its medium blade, or a potato ricer. Add the chick-peas to the onions and cook for another 5 minutes over medium heat, mashing the chick-peas into the onions with the back of a large slotted spoon, just as if you were making refried beans. The chick-peas have cooked enough when they are dry, thoroughly blended with the onions, and beginning to brown at the edges of the pan.

Stir in the green chilies and the cream and allow to simmer for a minute or two. At this point the chick-peas are ready to serve, but they can be set aside in their pan for a few hours and reheated without any harm. As they stand, the chick-peas will tend to turn stiff and acquire a darkened surface, so make sure on reheating to add a little water, and stir thoroughly. Feel free to adjust the texture of this dish to suit your personal taste, adding extra cream (or water) for a thinner consistency, extra olive oil for richness, and longer cooking for a drier texture.

Present at the table garnished with chopped *cilantro*, chopped scallion greens and lime wedges. If you are using bottled lime juice instead, stir in a teaspoon or two during the last seconds of cooking.

VARIATIONS:

Pureed Chick-Peas with Red Chilies and Tomatoes: Proceed exactly as above, but substitute 1 tablespoon powdered red chilies and ½ cup finely chopped tomatoes for the green chilies and cream. Crushed tomatoes packed with tomato puree work quite well here if you lack fresh, red-ripe ones; you can even use any *enchilada* sauce with tomatoes in it, such as the one on p. 79, in which case, omit the powdered chilies.

Baked Chick-Peas: Using either the basic recipe or the above variation, spread the finished chick-peas in a shallow 1-quart casserole or gratin dish. Sprinkle with 1 cup (4 ounces) shredded Monterey Jack cheese, and bake at 300° F. for 15 minutes, or until the cheese is melted and bubbling. Garnish with the *cilantro* and scallion greens, plus lime wedges, fresh, chopped tomato and shredded lettuce as you like. When elaborately garnished, a casserole of baked chick-peas can serve as a festive-looking vegetarian main dish—the amount given will serve 3 people—needing only warm tortillas, a table *salsa* and a green vegetable to complete it.

SPANISH RICE

Gummy tomato-flavored rice, which is how most of us think of Spanish rice in restaurants, makes a poor showing compared with the various delicious *sopas* Hispanic cooks dote upon. Although these rice dishes are called "dry soups" (*sopas secas*), the best of them are in a direct line with the marvelous pilafs and *pulaos* concocted from Valencia and Morocco to India. Put the restaurant rice out of your mind and try a few of the variations listed below—they will give you a new respect for Spanish rice.

As it happens, the villagers of northern New Mexico divide their allegiance between rice and corn-based preparations like *chicos* and *posole*, but as you go south toward Mexico proper, all manner of *arroz* dishes appear. In order to simplify the bewildering number of possible variations, I have outlined a basic *sopa* flavored with only onions and chicken stock, followed by all the additions.

For 4 people:

    2 cups chicken broth (or half broth and half water)
    3 tablespoons vegetable oil
    ½ medium onion, chopped
    1 garlic clove, chopped
    1 cup long-grained rice (converted rice gives a good texture to
      the finished *sopa*)
    Black pepper
    ½ teaspoon salt, if the broth is not already salty enough

The quantities and liquid called for are enough if you are baking the rice in a covered casserole. If you prefer instead to simmer the rice on the top of the stove, you may need as much as 3 cups of broth. Bring the broth to a boil and preheat the oven to 300° F. Heat the oil in an enameled 2-quart casserole (or any pot with a heavy lid that can be heated both on a burner and in the oven). Stir in the onion and garlic, cover the pot, and let sit over low heat for the onion to wilt, about 5 minutes.

Uncover the pot and stir in the rice. Continue to stir over medium heat until the rice turns translucent and then shows the first signs of browning. (Although this is the traditional Spanish way, you may like the rice better unbrowned, in which case cook it only until it turns translucent.) Take the pot off the heat, add the seasonings as needed, then carefully pour in the broth. Cover and bake for 20 minutes in the oven. Check to see if the rice is tender and the broth absorbed; if not, bake another 5 minutes. Let stand 5 minutes at room temperature, still covered, for the rice to continue steaming in its pot. Serve this basic *sopa seca* as a side dish to any New Mexican main course.

VARIATIONS:

These involve sautéing additional ingredients in a frying pan and adding the finished rice for only a brief cooking time. In this way, the garnishes remain in good condition instead of gumming up the *sopa* as it bakes.

Rice with Tomatoes and Garbanzos: Prepare rice as in basic recipe. Chop 4 to 6 canned tomatoes and ¼ onion. Drain 2 cups of canned, cooked *garbanzos* (chick-peas) and have them ready. Melt 2 tablespoons of butter in a 10- or 12-inch skillet, stir in the onion and cook for 3 minutes or so. Add the tomatoes and stir over high heat until the mixture starts to bubble. Add the *garbanzos* and the rice together, mix thoroughly, and let simmer uncovered for another 5 minutes to ripen the flavors. Garnish with sliced hard-boiled eggs and chopped green coriander. This particular *sopa seca* is a version of a popular dish in mother Spain and has been eaten in New Mexico since the beginning. If the rice does not have enough tomato to color it as much as you like, bake the basic rice with 1 cup of tomato puree in place of ¾ cup of the broth.

Rice with Tomato and Chilies: Prepare rice as in basic recipe. Chop 1 small onion, 1 bell pepper, 1 *jalapeño* and 4 to 6 canned tomatoes. (The peppers do not have to be roasted or peeled, merely deveined and seeded.) Heat 2 tablespoons of olive oil in a 10- or 12-inch skillet and sauté the onion, peppers and tomatoes until the mixture is wilted but the solids still a bit crisp. Stir in the finished rice *sopa*, season with a large pinch of oregano and simmer for 5 minutes until the flavors ripen. If this type of Mexican rice does not have enough tomato for your taste, add ½ cup of tomato puree and simmer 10 minutes over low heat with the cover on. Garnish with chopped green coriander. You can also substitute 2 Anaheim chilies for the bell pepper.

Green Rice: A refreshing and not at all stodgy version of *arroz verde* can be made by sautéing several green ingredients for a brief moment in butter, then tossing in the finished rice just to blend. Using your processor, finely chop 2 fresh Anaheim chilies and 1 *jalapeño* or *serrano* chili, stopping once to scrape down the bowl with a spatula. Set the chilies aside and finely chop ¼ cup green coriander (*cilantro*) with 4 green onions.

Heat 2 tablespoons of butter or olive oil in a 10- or 12-inch skillet and sauté the chilies in it for only a minute over high heat. Stir in the coriander and onion and toss for 15 seconds more. Add a large pinch of oregano or mint and then the baked rice. Any sort of fresh herb is excellent in *arroz verde,* even though parsley and basil, for example, would not be too authentic. A handful of mint (*yerba buena*) is delicious tossed in with a handful of piñons (pine nuts), particularly if you have also sautéed the nuts in butter beforehand.

Other garnishes for sopas: The rice dishes in New Mexico are traditionally rather plain, but you can be as elaborate and improvisational as you want, taking the Spanish kitchen as your authority. Chicken, shrimp, fresh peas, cubed young zucchini and almonds are just the beginning. All of them should be cooked lightly in olive oil or butter, then stirred into the *sopa* as it comes from the oven.

SUMMER RICE

Under this heading are grouped the recipes for steamed rice garnished with bits of fresh vegetables—peas, zucchini, ripe tomato, green onion— whatever the garden patch or the supermarket yields. All of them are simple concoctions to brighten a plain bowl of rice.

For 3 or 4 people:

2 cups water, salted with a scant teaspoon of salt
2 tablespoons butter
Dash black pepper
Dash paprika
1 cup rice (converted rice is recommended)

Bring the water, butter and seasonings to a full rolling boil in a heavy saucepan and preheat the oven to 300° F. When the water boils, add the rice, stir once or twice and cover the pan. Bring to the boil again over medium or low heat, then transfer the pot of rice to the oven. It will be cooked in 20 minutes, but should stand another 5 minutes, covered, at room temperature.

Made in this fashion, the rice also can sit in the oven for ½ hour after it is baked, but it will gradually begin to stick to the pan. (For softer rice, or if your saucepan is not a heavy one, increase the water to 2½ cups.)

Toss the finished rice with a fork, taste for seasoning, and garnish as in the following variations:

Rice with Green Peas: Defrost a box of frozen baby peas (*petits pois*) while the rice is cooking. Peas this small do not need to be cooked, merely heated through. When the rice has 5 minutes to cook, lightly stir in the peas, cover the pot again, and finish the steaming. Garden-picked baby peas should be added with the rice for the full cooking time.

Rice with Green Peas and Almonds: Prepare the rice as above, but reduce the butter to 1 tablespoon. In a small skillet, sauté a small handful of blanched, slivered almonds in 2 tablespoons of butter until lightly browned. Add one 10-ounce box of baby green peas, either defrosted or still frozen, and toss over high heat until just heated through but still sweet to the taste. Toss with the steamed rice.

Rice with Ripe Tomatoes: Cut 1 or 2 garden-ripe tomatoes into thin wedges and toss lightly with the steamed rice as it comes from the oven. Cover the pot for 5 minutes to allow the tomatoes just to warm through. Serve with a generous grinding of coarse black pepper and a sprinkling of vinegar (try the chili vinegar on p. 97). You can also add chopped parsley or green onion to the rice, or a few tablespoons of chopped red onion.

Rice with Mushrooms: Cook the rice as above but reduce the butter to 1 tablespoon. Drop a few sprigs of parsley into the processor with the motor running, then add 2 green onions cut into 1-inch lengths. Turn off the motor, place 4 to 8 large mushrooms in the bowl and process with repeated pulses until they are finely chopped but not watery. (All of this can, of course, be done with a chef's knife.)

Heat 2 tablespoons butter and 1 tablespoon olive oil to a foam in a small skillet. Add the mushroom mixture all at once. Sauté over high heat for about 2 minutes, or until the mushrooms are beginning to brown. Season with salt and pepper. Toss with the steamed rice.

Rice with Zucchini and Onions: Shred 1 small zucchini, using either the shredding blade of your processor or the coarsest holes on a four-sided hand grater. Finely chop 4 green onions or ½ small yellow onion. Sauté the zucchini and onion together in a few tablespoons of oil, exactly as described in the version with mushrooms above, stopping when the zucchini is still a bit crisp. Season with a pinch of dried (or fresh) oregano, thyme or fresh parsley; add salt and pepper. Toss lightly with the steamed rice.

Lemon Rice: The basic recipe or any of the variations can become lemon rice by tossing the finished rice with 2 teaspoons or more of fresh lemon juice. For a more bitter taste, place a slice or two of fresh lemon, un-peeled, on top of the rice as it bakes, but discard before serving.

Lime Rice: Garnish the finished rice or any of the variations with wedges of fresh lime to squeeze on at the table—only a few drops are necessary.

RICE AND POTATOES WITH CUMIN

Hispanic cooks are great believers in cooking rice with other starches such as *garbanzos* or potatoes, but many of us shy away from such combinations. That is a shame, because a simple preparation of spiced rice and potatoes is quite delicious and really not a great caloric hazard—one statistic notes that you would have to eat 11 pounds of potatoes to gain 1 pound of body weight. I highly recommend this version of rice and potatoes. It is hardly any more trouble than steamed rice alone, and the combination of flavors is surprisingly satisfying, considering the simplicity of the dish.

For 4 people as a side dish:

   2 medium boiling potatoes (12 to 14 ounces together)
   3 tablespoons butter
   ½ teaspoon (or more) whole cumin seed
   ½ teaspoon turmeric for color, optional
Generous dashes black pepper
   1 teaspoon salt
   1 cup long-grained rice (converted rice gives a good texture)
   2 cups water or chicken stock

Peel the potatoes and cut into 1-inch chunks (about 20). Preheat the oven to 300° F. and have ready a 2-quart saucepan or heat-and-flameproof casserole. Melt the butter until it foams, then add the cumin seed and optional turmeric. Stir for a minute until the cumin's aroma is released, but do not let it turn dark. Stir in the potatoes and toss well to coat them with butter. Add the pepper, salt and rice and stir another minute or so over high heat. Finally, pour in the water or stock, bring to a boil, then cover and place in the oven. Bake for 20 minutes, at which time the liquid will be absorbed and the rice dry and separate.

Remove the rice from the oven (though it can sit in the turned-off oven for up to 30 minutes if necessary) and let sit at room temperature for 5 minutes. Serve as a starch with any main dish.

POTATO GRATIN WITH GREEN CHILIES

In the Southwest, the combination of potatoes and green chilies (*papas con chiles*) usually means hash browns with the chilies added as the potatoes are frying in lard (see p. 206). For a lighter side dish that goes well with roasts, steaks or grilled meats, I like this potato gratin better. It is a straightforward adaptation of the classic French *gratin dauphinois* which you can vary as you like by substituting milk for the chicken broth, adding sautéed, chopped onions to the chilies, or crumbling some pre-cooked *chorizo* sausage over the top.

For 4 people as a side dish:

>   2 tablespoons butter
> 1½ pounds boiling potatoes, peeled
>   1 clove garlic, peeled
>   1 cup chicken stock
> ¼ teaspoon cumin
> Generous dash pepper
> ⅓ cup chopped, canned green chilies, or about 3 whole chilies, chopped
>   1 cup shredded Monterey Jack cheese (about 4 ounces)
> Salt

Preheat the oven to 425° F. Use half the butter to grease a shallow gratin dish or casserole with a capacity of 4 to 6 cups. Cut the potatoes into ⅛-inch slices by hand or with the slicing blade of a food processor. Bring the garlic, chicken stock, cumin and pepper to a boil in a small saucepan while you are slicing the potatoes. Have the chopped chilies and the shredded cheese at hand.

To assemble the gratin, arrange half the potato slices in the baking dish, evenly dot them with half the green chilies, then sprinkle half the cheese over. Salt very lightly or not at all, depending on the saltiness of the chicken broth. Repeat with another layer, using up the remaining potatoes, chilies and cheese. Remove the garlic clove from the boiling broth and carefully pour broth over the potatoes. Dot the surface with the remaining butter. Bake for 30 minutes, or until the surface of the gratin is browned and the potatoes are knife-tender. Allow to cool a few minutes and serve.

For a hotter chili flavor, either add 1 teaspoon canned chopped *jalapeños* along with the mild chilies or offer a chili *salsa* at the table for your guests to spoon over their portions of gratin at will.

BAKED WHOLE GREEN CHILIES

Green chilies that have been stuffed and fried in a batter, the traditional *chiles rellenos,* are considered substantial enough to serve as a main
course, but you can have that pure green chili taste as a vegetable dish,
too. The chilies are stuffed with tomatoes, onions, pinto beans or some
other savory filling, then simply baked in the oven with a coating of cheese.
One can easily eat 4 or 5 of these at a time, and with the availability of
good canned chilies, they no longer have a limited season.

The dish comes into its own, however, when the chilies are fresh from
the vine and home-roasted. The canned flame-roasted chilies in the markets
(the most widely circulated brand is Ortega) have a nice flavor, but they
are so thin-walled that stuffing them is a delicate business. If you can grow
your own thicker-walled *poblanos,* or if you happen upon some during the
short period in late spring or early fall when they seem to show up all at
once in the markets, use those and make as many *chiles rellenos* variations,
fried or baked, as you can invent.

For 4 people as a side dish:

> 12 whole green chilies, canned or fresh, already roasted and peeled
> (for the home method of roasting, see p. 64)
> 1½ cups, roughly, of filling (see below)
> 1 cup shredded Monterey Jack cheese
> Olive oil to drizzle over the chilies

You can stuff the chilies in one of several ways. If you have roasted
your own and peeled them without tearing the flesh, you show off your
accomplishment by making a slit in the side, leaving the stem intact, and
then pushing the stuffing in through the slit. Far less virtuosic is to stuff
the chilies through the opened stem end, a way that works with fresh
chilies and some of the sturdier canned ones. For the usual fragile canned
chilies, simply cut a slit down the side and open the chilies flat, spoon on
a scant 2 tablespoons of stuffing and gently reshape.

Whatever method you choose, stuff all the chilies and lay them close
together in a small casserole. Sprinkle the cheese over, drizzle a few teaspoons of olive oil over all, and let sit, lightly covered with waxed paper,
until you are ready to bake. Bake at 325° F. for about 5 to 7 minutes, just
until the cheese melts and the stuffing is heated through. Serve with
grilled meats or present a homemade red *enchilada* sauce on the side.

FILLINGS FOR THE CHILIES:

Your own taste and talent for improvisation dictate what you stuff the
chilies with. Here are a few of the more traditional choices:

Tomato and Onion: If you want to accentuate the freshness of your chilies, peel and seed a large fresh tomato, then chop it along with some green or sweet red onion, using about 3 parts tomato to 1 part onion. Flavor with chopped garlic and/or green coriander (*cilantro*) if you like, and season with salt and pepper.

Tomato and Cheese: Mix chopped fresh tomato, peeled and seeded, with an equal amount of shredded Monterey Jack cheese. Season with salt, pepper, perhaps a bit of cumin and cayenne. You can also add chopped *cilantro* or onion as you please, and skip the Monterey Jack cheese topping. Well-drained canned tomatoes can be substituted for the fresh if necessary.

Cooked Fillings: Mashed or refried pinto beans are among the commonest authentic fillings (see recipes on p. 296 for refried pinto beans and on p. 298 for a rich version of black beans mashed in butter). If you are using canned pintos, revive them in a skillet with a little oil and chopped onion cooked together. Mash the beans in the hot oil, season with garlic, oregano, cumin or whatever you think will perk up the flavor, then proceed with the stuffing. Refried beans with sour cream (p. 297) are quite delicious used as a filling.

Among the meat fillings, you can simply use the *chorizo*-flavored sausage on p. 103, or more complicated preparations like the spiced, ground meat called *picadillo* (p. 101) or the less traditional but nonetheless quite good shredded pork with spices called *carnitas* (p. 100).

GREEN CORN WITH LIME BUTTER

You know it is high summer when the fresh ears of sweet corn are ready for roasting and the Hispanic cooks start mashing butter with salt and lime juice to spread over them. The usual roasting method, which is unsurpassable, is to soak the whole, unshucked ears in water for a few hours or overnight, then to place them over charcoal or in the ashes of a barbecue pit—they are done after about 20 to 30 minutes when the husks are beginning to scorch on all sides and the interior is steaming.

If you are using a modern kettle barbecue, the timing is the same, as is the care you need to take to rotate the ears every 5 minutes or so to avoid burning on one side while the others remain raw. I particularly enjoy this treatment of corn on the cob when there are obliging guests on the premises who will undertake the job of peeling away the burning hot husks.

You can also get good results by roasting or steaming the corn using whatever method you are accustomed to. The lime butter is made as follows:

For 8 to 12 ears:

1½ sticks sweet butter, softened
2 tablespoons fresh lime juice
Salt to taste
Optional: ¼ to ½ cup fresh table *salsa* (p. 86)

Using a fork and a small bowl, mash the softened butter with the lime juice, adding the juice a tablespoonful at a time. Incorporate the salt now, if you like, or leave it to be sprinkled on by each diner. The option of adding fresh *salsa* to the lime butter is not authentic, but an improvisation by a friend of mine and a lover of the Southwest, Carl Fowler. He melts the butter in a small saucepan and stirs in the *salsa*; the flavored butter is presented at the table warm. For such a simple idea, it receives remarkable acclaim, so I pass it along.

CORN OFF THE COB

Cooking fresh vegetables with milk and green chilies is one of the most traditional ways among the old village cooks. In this simple sauté of corn and chopped mild chilies, you can make up for any lack of creaminess in store-bought white corn by adding dashes of fresh cream at the end. The sprinkling of Monterey Jack cheese called for to finish the dish is strictly optional, especially if your main dishes already include cheese.

For 4 people:

4 ears fresh white corn, kernels sliced from the cob with a paring
    knife—about 2 to 2½ cups. (Lacking fresh corn,
    substitute canned, whole-kernel white corn or frozen corn,
    defrosted.)
2 tablespoons butter
3 green onions, chopped
2 to 4 tablespoons chopped canned green chilies
Optional: 1 fresh or canned *jalapeño*, chopped, to add hotness
⅓ cup heavy cream
Salt and pepper
Optional: shredded Monterey Jack cheese

Save the milk from the fresh corn as you slice off the kernels, but drain the canned corn. Melt the butter in a 10-inch skillet, stir in the onions and chilies, including the optional *jalapeño*, and cook over medium heat just to wilt the onion for a minute or two. Add the cream and allow it to boil up for 1 minute, stirring if it threatens to overflow, then add the corn. Cover the pan and simmer gently for 2 or 3 minutes, or just until the kernels taste cooked. The finished dish should be fresh-tasting and creamy. Add salt and pepper to taste, then stir in the cheese off the heat, if using it, and serve immediately.

VARIATIONS:

In addition to the dish of corn with zucchini described on p. 318, you can combine other chopped, garden-fresh vegetables with the corn. A small new potato, already boiled and cut into cubes, would be quite authentic, as would chopped, seeded tomatoes (in which case reduce the cream a bit to accommodate the liquid of the tomatoes). Chopped sweet peppers, more onions and, in winter, yellow squash steamed and cut into small cubes, are all good.

Baked Indian Vegetables: If you gather as many of these garden vegetables as you can, place them all in a baking dish and bake, covered, for about 30 minutes, you will have a Pueblo-style vegetable casserole. Top this with generous amounts of shredded cheese.

BLUE CORNMEAL MUSH
Chauquehue

Some variety of cornmeal mush is eaten in every farming culture that raises corn. The New Mexican version, *chauquehue*, has the distinction of being colored blue (or cement-gray, depending on your color sense) since it uses the same roasted blue cornmeal that is the basis for *atole*, or corn gruel. The usual way of presenting the mush was as a "vegetable" sauced with red chili—it was the replacement for potatoes or rice, or a simplified substitute for *tamales*.

If you are curious to try *chauquehue*, there are two traditional preparations, differing only in their degree of stiffness:

1. Bring 3 cups of water to the boil with 2 tablespoons of lard or vegetable oil. Mix 1½ cups of packaged *atole* (roasted blue cornmeal—see p. 112) with 2 cups of cold water and 2 teaspoons salt. Stirring constantly, pour this mixture into the boiling water and simmer for 10 to 20 minutes. The result is a thick porridge to be served with eggs or meat dishes as grits would be in the South. As a sauce, try the basic *chile colorado* on p. 73, or if that proves too stark, the variation with tomatoes on p. 76. To a non-native palate, *chauquehue* is much improved by adding more

salt, black pepper to taste, and generous lumps of butter to the finished porridge.

2. Follow the same method as above but in the following proportions: 1 cup *atole*, 1 cup cold water, 1 cup boiling water, ½ teaspoon salt, and 1 tablespoon lard or vegetable oil. This *chauquehue* will become very thick. It is spread while still hot into a greased 8- or 9-inch-square cake pan and allowed to cool, then cut into squares like *polenta* to be sautéed in butter (or lard). Cut the squares about 2 or 3 inches to a side and fry them long enough so that they crisp up and begin to brown well. Serve with *chile colorado* of some sort, or with *chile verde* if you aren't bound by tradition.

POSOLE AS A VEGETABLE

Posole, or hominy, can be served as a starchy vegetable as well as in the full-dress version with pork on p. 266. In New Mexico restaurants, *posole* might be little more than hominy stewed in red chili sauce, perhaps with a bit of salt pork or chopped onion to flavor it. If you want to improvise on your own treatment, that is the way to start, using drained canned hominy and a portion of good red *enchilada* sauce. You have only to combine the two and simmer gently for half an hour. The version below is "company" *posole*, in that it uses both green and red chilies, and chicken stock in place of water. Do not worry over much about exact timings, for hominy, even when canned, is sturdy stuff—it can stand up to about as much slow simmering as you give it.

For 4 people as a side dish:

> 2 tablespoons vegetable oil
> 1 small onion, chopped
> 1 or 2 cloves garlic, chopped
> ½ teaspoon ground cumin
> ¼ teaspoon black pepper
> Pinch oregano
> 2 tablespoons powdered red chilies (hot or mild)
> 4 ounces canned, chopped green chilies
> 2 cups chicken broth
> 1 cup tomato puree (or about 8 whole canned tomatoes pureed in the processor)
> ¼ teaspoon salt
> 2½ to 3 cups canned hominy, white or golden, drained; or the equivalent in frozen *posole* which has been precooked according to the method on p. 267.

Heat the oil in a 2-quart saucepan, add the onion and garlic and cook over low heat with the pan covered for about 5 minutes to wilt the onion. Remove cover, raise heat to medium, and add the spices, oregano and red chilies. Cook for a minute, stirring, to ripen the seasonings, then add the remaining ingredients. Bring to a boil, cover and simmer over low heat for 30 minutes. The liquid around the *posole* should be only slightly thickened, the consistency of a thin sauce. If it seems too thick, add water, a little at a time.

STEAMED VEGETABLES WITH GREEN CHILI BUTTER

This is an invention for using garden-fresh tomatoes and green chilies when they are in season (although canned tomatoes and chilies will by no means lead to unrespectable results). It also fills a need for light, crisp vegetable dishes of the kind that traditional New Mexican cooking lacks. The method is very simple and impromptu. Steam enough vegetables for 4 people, using your favorite method and choosing from almost any that are fresh and good: broccoli, zucchini, new potatoes, cauliflower and corn on the cob are particularly suitable. When the vegetables have just about finished steaming, make the chili butter:

GREEN CHILI BUTTER:

> 2 red-ripe tomatoes, seeded and chopped into rough chunks
> 3 or 4 roasted, peeled green chilies (Anaheim, California,
>   *poblano* or even bell pepper), cut into rough chunks
> 4 to 6 tablespoons butter
> ¼ teaspoon ground cumin
> Salt and black pepper to taste
> Optional garnish: small handfuls of chopped green coriander
>   (*cilantro*) and green onion

Place the tomatoes and chilies in a food processor and use a pulse action until the vegetables are finely chopped but not liquefied (this can also be done by hand with a large chef's knife). In a pot large enough to hold all your steamed vegetables comfortably, with spare room for tossing them, melt the butter over medium heat. When it sizzles, add the cumin, stir for a few seconds, then add the tomato-green chili mixture. Allow to heat through, then add the steamed vegetables. Toss quickly, raising the heat if the vegetables are not steaming hot to begin with. Season to taste with salt and black pepper. Transfer to a serving platter or bowl, sprinkle with the optional *cilantro* and green onion for garnish and serve immediately.

GRATED ZUCCHINI WITH GREEN CHILI

Simple green vegetable dishes are welcome in New Mexico cooking, in which, in the past, even summer squash (*calabacitas*) was dried for storing and then cooked up with chilies. Here is a fresh zucchini sauté that takes only 10 minutes to prepare. Its fresh taste and startling green color contrast nicely with the earthy browns and reds of meats prepared with red chili. Following the basic recipe are two simple variations to help you cope with the flood of late-summer zucchini that delights beginning gardeners but overwhelms the cook.

For 4 people as a side dish:

2 medium zucchini
2 cloves garlic, peeled and chopped
¼ cup olive oil
4 Anaheim green chilies, seeded and cut into thirds
6 green onions, cleaned and trimmed of roots
Optional: 1 fresh *jalapeño* (for hotness), seeded, deveined and
    chopped into thirds
¼ cup green *enchilada* sauce (canned or homemade)
½ teaspoon salt
Black pepper to taste

The zucchini needs to be shredded before it is sautéed. You can do this by hand with the coarsest holes of an ordinary four-sided grater, or use the shredding disk of a food processor. Heat the olive oil in a 10- or 12-inch skillet and add the zucchini and garlic. Toss over medium heat for about 5 minutes—the zucchini will lose its raw taste but remain crisp and bright green.

Meanwhile, place the Anaheims and the green onions (and the optional *jalapeño*) in the processor, fitted now with the standard metal blade. Process until they are finely chopped, about 5 to 8 seconds (or chop by hand with a chef's knife). Add them to the zucchini when it is just done and sauté, again using tossing motions, for another minute. Add the green chili sauce, heat through, and season with salt and pepper. Serve immediately for freshest taste; if the vegetable has to wait, toss again over high heat to rewarm.

VARIATIONS:

Grated Zucchini with Cream and Cheese: Particularly if you choose to make your dish hot with the optional *jalapeño*, the addition of a little heavy cream helps balance the taste—it is also quite authentic. Begin with about ¼ cup, added at the same time as the green *enchilada* sauce, and finish the cooking by stirring in ½ cup of grated Monterey Jack cheese, which should be heated until just melted. This especially good variation can be further dressed up with slices of avocado and wedges of lime for garnish at the table. It is as compelling in its colors as a green dish can be.

Grated Zucchini with Avocado: Prepare 2 avocados while you are cooking the zucchini. The first is pureed in the processor and added to the zucchini along with the green *enchilada* sauce. The second is roughly chopped into ½-inch cubes and just stirred in as the dish finishes. The bland and unctuous avocado sets off the crispness of the zucchini. Garnish with lime wedges and chopped green coriander (*cilantro*) as the dish comes to the table.

ZUCCHINI WITH GREEN CHILI AND CORN
Calabacitas

Squash and corn began as Indian foods, but every Hispanic cook who came into Mexico or the American Southwest also learned to make a version of *calabacitas*, which combines them both. Sometimes the squash was browned with onions, particularly if the green squash had been dried and stored for winter. This version, though, is fresh and summery. All the vegetable flavors remain distinct, and the binding of cream and cheese just holds the *calabacitas* together—this is not the equivalent of a succotash stew. The variation on p. 319 does not taste very different from the basic recipe, but its use of green chili in quantity is more authentically New Mexican. *Calabacitas* is suitable for a vegetarian main course or as a side dish to serve with barbecued meats in the summer. These are only two uses among many for a vegetable that deserves to be appreciated everywhere.

For 4 people:

    2 cloves garlic, peeled
    2 Anaheim green chilies (or half a large bell pepper),
      seeded and cut into thirds
    6 green onions with the green tops left on, cut into 1-inch lengths
    2 medium zucchini, quartered lengthwise and cut into rough
      ½-inch chunks
    2 tablespoons olive oil
    1 tablespoon butter
    ¼ teaspoon salt
  Pepper to taste
  ⅓ cup heavy cream
    1 cup white corn kernels, either stripped from 2 ears of corn or
      canned (not cream-style)
    ½ cup shredded Monterey Jack cheese (about 2 ounces)

Drop the garlic into the food processor through the feed tube while the motor is running. Turn off the machine, add the chilies and green onions, and process until finely chopped, stopping at least once to scrape down the bowl with a rubber spatula. Add this chopped mixture to the cubed zucchini.

Heat the oil and butter in a 10- to 12-inch skillet, then add the zucchini and processed onion-and-chili mixture. Sauté over medium heat for 5 minutes, tossing occasionally. The zucchini will begin to lose its rawness but should not be allowed to brown. Add the salt, pepper, cream and the corn, if fresh; cover the pan and simmer over low heat for 5 minutes. Remove the cover and taste the zucchini, which should be just cooked but still somewhat crisp. If you are using canned corn, add at the end— only long enough to warm up.

Add the cheese off the heat and stir to incorporate and melt it—the residual heat of the cooked vegetables should be enough. If not, return to lowest heat for a few minutes, but be sure that the dish does not come near boiling, or the cheese will turn stringy. (If you are making the *calabacitas* ahead of time, set the pan aside before adding the cheese and canned corn; reheat just before serving and add as above.)

Serve the *calabacitas* as you would any green vegetable; it is also rich enough to eliminate the need for a starch in a light meal.

VARIATION:

Calabacitas with More Green Chili: Make exactly as in the basic recipe but eliminate the fresh Anaheim chilies. In their place, add either ½ cup green *enchilada* sauce (p. 80) or ½ cup (4 ounces) chopped canned green chilies. (The old mountain cooks would have roasted and peeled their own chilies, and no doubt their dish would have been the better for it.) For a hotter version, add 1 chopped *jalapeño* as well. Add the chilies with the cream.

DESSERTS

Chocolate-Piñon Torte
Coriander Cake with Pecan Topping
Boiled Lemon Cake • Drunken Prune Cake
Buñuelos • Buñuelos in Syrup
Sticky Sofa Pillows (Sopaipillas)
Madeira Cream Pie
"Spanish Pie" with Pumpkin Filling
Lemon-Cheese Tart (Quesadilla)
Almond Chess Pie • "Transparent" Pie
Double-Crust Pastry • Single-Crust Lard Pastry
Little Pies with Peach Butter and Piñons (Empanaditas)
Sweet Fillings • Aniseed Cookies (Bizcochitos)
Pumpkin Cookies • Piñon Tiles
New Mexico Pralines • Soft Custard (Natillas)
Bread Pudding with Wine and Cheese (Capirotada)
White Cocoa Flan
Flan with Pineapple and Lime
Indian Pudding with Pumpkin Custard
Rice Pudding with Carmel-Nut Sauce
Tequila-and-Lime Sherbet

CHOCOLATE-PIÑON TORTE

The recent vogue for flourless chocolate cakes was very welcome to me, for these low-slung, intensely chocolate-tasting desserts are much less finicky to prepare than the old layer cakes. The recipe given here is a small torte flavored with pine nuts, and it calls for but a modicum of flour to add body. It is perfectly possible to omit both nuts and flour, in which case the torte will puff like a soufflé in the oven and collapse as it cools. Such a "failed" soufflé is even moister and more chocolate-concentrated than the torte version.

Either batter will stick tenaciously to the pan, even a buttered and floured one, so do not neglect the step that calls for lining with foil. This cake is an invention, by the way—no indigenous New Mexico cookbook includes any chocolate cake as far as I have been able to find.

For 4 to 6 people:

>   3 ounces semisweet chocolate
>   1 ounce unsweetened chocolate
>   4 tablespoons (½ stick) butter
> Grated rind of 1 orange (reserving a generous pinch for garnish)
>   3 tablespoons piñons (pine nuts); if not available, substitute
>   blanched almonds
>   6 tablespoons sugar
>   2 tablespoons flour
>   4 large eggs, separated
>   2 tablespoons orange liqueur (Cointreau, Triple Sec or
>   Grand Marnier, for example)
>   ¼ teaspoon salt, if butter is not salted already
> For garnish: ½ cup heavy cream, 2 tablespoons sugar, 2 tablespoons
>   orange liqueur, and the reserved pinch of orange peel

Preheat the oven to 350° F. and grease an 8-inch round cake pan at least 2½ inches deep. Cut a circle of aluminum foil to fit the bottom of the pan, place inside, and grease or butter the foil. For added precaution against sticking, you can also lightly flour the foil lining.

Place the chocolate, butter and orange rind in a small skillet or saucepan with a cover over simmering water, or in a double boiler. Remove from the heat and stir thoroughly after the chocolate and butter have just melted. Set aside to cool slightly.

Grind the piñons, 2 tablespoons sugar and the flour together in the food processor until they reach the consistency of a fine meal, stopping the machine at least once to scrape down the bowl with a spatula. Do not overprocess or the nuts will turn into an oily paste.

Using an electric mixer, beat the egg yolks and 2 tablespoons sugar in a deep mixing bowl for a full 5 minutes at highest speed. The mixture should more than double in volume and reach the consistency of half-whipped cream. Briefly beat in the orange liqueur. Clean the beaters thoroughly. Beat the egg whites with the optional salt until soft peaks form, then beat in the remaining 2 tablespoons sugar until just incorporated.

Stir the piñon-flour mixture into the lukewarm melted chocolate and butter. Working deftly, fold this combined mixture thoroughly into the beaten egg yolks, using a broad rubber spatula. The chocolate will naturally sink to the bottom of the batter, so be sure to reach all the way down with your spatula, lifting the chocolate up and over the egg. Start folding in the egg whites, added all at once, after about a minute. It will seem to take a long time to incorporate all the chocolate so that the batter has no light streaks remaining in it, but if you work quickly and have beaten the eggs sufficiently, your cake will be light.

Gently transfer the batter to the cake pan and bake in the middle of the oven for 25 to 30 minutes. The cake may take another 5 minutes or so to finish baking, but it is done when the middle of the layer has risen and all but the very center is firm and spongy—a little jiggling in the middle is quite acceptable, particularly if you like tortes that are moist. Cool in the pan for 10 minutes, run a knife around the edge, and turn out onto a serving plate. Carefully peel away the foil after the layer is cooled to barely warm.

NOTE: Baked as directed, the torte will have a bit of a rind around the edges. For a cake that is moist throughout, cook in a water bath as follows: Have ready an ovenproof skillet or baking pan that is 1 inch or more wider than the cake pan. Before greasing the cake pan, set it in the larger pan and pour in enough water to come halfway up. Remove the cake pan and proceed to make the batter as directed. As you near the end, bring the water bath to a boil. Set it in the preheated 350° F. oven and set the batter-filled cake pan inside. Increase baking time to 40 to 45 minutes and lower the heat if you hear actual boiling—the water should just simmer. The cake is done when it tests firm to the touch throughout.

Serving the torte: The cake is delicious served plain, either warm or at room temperature. To garnish with whipped cream, beat the heavy cream until soft peaks form, then add the sugar, liqueur and reserved orange peel, and continue beating until stiff. Present the cream alongside the warm cake. If you wish to ice the cake with it, make sure the cake is thoroughly cold—chill in the refrigerator for 1 hour before icing. Chilling makes the torte cool enough to be covered with the whipped cream, but it somewhat impairs the flavor and texture of the cake itself.

CORIANDER CAKE WITH PECAN TOPPING

This informal cake is first cousin to pound cake and the innumerable Victorian butter cakes. The powdered coriander seed (not to be confused with green coriander leaves, or *cilantro*) gives it an elusive flavor. This cake is so rich with butter that really it is best on its own at teatime or as a special coffeecake for breakfast. Cut the cake while warm or at room temperature; refrigeration causes the butter to congeal.

For one 7- or 8-inch layer:

- 6 tablespoons sweet butter
- 1 cup unbleached white flour
- 1½ to 2 teaspoons ground coriander, depending on its freshness
- ¼ teaspoon salt
- 2 eggs
- 1 cup sugar
- ½ teaspoon vanilla
- ¼ cup milk

FOR THE TOPPING:

- 1 cup pecan halves
- 3 tablespoons butter
- 3 tablespoons sugar
- 1 tablespoon flour
- 1 tablespoon milk

Preheat the oven to 350° F. with a rack in the upper third. Grease and flour a 7- or 8-inch round cake pan. If you plan to serve the cake on a plate, line the pan—a spring-form type if possible—with a circle of waxed paper, but this is not necessary if you serve slices directly from the pan.

Melt the butter and set it aside to cool. Heap a measuring cup with flour, tap it on the table twice, and level off 1 cup with the back of a knife. Mix together the flour, salt and coriander. Set aside.

Beat the eggs in a bowl with an electric mixer until frothy. Add the sugar in a stream, still beating, then increase the speed to high and beat for 3 minutes more. The eggs will turn pale lemony yellow, thicken, and increase substantially in volume. Add the vanilla at low speed.

Add the flour and the milk to the batter alternately, beginning and ending with the flour and beating at lowest speed. Take no more than about 30 seconds to do this and be sure that the flour disappears into the batter before adding the next portion. Scrape down the sides of the bowl with a rubber spatula and beat a second or two more. Carefully fold in the butter with the spatula, working quickly to keep the batter light, but make sure that no floating spots of melted butter remain.

Immediately turn the batter into the prepared cake pan and bake at 350° F. for 30 minutes. The cake is done when it is lightly browned, completely risen, and the center just turned firm.

Prepare the topping when the cake is within 2 or 3 minutes of being done. The pecan halves can be left whole or coarsely chopped in the processor or blender. Mix the pecans and all the remaining ingredients in a small saucepan, bring to the boiling point and quickly spread with a metal spatula over the just-finished cake.

Raise the heat to 425° F., return the cake to the oven and bake 5 minutes more. If the topping is not tinged with brown yet, run the cake under the broiler for a minute or so—but watch it carefully, as pecans scorch easily.

Cool the cake in its pan and serve warm. Like other relatives of pound cake, this one forms a thick, sugary crust around the sides. If you want to show it off, run a knife around the edge of the pan after the cake has cooled for 10 minutes. Turn out upside down on a plate, then immediately flip it back over onto its serving plate—the topping will be none the worse for the experience.

VARIATION:

Spice Cake: Reduce the coriander to 1 teaspoon and add ½ teaspoon cinnamon, ¼ teaspoon nutmeg, and ¼ teaspoon cloves. Stir into the flour at the beginning and omit the pecan topping. Bake in the round pan or in a 9- by 5½-inch loaf pan.

BOILED LEMON CAKE

Anything called "boiled" sounds as if it were dredged up from one of those Victorian cookery manuals written in a time when boiled milk, boiled beef and stewed fruit were considered to be healthy, aesthetic concerns be damned. In fact, this is a rather new recipe, adapted from one published by James Beard in a recent cookbook, *The New James Beard*. His recipe was for an orange and almond cake and began with boiling a whole orange for 30 minutes. This heavy, moist, intensely lemony version is unrelated to Santa Fe traditions, but its tartness is a perfect foil for Mexican cooking. The bitterness of the boiled lemon peel is set off by the cake's whipped-cream topping, or at least with dollops of cream to the side. A garnish of raspberries or blueberries adds a nice touch, but it is not essential.

To recreate James Beard's original, substitute 1 whole navel orange for the lemon and lime called for here, and decrease the sugar to ½ cup.

For 4 to 6 people:

  1 lemon
  1 lime
  Water for boiling fruit
  ¾ cup blanched, slivered almonds
  ⅔ cup sugar
  3 large eggs
  3 tablespoons all-purpose flour
  ⅛ teaspoon salt
  1 teaspoon baking powder

FOR THE TOPPING:

  ¾ cup whipping cream
  Sugar to taste
  ¼ teaspoon vanilla

This recipe makes a single round layer cake 7 or 8 inches in diameter; if you plan to serve more than 6 people, double the recipe and bake the cake as a single layer in a 9- by 13-inch pan—it will take about 1 hour.

Bring 2 quarts or more of water to a boil in a saucepan, and while it is heating, peel away the skins, pith and all, from the lemon and lime. You do this by first quartering the fruits lengthwise, then stripping away the peel with your fingers. It usually takes a small incision with a knife to get the peeling started; otherwise it is easy to accomplish. Discard the lime peel, which can never be boiled enough to remove its bitterness, but keep the lemon peel. Carefully pick the seeds from the lemon and lime flesh. Set aside the flesh of both. Drop the lemon rind into the water and boil for about 20 minutes. If you do not like the bitter taste of lemon oil, change the water and boil again for 10 minutes more. Take out the rind and set it aside.

Preheat the oven to 400° F. Line the cake pan with a circle of waxed paper.

The batter is now mixed in the food-processor bowl in several continuous steps. First, place the almonds and the sugar in the bowl and grind them to a fine powder, stopping at least once to scrape the sides and bottom of the bowl with a rubber spatula; this will take about 2 minutes. Set almonds and sugar aside.

Process the lemon rind with the lemon and lime pulp until they are pureed but still show bits of rind—this might take as little as 15 seconds. Remove to the bowl with the almonds and sugar.

Place the eggs in the processor and mix until frothy. Add the flour, salt and baking powder. Mix for a few seconds only, to incorporate the dry ingredients. Now add the reserved fruit mixture along with the almonds and sugar and process for about 5 seconds to achieve a uniform batter, stopping once to scrape the bowl with a spatula.

Turn the batter into the cake pan and bake for 35 to 45 minutes. The cake is done when it draws away from the sides of the pan and a knife inserted in the middle comes out clean. It may seem done when in fact the center is still mushy, so do not be hasty. It is hard to overcook this batter, and the top usually does not brown. Cool the cake in its pan for 10 minutes and turn it out onto a serving plate.

Whip the cream until stiff and sweeten to taste when halfway done, starting with about 2 tablespoons of sugar. Beat to dissolve the sugar; add the vanilla and finish beating. Top the cake when it is thoroughly cool, or, if time does not permit complete cooling, sprinkle the cake with powdered sugar and present the whipped cream on the side. Because of the cake's bitterness, the cream is more or less a necessity.

DRUNKEN PRUNE CAKE

Even before the planting of orchards, the Indians found wild plums in the countryside around Santa Fe, which the Spanish and later the Anglo pioneers continued to gather and dry into prunes. This delightful cake, whose prune filling is soaked in Madeira and laid on a cushion of pastry cream, comes from Basque cookery. I am not sure any local prune cake was ever made exactly like this, but the *Vascos*, or Basque shepherds, still run sheep throughout the Southwest.

Once the prunes are plumped in wine overnight, there is not much to assembling the cake. Making the orange-flavored custard may seem like extra trouble, but the finished cake is so rich that it needs no icing. Plan to produce this dessert at holiday time in place of English-style fruitcake, for no one is likely to have seen quite its like before.

For 1 large 9-inch cake, serving at least 8 people:

PRUNES AND WINE:

  20 prunes (about 1¼ cups), pitted
  ½ cup Madeira or ruby port (or ½ cup orange juice)

CAKE BATTER:

  3 large eggs
  1 cup sugar
  ¾ cup butter (1½ sticks)
1½ cups unbleached white flour
  2 teaspoons baking powder
  1 fresh orange (grate the peel and set aside, and squeeze the juice—you will need ⅓ cup)
  1 teaspoon vanilla
  ¼ teaspoon nutmeg
Scant ½ teaspoon salt, if the butter is unsalted

CUSTARD:

  ⅓ cup sugar
  1 tablespoon plus 1 teaspoon cornstarch
  ¾ cup scalded milk
  2 egg yolks
Grated orange peel (above)
  1 teaspoon vanilla

Cut the prunes into quarters with kitchen shears, place in a small bowl with the wine, cover and allow to plump at room temperature overnight. If you are short of time, the prunes can be plumped almost as well by setting the covered bowl containing the prunes and wine in a pan of simmering water for 30 to 60 minutes, depending on the dryness of the prunes. (For a cake without wine, plump the prunes in ½ cup fresh orange juice.) Have the prunes at room temperature by baking time, whichever method you choose.

Preheat the oven to 400° F. and place a rack in the middle. Grease and flour a 9-inch springform pan, or a regular 9-inch cake pan at least 2 inches deep, preferably coated with a nonstick surface. (If you are skillful at spreading batter thin—see the assembly procedure below—it is possible to make a 10-inch cake; in that case, reduce baking time to 45 to 50 minutes.)

Cream the eggs, sugar and butter in a food processor for about 15 seconds, stopping once to scrape the bottom and sides of the bowl with a rubber spatula. The butter and sugar may still be grainy, but that is all right. Add the flour, baking powder, orange juice (not the peel), vanilla, nutmeg and optional salt. Process for 5 seconds or just until a smooth batter is reached. Stop at least once to scrape the bowl with a spatula. Set the batter aside in the processor bowl while you make the custard.

For the custard, first mix the sugar and cornstarch together in a small saucepan, then pour in the scalded milk in a steady stream, stirring constantly to prevent lumps. Whisk in the egg yolks and place over low heat. Stir constantly until the custard thickens, but don't let it boil. Be patient and resist the urge to raise the heat—it will take a good 8 or 10 minutes before the custard is as stiff as mayonnaise. Remove from the heat, stir in the grated orange peel and vanilla and set the pan in cold water; beat for a minute to cool the custard.

Assembly and baking: Using an ordinary table knife, spread a scant half of the cake batter in a thin, even layer across the bottom of the prepared cake pan. Drop the custard by spoonfuls all over the surface of the batter and in turn spread it evenly with your knife—but leave a margin of ½ inch around the outside and try not to disturb the cake batter.

Dot the custard layer completely with the prunes and drizzle any remaining wine over. Now form the top layer of batter, dropping it by spoonfuls all over the prunes and spreading as evenly as you can with your knife. Cover the filling well enough so that no prunes are left peeking out.

Level the top, making sure that there is no hump in the center. Bake in the middle of the oven for 50 minutes to 1 hour. Since the outside of the cake cooks much quicker than the center, turn the heat down to 350° F. for the last 15 minutes of baking time to prevent overbaking. The cake is done when the center is risen and browned and the sides drawn away from the pan. Inserting a knife into the middle of the cake is only a rough test. It should not come out heavily coated, for that means the batter is still raw, but it should look moist, since you want the custard to remain soft. Cool the cake in the pan thoroughly, loosen the edges with a knife and remove the outside of the springform. Dust with powdered sugar and keep covered with plastic wrap.

This cake is delicious served plain or with a dollop of whipped cream on the side, perhaps spiked with a teaspoon or so of the same wine that plumped the prunes. The slices are also good slightly rewarmed.

VARIATION:

A simpler Prune Cake with Piñons: If you do not want to bother with the layering and custard making, simply make the batter and plump the quartered prunes as directed. Fold the prunes into the batter, adding the grated peel of 1 orange and 1 cup of shelled piñons or any other chopped nut, and you will have a generic Spanish prune-and-nut cake. Bake in a deep 9-inch round cake pan lined with buttered and floured waxed paper for 50 to 55 minutes. Turn out on a serving plate after the cake cools and dust with powdered sugar. Serve warm or lukewarm with whipped cream on the side. A 10-inch layer would take only about 45 minutes, but either size will be done when the cake draws away from the sides of the pan and a knife inserted into the middle comes out clean.

BUÑUELOS

When bread dough is fried like a fritter and then served with honey or a sweet syrup over it, the preparation is called *buñuelos*. Sometimes this word (and the dough) is used interchangeably with *sopaipillas* (see p. 127), the puffed "sofa pillows" that appear on the menus of all authentic Southwestern restaurants. If you wish, you can adapt the recipe below by using *sopaipilla* dough—since the latter is a quick bread that doesn't require rising, it is made in a fraction of the time as the yeast dough given here. You will still have a perfect right to call your fritters *buñuelos*. (Plan on about 8 to 10 fritters from *sopaipilla* dough based on 1 cup of flour.)

Another extremely delicious base for fritters is the saffron-and-egg bread on p. 140. Such a dough, bathed in wine syrup with raisins (p. 333) would make a very grand batch of *buñuelos* indeed, but the basic dish is more homey, meant to be eaten with pleasure in the heart of one's family.

The recipe below is for fritters with a sweet filling, and they need no further sweetening. The more common practice is to dip the *buñuelos* for a minute in syrup and then serve them up sticky-sweet. For that, see the recipe on p. 333.

For 12 large fritters, serving 4 people:

> 1 package active dry yeast
> ¼ cup warm water
> 1 tablespoon sugar
> 7 tablespoons milk
> 2 tablespoons shortening
> ¼ teaspoon salt
> 1½ cups unbleached all-purpose flour
> Vegetable oil for frying

FOR THE FILLING:

2 tablespoons butter
4 tablespoons brown sugar
3 tablespoons piñons (pine nuts) or almonds
¼ teaspoon cinnamon
Dash powdered cloves

Sprinkle the yeast into a cup that contains the warm water mixed with the sugar and set aside for 10 minutes; the yeast should froth up and smell yeasty. Heat the milk, shortening and salt in a small saucepan until the shortening melts, then set aside to cool to lukewarm. Place the flour in a mixing bowl, add both the yeast and milk mixtures, and stir vigorously with a wooden spoon to incorporate the ingredients.

Turn the dough out onto a lightly floured board and knead heartily for 5 minutes. An easy kneading technique is to push down on the dough with a rocking motion of the heel of one hand, then fold the dough in two and repeat the motion. After rocking and folding for the required period, the dough should be smooth and elastic, not at all sticky against the board, and resilient enough that a dimple poked into it with your finger begins to spring back.

Wash out the mixing bowl and pour a scant ½ teaspoon of oil into it. Roll the ball of dough around in the bowl to coat it with a film of oil, then place the dough inside the bowl. Cover with a piece of foil and set in a warm place (75 to 80° F.) until the dough rises and doubles in bulk. This happens very quickly at 7,000 feet above sea level in Santa Fe, but begin checking after 1 hour. (If you are making the dough a day ahead, allow it to rise overnight in the refrigerator with a plate and at least 2 pounds of canned goods on top to keep it from overflowing. The rising can finish in the morning if need be.)

When you are ready to fry the *buñuelos*, punch the dough down and divide it into 4 pieces, each of which makes 3 fritters.

Combine all the ingredients for the filling in a food processor and blend until smooth, stopping at least once or twice to scrape down the bowl with a rubber spatula.

Heat about an inch of vegetable oil in a skillet or electric wok. Set the temperature at 375° F. or heat until a scrap of dough starts to bubble hard as soon as it hits the oil.

To form the buñuelos: Divide each quarter-portion of dough into 3 pieces. Pat each piece in your hands to make a 4-inch circle, simply stretching and pressing until the shape is roughly formed. Place on a board before you, draw a deep line down the center of the circle with the back of a knife, taking care not to cut through the dough, and spread about a teaspoonful of filling across one side of the circle, but not all the way to the edge. Fold the circles in half, press the edges all around with a fork to seal them and set aside. Repeat with the remaining pieces of dough, then fry the fritters until they puff and brown, a few at a time. This will take about 1 minute or so per side. Drain on paper toweling and keep warm while you finish the batch. Serve immediately, either alone as a snack or perhaps buttered to go with tea or coffee. *Buñuelos* are also good as a simple meal with nothing more elaborate than good cheese on the side.

BUÑUELOS IN SYRUP

This is the traditional way to prepare *buñuelos*, or bread fritters: first fried, then dipped while still warm in a dark syrup of brown sugar, wine and raisins. If making a yeast dough seems like too much trouble for such a homey dessert, by all means use a baking-powder dough instead, such as the one for *sopaipillas* on p. 127. The saffron-egg dough on p. 140 makes fritters of such delicate richness that they should go directly to Paradise, making sure that the beautiful wine syrup comes along.

For 12 buñuelos, serving 4 people:

**Dough from the preceding recipe, or one of the doughs
    suggested above
Vegetable oil for shallow-frying**

WINE SYRUP:

   ⅔ **cup dark brown sugar**
   ½ **cup sweet wine, such as Madeira or Port**
   ½ **cup water**
   ¼ **teaspoon cinnamon**
Grated peel from half a lemon or orange
   ⅓ **cup raisins**

Combine the sugar, wine, water and cinnamon in a saucepan and bring to a boil. Let boil until barely beginning to thicken, about 3 to 5 minutes. Remove from heat, and stir in the grated peel and raisins. Keep warm for pouring over the finished fritters. This syrup can also be used for the *sopaipillas* on p. 334.

Review the procedure for making *buñuelos* outlined in the preceding recipe and follow it in every step, but with these changes: pat out your circles of dough without filling them and proceed directly to frying in the oil, taking about a minute to brown the fritters thoroughly on each side.

Make the entire batch, arrange on a serving tray while piping hot, and pour the warm syrup over. After letting the *buñuelos* soak in the syrup for only a minute, serve as a dessert or at teatime.

STICKY SOFA PILLOWS
Sopaipillas

Little fried breads dropped into syrup are an old-time dessert among the mountain villagers. They usually sweetened their *sopaipillas*, or "sofa pillows," in a caramel syrup spiced with cinnamon, but this version with honey and butter is just as appropriate. You would not think that such a Simon-simple sweet could be so nice, but as long as you keep the bread warm and serve it as soon after dipping as possible, the results are quite satisfying.

Northern New Mexicans traditionally do not eat sweets with their chili dishes, but the combination is complementary, so take Caribbean cooking as your justification, if you need one, and try these sticky sofa pillows with the pork and red chili on p. 270, or with any other very hot meal dish that you like.

For 12 to 16 small pillows:

The dough for *sopaipillas* on p. 128
  2 **tablespoons butter, melted**
¼ **cup honey**
½ **cup sugar and ½ teaspoon cinnamon, mixed together**

The basic procedure for rolling and frying the *sopaipillas* is exactly as given in the main recipe on p. 127. Cut the dough into 2-inch squares, small triangles or oblongs, instead of into larger shapes.

As you are frying, have ready a honey syrup made of the melted butter and the honey mixed together and kept slightly warm. As each pillow is done, dip it into the syrup, turn it to coat the other side and remove immediately.

Now roll the dipped pillow in the cinnamon sugar. Set the dipped and sugared morsels on a plate in a warm place, but do not place them in a hot oven or the sugar will dissolve. Serve at once.

NOTE: Although dipping has to come at the last moment, the actual frying can be done ahead of time; be sure to reheat the *sopaipillas* briefly in a 300° F. oven before dipping.

MADEIRA CREAM PIE

This is one of several desserts to use Madeira, a sweet, buttery wine that was immensely popular in the last century, but now is mostly forgotten as a beverage. The nesselrode-like filling of fruits and nuts also strikes an old-fashioned note. Although the pie itself has no specific connection with the West, it is akin to the kind of rich pastry that pioneer women and their descendants prided themselves on.

For one 9-inch pie, serving 6 people:

Pastry for a single-crust pie (p. 345)
⅓ cup Madeira, preferably a sweet variety like Bual or Malmsey
½ cup raisins
½ cup chopped dates
6 tablespoons unbleached all-purpose flour
⅓ cup sugar
¼ teaspoon salt
2 cups milk, scalded
1 egg plus 2 egg yolks
2 tablespoons butter, cut into 4 pieces
½ cup coarsely chopped pecans
¼ teaspoon cinnamon
½ cup heavy cream whipped with 1½ tablespoons sugar
  and ½ teaspoon vanilla

Preheat the oven to 400° F. Roll out the pastry and fit it into a 9-inch pie pan (measured across the top), making sure that the dough overlaps well onto the margin of the pan. Prick the bottom and sides of the pastry at ½-inch intervals with a fork and chill for 10 minutes. Bake at 400° F. for about 12 minutes, or until the finished shell is crisp and just beginning to color—it should be no darker than blond. (Look in after 5 minutes of baking to see if the sides of the shell are falling down. If so, remove it from the oven and push up the sagging spots with the back of a spoon, then continue the baking.) Set the shell aside to cool.

Heat the Madeira to lukewarm in a small saucepan, then pour over the raisins and dates and set them aside to steep while you make the cream filling.

Mix the flour, sugar and salt well in a 2-quart saucepan, then pour in the scalded milk all at once and stir briskly to combine them. Heat over a medium-low flame, stirring constantly to prevent lumps from forming, until the filling comes to a boil, then let boil slowly for 2 minutes. Remove from heat.

Whisk the egg and egg yolks thoroughly in a measuring cup, then rapidly stir them into the boiled filling. Return to heat and cook, stirring constantly, until thickened—about 2 minutes—but do not boil. Remove from the heat and stir in the butter, then add the pecans and cinnamon, along with the fruits and their wine.

Pour the filling into the baked shell and chill for at least 2 hours. The filling must be thoroughly chilled or it will run when the pie is cut.

Just before serving, whip the cream until thickened but not yet stiff, add the sugar and vanilla, then finish whipping until the cream holds stiff peaks. Spread in a thin layer over the surface of the pie and chill until serving time. (The whipped-cream topping will hold its shape under refrigeration for a few hours at most, after which it begins to separate.) You can decorate the center of the pie with a few pecan halves and raisins if you like.

"SPANISH PIE" WITH PUMPKIN FILLING

A pie becomes Spanish, at least in Santa Fe, when it is a thin, double-crusted disk filled with a scant half-inch of fruit—in this case a puree of candied pumpkin. The amount of dough called for below will make a lovely 10-inch pastry. If you are not yet confident about your ability to work with such large circles of fragile dough, cut the dough into about 16 smaller circles and make pumpkin *empanadas* (p. 338).

Unlike the similar pie filled with turkey on p. 160, this sweet version is shaped directly on the baking sheet, which is less complicated than working with a flan ring. I urge you to try this kind of pie, for the tender crust and intensely candied filling are very different from any other American pastry. If you become enthusiastic about "Spanish pie," see the list of alternative fillings on p. 347. Any of them will do beautifully for either the large pie or the small *empanadas*. Allow about 1½ cups of filling for either method.

For one 10-inch pie or about 16 empanadas:

PUMPKIN FILLING:

 2 tablespoons butter
 1 cup dark brown sugar
 1 cup pumpkin puree, fresh or canned
   (but not presweetened pumpkin pie filling)
 1 teaspoon cinnamon
 ⅛ teaspoon powdered cloves
Grated peel of half an orange
Chilled pastry for a double-crust pie from p. 343
Egg wash made of 1 egg whisked with 1 teaspoon water
Cinnamon sugar (about ¼ cup), using ½ to 1 teaspoon cinnamon

Melt the butter in a small saucepan and stir in the brown sugar. Allow to heat for a few minutes, then stir in the pumpkin and the spices. Stir over medium heat until enough water evaporates from the pumpkin to make it stiff enough to hold its shape well when a bit is picked up in a spoon—about 3 to 5 minutes. Remove from heat and stir in the grated orange peel. Cool completely in the refrigerator before filling the pie.

Assembling the pie: Divide the pastry into two portions, refrigerating one while you roll out the other. Roll out the first part into an 11-inch circle. Transfer the circle to a baking sheet by folding it into quarters, gently lifting it with your hand or a broad spatula underneath for support, and then just as gently unfolding it on the sheet. (Refrigerate for 5 minutes if the pastry seems soft and warm.) Spoon a thin, even layer of the cooled pumpkin filling over, using a cake spatula or a broad knife. Leave a ½-inch margin all around.

Refrigerate this first circle while you roll the second part of the dough into another 11-inch circle. Once again fold it up into quarters and gently unfold it on top of the filled bottom circle of dough.

This is the only point where a mishap might occur. If the top circle rips in transit, re-form the dough into a ball, chill if necessary, and roll again. If it splits upon touching the filling, try to draw it together; a few tears can always be masked with sugar after baking. If you want to eliminate the danger of tearing your pastry altogether, consult the directions for the Spanish turkey pie on p. 160 shaped with wedges of top crust.

Gently press the two layers of pastry together all around the edge, then follow up with a crimped border by pinching edges together all around with your thumb and forefinger. Glaze the top of the pie with egg wash, allow to dry for a few minutes, and brush again with a second wash.

Chill the pie once more while the oven preheats to 425° F. Place a rack in the upper third. Bake the pie for 25 minutes, or until lightly browned.

You can then finish it in one of several ways: either remove from the oven when the baking has 5 minutes to go, brush again with egg wash, dust heavily with cinnamon sugar and return to the oven, or sprinkle with sugar after the pie is baked; or leave plain and unsugared. Serve the pie warm or tepid, but not cold, cut into large wedges. Even a big circle of this size feeds only about 6 people.

VARIATION:

Pumpkin Empanadas: Divide the dough in half and cut out each part into about 8 small circles, 4 inches across. Fill with a generous tablespoon of filling. Fold each circle into a half-moon, press the edges into a crimped border and wash with egg glaze. Bake in a 425° F. oven for about 15 minutes, or until nicely browned. Sprinkle the cooled *empanadas* with cinnamon sugar and allow 3 or 4 per person. Be sure to see p. 347 for alternate fillings. The *empanaditas* of Christmas should be in the repertoire of any Santa Fe cook.

LEMON-CHEESE TART
Quesadilla

As defined in modern Mexican cookbooks or on restaurant menus, a *quesadilla* is a baked or fried flour tortilla stuffed with cheese. An earlier generation of New Mexican cooks also applied the word to a puffy cheese tart, sometimes sweet, sometimes savory. Both usages appear in this book, but the possibility for confusion is lessened by the fact that the tart version I give here is a dessert, so its relationship to any appetizer is fairly remote. Besides being moderately sweet, this *quesadilla* is flavored with lemon, giving it a fruity tartness that is very welcome after a typical Southwestern meal.

The ingredients in the filling do not differ very much from those in a conventional cheesecake, but the texture of the cooked product is quite different—lighter and impeccably smooth. As baked by hill-country cooks in the Santa Fe area, such tarts no doubt were more rustic than this, and the use of sheep or goat cheese instead of cow cheese imparted an unusual basic taste—not what we are used to in a dessert. Another detail worth noting is that unlike other versions of puffy cheese tarts I have tried, this one sinks very little as it cools.

For 6 people:

Pastry for a 9- or 10-inch pie shell
   2 cups large-curd cottage cheese
   3 ounces cream cheese
   1 large egg plus 2 yolks
   1 cup sugar
   2 tablespoons flour
 ⅛ teaspoon salt
Scant ⅛ teaspoon nutmeg
Grated peel and juice of 1 lemon, plus extra juice (if needed) to
   make 6 tablespoons
 ½ cup whipping cream
   2 egg whites

Roll out the pastry to fit a 9- or 10-inch pie pan, measured across the top, making sure that the pan is deep enough to accommodate a large amount of filling—about as much as for a deep-dish apple pie. The pastry shell will be filled to the rim with the cheese batter, which will puff as it bakes but will not overflow. Place the pastry-lined pan in the refrigerator while you prepare the filling, allowing at least 15 minutes for it to rest.

Preheat the oven to 350° F. with a rack set in the upper third.

Place the cottage cheese and cream cheese in a food processor or blender and puree until quite smooth, about 3 minutes. If your machine clogs up or does not run smoothly, add the whole egg at this time to make the mixture less stiff. Taste the pureed cheeses to make sure that there is no trace of a grainy texture, then add the egg (if you have not already done so), the egg yolks, sugar, flour, salt and nutmeg. Process to blend them in, stopping once or twice to scrape down the sides of the bowl or blender jar with a rubber spatula. With the machine still running, add the lemon peel, lemon juice and cream. Continue processing until the filling is uniformly smooth, stopping to scrape down the bowl as needed.

Using a portable mixer or a hand whisk, beat the egg whites in a small, narrow-sided bowl of 6- to 8-cup capacity until soft peaks are formed. Continue beating a little further but not so much that the whites dry out or lose their glossy finish. Pour the cheese mixture over the beaten whites, then fold them in with a rubber spatula, working rapidly and deftly so that you lose a minimum of fluffiness. Since the filling is fairly liquid, be sure to reach your spatula to the very bottom of the bowl, lifting up the part of the filling that tends to remain under the floating egg whites.

When you are satisfied that the whites are thoroughly incorporated, pour the filling into the reserved pie shell. This amount of filling nearly overflows many pans, so it may be easier to fill the shell after you have placed it on the oven rack. Bake at 350° F. for 1 hour, or until the tart is puffed, lightly browned, and shows no jiggling in the middle. It can also be tested by lightly pressing your finger in the center, which should feel firm and not wobbly to the touch.

Serve warm or at room temperature, not chilled. Leftovers may be refrigerated without changing the taste or texture, but they should be brought back to room temperature before serving.

I find that the delicate taste of this dessert stands out best when it is presented alone, but if you like to garnish cheesecake with crushed straw-berries or pineapple, these go very well with *quesadilla* also.

ALMOND CHESS PIE

Chess pies are meant for keeping (the name may be a variant on "chest pie"), which they do without refrigeration because the high sugar content of the filling causes a crisp, sugary insulating crust to form as the pie bakes. Practically unknown today outside the South, these pies traveled every-where with pioneer women in the last century. One recipe that won ribbons at the New Mexico state fair in the 1950s was unaltered from an original written out in Kentucky in 1829.

The version given here does not taste like an antique—it is fully as good as pecan pie and even sweeter. (If you want to try the full dose of sugar, which also produces a thicker crust, increase the amount to 2 cups.) The addition of almonds is not traditional, but without it the pie tastes of sugar and not much else. Since this rich pie is served in small portions, one 9-inch pie can serve 8 to 10 guests.

For one 9-inch pie:

> Pastry for a 9-inch pie, based on 1½ cups of flour and 8 tablespoons
>   of shortening (see pp. 344–45)
> 3 extra large eggs or 4 large
> 1½ cups sugar
> 1 tablespoon white or yellow cornmeal
> ¼ teaspoon salt
> ¼ teaspoon almond extract
> ½ teaspoon vanilla
> 4 tablespoons sweet butter (if salted butter is substituted,
>   omit the salt above)
> ⅓ cup buttermilk (or 5 tablespoons milk mixed with 1 tablespoon
>   lemon juice)
> ½ cup (about 2 ounces) almond slices
> Optional: sweetened whipped cream for garnish

Preheat the oven to 300° F.

Roll out the pastry and fit it into a 9-inch pie pan (measured across the top). Use a fairly deep pan suitable for deep-dish fruit pies so that the filling, which swells as it bakes and then sinks as it cools, does not overflow. Crimp a decorative edge around the shell and set aside in the refrigerator while you prepare the filling.

Mix the eggs and the next 5 ingredients with an electric mixer (or a vigorous hand whisk) until they are well blended. It is not necessary to beat so long that the sugar dissolves, since you are after a sugar crust on the finished pie.

Melt the butter in a small pan, remove from heat and pour the buttermilk in. Blend into the filling with the mixer at low speed for about a minute to make sure the filling is homogeneous. Beat in the almond slices at lowest speed.

Pour the filling into the pastry shell and bake at 300° F. for about 1 hour. You will not be able to test the center for doneness without cracking the sugar crust, but the crust and the pastry should be browned. If experience with your oven makes you suspect that the center is not set (it may also look sunken), bake another 10 minutes. Cool at room temperature.

Serve the pie tepid or cool—not cold—in small wedges. Garnish with lightly sweetened whipped cream if you wish to cut the pie's sugariness.

VARIATIONS:

Pecan Chess Pie: The basic recipe is first cousin to pecan pie, a favorite in the nut-growing areas of New Mexico, as it is in Texas. To convert it into a pecan pie, substitute 1 cup dark corn syrup for ½ cup of the sugar, 1½ cups whole pecan halves for the almonds, and eliminate the almond extract. Bake at 350° F. Watch the baking time so that the pecans do not over-brown, checking for doneness after 45 to 50 minutes.

Walnut Chess Pie: Follow the first variation but use walnut halves in place of the pecans. Replacing the buttermilk with ⅓ cup walnut cream liqueur would add a sumptuous note.

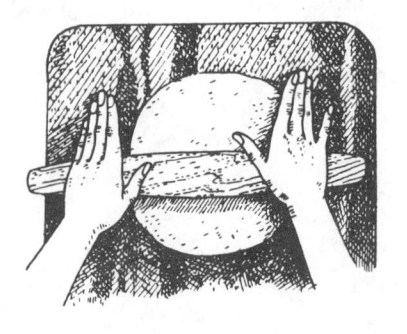

"TRANSPARENT" PIE

This, too, is a chess pie, due to its sweetness and good keeping potential. Even when chess pies contained cream and looked opaque, the old cooks were apt to call them "transparent" pies. This small one, just the right size for four people in the mood, does at least look translucent, rather like a nutless Southern pecan pie.

For 4 people:

> Pastry for a 9-inch pie (measured across the top) using 1¼ cups
> flour and 6 tablespoons shortening
> 4 large eggs
> 1 cup sugar
> ⅓ cup light corn syrup
> 1 stick (4 ounces) sweet butter, melted and set aside to cool
> ½ teaspoon vanilla
> Scant ¼ teaspoon salt
> 1 tablespoon yellow or white cornmeal
> 1 tablespoon white or cider vinegar

Preheat oven to 400° F.

Roll out the pastry to fit into a 9-inch pie pan, crimp a border around its edges and set aside in the refrigerator while you prepare the filling.

Using an electric beater or beating with a whisk, add all the ingredients listed in order. Make sure that the eggs are thoroughly beaten, that the sugar is well incorporated, and so on. The process of making a smooth filling will take you only 2 or 3 minutes. It is also possible to mix the filling in a food processor, but it tends to splash about a bit too much.

Pour the filling into the reserved pie shell, place in either the lower third or the middle of the oven, and bake for 15 minutes at 400° F. Turn heat down to 350° F. and bake 15 minutes more. The pie filling should be well puffed and browned, the crust a pale tan. If after half an hour the filling is still sunken or liquid in the middle, continue to bake until it is set, but do not cook so thoroughly that the edges have begun to dry out. The pie is cooked enough even if the center jiggles slightly, as long as it has risen.

Cool to room temperature and serve, garnished with whipped cream if you desire. Chess pies taste best if they are not refrigerated.

VARIATIONS:

Lemon Transparent Pie: The pie above was also known as "vinegar pie." Its rusticity is lost when you substitute 2 tablespoons of lemon juice for the vinegar and add the grated rind of a fresh lemon. You will, however, have made a good pie in itself—a lemon chess pie.

Not-Transparent Pie: Substitute brown sugar for the white, and honey for the corn syrup. This one will be decidedly opaque, but still good.

DOUBLE-CRUST PASTRY

The quantity of pastry given below will make enough dough for one double-crust tart measuring 8 or 9 inches (or the flat 10-inch "Spanish pie" on p. 336). Besides being very quick to produce in a food processor, it does not require a cool kitchen. The dough is handled so briefly that even the high butter content presents no problem. Work quickly, never pressing the pastry with the palm of your hand, and the dough will remain cool even if you are roasting meats or boiling pinto beans in a small kitchen. Unlike the usual processor recipes, this does not require frozen butter, because the metal blade of the machine does not work long enough to heat up.

For one 8- or 9-inch double-crust pie:

1 large egg
1 tablespoon cold water
2 cups unbleached flour
1 teaspoon salt
7 tablespoons cold butter, cut into 5 pieces
3 tablespoons cold lard or vegetable shortening

Whisk together the egg and water and set aside.

Place all the other ingredients in the processor bowl and blend until a uniform meal is produced—about 8 seconds—stopping once to scrape the bottom and sides of the bowl with a rubber spatula. Turn off the machine, remove its cover, and pour in the egg and water. Process for 3 seconds more, scrape down the bowl and process for another 3 seconds. The dough should be uniformly moistened, but not nearly so processed that it has begun to draw together into a mass.

Place mixture in a mixing bowl and work the dough into a mass with twisting motions of the knuckles of a fist. By using 5 or 6 twisting motions, then turning the dough over in the bowl and giving it 3 or 4 more thrusts, you should achieve a mass, fairly moist but not at all wet, with some unincorporated bits still lying around. Place the massed dough and the bits in a plastic bag or plastic wrap and chill in the refrigerator for 30 minutes, or until the dough is needed. Pat the mass into a flat disk after it is in the bag to hasten the cooling process.

Even with the egg added as a reinforcement, this is quite a fragile dough. If it cracks when you attempt to roll it out (a common occurrence when the dough is well chilled) let it rest at room temperature for a few minutes. Or crumble the pastry back into the processor bowl, sprinkle 2 teaspoons of water over and blend for 5 or 8 seconds. This will give it enough extra cohesion to handle well.

SINGLE-CRUST LARD PASTRY

Lard is far and away the most authentic traditional shortening for "Spanish pies," *empanaditas* and the pies of every stripe made by pioneer women. Although this is not meant as a historical cookbook, I would here like to point out some virtues, besides its ready availability, that all those generations of Indian, Spanish and American cooks saw in lard.

Flaky pastries made from butter are both fine and fragile. Too much hand contact warms them up beyond the point where they are firm enough to manipulate easily, and even a moderately warm kitchen will reduce them to pasty oiliness in short order. Lard has none of these problems. Although you do chill a lard dough, it can be handled without undue concern. It rolls out stiffly, once cooled, since lard as an animal fat congeals to a stiffer texture than other shortenings, but the stiffness is not transmitted to the cooked product. As long as it is not cold, lard pastry is quite tender.

The second benefit is that lard pastry does not easily absorb liquid from the filling placed over it. A chess pie, whose liquid filling often soaks the bottom crust into mush, cannot harm a lard crust—hence all the Southern recipes for pecan pie that inevitably leave butter out of the pastry dough (although a good flaky crust can be made mixing lard and butter).

The drawback to lard pastry in our age of cholesterol fears is obvious, however. A lard pastry also coats the roof of the mouth with an unmistakable film. All that aside, such pastry is worth making once for nothing more than the experience of handling a dough that works and acts entirely unlike fine butter pastry.

For a single-crust 9-inch pie:

   1¼ cups unbleached all-purpose flour
   ½ teaspoon salt
   1 teaspoon sugar
   6 tablespoons lard
   3 to 4 tablespoons cold water

Because lard pastry is a relatively tough product, you do not have to worry about ingredient temperatures as much as when a finer shortening is used. The lard should be kept refrigerated and the water should come from the cold tap—no ice water is necessary.

Place all ingredients but the water in a food processor and reduce to a flaky meal by using 6 to 10 fast bursts. With the machine off, remove the top from the processor bowl. Sprinkle 2 tablespoons water over the mixture and once again give it 3 or 4 bursts, just enough to distribute the water evenly. Add extra water, a tablespoon at a time, if needed. Do not attempt to make the mixture look like a cohesive dough yet, or process it long enough to form a ball, but there should be no dry flour left.

Scrape dough into a medium mixing bowl and work it with the knuckles of your fist until a crumbly pastry forms. Use quick, jabbing twists, for you are trying to form flakes of lard and flour, not a homogeneous mass. After the dough begins to draw together, wrap it in plastic wrap and refrigerate ½ hour to allow the dough to relax and absorb moisture. A dough that still looks completely crumbly may need a teaspoon or so of cold water sprinkled over it, but no more. Once chilled, the dough is ready to be formed into a ball and rolled out as usual.

VARIATION:

Lard-and-Butter Pastry: In place of 6 tablespoons lard, use 4 tablespoons butter and only 2 of lard. This is the everyday pastry I have used for a decade.

LITTLE PIES WITH PEACH BUTTER AND PIÑONS

Under the Spanish name of *empanaditas,* little pies appear as one of the choicest delights of Christmas. Under the English name of "fried pies," they sound heavy and dull, which has banished them from American cooking outside the most unregenerate regions of the South. In truth, the frying in half an inch of oil leaves the turnovers light and flaky, particularly if the oil is hot enough to prevent it from soaking into the pie dough. The filling in this recipe calls for peach butter and piñon nuts, giving a marvelous intensity of fruit, but any of the sweet filling listed on p. 347 would also do very well. The most traditional filling in northern New Mexico is probably dried fruit, especially apples, which have been softened in water.

For 16 turnovers:

PASTRY DOUGH:

- 2 cups flour
- ½ teaspoon baking powder
- ½ teaspoon salt
- ¼ teaspoon cloves
- ½ teaspoon cinnamon
- 2 teaspoons sugar
- 6 tablespoons lard, cut into 12 pieces (or 4 tablespoons butter and 2 tablespoons lard or vegetable shortening)
- 6 tablespoons cold water

FILLING:

- ½ cup shelled *piñons* (pine nuts) or blanched almonds
- ¼ cup peach butter (or apple butter)
- Grated peel of half a lemon
- ¼ cup dark brown sugar
- Vegetable oil for shallow frying
- Powdered sugar

Place all the pastry ingredients except the water in the bowl of the food processor and blend until a coarse meal is achieved—about 5 seconds or so. Stop the machine, add the water by sprinkling it around the surface of the flour mixture and process a few seconds more to incorporate it, but not long enough to form a ball. Pour the dough into a bowl and press it with twisting jabs of your knuckles until it draws together into a mass. Turn the mass over and repeat. Place the ball of dough into a plastic bag and chill while you make the filling.

Place all the ingredients for the filling in the food processor and blend until a chunky, amalgamated texture is reached, about 5 seconds, stopping once to scrape down the bowl with a rubber spatula. The filling is most appealing when the piñons retain a definite texture.

Rolling and frying the empanaditas: Cut the chilled dough in half, then cut each half in half again. Each of these quarter portions will make 4 turnovers. Place the dough you are not working on back in the plastic bag and cut the portion in front of you into 4 pieces. Roll each piece out on a floured board to a 3-inch circle, cutting it precisely, if you like, with a doughnut or biscuit cutter. Place a good teaspoon of filling in the middle of the circle, moisten the edge all around with a forefinger dipped in water, and fold the circle into a half-moon shape. Crimp the edge by pressing along it with a fork; turn the *empanadita* over and crimp again. Set the finished turnover aside and roll out 3 more in the same fashion.

Pour a good ½ inch of oil into a skillet or electric wok and heat it to 375° or until a scrap of dough bubbles quite hard as soon as it lands in the oil. If the oil starts to smoke, it is too hot. Drop in the turnovers and fry until they are brown on both sides—this will take from 2 to 4 minutes. Drain the browned pastries on paper toweling, cool briefly, and sprinkle with powdered sugar, using either a fine sieve or a flour sifter. Rolling and frying the whole batch of 16, which is enough for 3 or 4 people, takes about 30 minutes once you are organized, since you can roll out one batch while the preceding one is frying. Serve warm or tepid as a dessert.

These little pies are best served soon after making, but they keep fairly well at room temperature if you must make them ahead. Rewarm before serving.

VARIATION:

Baked Empanaditas: Frying these little pies appears to be more common in the Southwest than in Mexico, where they are customarily baked. Make all the turnovers and place them on a cookie sheet. Brush with an egg wash made of 1 egg beaten well with 1 teaspoon milk. Bake in a 375° F. oven until browned, about 15 to 20 minutes. Dust with powdered or granulated sugar as above.

SWEET FILLINGS

Santa Fe cooks use sweet fillings for their baked turnovers called *empanadas,* or for the smaller, choicer ones, often deep-fried, which are given the diminutive name *empanaditas.* Any of the fillings below will also do very nicely for the Spanish style of round double-crusted tart. Finally, if you are fairly adventurous and have looked into sweet *tamales,* feel free to fill them with these alternative stuffings, too.

Dried apples, nuts and raisins are the most authentic sweet fillings, followed by candied fruit, various preserves and conserved fruit such as the candied pumpkin filling on p. 337. The use of apple or peach butter, as on p. 346, is associated in my mind with pioneer women cooks, but of course they had orchard fruits and nuts, too. Some of the most curious among them might have even known that candied pumpkin came down from the original Indians in New Spain. Experiment with various combinations, but fillings which are particular to one dish, such as the almond-custard filling for chess pie on p. 340, are probably best left for that use.

I have not given proportions for the ingredients because, being a matter of the cook's preferences, none of these fillings needs exact proportions. The overall amount you will need is also variable, ranging from a bare teaspoon for each tiny *empanadita* to over a cup for a large "Spanish pie."

Dried Apples with Nuts and Raisins: The old mountain cooks plumped their winter-stored dried apples in hot water, but you can let store-bought dried apples sit for a few hours in rum or a sweet wine like Madeira. Chop them fine or coarse and mix in raisins and piñons (or almonds). The filling is now ready or it can be improved with a little ground cinnamon, clove and grated peel of fresh lemon or orange. Sometimes this filling was stewed for 30 to 45 minutes (and cooled) before use.

Candied Fruit Filling: Use good-quality candied fruit of one kind, such as cherries, citron or pineapple, avoiding the chopped confetti mixes sold in the supermarkets, and plump in hot water (or substitute a few table-spoons of rum or brandy if you like) for an hour or two. If the candied fruit is well made and the liquor is pure in taste, there is no need for any-thing else. Mixing pineapple and coconut with rum during the plumping process is particularly nice.

Coconut and Brown Sugar: Mash together some flaked or fresh coconut with brown sugar. Moisten with lime juice and a little honey, then flavor to taste with powdered ginger. Like most of the other fillings, this is a wintertime preparation, but it is distinctly tropical compared to dried apples or pears.

Apricot Preserves and Almonds: Heat some apricot jam until it melts, and then stir in finely ground blanched almonds. The mixture should be thick enough to hold its shape in a spoon. Flavor with almond extract, cinnamon or perhaps some grated orange rind, adding only a trace at a time.

ANISEED COOKIES
Bizcochitos

Aniseed cookies are traditional for Christmas in New Mexico. Like other preparations that appear nowhere else in the country, they have an antique European air, this time of a very old style of seed cookie. Tradi-tionally, the shortening employed is lard, which the cook whips as light as cream with her hands. The recipe below calls for several alternate shortenings. Substituting butter or margarine, while not authentic, would be more delicious. In texture, *bizcochitos* fall halfway between sugar cookies and shortbread. New Mexican children expect their cookies to be cut into fancy shapes, the favorite being a fleur-de-lis, or iris, but round *bizcochitos* are also common.

For 2 dozen cookies:

½ cup vegetable shortening, lard, or unsalted butter or margarine
⅔ cup sugar
1 egg
1 teaspoon aniseed (or ⅛ teaspoon anise extract)
1 tablespoon brandy
1½ cups unbleached all-purpose flour
1 teaspoon baking powder
¼ teaspoon salt
¼ cup sugar mixed with ¼ teaspoon cinnamon for dredging

Preheat the oven to 350° F. and have 2 ungreased cookie sheets ready. Combine the first 5 ingredients in the food processor and blend until the shortening and sugar are creamed, about 5 to 10 seconds, stopping once to scrape down the bowl with a rubber spatula. With a fork, mix the flour, baking powder and salt in a mixing bowl. Still using the fork, add the shortening mixture from the processor and keep blending until no loose flour appears in the bowl and the cookie dough begins to draw into a mass.

At this point, you can either pat out 2½-inch rounds, just under ¼ inch thick, or you can chill the dough for 15 minutes and then roll it out on a lightly floured board with a rolling pin. Rolling out enables you to cut fancy shapes if you like. A quick method is to place a tablespoon of dough on the board and flatten it into a circle with the bottom of a glass or cup.

However you shape them, dredge one side of the *bizcochitos* in the cinnamon sugar and arrange close together with the sugared side up. Bake 10 minutes at 350° F., or until the cookies turn a pale blond. Cool for 5 minutes in the pans, then transfer to a cooling rack. Cookies cut thicker than ¼ inch will be softer, once baked, than thin cookies. The dough can also be baked at 375° F. for 15 minutes, in which case the cookies will be browned and crisp. Store in a cookie jar or paper bag, where they will keep for at least a week.

PUMPKIN COOKIES

The Pueblo bakers are known for their sweet pumpkin bread, which is so similar to the quick breads found in standard American cookbooks that one wonders if they have borrowed from pioneer cooks. Baked as cookies instead of a loaf, the batter makes soft mounds like free-standing muffins—

and, in fact, you can butter them and eat them as hot, sweet muffins if you like. Here they are iced with a simple sugar-and-milk glaze, a touch that no child could resist.

For 24 cookies, each about 3 inches across:

    ½ **cup honey**
    ⅔ **cup brown sugar**
    ¾ **cup butter (1½ sticks), cut into small chunks**
    1 **cup solid-pack canned pumpkin, unsweetened**
    2 **teaspoons baking soda**
    1 **teaspoon salt**
    ½ **teaspoon ground cinnamon**
    ½ **teaspoon grated nutmeg**
    ¼ **teaspoon ground cloves**
    1 **teaspoon vanilla**
Grated rind of 1 orange
    2 **large eggs**
    2 **cups flour**
    ⅔ **cup raisins**

FOR THE GLAZE:

    1 **cup powdered sugar**
    2 **tablespoons milk**
Few drops vanilla
Dash cinnamon
    24 **to 48 pecan halves**

Preheat the oven to 375° F. and lightly grease two baking sheets if they are not the nonstick kind.

Combine all the dough ingredients but the flour in the bowl of a food processor or an electric mixer. Blend until a smooth batter is formed, about 15 seconds, stopping once to scrape down the bowl with a rubber spatula. Add a cup of the flour and blend for a second or two, then add the remaining cup and process for 3 to 5 seconds to blend, stopping once to scrape the bowl again. Stop when the batter is just mixed, or it will toughen. Add the raisins with a few short pulses or stir them in by hand.

Drop the cookie dough by large tablespoonfuls onto the baking sheets, spacing them close together but not touching. Bake at 375° F. for 12 to 15 minutes. The cookies will be springy to the touch, lightly browned underneath and just colored on top. Cool thoroughly.

Mix together all the ingredients for the glaze except the pecans. Drizzle by spoonfuls over the barely warm cookies, and press 1 or 2 pecan halves firmly onto the glaze of each.

PIÑON TILES

The wonderful, lacy cookies called *tuiles*, "roof tiles," are usually made in Europe with almonds, but they adapt perfectly to New Mexico piñons (pine nuts), giving you a crisp accent to go with creamy-soft desserts like the soft custard, *natillas*, on p. 353. These cookies must be handled very delicately during the moment when you shape them into tiles, but you can skip that part and leave them flat if you like. (Santa Fe, as it happens, was built with flat adobe roofs anyway, not the curved red tiles of Spain or Mexico.) The tiles are best lifted off cookie sheets lined with a nonstick surface like Silverstone or Teflon II, since even the least sticking will cause them to rip.

For 2 dozen cookies:

> 6 tablespoons sweet butter, cut into 12 pieces
> ½ cup sugar
> 2 egg whites
> ⅓ cup flour
> Dash of salt, if the piñons are not salty already
> Grated peel of one lemon
> 1 cup shelled piñons

Preheat the oven to 400° F. and butter 2 nonstick cookie sheets.

Place the butter, sugar, egg whites, salt, flour and lemon peel in the bowl of the food processor, along with ½ cup of the nuts. Process for about 10 seconds until a batter is formed, stopping once to scrape down the bowl with a rubber spatula. Add the remaining ½ cup of piñons and blend just a second or two to incorporate.

Drop the batter by teaspoonfuls about 1½ inches apart onto the baking sheets—this amount of batter should yield 24 cookies. Bake at 400° F. for 8 to 10 minutes, or just until the edges of the tiles are golden brown but the centers remain uncolored. Remove from the oven and let cool for about 2 to 3 minutes. The tiles should be firm enough to lift up without ripping, but still flexible enough to curve into tile shapes. (If you have had no experience with tile cookies, bake only half a batch at one time so that you will have leisure to form the shapes.) To form the tiles, bend each cookie over a rolling pin, let it cool for a few seconds, and then transfer to a cooling rack. If the tiles begin to crack at any point, leave them flat. Serve alone with tea, coffee or the Mexican chocolate on p. 372, or as an accompaniment to *natillas* (p. 353). The tiles store well in a paper bag once they are thoroughly cooled.

NEW MEXICO PRALINES

Like Creole pralines and Texas pralines, the New Mexico version indicates the presence of commercial pecan orchards in the southern part of the state—one also sees the name "Las Cruces pralines" in tribute to a town where such orchards are abundant. Unlike Mexico, where there exists a variety of *dulces*, or candy, the one invariably referred to in New Mexico is this one. New Mexico pralines are so sweet that one needs but one or two after a meal, accompanied with strong coffee. An interesting note is that experienced eaters consider sweetness to be the best antidote for hot chilies.

Praline candy is boiled to the same point as fudge, but it does not need beating to make it harden. Use a candy thermometer to determine when the hot batter has cooled to about 200° F., and then drop puddles of it onto waxed paper. The thin praline patties will attain their proper consistency as soon as they cool completely.

For 2 dozen candies:

>   1 cup sugar
> ½ cup dark brown sugar
> Dash salt
>   1 tablespoon corn syrup
>   3 tablespoons butter
> ½ cup milk
>   2 cups pecan halves
> ½ teaspoon vanilla

Combine the first 6 ingredients in a 2-quart saucepan and stir over low heat until the mixture is about to come to a boil. Be patient in your stirring, as the sugar has to be dissolved and incorporated into the rest. Stir for a good 2 minutes when the candy is near the boil, then cover the pan and boil gently for 3 more minutes. Uncover the pan, insert a candy thermometer and allow to cook slowly until a soft ball is reached (250° F.).

Remove the pan from the heat and let sit undisturbed until the thermometer drops to 200° F.—the batter should be as thick as honey. Remove the thermometer, stir in the pecans and the vanilla and drop the batter by tablespoonfuls onto waxed paper. You will need several square feet of paper, for the batter puddles and spreads into thin patties. (For chunky pralines, allow the temperature to drop to 175° F. before adding the nuts.)

Allow the candy to cool thoroughly, after which it can be stored at room temperature in a closed container. If you plan to store the pralines for any period, wrap them individually in plastic wrap.

SOFT CUSTARD
Natillas

Hispanic cooks love to make custards, but in the desolate reaches of
New Mexico, where eggs and milk once were scarce, the local custard,
natillas, was often based on canned, evaporated milk thickened with flour.
In the standard recipe, egg whites were folded into the custard, but the
version here is based on another traditional New Mexican technique—the
custard is poured over dollops of poached egg white, very much like
the French floating island. In deference to the newfound prosperity of
Santa Fe, the custard has a full complement of milk, cream, and eggs.

For 4 people:

THE POACHED EGG WHITES

    4 egg whites
Dash salt
½ cup sugar

THE CUSTARD:

    4 teaspoons cornstarch
½ cup sugar
⅛ teaspoon cinnamon
Dash nutmeg
    4 egg yolks
    2 cups milk, scalded
½ cup light cream
    1 teaspoon vanilla
Powdered sugar for glazing

The procedure for making these *natillas* is first to poach the egg whites
in simmering water, then make the egg custard separately and glaze the
assembled pudding under a hot broiler. Place the egg whites in a bowl
with the salt, whip with an electric mixer until soft peaks are reached,
then gradually sprinkle on the ½ cup sugar, still whipping, until glossy,
stiff peaks are reached and the sugar is dissolved.

Bring 1 inch of water to a boil in a wide, shallow frying pan, and turn
the heat down so that the water simmers with only an occasional bubble
breaking the surface. Drop the egg whites into the water by large dollops.
They will swell and poach in a minute or two. Turn them over if they are
large enough to need poaching on both sides. Drain on paper toweling.
You will have to make two batches if you are using a 10- or 12-inch skillet.

To make the custard, mix the cornstarch, sugar, cinnamon and nutmeg in a bowl, add the egg yolks and beat at low speed with a portable electric mixer. Gradually pour in the scalded milk, blend thoroughly and add the light cream. Pour the custard into a small saucepan and heat, stirring, over low heat. The custard will take about 8 to 10 minutes to thicken. The custard has to cook until the starch loses its raw taste—but do not try to hurry the process by turning up the heat—the custard should not boil. Remove from heat and add the vanilla.

Assembling the pudding: Carefully place the drained egg whites in a shallow baking dish from which you can serve the *natillas*. Pour the egg custard over and chill in the refrigerator for at least 2 hours. When you are ready to serve, sprinkle the entire surface with powdered sugar from a sieve, run the pudding close to the heat under a hot broiler to brown the peaks and as much of the rest of the sugar as you can, and serve. As an accompaniment, the crisp piñon cookies on p. 351 are lovely with this bland, soft and delightful dessert.

VARIATION:

For Natillas Without Starch: Soft custards are, in truth, much better if they are not thickened with starch. Omit the cornstarch from the custard mixture and increase the egg yolks to 6 or 7. Cook over low heat as in the basic recipe, making sure that the eggs really thicken enough to coat a spoon well, but do not allow the custard to come near the boil (no more than 175° F. on a candy thermometer).

BREAD PUDDING WITH WINE AND CHEESE
Capirotada

The New Mexican version of bread pudding is made not with milk and eggs but with caramel sauce, cheese and sweet wine, giving an intensity of flavors that raises this *sopa*—here is yet another food called "soup"—far above a cottage dessert. Without such niceties in it as raisins and nuts, and certainly without wine, the pudding is a favorite Lenten dish. An old name for this dish that is still commonly used, especially on restaurant menus, is *capirotada*.

For 6 to 8 people:

> 8 ounces good French bread—one small loaf or about
>   6 French rolls
> 1 cup sugar
> 1½ cups water
> 1 teaspoon cinnamon

   4 tablespoons sweet butter
   1 cup sweet wine (preferably Madeira, but Tokay or even Greek
      Mavrodaphne will be good)
   ¾ cup piñons (substitute blanched, slivered almonds or chopped
      pecans if piñons are not available)
   ¾ cup raisins
   1 cup shredded Monterey Jack cheese (about 4 ounces)
Sweetened whipped cream for garnish, if desired

Preheat the oven to 350° F. Butter a shallow baking pan that will accommodate the bread in 1 or 2 layers.

Tear the bread roughly into bite-size pieces with your hands, place the
pieces on a baking sheet and toast lightly in the oven, checking after about
10 minutes.

Meanwhile, place the sugar in a heavy saucepan over medium heat.
Cook without stirring until the rim around the sugar is beginning to melt,
then start stirring with a metal spoon. As the sugar melts and begins to
turn straw-colored, turn the heat down to low; continue to stir until the
sugar is melted and the color of dark honey, but be careful not to burn it.
Remove the pan from the heat and pour in the water a teaspoonful at a
time. The sugar will boil up madly, but keep stirring and adding the water
very slowly; it all will be incorporated into a thin caramel syrup. If lumps
of hard caramel remain, return the pan to the heat and boil until they
dissolve. NOTE: To remove caramel from the metal spoon and the pan, let
them soak in cold water overnight.

Add the cinnamon and butter to the caramel sauce while it is still hot.
Place the toasted bread in the prepared baking pan; carefully spoon the
sweet wine over every piece. Sprinkle the nuts and raisins over, and then
an even coating of the cheese. Pour on the caramel syrup, once again
being sure to reach all the bread, and bake at 350° F. for 30 minutes.

It is usual to cover the pan with foil while it is baking, which results
in a pudding as soft as custard. On the other hand, if you like a crisp
crust, bake uncovered, but look in after 15 minutes or so to make sure that
the cheese is not browning; it is meant to melt into the general texture of
the pudding. Cover with foil any time the pudding seems browned enough
during the baking period. Serve warm or cold, as is or garnished with
whipped cream to cut the *capirotada*'s intense sweetness.

WHITE COCOA FLAN

Only once did I see printed an old trick for making coffee ice cream that was white instead of brown (as I recall, it was meant to be served to Austrian aristocracy). The trick was to soak a handful of coffee beans for an hour or so in cold milk or cream, which was then used for making the ice cream, imparting a suitably noble ivory color instead of mocha. I liked the idea of an illusionary taste going into *flan*, the caramelized custard which is universally known via Mexican restaurant menus. My coffee beans, though, always colored the cream, just as if I were using powdered coffee crystals (which is the usual method for making coffee *flan*), until it occurred to me that white crème de cacao would work a similar trick—and so it does.

If you do not care about the white-cocoa flavor in the first place, omit the liqueur and make your custard without it, but by no means skip the caramel, which always seems darker and more burnt when made by the hands of Spanish cooks than by their French counterparts. Long familiarity has not worn out the appeal of *flan*. It is one of the few desserts so light that overstuffed diners never pass it up—the restaurateurs know what they are about when they put it on the list—and it is even better made by home cooks, because we are less likely to skimp on the eggs.

For 4 people:

   ½ cup sugar plus 2 tablespoons water for making the caramel
  1¼ cups milk
    1 cup half-and-half
    1 stick cinnamon
    3 or 4 tablespoons white crème de cacao
   ½ cup sugar
    4 large eggs
    2 egg yolks
    1 teaspoon vanilla
   ⅛ teaspoon salt

Making *flan* is an uncomplicated process, especially when you have had experience in caramelizing the sugar, but it takes time—about 1 hour for baking the custard in its water bath, followed by at least 3 hours of chilling. On the other hand, it must be made the day it is to be eaten, since custards without starch will weep if they are kept standing, and the solid part will turn pasty.

To caramelize the mold: Have ready a 6-cup metal or enamel mold that is at least as thick as a thin saucepan and flat-bottomed. Place the sugar and water in it and stir over medium-low heat until the sugar dissolves, which should be just as the syrup comes to the boil. Place a lid on the mold and let the syrup boil gently for a minute, then uncover and cook over medium heat without stirring or moving the pan. Watch the color as it turns from transparent to a light straw. If you notice that some spots of syrup are turning brown before the rest (this invariably happens, since molds all have hot spots), turn down the heat to low and begin to stir the syrup. Remove from heat when the caramel is a good honey-color; do not overcook or the caramel will taste burned. Handling the mold with pot holders, tilt in all directions to coat the mold with caramel along its sides. Set aside to cool.

Scald the milk and half-and-half together with the cinnamon stick. When the milk steams and begins to form a skin, remove from heat and add the crème de cacao. Let steep for 2 minutes, then remove the cinnamon. Blend all the remaining ingredients smooth with a whisk, electric mixer or blender, and then blend in the scalded milk mixture. Set aside while you prepare the water bath.

Preheat the oven to 325° F. Stand the caramelized mold in an oven-proof skillet or other pan wide enough to hold it with at least 1 inch of space all around. Bring water to a boil in a teakettle. Pour the custard through a sieve into the mold, then pour the boiling water into the surrounding skillet until it reaches about halfway up the mold. Carefully transfer to the oven—you can move the skillet and mold in separate trips —and bake for about 45 minutes, or until a knife inserted into the center of the custard comes out clean. Since the silky texture of well-made custards is spoiled if they boil, turn down the oven heat at the first sign that the water in the bath is about to boil, even if that means that the *flan* may take longer to bake.

Remove the mold from the oven and place it directly into another bath of cold water—this aids the cooling—for about half an hour. Refrigerate for at least 3 hours until thoroughly cold.

To serve, run a knife around the sides of the *flan*, dunk the bottom into hot water to melt the caramel a bit, then hold a wide serving plate over the mold. Flip the two together with one deft motion, and the custard will fall out with a delicate plop. Sometimes quite a bit of syrup comes out with it, so make sure your plate has a rim. Heat 2 tablespoons of water in the mold over medium heat to create more caramel sauce, stirring to loosen as much of it as you can from the mold. For the most spectacular presentation of your *flan*, heat ¼ cup of rum to lukewarm either in the mold or a separate saucepan, carefully ignite it (after the *flan* has been unmolded) and pour over the unmolded custard as it comes regally to the table.

Traditional Flan: Besides the pineapple-and-lime *flan* below, the most important version is a plain one, which omits the crème de cacao. Mexican cooks would still leave in the cinnamon, however, and they might add a few drops of almond extract. In the New Mexico villages, where fresh milk was not always at hand, the cooks became accustomed to making their *flan* with canned evaporated milk, and even some modern recipes call for it.

If you like the idea of liquor-flavored custards, you can substitute rum or brandy for the crème de cacao; restaurants are quickly popularizing a version that calls for Amaretto. For coffee *flan*, add 2 tablespoons of coffee crystals to the scalded milk.

Flan with Nut Sauce: Make the traditional recipe above or the cocoa-flavored one, but heat 2 tablespoons of water in the mold after the custard has been turned out to make more caramel sauce for the unmolded pudding. As you are stirring up the caramel over medium heat, add ½ cup ground pecans. Dilute with a little more water or 1 tablespoon dark rum as needed, then spoon the nut sauce over the portions after they are cut. This is a delectable variant.

FLAN WITH PINEAPPLE AND LIME

This absolutely wonderful variation upon the traditional New Mexican *flan* is also very different from it. Where *flan* is creamy, this dessert is textured with crushed pineapple; where *flan* is bland, this tastes sharply of lime, but it retains the caramel coating of the old dessert and looks just as dramatic unmolded in a moat of caramel sauce. The sweet tartness of the pineapple makes it very welcome after a dinner containing green chili, onions and garlic. Like all unmolded custards, it must be well chilled to hold its shape, but do not be afraid to turn it out of the mold—seeing the glistening brown caramel over the top is all the charm.

For 6 people:

> ⅔ cup sugar, for caramelizing the mold
> 1 large can (15 ounces) crushed pineapple packed in its
>   own juice
> 4 large eggs
> ¼ cup sugar
> 1 can (14 ounces) sweetened condensed milk
> Juice and grated rind of 1 lime, plus enough additional lime juice to
>   make ¼ cup

Caramelize a 6- to 8-cup mold, using the ⅔ cup of sugar, according to the directions in the recipe for white cocoa flan on p. 356.

Preheat oven to 350° F.

Set aside the mold to cool, and prepare the custard: Whisk the eggs thoroughly in a mixing bowl, either by hand or electric mixer. Add the ¼ cup of sugar and beat until well incorporated. Add the condensed milk, grated lime peel and lime juice. Mix thoroughly and finally, add the crushed pineapple along with its juice. Pour the custard into the cooled mold, and set the *flan* to bake in a water bath (see p. 357).

Bake for 45 minutes. The *flan* is done when the center looks firm and is no longer jiggly. Cool thoroughly and chill until serving time. Since this dessert is quite dense, cooling can take 4 hours or more in the refrigerator. The fastest way to cool it is first to let it sit for an hour in a cold-water bath, then refrigerate to chill.

To serve: Run a knife around the edges of the *flan*, hold the serving plate over the mold, and flip plate and mold over deftly in one smooth motion. If the *flan* is cold, it will slip easily out of its mold, and the custard will stand firm without spreading. (A *flan* that starts to collapse can be rushed to the table or served with a spoon.) Place the mold over a low burner and stir about ¼ cup water into the remaining caramel until a sauce is formed. Sometimes this happens rapidly, sometimes the caramel hardens when the water touches it and has to be dissolved again by a few minutes of patient stirring. The wait is well worth it. Allow the caramel sauce to cool and spoon it over the portions of *flan* after they are cut.

VARIATION:

Cuban Flan: You can alter the *flan*'s taste by substituting 3 tablespoons dark rum for the lime peel and juice. A little rum can also be added to the mold at the time you are heating it for the caramel sauce.

INDIAN PUDDING WITH PUMPKIN CUSTARD

Practically the first food that the Indians bequeathed to Europeans was the sweetened corn gruel called *atole* (see p. 191), to which the New England colonists added eggs and the name "Indian pudding." Like *atole* itself, Indian pudding is little more than cornmeal, molasses and milk, but the dish was so popular that pioneer wives carried it West two centuries later. As a cottage dessert, it survived well into the 1950s in general American cookbooks, but I doubt if it is made with any regularity now outside Boston. The version below is a traditional Indian pudding. The pumpkin custard that goes over it, however, is an invention contrived to perk up the rather stolid taste of the traditional pudding and thereby attract more cooks to try it. Not only is the heritage of this dish centuries old, but the warm, inviting smell of the corn custard and its flannel-soft texture have an instinctive appeal.

For 4 people:

> 3 cups scalded milk
> ⅓ cup yellow cornmeal
> 1 cup cold milk
> 2 large eggs
> ½ cup molasses, light or dark
> ½ cup sugar
> ½ teaspoon salt
> ½ teaspoon cinnamon
> ½ teaspoon powdered ginger
> 4 tablespoons butter

PUMPKIN CUSTARD:

> ¾ cup half-and-half
> ¼ cup solid-pack canned pumpkin, unsweetened
> 2 egg yolks
> 3 tablespoons honey
> ½ teaspoon vanilla
> 1 or 2 tablespoons dark rum

For this dish, use a double boiler or improvise one by placing a metal bowl over a saucepan containing 1 inch of water, but do not let the bottom of the bowl touch the water. Bring the water to a boil and pour the scalded milk into the bowl or the top of the double boiler. In a separate bowl, stir the cornmeal into the cold milk, then gradually pour this mixture into the scalded milk, stirring constantly. Cook for 20 minutes with an occasional stir to prevent lumping. The cornmeal will swell and begin to thicken in the milk.

As the mixture nears the end of its cooking time, preheat the oven to 325° F. Combine all the remaining pudding ingredients except the butter in a food processor and blend for about 5 seconds. Stir this into the cornmeal-milk mixture, add the butter and mix thoroughly.

Transfer the pudding to an ovenproof bowl if necessary and bake for about 1 hour, then test to see if the center of the pudding is firm to the touch; a knife inserted into it should come out clean. If in doubt, bake 15 minutes more. Serve the warm pudding directly from its bowl. Hot from the oven, with only a few minutes to cool, the pudding can be eaten in the conventional way with vanilla ice cream or sweetened whipped cream. But it is even better served warm, not hot, with the pumpkin custard sauce you make as follows:

Blend all the sauce ingredients except the vanilla and rum in a small saucepan using a whisk. Cook over medium heat, stirring constantly, until the custard thickens enough to heavily coat a spoon—about 5 to 8 minutes —but do not let it get near the boil (it will thicken at 175° F., which is barely too hot to touch with your finger). If the custard by chance begins to curdle, it can be rescued by immediately transferring it to a food processor or blender and blending for 10 seconds. Remove from the heat, stir in the vanilla and rum and process for 10 seconds if the pumpkin seems too grainy for your taste. Serve warm, cool or chilled.

RICE PUDDING WITH CARAMEL-NUT SAUCE

Cafeteria-style rice pudding, a dessert no hobgoblin could wish worse, tends to make anyone skeptical that a rice pudding can ever be good. This Spanish pudding is quite fine, however, and it becomes even better with a simple caramel-nut sauce to go over it. Since the rice *sopa* itself is no trouble to make (the Hispanic cooks call this, too, a "soup"), the extra effort spent over the caramel is not too much to ask, and it is well worth it. Even though we think of rice pudding as a cottage dessert, or an institutional punishment, you will be safe offering this delicious version at a dinner party. The variation with poached pears is even more elegant than the basic recipe. Both are so sweet and rich that small portions, accompanied by strong coffee, are called for.

For 4 people:

    1 quart milk
    3 tablespoons butter
    ½ cup long-grain rice
    ⅔ cup sugar
    ¼ teaspoon salt
    1 cinnamon stick
    1 teaspoon vanilla
    2 large eggs, separated

FOR THE CARAMEL:

    ¾ cup sugar
    7 tablespoons water
    ½ cup pecans, finely chopped
    2 or 3 tablespoons dark rum

Preheat the oven to 300° F. and scald the milk in a saucepan or in the casserole in which you are going to bake the pudding, if the casserole is flame-proof. Stir in the butter, rice, sugar, salt and cinnamon stick. Transfer to the oven and bake, uncovered, for about 2½ hours, stirring every 20 minutes or so during the last hour. As the pudding shows signs of boiling, keep turning down the heat gradually, and stop the cooking when the rice is thick and the milk all but absorbed. Some cooks consider the rice done when there is still a good deal of thickened milk left; others bake the pudding until nothing remains but swollen rice—in any event, do not let the rice brown around the edges or on the bottom.

Remove the rice from the oven, take out the cinnamon stick, and let rest for 5 minutes. Rapidly stir in the vanilla and egg yolks. Whip the egg whites until stiff, but still satiny, then fold them into the warm pudding. Set aside while you prepare the caramel sauce.

The directions for making caramel are given on p. 356 in the recipe for *flan*, but for this rice pudding you caramelize the sugar in a saucepan rather than directly in the mold. Here is a brief repetition of the main points: place the sugar and 3 tablespoons of water in the saucepan, slowly bring to a boil over medium heat, then caramelize the sugar without stirring. When the caramel is the color of honey, remove from the heat and drizzle in the remaining 4 tablespoons of water, stirring constantly. The caramel will bubble furiously, and sometimes it will turn hard rather than cooperate and become a thick sauce. If that happens, simply return the pan to low heat and continue cooking until the caramel dissolves again, adding a little water if needed to reach the desired consistency. Stir in the pecans and the rum flavoring. The finished sauce will be the consistency of maple syrup and well textured with nuts.

Divide the finished pudding into individual portions (or transfer to one decorative bowl) and spread on the warm caramel-nut sauce. Serve either warm or at room temperature. If you have to hold the pudding for any length of time, add the warmed sauce an hour before serving. To rewarm the pudding, cover with foil and set over a pan of simmering water.

VARIATIONS:

Rice Pudding with Poached Pears: This is a delicious combination of flavors and very easy to achieve if you simply place slices of drained, canned pears over the warm pudding before adding the caramel sauce; do this near serving time since the caramel tends to cause the pears to weep and thin the sauce. If you want to poach your own pears, make a syrup of ½ cup water, ½ cup dry white or vermouth, ¾ cup sugar and 1 tablespoon lemon juice. Bring the ingredients to a boil in a saucepan, boil for 5 minutes, then reduce to a simmer. Peel, core and section 3 pears which are still somewhat hard and immediately drop the slices into the syrup so that they do not turn brown. Poach until knife-tender (the time will vary from 2 to 5 minutes depending on the hardness of the pears—Bartlett pears generally cook more quickly than the harder Bosc or Anjou). Remove the slices and allow to cool in enough syrup to barely cover; chill until needed.

Lemon Rice Pudding: If in your memory rice pudding is a stodgy dessert, liven it up with lemon. Proceed as in the basic recipe, but add the grated peel of 1 lemon along with the vanilla. This variation can be served without the caramel sauce, if you like, since the lemon flavor is distinct enough to stand on its own.

TEQUILA-AND-LIME SHERBET

Simple tricks can turn out the most memorable dishes, as witness this sherbet. It is light enough to qualify as "sea-foam" sherbet, the airiest kind made in France, but the method behind it is absurdly simple, involving little more than a frozen mush to which beaten egg whites are added. The only precaution in making a sherbet with liquor in it is to keep the ingredients cold at all times. Be sure, then, that you use a metal bowl and set it on the bottom of your freezer compartment, directly against the metal surface. An average freezer compartment set to "medium" will make this quantity of sherbet in about 3 hours minimum, but it helps to freeze it thoroughly, which adds another hour or so to the timing.

For roughly 1 quart, serving 4 people:

> **6-ounce can limeade concentrate, barely thawed**
> 1 **cup water**
> 2 **tablespoons aromatic tequila, preferably the amber or**
>   *añejo* **variety**
> 2 **egg whites**

Combine the limeade concentrate, water and tequila in a 2-quart metal or glass bowl and set it onto the bottom of the freezer compartment. Setting the temperature at medium to coldest, freeze to a mush, stopping at least once to beat the half-frozen mush with an electric mixer at highest speed. This step, which helps to make a finer grain in the finished sherbet, should take only a few seconds—the mixture must never turn liquid again.

When the mush is set, but not too solid, beat the egg whites until they form soft mounds, not stiff peaks. Working quickly, remove the mush from the freezer and beat it up for a few seconds with the same beater you used for the egg whites. Using a rubber spatula, rapidly fold in the beaten whites until thoroughly incorporated into the sherbet and return to the freezer until serving time. Since this sherbet melts quickly once taken out to room temperature, spoon into chilled serving cups and serve immediately.

VARIATIONS:

Margarita Sherbet: Although the basic recipe is already a delicious pairing of lime and liquor, you can come closer to the taste of a Margarita cocktail by adding 1 teaspoon freshly grated orange peel to the limeade. Sprinkling a little salt over the sherbet at serving time is definitely a matter of personal taste.

Tequila and Sherbet: Chill tequila in the freezer before serving time and spoon a few tablespoons into the serving dishes. Scoop out the sherbet onto the tequila, but do not pour the tequila directly over the sherbet, which will cause it to melt almost immediately, and do not add more tequila to the mush, since that will make it very difficult to freeze in a home freezer.

BEVERAGES

Beer
Table Wines
Sangría
Margarita
Sangrita
Mexican Eggnog (Rompope)
Mexican Chocolate
Champurrado

BEER

With Mexican food, beer is good, and it matters not at all if it comes from Mexico. German-speaking immigrants built the breweries there, imitating the same Viennese, Bohemian or Munich styles that were traditional at home. One of the best medium-weight lagers from Mexico is still called Bohemia, though only a dyed-in-the-wool beer taster could distinguish it from the countless other Pilsner-style lagers of the world. In the last century, when Mexico gained its brewing heritage, the dark beers from Munich set the standard, and it surprises people today when they discover that this bygone Teutonic fashion is still very good with chili and tortillas. Two dark beers commonly imported to the U.S. are Tres Equis (labeled with three large X's) and Negra Modello, probably the best product from the Modello *cervezería*, or brewery. The most popular import, Dos Equis (labeled with two X's), is a rich enough lager so that diners who first experience it in restaurants after being used to light American beer distinctly think of it as somehow especially Mexican. It is not, but unlike most bulk-produced American beers, there is at least something to it which does not utterly disappear in the presence of red chili sauce.

All of these imports are worth trying. I have found only scattered enthusiasm at tastings for Tecate, the workingman's beer from Mexico City, or for Carta Blanca, a Budweiser-style beer I remember seeing in the U.S. when no other was readily available. Recently, as imported beer connoisseurship began to make a mark in the restaurant trade, two excellent beers, Superior and Bohemia, both of about the same heft as Carta Blanca, have attracted a following. They are my first choices among lighter Mexican beers, but I would not attest that they are in any way superior to good German beers, and certainly not the equal of the best imports like the true Pilsner Urquell.

As far as I know, none of these beers has a legitimate claim to snobbery, as all are products of huge commercial brewing combines and deserve no more status as rarities than everyday U.S. beer. Like the other drinkers of the world, Mexicans are tending evermore toward a uniform taste for pale lagers, and if they haven't embraced the near-tastelessness of our beers, the Mexican contenders are hardly the stuff of a latter-day Munich.

A minor cult for sprinkling lemon juice and salt in the top of a can of Tecate, widely publicized by the company as a habit of Mexican drinkers, is flickering here and there throughout the Southwest. Modern advertising has also carried it with great speed to New York City, but I have nowhere seen people drinking beer over ice with a lemon slice in it, which is an authentic practice, too—I suspect that it came to Mexico from Germany along with the old brewers, for the bottles of light summer beer you see in Bavaria with yeast floating at the bottom are frequently drunk over ice with lemon. If you have never tried this practice, or never thought of matching chili dishes with dark beer, both are worthy of experiment.

TABLE WINES

We discover in the early records that grapes were among the first culti-vated crops planted by the Franciscan and Jesuit Fathers in New Spain, but it is a surprise to find almost all of the Rio Grande valley planted to vineyards by the middle of the 1800s. A great deal of this country was vineyard a hundred years ago, spread over many more regions. And our predecessors drank more often than we do. The early Anglo travelers to Santa Fe found wine and brandy on the table at breakfast, lunch and dinner. Fine table wines from France made their way up the trail from Mexico, but they arrived at three-year intervals, we are told, so the need for sacramental wine and wine for daily drinking had to be met by local growers.

The standard appears to have been set by the mission wine makers at El Paso del Norte (roughly the same location as the present El Paso, Texas) who fashioned their "clarets" and "Cognacs" along European lines. Their whiskey, in fact, was grape brandy; bourbon whiskey did not show up until the American occupation of Santa Fe. Even though the El Paso wine no doubt suffered from the hot, long trip in barrels or metal containers rather than bottles, we know that Santa Feans enjoyed what they got, and that included the Americans who came after the 1840s.

Yet their tastes are not ours. I cannot recommend that you blithely drink wine with New Mexican food, because some of the strongest flavors in the cooking—chilies red and green, cumin and other spices—are not friendly to wine. The primary consideration might simply be the heat of chili dishes, which numbs the palate beyond the reach of table wines. Do drink all wines on an experimental basis to begin with. Now that California wines amount to 70 percent or more of our national consumption (at least in the West), it is helpful to know what wines are both good and appropriate with hearty, highly seasoned dishes. Among the California whites, table wines made from Gewürztraminer, Sauvignon Blanc (also labeled Blanc Fumé or Fumé Blanc), and Chenin Blanc grapes are likelier matches for Santa Fe cooking than the refined Chardonnays and Rieslings. Among the reds, the choosing is not really a delicate matter, for California practice is to stuff the young wines full of fruit and tannin with little realistic expectation of letting them age. Zinfandels in particular are now so common in the raw, big-gun style that they can be readily recommended. They are also considerably cheaper than Cabernets and Pinot Noirs, the best of which are well left to accompany grilled meats and roasts that are not sauced with chili. Thanks to the unslaked demand for white wines in the last decade, many red wines are also good value in the marketplace. Even the coarser ones are likely to surpass the dubious barrels of old El Paso.

SANGRÍA

The latest wave of popularity for *sangría* has come and gone, and in truth this drink can be cloying once the sugary combination of red wine and oranges sets in too strongly on the palate. The first fine taste of it, though, is quite refreshing on a July afternoon if there is air and shade and the dryness of the Southwest. I have come to think that a little orange peel goes a long way if you plan to drink more than one glass of this punch.

For 4 people:

  ½ to 1 whole orange, cut into thin slices
  ½ to 1 whole lemon, cut into thin slices
  1 bottle dry red wine
  ¼ cup brandy
  2 to 4 tablespoons sugar
Soda water to taste

Combine the unpeeled fruit and wine in a pitcher and allow to chill for 1 hour. Add the brandy and 2 tablespoons of sugar, then taste to see if the sweetness is right. Add more sugar and brandy as desired. Pour the *sangría* straight up or over ice in large wineglasses and dilute at the last moment with soda water for a spritzer effect.

MARGARITA

Margaritas have become the mandatory Southwestern cocktail in the last decade, but they are seldom if ever made according to the classical formula, which called for equal parts of lime juice, tequila and Triple Sec. Assuming that you use an ounce of each ingredient, the drink turns out rather like a Daiquiri. Today's Margaritas are tall limeade coolers, commonly as large as singles-bar Bloody Marys, with scarcely a quarter of the liquid made up of alcohol. The preferred glass is a large, narrow-necked chimney, looking something like the top of a hurricane lamp, but oversize balloon-type Burgundy glasses are also encountered.

For 1 drink:

  Salt
    1 or 2 ounces (2 to 4 tablespoons) tequila
    1 ounce (2 tablespoons) Triple Sec or Cointreau
    1 cup limeade (or limeade and lemonade combined if you want a
      less acidic mixer)

Arrange a layer of coarse-grained or kosher salt in a saucer. Dip the rim of a tall cocktail glass of 12-ounce capacity into a shallow saucer of water to wet it, then into the salt. Mix the liquors and the limeade and shake with ice if the limeade is not refrigerated. Otherwise, simply pour the liquor and limeade over ice cubes in the glass. Stir well and garnish with fresh lime wedges if you like.

SANGRITA

Though it lags far behind the Margarita, *sangrita* is one of the few other Mexican cocktails to achieve a measure of popularity in the Southwest. Its tomato-juice-and-chili taste would resemble a Bloody Mary except that onion and fruit juice are also added. The result is a hot-and-sweet combination that is something of an acquired taste. In its birthplace *sangrita* is drunk in small glasses without any liquor, serving as a chaser to straight tequila. You can present it that way, or with the liquor added, as in the recipe below. If the taste is too peculiar for your guests, you can achieve some of the same effect by making Bloody Marys with tequila in place of the vodka, plus considerably more lime juice to taste.

For 5 cups of sangrita:

   ¼ medium onion
   1 or 2 whole *serrano* chilies (if you substitute the larger
      jalapeños, devein and seed them first)
Juice of 1 orange
Juice of 2 limes
   1 teaspoon sugar, or more to taste
   ½ teaspoon salt, or more to taste
   4 cups tomato juice
Tequila, to serve either in the drink or with it
Lime wedges for garnish

Combine all the ingredients except the tomato juice, tequila and lime garnish in an electric blender and blend until liquefied. Mix with the tomato juice and chill until serving time. Taste for salt and sugar, adding more if you like. Serve the *sangrita* in small tumblers as a chaser to tequila; or mix a cocktail consisting of ½ cup of the mix stirred with 1 or 2 ounces of tequila (2 to 4 tablespoons). Garnish either version with lime wedges.

MEXICAN EGGNOG
Rompope

Rompope, the Mexican equivalent of eggnog, differs only in using milk boiled down with sugar in place of the usual cold milk or cream. The same effect can be realized with sweetened condensed milk, as in this recipe, which makes a concoction rich enough to be mistaken for custard. It should be taken in quite small glasses, the way New Mexicans in fact might drink theirs, as a social afternoon drink as well as a holiday one. The addition of whiskey to the customary rum marks the Anglo influence in this version.

For about 1½ quarts, or at least 24 servings:

   2 cups sugar
   8 egg yolks
   ⅔ cup light cream
   1 teaspoon vanilla
   1 can (14 ounces) sweetened condensed milk
   2 cups light or dark rum
   ⅔ cup bourbon

Beat the sugar and egg yolks together by hand or electric mixer in a mixing bowl until well combined, then beat in the other ingredients, one after another, until the sugar is dissolved. Store, refrigerated, in a glass jar for no more than a few days.

MEXICAN CHOCOLATE

Chocolate, or what we would call hot cocoa, was a rage among the Spaniards when they first began to learn from the Aztecs about hitherto unknown food and drink in New Spain. The Aztecs reserved it for kings and priests, who partook of chocolate (or "bitter water") as a potent ceremonial drink. The Spanish at first also restricted it to the upper classes, and even within modern memory some Mexican men would indulge themselves with cholocate while the women drank corn gruel. Now that chocolate is no longer considered intoxicating, the potion is saved for children. Mexican chocolate is no more than a tablet of sweetened chocolate dissolved in a cup of hot milk. The only reason that the flavor seems exotic to us, assuming we actually procure the real Mexican chocolate tablets, is that they are spiced with cinnamon, clove, vanilla and crushed almonds.

New Mexicans of a conservative persuasion may still be taking their chocolate at breakfast, lunch, dinner or midnight and it cannot help but bring to their minds memories of Christmas Eve or a wedding breakfast. The following recipe takes account of the Aztec taste for chocolate in that it is distinctly bitter and sweetened with honey in place of sugar. The egg is not really necessary, but it gives a high froth, which is desirable. Real lovers of Mexican chocolate froth theirs up while it is heating with the aid of a decoratively notched stick called a *molinillo*. As much as I like this drink, its own special implements are not necessary.

For 2 people:

          3 tablespoons powdered cocoa
          2 tablespoons honey
      ¼ cup hot water
    Generous dash cinnamon
    Scant dash cloves
    Small pinch of salt
          1 teaspoon instant coffee
          2 cups milk
          1 egg
      ¼ teaspoon vanilla

Place the first 7 ingredients in a small saucepan and stir over medium heat until the mixture reaches the boiling point. Simmer, still stirring, for 30 seconds, then stir in the milk. Let sit over heat until the chocolate is too warm to touch, but not boiling. Meanwhile, beat the egg with an electric mixer for a minute or so, until it is frothing. Add the vanilla. When the chocolate is hot, pour it over the egg and immediately beat at highest speed for about 15 seconds, long enough to achieve 1 inch or more of foam. Pour into mugs and drink with a sprinkling of cinnamon on top if you like. Native New Mexicans have learned that you can get the semblance of a froth with no effort by floating a marshmallow in their chocolate, but that, naturally, is not the Aztec way.

CHAMPURRADO

Champurrado is a peculiar drink beloved by anyone whose roots sink deep in the Spanish past of New Mexico. It is essentially hot chocolate thickened with blue cornmeal. Nothing in the way of cookbook prose can make it sound much better than it is—a thin gruel which the old people found ultimately nourishing. If you want to try *champurrado*, first obtain roasted blue cornmeal, sold as *atole* in the Southwest. Dissolve ¼ cup of it in ½ cup cold water. Next make the recipe for Mexican chocolate on p. 372, proceeding to the point where you bring the chocolate just under a boil, and add the milk. Add the *atole*-and-water mixture, stirring constantly. Still stirring, bring the *champurrado* to a boil, lower the heat and simmer, stirring often, until the *atole* is cooked through and the whole concoction thickened, about 10 minutes. *Champurrado* needs no frothing but is drunk hot as soon as it is thick. Serves two.

SOURCES FOR INGREDIENTS

This book was written to take advantage of the Mexican foods sections of ordinary supermarkets. Their supplies of quality-grade tortillas, chilies, and cheeses have blossomed over the last decade, a very helpful thing for the serious cook. If your local markets do not yet stock the ingredients most often called for in the recipes, then my advice is to ask the manager to make a special order for you. Only if that fails—and it shouldn't, since supermarkets can order from national distributors such as Ortega and Old El Paso—would I turn to mail-order sources.

Among the products you will want to see stocked in your supermarket are—

Mild green chilies, whole or in strips, 8-ounce cans or larger.
Chopped *jalapeños* (not pickled), 2-ounce cans
Tomatoes packed with *jalapeños*
100% pure powdered red chilies, both mild and hot
Fresh corn and flour tortillas for the refrigerator case (not canned or frozen)
Pinto, black, and red kidney beans, both dried and canned
Monterey Jack cheese

The list could go on to include less common ingredients, such as shelled, roasted piñons (not easily found outside large cities), whole red chilies, fresh *poblano* chilies, and so on, but none of these are exactly staples. If your grocery manager seems unwilling to cooperate with you except on inconvenient terms—such as asking you to commit yourself to buying a whole case of canned chilies—keep looking until you find a more cooperative store. They are almost always out there.

Mail-order sources: We are presently riding a wave of interest in mail-order gourmet foods, so it is tempting to list sources for all manner of exotic ingredients. I think, however, that a few reliable sources are all that any practical cook needs—there is nothing quite so dismal as opening a package and discovering that you indeed did order two pounds of *ancho* chilies and half a case of jalapeño jelly. The sources listed here will supply you with good dried red chilies, piñons, and *ristras*, all of which are welcome if you learn to love Santa Fe cooking.

Albuquerque Traders
P.O. Box 10171
Albuquerque, NM 87114   *phone:* (505) 897-1650

Casados Farms/Dos Ves Inc.
Box 1269
San Juan Pueblo, NM 87566

Casa Moneo
210 West 14th St.
New York, NY 10011   *phone:* (212) 929-1644

Jane Butel's Pecos Valley Spice Co.
142 Lincoln Ave.
Santa Fe, NM 87051   *phone:* 1-800-HOT TACO

GENERAL INDEX

RECIPE INDEX

ABOUT
THE AUTHOR

Huntley Dent was born in Mississippi and educated at Harvard, where he studied American history. His interest in Southwestern regional cooking grew out of extensive travel throughout the West after he moved to Denver in 1973. Dent reviewed restaurants and wine for *Denver Magazine* for four years. He is also interested in East Indian cuisine and the new cooking of California.